O

Father,
Who art in Heaven,
hallowed be Thy Name.
Thy Kingdom come.
Thy Will be done, on earth as it is in Heaven.
Give us this day our daily bread,
and forgive us our trespasses,
as we forgive those who
trespass against us,
and lead us not
into temptation,
but deliver us
from evil.
Amen.

"This is our great hope and our petition: 'Your Kingdom come'—a kingdom of peace, justice, and serenity, that will re-establish the original harmony of creation."

–Pope St. John Paul II.

Available from:
www.DSDOConnor.com
www.ProclaimTheKingdom.com

Published on The Feast of Christ the King. November 21st, 2021.

ISBN 978-1-957168-00-5 (Paperback)
978-1-957168-01-2 (eBook)

On the Title, Subtitle, and Cover Images: The main cover image is Gustav Doré's depiction of Dante's vision of Heaven described in *The Divine Comedy* (Paradiso, Canto 31). Embedded within it is a photograph of earth from space. The superimposition is meant to illustrate God's plan: one single will—the Divine Will—animating both Heaven and earth. (Wikimedia Commons.)

As Christians have always believed, the world's ultimate destiny, the Supreme Good of each person's life, and the proper object of supernatural Hope is none other than the Beatific Vision; commenced individually upon a soul's entrance into Heaven after death, and universally for the elect upon the General Resurrection and Last Judgment with Christ's Second Coming in the flesh, which will only occur at the very end of time. But as Heavenly realities enjoy corresponding temporal ones, we shall see the world's "Penultimate Destiny" achieved in time—that is, on earth, within history—a destiny whose essence likewise defines each Christian's mission here and now, and is described by none other than the climax of the Greatest Prayer: the Our Father's third petition. ***Fiat Voluntas Tua sicut in Caelo et in terra.*** **Thy Will be done on earth as it is in Heaven.**

Thy Will Be Done

The Greatest Prayer, the Christian's Mission, and the World's Penultimate Destiny

By Daniel O'Connor

Dedication

In honor of the Passion of the Christ, the ultimate display of love, which Our Lord suffered freely and willingly for each one of us.

May His love thus revealed be ever before our eyes, and may we satiate His thirst on the Cross by entrusting all souls to His Divine Mercy, by remaining ever with His Holy Mother, whom He gave to us from the Cross as our own Mother, and by consoling His Pierced Sacred Heart in the Holy Eucharist.

Introduction

This book is about the Greatest Prayer: The Our Father. The only prayer that the Son of God Himself taught and commanded us to pray. Specifically, this book is about that extraordinary prayer's greatest petition:

Thy Will be done on earth as it is in Heaven. (Matthew 6:10)

As the Our Father is the supreme prayer of Christianity, our efforts to contemplate its own climax will certainly lead us to better understand the true depth and breadth of the Christian's Mission and the World's Penultimate Destiny.

The audacity of this simple assertion may confound some, but whoever is taken aback should consider: how could it be otherwise? Would the all-knowing Second Person of the Blessed Trinity have failed to endow these superlatively important words with a degree of meaning proportional to the exaltation which He deigned from all eternity to bestow upon them?

Words that, for two-thousand years, have shone like the sun among all the prayers of the Church? Words of prayer that—more than any other words—Christians everywhere throughout history have ever lifted up to Heaven from the very depths of their hearts? Words prayed during the most solemn moments of each Holy Sacrifice of the Mass from the time of the Apostles to today? Words that even the hitherto apathetic socialite and avowed atheist cannot help but cry out as the airplane hurtles to the ground, and that even the holiest of saints affix as the pinnacle of prayer? Words no Christian child neglects from his most tender years and no soul on his death bed forgets even in the throes of agony?

Certainly not.

Trusting, therefore, that our Blessed Lord would not have committed this sacred prayer to the Church as her most substantial plea without ensuring that within its own heart lies the key to a Christian's mission—both in regard to his own salvation and sanctification and in his role to play within the culmination of history itself, we shall now proceed to inquire: What does this prayer mean for both ourselves and the entire world?

Allow me to spoil the plot for you right from the onset. It means a radical transformation of all, in the most glorious imaginable manner. Achieving this transformation, however, requires that we first know what God wishes to do, that we desire and ask for the total fulfillment of His Will in our lives and in the entire world, and that we cooperate with His plan moving forward. I have written this book to strive to aid in such an achievement (though I will rest content if, after reading it, you are merely left with a burning desire to pray the Our Father more frequently, more fervently, and more faithfully than ever before—believing in its power and promise with your whole heart, mind, and strength, and striving to live the rest of your life in accordance with its dictates).

As the third decade of the third millennium is now at hand, and we draw near the two-thousandth anniversary of Our Lord revealing this prayer and sealing the certainty of the promise of its third and supreme petition—a promise of the imminent "Third Fiat"—with the absolute assurance provided by His Resurrection, the urgency of the task before us is without precedent or parallel.

"**Rise, let us be on our way**." (John 14:31)

Some notes before proceeding: 1) If you have already heard of "Luisa Piccarreta," then you may wish to first consult the brief "Notes on Luisa's Revelations" section in Chapter 12 (Part Four). Parts One through Three, however, do not deal with this mystic at all. Moreover, there are no direct quotes from her private revelations anywhere in this book, therefore all that follows may be comfortably approached by anyone at all, no matter how strictly he interprets the implications of certain existing ecclesial notifications. 2) Where appropriate, portions from my previous books, *The Crown of History* and *The Crown of Sanctity* (available at DSDOConnor.com), are used here, though the majority of this book's content is original. Needless to say, any material from any other authors will be clearly displayed as a quotation and cited. 3) When quotations are presented in this book, some lines or phrases may be **bolded**; this emphasis has been added by me, unless otherwise noted. 4) Bible quotes will generally be taken from the RSVCE or the Douay-Rheims translations.

TABLE OF CONTENTS

Preface: My Journey

As my radical unworthiness to have authored these pages before you is beyond question, I will here share some of my own story in order to make it clear why I nevertheless felt compelled to write this book, and to lay bare just what my motive is.

A cradle Catholic, I grew up believing the Faith. A typical Millennial, I only lukewarmly practiced it. I attended Mass most Sundays and prayed the Our Father each day, but there was little Christianity of note beyond this in my life, and the behavior of my youth was often indistinguishable from the average promiscuous, intemperate, wild partying teenager of the day. While living that sinful lifestyle, I began studying mechanical engineering at RPI (Rensselaer); for, despite my sinfulness, I was dead set on saving the world through my ideas for certain inventions which I had begun designing and prototyping.

Embarking upon my freshman year, however, I did not know that it would ironically be at this institution – whose very motto urges its students to "change the world" – where I would discover that the change this world needs has nothing to do with the technological ones it existed to produce. For it was there, at RPI, that I realized no invention would save the world, but only something much simpler, though infinitely higher. My path to this recognition began when, shortly after enrolling, I finally acknowledged that my sins were tearing my soul to shreds, and immediately vowed to radically change my life forever. I still remember experiencing this revelation of the Divine Will; I still recall that precise moment of immense Heaven-sent clarity dawning upon my mind like the rising sun. It presented itself without invitation as I was merely amid my ordinary daily endeavors, and seared forever into my soul the recognition of one simple fact that took no heed of the rationalizations I had, until that moment, concocted: I knew the Will of God, and I was not doing it. There was nothing left to wait for. It was I who had to change, not God, and no delay could be justified. The vow followed immediately on the very spot I was standing.

This foundation of my awakening to a genuine life of Faith now being laid, I nevertheless had (and still have!) much room to grow. Providentially, in my junior year I found myself living in an apartment located just one block away from a Church with daily Mass and Perpetual Adoration. I began to frequent both, and soon became a go-to substitute for many nocturnal adoration hours. This precious midnight time with Jesus in the Blessed Sacrament made me realize that, ultimately, all that matters is becoming a saint. I also began devouring knowledge of the Faith. I can relate to the many conversion stories one often hears of Protestants coming into the Catholic Church and then, being utterly blown away by the Sacred Tradition we are blessed with, proceeding to bury themselves in books. From this era of my life, I recall most fondly my time reading the *Imitation of Christ* and the works of St. Louis de Montfort, St. Francis de Sales, and St. Alphonsus Liguori.

At that time, I had never heard of the Servant of God Luisa Piccarreta (and, if you haven't either, worry not; you'll never forget her after finishing this book), but the Holy Spirit inspired within me an unshakeable conviction that St. Alphonsus' work, *Uniformity With God's Will*, contained the ultimate key to becoming a saint—a key summarized perfectly in the four words of its title. Therefore, from the day I read that treatise from this great Doctor of the Church onward, my eyes remained ever affixed on *The Will of God* as the supreme principle of all things. Little did I then know that this book of St. Alphonsus' was the introduction to and foundation of the very theme that would later become the overarching mission of my life.

Many adventures in the Will of God followed (some of which can be read about in the Preface of my 2019 book, *The Crown of Sanctity*)[1], and His Will ultimately led me out of the engineering industry, where my professional career began at the GE (General Electric) Global Research headquarters, and into the old, dilapidated, and abandoned St. George's Church rectory in Utica, New York. I was to begin a new apostolate and job—living there while working with several others to convert it into a transitional home for homeless young men. It was to be called the John Bosco House, and once we had it ready, I served there as the live-in "house father" or "big brother" to the residents we welcomed.

Friday of the initial week working there consisted in a particularly grueling day of manual labor spent preparing the house's floors, and I was eager to take a break from work and head off to evening Mass at the nearby parish. So off I went to attend daily Mass as I did each ordinary, uneventful day. But as I entered the church, instead of seeing the usual celebrant, I noticed in the sanctuary a priest I did not know. After an announcement was made, I realized that I had not come to the ordinary Friday evening Mass, but had rather stumbled upon the beginning of a weekend-long retreat given by Fr. Joseph Iannuzzi on a topic I knew nothing about: *the Gift of Living in the Divine Will in the writings of the Servant of God Luisa Piccarreta*. What followed

---

[1] A free eBook is available at www.DSDOConnor.com

were two days of utter holy amazement that I will never forget.

The adventure of God's Will went on, and I continued to both study the "Gift of Living in the Divine Will" and strive to receive this Gift. After several months, the Will of God led me (through another intervention of immense clarity) to begin studying as a seminarian at Holy Apostles College & Seminary in Cromwell, Connecticut—even though God had made it equally clear that He was not yet revealing to me my ultimate vocation at that time.

Each month at Holy Apostles, one day was set aside as a "Day of Recollection," in which the seminarians kept total silence as they prayed and attended a retreat given by a priest. It was my first day of recollection as a seminarian, and I entered the chapel that morning eager to receive whatever edification it might be God's Will to impart through the priest's lips, though I was entirely uninformed as to both the topic and the priest for the retreat. When I looked towards the sanctuary, I saw to my great surprise a familiar face. I immediately knew I would not be disappointed, for the holy amazement on the Divine Will that I had received from this very priest ten months earlier and hundreds of miles away was alive and well. I left the chapel knowing that God had called me to continue studying these most sublime private revelations on His Holy Will, given to the Servant of God Luisa Piccarreta, and to do my humble best to introduce others to the same. Ever since then, it has been the overarching passion of my life.

God's clear guidance to me did not end that day, and He revealed that—as blessed and grace-filled a time as my one semester as a seminarian was—His Will for me was not priesthood, but marriage. An amazing wife (Regina, to whom this book's existence owes an immense debt of gratitude!) and four beautiful children (Joseph, David, Mary, and Luisa) later—along with a Master's in Theology, five years so far spent teaching college philosophy and religion, four years so far working on my PhD in philosophy, and many other apostolates—the Will of God remains the supreme principle in my life. In spite of my own sinfulness and unworthiness, I have always and will always do everything I can to invite others into an ever-deeper dedication to and love of Jesus' Divine Will. Please join me in this mission.

Prologue: My Exhortation

Of the "many adventures" referred to above, some included cross-country road trip pilgrimages. During their countless hours spent traversing endless miles of highway, I often enjoyed listening to Catholic Radio and hearing different conversion stories. One among the myriad, however, will always stand out in my memory.

The speaker (a former Protestant) recounted what preceded his conversion, and he told of the pivotal moment of Heaven-sent clarity that dawned upon his conscience. In this epiphany, he recognized that the crux of his antagonism toward Catholicism was found simply in the fact that Catholics took Our Lord's most important words in the Gospel at face value, while he was too afraid and timid to do the same. "Take, eat; this is my body." (Matthew 26:26) "Whose sins you shall forgive, they are forgiven them." (John 20:23) "You are Peter, and upon this rock I shall build my Church, and the gates of hell shall not prevail against it." (Matthew 16:18) "Behold thy mother." (John 19:27)

He then realized that he did not need to spend any more time debating with himself or others; he only needed sufficient Faith to trust that Jesus meant what He said, and sufficient courage to follow through with the implications of that Faith.

Now, if Our Blessed Lord meant any words of His to be taken absolutely seriously, at their face value, and without a shred of doubt about their implications, then those words would certainly be none other than the greatest petition of the Greatest Prayer—"Thy Will be done on earth as it is in Heaven." (Matthew 6:10) On our part, therefore, affixing our attention on these words and intensifying our zeal for living out the full glory contained within them will not go unrewarded. But if you find yourself struggling with that notion, I bid you consider just one question before putting this book down: *Why not?*

Why not believe that the greatest petition of the Greatest Prayer will not go unanswered? *Why not* believe that the Our Father contains no ill-advised requests, but rather encapsulates the very blueprint and purpose of the Faith and of History itself? *Why not* believe that Jesus desires what His Own Divine lips pronounced at the Gospel's climax to be taken *at its word*?

If you cannot yet bring yourself to fully believe it, then at least *consider* it while this book is in your hands. On Judgment Day, you will doubtless find yourself regretting many things you had chosen to do with your precious few moments of time on this earth. Reading this book, to the very last page, will not be one of them. Before you make it to that page, however, I anticipate a temptation that will arise in your mind: the temptation to regard God's promises as too good to be true. We will save addressing that temptation for this book's Epilogue, where we will complete the very thought we have here begun.

Part One: The Our Father Itself: The Promise and The Call of The Greatest Prayer

"For He did not at all say, 'Thy will be done' in me, or in us, but everywhere on the earth; so that error may be destroyed, and truth implanted, and all wickedness cast out, and virtue return, and no difference in this respect be henceforth between heaven and earth."

–St. John Chrysostom, Father of the Church

1. On the Our Father as a Whole

"Jesus laid bare the fundamental longing of His soul when He taught us to say: 'Thy will be done on earth as it is in Heaven.'"

–Servant of God Archbishop Luis Martinez

In the sixth chapter of the Gospel of Matthew,[2] Our Lord Jesus Christ teaches us the Greatest Prayer: the Our Father. The prayer everyone around the world knows by its other simple title, *The Lord's Prayer*. The prayer whose sublime words are committed to more memories than any other words ever written or spoken in his-

[2] Although another version of the Our Father is found in the Gospel of Luke, it is the version in the Gospel of the Apostle Matthew that is more complete and which was adopted by the Church, including in her liturgy (cf. *Catechism of the Catholic Church* §2759), from the very beginning up to the present day. This is not to imply that the Gospels contradict each other (they do not); it is only to say that no single Evangelist's Gospel gives the entire story, and in the case of the Lord's Prayer, Matthew's Gospel provides the fuller account. We know this, for example, from "Matthew's" Our Father being the one included in the *Didache* and other sources. There is no doubt, therefore, that *the* Lord's Prayer is the version found in Matthew's Gospel. Indeed, it has been rightly said that "the New Testament was a Sacrament before it was a Document," and accordingly, the Our Father was prayed incessantly by the Church well before the Gospels were written.

tory. The prayer that, "At the Savior's command and formed by Divine Teaching, *we dare to say*" at the pinnacle of each Mass, as we stand before Almighty God Whose Real Presence descended upon the altar only moments earlier.

The revelation of this prayer is itself the midpoint and climax of the most famous homily in history (the Sermon on the Mount), whereafter the crowds "were astonished at his teaching, for he taught them as one who had authority, and not as their scribes." (Matthew 7:28) Doubtless, this astonishment was provoked by what must have been emblazoned upon their minds like lightning while they sat under the midday sun, by the warm water of the sea of Galilee, and upon the soft grass of the Mount of Beatitudes as they gazed upon the very Creator of it all. For there, they heard the Son of God Himself praying—and thus guaranteeing—the Coming of the Kingdom, wherein the Will of God shall be accomplished on earth as in Heaven.

Of all the things Christians around the world have done for 2,000 years, praying the Our Father is the most recognizable and the easiest to trace back to the beginning of the Faith. Written during the First Century, the *Didache* itself (the "Teaching of the Twelve Apostles"), although brief, does not fail to command praying the Our Father three times a day. The Fathers of the Church—true Patriarchs of early Church history who established the permanent foundations of the Faith—provide countless commentaries on the Lord's Prayer, and all agree regarding its centrality and supremacy.

We know that any unanimous consensus of the Fathers of the Church is, by that fact alone, rendered a dogmatic truth,[3] so there is no danger we might stray from realms of safety by speaking too highly of the Lord's Prayer or focusing too passionately on its essence. Quite the contrary, to deepen one's understanding of the Our Father is to deepen one's understanding of Christianity itself. To dive more deeply into the *center* of the Our Father is to cooperate with the Holy Spirit most powerfully to "renew the face of the earth."

> Sanctify your whole Church in every people and nation; pour out, we pray, the gifts of the holy spirit across the face of the earth; and, **with the divine grace that was at work when the Gospel was first proclaimed, fill now once more the hearts of believers.** (Collect for the Feast of Pentecost. Roman Missal.)

It is always wise, however, for a Catholic who seeks greater understanding of the Faith to turn first to the Catechism, and this is what we will now do.

---

[3] A guarantee given by the Council of Trent and the First Vatican Council.

The Catechism on the Our Father

> "The Lord's Prayer is the most perfect of prayers."
> –St. Thomas Aquinas

While relaying the essence of this prayer, the current *Catechism of the Catholic Church* exalts the Our Father as "**the fundamental Christian prayer**," (§2773) and "**the quintessential prayer of the Church**." (§2776) Its presentation begins by quoting the Church Father Tertullian's teaching, "The Lord's Prayer 'is truly the summary of the whole gospel,'" (§2761) and it goes on to quote St. Thomas Aquinas who, in the *Summa Theologica*, affirmed with directness: "The Lord's Prayer is the most perfect of prayers." (II-II, Q83, A9)

Having established the supreme status of the Lord's Prayer in the Christian Faith, the Catechism then insists we regard it *mystically*, lest this prayer be mistakenly considered no more than several petitions that we present to the Lord and promptly forget:

> Since our **prayer sets forth our desires before God**, it is again the Father, "he who searches the hearts of men," who "knows what is the mind of the Spirit, because the Spirit intercedes for the saints according to the will of God." **The prayer to Our Father is inserted into the mysterious mission of the Son and of the Spirit ...** In the Eucharistic liturgy the Lord's Prayer appears as the prayer of the whole Church and there reveals its full meaning and efficacy. Placed between the [Eucharistic prayer] and ... communion, the Lord's Prayer sums up on the one hand all the petitions and intercessions expressed in the movement of the epiclesis and, on the other, knocks at the door of the Banquet of the kingdom which sacramental communion anticipates. (§2766, 2770)

Here, the Church teaches that the Our Father is more than a mere request. It is also that which:

1) Must order our desires themselves
2) Is inserted into the "mysterious mission" of the Holy Trinity
3) Is the ultimate link between Heaven and earth (for it *"knocks at the door of [Heaven],"* and within it is summed up *"all the [Liturgy's preceding] petitions and intercessions ..."*)

Considering the first teaching, we can see that forming our own desires—and, even more, *inflaming* them—according to the model of the Our Father[4] is synonymous with Christianity itself. As St. Augustine

---

[4] Among the Our Father's many titles is "The Model Prayer."

said: "Run through all the words of the holy prayers [in Scripture], and **I do not think that you will find anything in them that is not contained and included in the Lord's Prayer**." (Epistle 130)

Our considerations of the second teaching will constitute much of the remainder of this book, wherein we will see that God has now given greater clarity regarding the Holy Trinity's "mysterious mission" that permeates the supreme petition of the Our Father prayer, which itself penetrates into the Heart of God and stands as the guiding principle of 2,000 years of Sacred Tradition (millennia which now approach their culmination in the fulfillment of that very principle; as St. Thomas Aquinas taught, *all things find their perfection in returning to their origin.*[5])

On this point, we must tangentially note that the Church proposes neither to settle nor exhaustively describe, within her Magisterium, what exactly is contained in all the details of this "mysterious mission;" therefore, we must disregard the arguments of those who claim that the eschatological dimension of this mission's achievement consists in nothing other than waiting for the end of time to arrive. No opinion could be more mistaken than the one which holds that all we are doing—when praying in the Our Father for God's Will to be done on earth as in Heaven—is praying for the end of the world.[6] As the Church Historian Professor Jacques Cabaud wrote: "*Is there anybody in his right mind who would say: "Please Lord, we beg of you, do destroy this world which is unworthy of your divine concern"? Nobody would be caught expressing himself in this fashion. [The Kingdom] will come at the right moment. You should petition for its coming with faith, perseverance and a joyful heart.*"[7]

The Catechism's third teaching, which presents the Our Father as the link between Heaven and earth, leads us to our next chapter, as it is precisely in this Supreme Prayer's Supreme Petition that we see this "link."

---

[5] Cf. *Summa Contra Gentiles*. Book II. Chapter 46, §5

[6] By that logic, whoever prays to grow in holiness is merely begging to die, since the afterlife contains the supreme holiness. Clearly, however, sanctification is not suicide, and neither is praying the Lord's Prayer comparable to the motive of some fictional supervillain who only desires the end of the world!

[7] Jacques Cabaud. *On the End Times*. Chapter 1.

2. The Supremacy of the Third Petition

"Thy Will be done on earth as it is in Heaven."
"*Fiat Voluntas Tua sicut in Caelo et in terra.*"
–Matthew 6:10

Before delving even more deeply into the supreme petition of the Our Father, we should consider why—even among other petitions which are themselves so greatly exalted—we know it enjoys such a lofty rank.

> "When the disciples asked him to teach them to pray, he gave them the Our Father, **the core of which is undoubtedly 'thy will be done, on earth, as it is in heaven.'"** -Fr. Romano Guardini[8]

The Crescendo of the Lord's Prayer

> "Conformity with the holy will of God [is] and ought to be the rule of a Christian life. This it is that we implore, when we address these words to God: 'Thy will be done.'... God vouchsafes to propose to us, as the sole corrective of all our evils, a conformity to his holy will ... he commands us to regulate all our thoughts and actions by this standard." –Catechism of the Council of Trent

The first reason for the third petition's preeminence is found in the impeccably structured design with which Jesus imbued the Our Father. Dr. Scott Hahn explains:

> The Lord's Prayer is one unified, compact, model prayer consisting of seven petitions, divisible into two parts: the first "God-ward," the second "us-ward." **No work of poetic art was ever more perfectly crafted.**[9]

Indeed, the poetry displayed is perfect, and from it we see revealed the hierarchy of the prayer's contents. The prayer begins precisely *where we are* already—"*Our* Father..." God's proximity to us is displayed in the most intimate way—through true Paternity. Herein the tone is set for the remainder of the prayer, imbuing it with the trust and certainty which comes from knowing that God is not only all powerful, but also overflowing with love for us. For we are His children, and He cannot deny what we, in faith, ask of Him through His

---

[8] *The Lord*. Part II. Chapter VI.

[9] *Understanding "Our Father"*. Introduction.

only begotten Son. The prayer then ascends higher and higher; acknowledging, despite God's immanence, that He is also transcendent—His dwelling is in Heaven—, hallowing His Name, and imploring the coming of His Kingdom. Then, at last, it reaches its pinnacle and climax; the petition which encapsulates just what the greatest temporal establishment of His Kingdom consists in, and the petition containing within itself all the petitions that follow thereafter—***Thy Will be done on earth as it is in Heaven!*** Theologian Fr. John McMahon describes this structure as resembling a rainbow:

> The Pater Noster, the family prayer of the Church, has an arc like the rainbow, which springs up from the earth, touches the clouds, and then sweeps down to earth. We lift our hearts to God in its mounting petitions: 'Hallowed be Thy Name: Thy Kingdom come,' until we reach the apex of the arc in: 'Thy Will be done on earth as it is in Heaven.'[10]

According to another Biblical scholar, the Our Father is like a "hymnic prose poem;" a prayer which has:

> ... synonymous poetic parallelism between the first half, about God's name, kingdom, will, and the second half, about our bread, debt, and temptation ... Furthermore, **each half is itself in crescendo or climactic parallelism building up through the three component challenges ... "Name" and "kingdom" come to a climax in "will."**[11]

The analysis is straightforward even if subtle: *first in intention is last in execution*[12] (a philosophical theme we will apply to history itself in another chapter); what is greatest in a given presentation comes not first, but last. Why, then, is not the *seventh* petition the Our Father's greatest? Because, as Dr. Hahn points out, the prayer has two parts; halves which, though parallel and interdependent, have their own structure and their own distinct climax. Accordingly, the greatest petition of the Our Father's second part is that we be "delivered from evil." This supplication itself, however, is clearly not as great as praying for the accomplishment of God's Will, since His Will is not exhausted by mere deliverance from the evil one.[13] He also Wills, for example, that

---

[10] Monsignor John T. McMahon, PhD. "Rosary Talks with Mary." Australian Catholic Truth Society. No. 1073. 1949

[11] John Crossan. *The Greatest Prayer*. Page 115. (Nota Bene: I do *not* recommend this book, though it does contain a few morsels of wisdom.)

[12] Cf. Thomas Aquinas. *Summa Theologica*. I-II. Q1. A1.

[13] Many Scripture scholars have argued that a better translation of the last petition in the Our Father's original Greek is that we be delivered "from the evil one," not merely that we be delivered "from evil."

we become like Himself as much as is possible for a creature—a destiny far surpassing mere absence of bondage to the devil. Therefore, we are left acknowledging the Our Father's third petition as the greatest.

Admittedly, this pattern does not hold in all cases. For example, a set of instructions or a list of objectives generally yields its primacy to the first item presented. (The first of the Ten Commandments is the greatest; the first of the Seven Gifts and Twelve Fruits of the Holy Spirit—wisdom and charity, respectively—are greatest, etc.) But the "best wine saved for last" (cf. John 2:10) pattern does hold in those cases wherein what is being considered is a choreographed whole; when it is something that, within itself, bears a dramatic structure: a novel, a song, a movie, a poem—and, yes, a well-composed prayer.[14]

The Petition Containing All Others

> "'Your will be done on earth as it is in heaven.' **There cannot be a greater prayer** than to desire that earthly things should deserve to equal heavenly ones." –St. John Cassian (Father of the Church)

The second reason we know the Our Father's third petition is supreme is a philosophical one: *the whole is greater than the part*. In other words, what is contained within another thing cannot itself exceed that thing; for the container is always greater than the contained. Of the Our Father's seven petitions, six of them are contained within the one remaining plea that, simply, God's "Will be done on earth as it is in Heaven." God *Wills* our protection and nourishment, our forgiveness, and our deliverance from temptation and evil, therefore beseeching any such particular supplication of Him can never be greater

[14] This pattern certainly holds for the Hail Mary prayer; it, too, is divided into two parts, with the first half glorifying Our Lady, and the second half being directed more toward our own needs. Likewise, here, it is the final words of the first half that contain the prayer's own greatest exaltation of Mary and which are, therefore, the greatest of the whole prayer. For neither Our Lady being hailed, nor her fullness of grace, nor her abiding with the Lord, nor her being most blessed of women are themselves exaltations so glorious as the fact that Jesus Himself is the fruit of her womb. The first half of the Hail Mary, then, closes with a benediction of the Lord and a pronouncing of His Most Holy Name, the name at which "every knee shall bow in Heaven and on earth" (Philippians 2:10), which simultaneously acknowledges the Virgin Mary's supreme title: Mother of God. This concurrent pronouncement of the Name Above All Names and recognition of the greatest creature's greatest title is itself a concurrency in which is found the greatest part of the Hail Mary prayer. The revelations to St. Catherine of Genoa confirm this, as we will see in Part Two. As the Hail Mary and the Our Father fit as perfectly together as the Mother and the Son themselves, we should not be surprised to see that the exaltation of the petitions within them follows a similar arrangement.

than merely beseeching that His Will be done. Similarly, the fulfillment of God's Kingdom is found in His Will being done on earth as in Heaven, whereupon His name is also fully sanctified and hallowed among His creation. The whole of the Our Father—and, in fact, the whole of Christianity—is contained in *God's Will being done on earth as in Heaven*. No part of this whole, therefore, can surpass the totality to which it belongs.

The Opposite of Pagan Babbling

> "[Jesus] did not ask us to compose a prayer of ten thousand phrases and so come to him and merely repeat it... But if he already knows what we need, why do we pray? Not to inform God or instruct him but to beseech him closely, to be made intimate with him, by continuance in supplication." –St. John Chrysostom

The next reason for the third petition's preeminence derives from the context of the Our Father in the Gospel itself. It is precisely this phrase, "Thy Will be done," which is most in accord with the admonition Jesus gave us immediately before teaching the Our Father; the admonition which, as He tells us, contains the key to properly understand and approach this prayer:

> ... in praying do not heap up empty phrases as the Gentiles do; for they think that they will be heard for their many words. Do not be like them, for **your Father knows what you need before you ask him. Pray then like this: Our Father ...** (Matthew 6:7-9)

Indeed, if our Heavenly Father knows what we need before we ask Him, then the greatest thing we can beseech of Him is simply that *His* Will, *not ours*, be done. He knows what is best for us and for the world, and He is not in need of our counsel. The greatest act of faith and trust, therefore, is to submit entirely to His Will and implore its fulfillment, without even needing to know the details of what it portends.

This posture of total abandonment to the Divine Will—insisted upon by Jesus as the very prerequisite for praying the Our Father, and also contained within the same prayer's third petition—is the very opposite of the "heaping up of empty phrases" like the Gentiles (or, as other translations put it, "**babbling like the pagans**"), who "think that they will be heard for their many words."[15] For "Thy Will be Done" is not only the most powerful and exalted prayer; it is also the prayer which is the simplest, shortest, and most imbued with a child-like Faith, Hope, Love, and Trust in the One to Whom it is directed.

Illustrating well this contrast is the prophet Elijah's triumph over the priests of Baal (cf. 1 Kings 18). The priests of the false god, seeking to have their own offering consumed by fire, spent all day crying out to their idol with a barrage of supplications, beseeching its intercession, and supplementing their *heaping up of empty phrases* by cutting themselves with swords until their blood flowed freely. Thus they "raved on until the time of the offering of the oblation, but there was no voice; no one answered, no one heeded." (1 Kings 18:29) Elijah, afterward, offered a few simple words of sincere prayer consisting in three petitions which are not dissimilar from the Our Father's first half. First, he glorified God's name (v.36), then he asserted his own obedience to God, and finally he requested that God intervene so that "people may know that thou, O Lord, art God." (v.37) Immediately, fire came down from Heaven and consumed his own offering, vindicating the one true God against Baal and his priests. By this, not only was the God of Israel thus vindicated; so, too, was the humble, simple, childlike, and trusting approach to prayer. The very approach which Jesus admonishes us to adopt in the Our Father and which is exemplified above all in its third petition.

> "'Thy will be done' is the essential formula for obedience and for charity, for 'God is charity.' That is also the whole meaning of life in one sentence. The meaning of life = sanctity = 'Thy will be

---

[15] Make no mistake; avoiding "pagan babbling" does not mean praying little, praying rarely, or avoiding "vocal" or "repetitious" prayer. Quite the opposite, our calling as Christians is to be in "continual prayer" (cf. 1 Thessalonians 5:17), which should be a loving conversation from the heart between a child and his Father. The point is that it must not become an exasperated delineation and detailed description of every single thing one has decided he needs, lest - the babbling pagan frets — something be overlooked, and grace be thus neglected on account of a failure to sufficiently meticulously tell Heaven what to do. The proper way of praying—as a loving conversation—can indeed exist even when we are reciting established or "repetitive" prayers; e.g., the Rosary (which we should recite very often without any fear that even hours a day spent thus praying constitutes "pagan babbling"). Furthermore, we can, and should, present our specific temporal needs to God in prayer, but this should not constitute the majority of our prayers. Moreover, even while presenting them, we should often return to that blessed state of peaceful rest in God's Will which is more concerned with loving and trusting Him than with getting something out of Him. In this rest, we remain absolutely sure that God knows best, and He will bring His designs about, no matter what. In this way, we will be protected from the very superstition, scrupulosity, legalism, and mistrust that characterize the pagan religions to which Jesus presents the Our Father as a counterpoise.

done' = charity. It's so simple that it's hard." -Dr. Peter Kreeft [16]

The Greatest and the "Least Useful"

> "The workings that befall you receive as good, knowing that apart from God nothing comes to pass." –*The Didache*

In one ironic sense, beseeching the fulfillment of the Will of God—which is, without a doubt, the Greatest Prayer—is in a way the most "useless" prayer, since nothing and no one can thwart God's Will, and it shall in fact be done whether or not we supplicate for its accomplishment. On the other hand, asking for forgiveness, for one's daily bread, for deliverance from evil, etc., might seem like much more "useful" endeavors. But the greatest things always appear in one sense the most "useless."

Whatever is distinguished by its "usefulness" only exists for the sake of some other superior reality. We call medicine useful because it can contribute to the superior reality of health, but if we are already healthy, then we do not bother with it. In contrast, those things which are so exalted that we desire them for their own sake are not deemed useful, since to so regard them would be unworthy of their dignity. We would rebuke another for justifying enjoying a meal with family, appreciating a beautiful landscape, or creating a stunning work of art on account of the "usefulness" of such things.

If this pattern holds for the goods of natural life, then it is even more true in the spiritual life. There, we must do many things; but not all that we do in this realm is done entirely for its own sake (e.g., going to Confession so as to be absolved, mortifying one's flesh so as to grow in discipline). For man's supreme and innermost calling is at once simpler and more profound: to participate in the life of his Creator. And since man has a free will, he is capable of the most glorious possible manner of participation in that Divine Life. While rocks, trees, and animals each participate in the Divine Life by unknowingly testifying to the beauty of the One Who created them, man can do infinitely more. Man can *freely* choose to desire, ask for, and cooperate with the total accomplishment of the Will of God instead of his own self-will.

---

[16] *Practical Theology*. Page 435

Therefore, since will is supreme in both God and man,[17] it follows that the essence of man's ultimate calling (likeness with his Creator) is above all discovered in the simple plea, *Thy Will be done on earth as it is in Heaven!* To constantly speak these words with all our heart, soul, mind, and strength is the greatest thing that man can do; even to the point of rendering him invincible, as Pope St. Leo the Great taught when he said:

> They who have peace with God and are **always saying to the Father with their whole hearts "thy will be done,"** can be overcome in no battles, and can be hurt by no assaults. (Sermon XXVI. On the Feast of the Nativity)

Moreover, while beseeching the accomplishment of God's Will may appear "useless" from a worldly perspective, it is the *most useful thing possible* from a Divine perspective; both as regards the glory of God and the happiness of man. As the Servant of God Archbishop Luis Martinez—spiritual director of Blessed Conchita—taught:

> We certainly cannot add one iota to [God's] goodness and felicity... But there is a good that we can do to God, accidental and extrinsic to His fullness: we can lovingly fulfill His will. **The will of God is to reflect Himself in creatures... The fulfillment of that will is His glory: the end of all His works and the end of all His creatures. Their happiness consists in co-operating in its accomplishment.** (*The Sanctifier*. Chapter XVI)

The Surety of its Fulfillment

> "To pray 'Thy will be done on earth, as it is in heaven' is to pray that men may be like angels, that as angels fulfill God's will in heaven, men may fulfill his will, instead of their own, on earth. No one can say this sincerely except one who believes that every circumstance, favorable or unfavorable, is designed by God's providence for his good..."
>
> –St. John Cassian

We must indeed regard the fulfillment of the Our Father's third petition as certain. But as we are here comparing the third petition with the other six contained in the same prayer, a conundrum might appear: "*If the fulfillment of the Our Father's petitions is a guarantee, then*

[17] Though disputed by some, this assertion will be covered in a later chapter. For now, suffice it to say that it should not be taken as implying any of the deeply problematic extreme voluntarist positions put forth by philosophers like Ockham.

what of those who are not forgiven – souls in hell – even though the Lord's Prayer supplicates for our forgiveness? Doesn't this show that the Our Father's petitions might not be so certain?"

The answer is simple: *all* the petitions of the Our Father will certainly be fulfilled. But they will be fulfilled *as Jesus stated them.*

Accordingly, all of the four petitions of the Our Father's second half are offered for "us" ("give *us* ...forgive *us*... lead *us* ... deliver *us*..."), and no promise is implied within the prayer regarding who exactly is numbered among the ranks signified by "us." In appreciation of God's infinite Mercy, we can be assured that this "us" will incorporate all who sincerely desire to be counted among Christ's flock and allow themselves to be saved. But neither is a promise made nor implied that the "us" refers to *all.*

On the other hand, the Our Father's first three petitions are not likewise circumscribed. God's name *will* be hallowed, for "at the name of Jesus, every knee shall bow" (Philippians 2:10). God's Kingdom *will* come, for "the kingdom of the world has become the kingdom of our Lord and of his Christ" (Revelation 11:15) and "it is your Father's good pleasure to give you the kingdom." (Luke 12:32) The temporal fulfillment of this Kingdom is found precisely in His Will being done on earth as in Heaven, which *will* happen, for the saints "shall reign on the earth," (Revelation 5:10) and Christ has indeed been lifted up even after promising, "And I, if I be lifted up from the earth, will draw all things to myself." (John 12:32) Assuredly, each of these things will transpire precisely as the Our Father promises they will, and there is nothing within the prayer that warrants supposing its first three petitions might contain a subtle caveat.

Were one to offer a qualification that mitigates the prayer's certainty, he would be guilty of what the last warning in Scripture insists we never, ever do; that is, add or subtract from it (cf. Revelation 22:18-19). To suppose that "Thy Will be done on earth as it is in Heaven" means something other than "Thy Will be done on earth as it is in Heaven" is to attempt to inject into Scripture something not only foreign to but also in contradiction of its clear teachings. The Bible's final exhortation does not in vain warn against such a crime. No Christian may ever, as the axiom says, "place a comma where God has put a period," and woe to one who seeks to place a footnote on what God has rendered absolutely clear on its own.

From the beginning of Christianity, the Fathers of the Church knew all this very well and insisted upon the reality of the fulfillment of the *clear* sense of the Our Father prayer (as we will see in greater detail in Part Five). Recalling the teachings of the greatest Father and

Doctor of the Eastern Church, St. John Chrysostom, we find the following:

> For **He did not at all say, "Thy will be done" in *me*, or in *us*, but everywhere on the earth**; so that error may be destroyed, and truth implanted, and all wickedness cast out, and virtue return, and no difference in this respect be henceforth between heaven and earth. "For if this come to pass," saith He, "there will be no difference between things below and above, separated as they are in nature; the earth exhibiting to us another set of angels." (Homily XIX, §7)[18]

The observation of this great Father is as clear as its implications are certain: *There are no asterisks on the third petition.* Jesus prayed it. *It. Will. Happen.*

The Importance of Hierarchy

> "Here appears the wonderful hierarchy of knowledge: division below, unity on high."–Fr. Garrigou-Lagrange

A word is in order on the legitimacy and importance of the task we have undertaken in this chapter. For none should worry that there may be something scandalous or distracting about these comparisons which seek to ascertain what is supreme within the Lord's Prayer. Of course, the entire Our Father is certainly *extremely* important; and *all* of Scripture is very important. This fact, however, does not change another one: God's works are hierarchical, like a symphony or a castle; not blandly uniform, like elevator music or a warehouse.[19]

In our Faith, hierarchies exist everywhere we look. All the virtues are utterly necessary; the supernatural virtues, however, exceed the moral virtues. Each supernatural virtue is required, but charity surpasses faith and hope (cf. 1 Corinthians 13:13). Seven Sacraments have been given to us, but the Blessed Sacrament surpasses all the rest. Nine choirs of angels exist; each of sufficient beauty to astonish the world, but the Seraphim occupy the position closest to God.

---

[18] This teaching of Chrysostom's is also quoted in *the Catechism of the Catholic Church*, §2825

[19] Perhaps, for example, no one is currently writing a doctoral dissertation on the "supreme importance" of St. Paul asking Timothy for the return of the cloak he left with Carpus (cf. 2 Timothy 4:13). The Church will manage to survive without such an exposition. But many are likely working on ever-deeper writings extolling the glories of Mary by commenting on her "fullness of grace." (Luke 1:28) Surely, the importance of this dignity enjoyed by Our Lady still must be better appreciated by the Church, and the Scriptural verses which signify it are so important that they deserve even more attention than St. Paul's cloak.

This list will not be prolonged, lest we find ourselves here reviewing the entire content of our religion, for not one corner of it will be found without hierarchy. God did not in vain provide these hierarchical structures, therefore the effort we put into prayerfully considering what exactly enjoys supremacy within the various realms of our Faith—far from constituting a scandal or distraction—is, rather, *necessary* for making the best use of this brief time we are given on earth for the mission of becoming saints. No businessman neglects to consider what products are most profitable for him to sell. Likewise, we—to whom Our Lord recommends the astuteness that the worldly apply to their own occupations (cf. Luke 16:8)—should not neglect to have our eyes fixed, like a tiger in pursuit of its prey, on the supreme principle of the spiritual life. In order to do so, we must first endeavor to discover just what that principle is. Hence, the present inquiry.

Let us now examine how this very petition is not only supreme in the Lord's Prayer, but also encapsulates the supreme principle of *all* Scripture.

> "The Saints, with scarcely a single exception, failed not to make the principal gift contemplated by this Petition [The Our Father's Third] the object of their fervent prayers to God." -Catechism of the Council of Trent. Part IV.

3. "Fiat": The Greatest Theme of Public Revelation

"Divine and active Love burned in My heart, and had as its main motive to carry out the Divine Will on behalf of man. The Redemption was naught but the faithful accomplishment of this Divine Will."
–Jesus to Blessed Conchita[20]

The simple but earth-shattering sentiment expressed by the words "Thy Will be done,"—or, in Latin, "Fiat Voluntas Tua," which can be shortened to simply "*Fiat*,"—is not only supreme among the petitions of the Our Father prayer. It also best encapsulates the most dramatic Scriptural moments of utmost importance, and best summarizes the loftiest Biblical expositions of Heaven-sent clarity which speak most powerfully to the truths of God and His creation.

The Creating Fiat and the Fiat Heralding Redemption

"The greatest event in our history, the Incarnation..."
–Pope Benedict XVI

In *the* beginning, it is none other than *The Fiat* that is revealed, in Scripture's third verse, as establishing the fundamental principle of creation itself:

> And God said, "**Let there be light**"; and there was light. (Genesis 1:3. RSVCE). Dixitque Deus: **"Fiat lux."** Et facta est lux. (Genesis 1:3. Latin Vulgate).

"Fiat," Latin for "so be it" or "let it be done," is the first word spoken by God in Scripture. History itself began with its utterance. Before the Divine pronouncement of this word, "the earth was without form and void, and darkness was upon the face of the deep." (Genesis 1:2) Therefore, only thanks to *The Fiat* does anything but God Himself exist. As "existence is our first and greatest good" (Aristotle) and gratitude should be proportioned to the value of the gift which inspires it, what follows is that no act is so deserving of our thanksgiving and

---

[20] Juan Gutierrez Gonzales, M.Sp.S. *Priests of Christ*.

praise as God's own *Fiat*; that no prayer is so exalted and meritorious as one which glorifies this *Fiat*; and that no deed we ourselves can do will ever be as powerful and pleasing to God as simply pronouncing our very own *Fiat*.

This most exalted of all words was not only the instrument for God bringing creation into existence and thus initiating history itself, but it was also the instrument—on the lips of a certain virgin from Nazareth—for God undertaking the single greatest event *within* history: the Incarnation.

> And Mary said: Behold the handmaid of the Lord; **be it done to me** according to thy word. (Luke 1:38. Douay-Rheims.) Dixit autem Maria: "Ecce ancilla Domini: **fiat mihi** secundum verbum tuum." (Luke 1:38. Latin Vulgate.)

The primacy of Mary's *Fiat* (and the Incarnation of the Word that it precipitated) among the works told in Scripture and all those the world has ever seen, is without question. Not even in the Paschal Mysteries themselves was what transpired so incomprehensibly glorious. For in each such Mystery, the God-man *did something*—suffered, died, rose, and ascended; but upon the Annunciation, the Fiat of Mary, and the Incarnation, the Eternal God Himself *became* the God-man. As Pope Benedict XVI teaches:

> ... The moment when the angel of the Lord came to Mary with the great announcement of the Incarnation, [she] gave her reply...[then transpired] **the greatest event in our history, the Incarnation; the Word became flesh** ... she placed her entire being at the disposal of God's will... **The will of Mary coincides with the will of the Son** in the Father's unique project of love and, **in her, heaven and earth are united,** God the Creator is united to his creature ... John XXIII issued an invitation to contemplate this mystery, to "reflect on that union of heaven and earth, which is the purpose of the Incarnation and Redemption."[21]

Here, Pope Benedict—quoting Pope St. John XXIII—insists that *the* purpose of the Incarnation and Redemption (that is, *the purpose of Christianity itself*) is the "union of heaven and earth," and he likewise insists that this union is found in the *Fiat* of Mary, made possible by the union of *Mary's will with the Divine Will*. Expounding upon the same event, the *Catechism* notes, "**'Fiat': this is Christian prayer:** to be wholly God's, because he is wholly ours." (§2617) In other words, the *Fiat* is not just a Scriptural illustration of an advisable devotion, but

---

[21] Pope Benedict XVI. Pastoral visit to Loreto. October 4, 2012

rather must be regarded as the essence of a Christian's *entire life*. Similarly, Benedict also taught:

> To be 'devoted' to the Immaculate Heart of Mary means therefore to embrace this attitude of heart, which makes **the fiat—'your will be done'—the defining center of one's whole life**. (Cardinal Ratzinger. *The Message of Fatima.*)

Should one claim that this admonition applies only to those inclined to devotion to the Immaculate Heart, let him be reminded that Jesus gave the Virgin to us as our mother (cf. John 19:26). Marian devotion is not optional; it is inseparable from Christianity. As we see here, however, such devotion is essentially a means (albeit a necessary and supreme means) to rendering the Our Father's third petition the "defining center of one's whole life." It therefore follows that the fundamental call of all Christians is ensuring that the Divine Will is "the defining center" of one's own life.

From these two Scriptural passages alone—the *Fiat* of Creation and the *Fiat* of Mary's Annunciation—the Our Father's third petition stands so exalted as to merit our most wholehearted devotion and resolute attention. The Gospel, however, presents another *Fiat* that also commands our imitation.

The Fiat of the God-man

> "And again he prayed in the same way, saying, "My Father, if this cannot pass unless I drink it, your will be done." It is clear here that his human will is in full harmony with God's will. This harmony is what we must always seek after and follow." –St. John Chrysostom

While the Catechism teaches that *Fiat* is the essence of the Blessed Virgin's prayer, it also presents the same principle as the essence of the prayer of her Divine Son:

> [Jesus echoes] his mother's Fiat at the time of his conception and [prefigures] what he will say to the Father in his agony. **The whole prayer of Jesus is contained in this** loving adherence of his human heart to the mystery of the will of the Father (cf. Eph 1:9) (§2603)

Jesus, though God incarnate, was also truly man and thus, like us, had a human will. Moreover, the "whole" of His prayer—as we see here illustrated in Church teaching—is "contained" in the "adherence of his human heart" (that is, His human will) to the "will of the Father" (that is, the Divine Will). As all of Jesus' acts *were* prayer itself (He of all people did not fail to "pray without ceasing" [1 Thessalonians 5:16]), we know that the paradigm of His entire life is none other than the union of His human will with the Divine Will. No other description of His operation better captures its essence, and no other aspect of His life commands our imitation more than this "living in the Divine Will."

Apart from being God's first word anywhere in Scripture, "Fiat" is also what He essentially says first in the New Testament. The opening words Jesus speaks in the Bible are "Let it be so..." (Matthew 3:15). Such was His response to John the Baptist's protestation that it is Jesus who should be baptizing him, not vice versa. But Jesus insisted that such a baptism was "fitting for us to fulfill all righteousness" (Matthew 3:15)—*it was the Will of God*. Here, in brief, we see that Jesus' first admonition—His very first word—in the Gospels was simply to commend submission to the Divine Will in a matter at first perplexing to human understanding.

The first Biblical words of Jesus, therefore, in essence say "Fiat." So do His final ones. The closing of His "Seven Last Words from the Cross" are, **"Father, into thy hands I commend my spirit!"** (Luke 23:46) Of this exclamation, Fr. Peter Stravinskas teaches: *"Jesus died resigned to the Will of the One Who sent Him ... it is an active resignation, which sums up His entire life: "As a man lives so shall He die."*[22] To commend one's spirit—that is, one's very life—to the Father is exactly this: to willingly submit oneself entirely to the Will of God. Addressing His Father, Jesus says, "into thy hands" (to the Divine Will), "I commend" (submit and entrust) "my spirit" (Jesus' human soul and human will). This act is certainly also a *Fiat*, and at this point none should be surprised to see that the Son of God ensured that the last act of His pre-Resurrection earthly life reflected the Our Father's third petition.

But the last word of Christ on the cross did not, perhaps, contain the ultimate drama of the Passion. According to several mystics, this drama reached its summit in the Garden of Gethsemane, wherein Jesus took upon Himself all the sins of the world—from the sin of Adam up to the last sin that will ever be committed—and experienced in advance, inside Himself, the entire course of the Passion that would follow in the remaining eighteen hours.[23] It was during this extreme

---

[22] Peter M.J. Stravinskas. *The Seven Last Words from the Cross: "Into Your hands I commend My spirit."* March 29, 2018. Catholic World Report

[23] Consider that, of all the 14 Stations of the Cross and 5 Sorrowful Mysteries, only one is described *subjectively; the Agony in the Garden*. That is, it is only this event of Christ's

moment in which Jesus, now in such agony that His Precious Blood burst forth from His pores, echoed the supreme petition of the prayer He had taught earlier on the Mount of Beatitudes:

> Father, if thou wilt, remove this chalice from me: but yet **not my will, but thine be done.** (Luke 22:42)

As the Agony in the Garden saw Jesus enduring the ultimate suffering of His entire Passion, it would only be reasonable to anticipate that His response to such suffering would likewise encapsulate the decisive principle for all Christians. And this is precisely what his response entailed: *Thy Will be done.* Pope Benedict XVI, relaying a teaching of St. Maximus the Confessor on this moment in the life of Christ, explains that:

> ... in Jesus' prayer, **"not my will but your will"... [he] recapitulates the whole process of his life** ... [God's will] is the very place where we find our true identity. God created us and we are ourselves if we conform with his will; only in this way do we enter into the truth of our being... redemption is always this process of leading the human will to communion with the divine will. It is a process for which we pray every day: "May your will be done."[24]

Imagine how attentively a student would sit up and listen if, on the last day of class, the teacher announced that he would summarize ("recapitulate") all the lessons of the semester in one simple phrase. Benedict is doing that for us here, and not for a mere school lesson, but rather for "the whole process" of Jesus' life—a life that bears all of Christianity and all of humanity's past and future within itself.

From Benedict's accurate account of the drama of Gethsemane alone, therefore, we see clearly revealed the Christian's Mission and the World's Penultimate Destiny: *Thy Will be done.* Everything is in that prayer. No effort to dive more deeply into it could ever be ill-advised, and no time spent building upon its foundation will ever go unrewarded.

> "The watchword of the Passion, as indeed of His whole life, was 'Thy Will be done!' That motto is written large across the Sacred Heart for the Father to read." -Fr. Robert Nash, S.J.

Passion which we primarily refer to not by way of physically describing what transpired (e.g., the scourging at the pillar, the crowning with thorns), but rather by referring to what Jesus Himself experienced during it (agony).

[24] Pope Benedict XVI. Lectio Divina with the parish priests of the Diocese of Rome. February 18, 2010.

The Passion of Jesus' 33 Years

> "The soul's free will is what I seek, what I came to earth to look for, what I desire to possess in all its fullness, what satisfies Me. The culmination of transformation into Me lies in joining this will to Mine on all levels and in all fullness."
>
> –Jesus to Blessed Conchita[25]

Not only, however, was Jesus Himself conceived in the womb of the Virgin upon her *Fiat*; not only was the *Fiat* the supreme petition of the only prayer He ever taught; not only was the *Fiat* the last word He spoke on the cross and the word He spoke in His supreme moment of agony—the *Fiat* was, moreover, the defining theme of His whole earthly life. For indeed, *He lived as He died*, and His words and deeds during His public ministry also demonstrate that the accomplishment of the Divine Will was the paradigm and the passion of all the years He spent on earth.

> My food is to do the will of him who sent me. (John 4:34) I have come down from heaven, not to do my own will, but the will of him who sent me. (John 6:38)

Confirming that the Divine Will was the standard of Jesus' life, the Servant of God Archbishop Luis Martinez teaches that:

> ... ordinarily, [Jesus] hid His tenderness with a veil of divine serenity... but when it was a question of His Father's will, far from concealing His desire to fulfill it, He was pleased to show it in all the circumstances of His life. (*The Sanctifier*. Chapter XVI.)

The Servant of God goes on to explain that "the secrets of the soul of Jesus" are found in the Book of Hebrews: "When Christ came into the world, he said... '**Lo, I have come to do thy will, O God**,' as it is written of me in the scroll of the book." (Ch. 10:5,7) He says that in this passage, we see:

> ... a revelation of the depths within Jesus: we know what He felt, what He said, and what He longed for in the beginning of His life; He came to do the will of His father, and the full accomplishment of that will was His oblation on Calvary... For Jesus, **the will of His Father was the foundation of His relationship with souls ... In [the Our Father,] we find these words that seem to come forth as a triumphant cry from the depths of His soul: "Thy will be done on earth, as it is in Heaven."** He wished to

[25] *Priests of Christ*. Concepción Cabrera de Armida. Society of Saint Paul, 2015. *imprimatur*, Domenico Di Raimondo Romo, M.Sp.S. May 30, 2004. Page xxvii

> tell us in our own language how avidly He sought to do the Father's will and how that will was His very life... the very foundation of His soul... The will of God is the norm of perfection, the secret of happiness, and the repose of love... (*The Sanctifier*. Chapter XVI)

Lest anyone—despite recognizing that the Divine Will was the unquestionably supreme principle of Jesus' life—forget that *we* are called to *imitate* Christ and model our entire lives after His, Jesus teaches explicitly that our adherence to the Will of God is what renders us His Own: "**Whoever does the will of my Father in heaven is my brother, and sister, and mother**." (Matthew 12:50)

Neither healing the sick, nor raising the dead, nor forgiving the sinners, nor bestowing power to cast out demons, nor anything of the sort, is so glorious a gift as what is here described: the adoption of Divine Sonship. Jesus could not have given a greater promise than one which offers incorporation into His Own Divine family, as is here pledged to whoever does the Divine Will.

But if such a lofty promise fails to motivate a slothful soul, he should be reminded of Jesus' teaching that salvation itself depends upon doing God's Will:

> Not every one who says to me, 'Lord, Lord,' shall enter the kingdom of heaven, but he who does the will of my Father who is in heaven. (Matthew 7:21)

We have already settled that the Divine Will is the object of the greatest petition of the Greatest Prayer; that it is the fundamental principle of Scripture itself; that it is the very life and breath of Jesus Christ and His Most Holy Mother. Now we see that it, and it alone, is the key admission to eternal glory.

All these truths about the Divine Will are found within the foundation of the Faith itself: Public Revelation. In laying this foundation down, however, God neither intended for it to remain strictly a bare foundation, nor did He desire that only tents be pitched upon it. *He laid it down to build on it,* and He immediately commenced that work upon the foundation's completion. Perhaps no one who has read thus far will be surprised to see, therefore, that the very principle which was supreme in Scripture remained supreme in the Age of the Church. But everyone, I think, will be astonished to see just how gloriously the Holy Spirit inspired the saints to develop this principle. In Part Two, we will see that development.

Part Two: The Divine Will and Sacred Tradition: Paradigm of The Holy Spirit's Work in Church History

"The Holy Spirit is at work with the Father and the Son from the beginning to the completion of the plan for our salvation. But in these "end times," ushered in by the Son's redeeming Incarnation, the Spirit is revealed and given, recognized and welcomed as a person. Now can this divine plan, accomplished in Christ, the firstborn and head of the new creation, be embodied in mankind by the outpouring of the Spirit..."
–*Catechism of the Catholic Church*, §686

4. The Holy Spirit's Work After Public Revelation

"Certainly there is progress [in the Church], even exceedingly great progress! For who is so envious of others and so hateful toward God as to try to prohibit it? ... It is necessary, therefore, that understanding, knowledge, and wisdom should grow and advance vigorously in individuals as well as in the community, in a single person as well as in the whole church, and this gradually in the course of ages and centuries."
–St. Vincent of Lérins

From Part One, we have seen that the accomplishment of the Divine Will on earth as in Heaven – the *Fiat* – is the supreme principle of both the Lord's Prayer and the whole of Public

Revelation itself, especially concerning the lives of Jesus and Mary. As all true development in the Church respects continuity, this same principle could not fail to remain the key to the growth of the Church's Sacred Tradition throughout her history. The same Holy Spirit Who inspired each word of Public Revelation (Sacred Scripture) is even now the "soul of the Church" (Catechism, §797), and He did not forget, upon the completion of the Deposit of Faith with the death of the Apostle John, the essential principle that defined His work two thousand years ago.

Considering the analogy at the conclusion of the last chapter, Public Revelation now standing complete does not entail a cessation of the Divine conquest it describes any more than a house's foundation being complete means construction is done. Quite the opposite, the closing of the age of Public Revelation, as well as the opening of the Age of the Church at Pentecost, only commenced a new phase in the same fundamental conquest. Moreover, far from being in any way less important than what had transpired before, this new phase brings an *acceleration* of God's intervention in the world directed at the accomplishment of His Will.

This acceleration is imparted by the fact that the climax of the greatest story ever told—The Story of History—has now occurred. For we have experienced the Incarnation, death, and Resurrection of the Lord. The tides have turned, the gates of Heaven have opened, and the ancient enemy's fate is sealed; therefore, we are—as of two thousand years ago—in the "end times" (Catechism, §686), wherein the "divine plan, accomplished in Christ" can be "embodied in mankind by the outpouring of the Spirit." (Ibid.) We are now awaiting *and participating in* The Greatest Story's *dénouement*—that is, the completion of the fulfillment which its *own* pages will see before the book is closed, whereupon eternity commences and the Story's "happily ever after" begins: God forever being "all in all," (1 Corinthians 15:28) as we stand together, "Saints among the Saints in the halls of heaven." (Roman Missal) We will explore this dynamic more carefully in Part Five, but for now it suffices to acknowledge that the *climax* and the *dénouement,* while perfectly united in substance, are also distinct in execution.

Unlike the Israelites of the Old Testament who had Public Revelation *in process* but not yet complete, we now need not wonder what exactly our mission is, or what its central facts are: we know both with certainty and with closure. The Our Father's promise and prophecy of the Will of God being done on earth as in Heaven is the mission.

The contents of the Creed are the central facts. As St. Augustine taught:

> One of the prophets, anticipating the time of God's grace, declared: And it shall come to pass, that whosoever shall call on the name of the Lord shall be delivered. **Hence the Lord's Prayer.** But the apostle, when, for the purpose of commending this very grace, he had quoted this prophetic testimony, immediately added: How then shall they call on Him in whom they have not believed? **Hence the Creed.** (St. Augustine. *Enchiridion of Faith, Hope, and Love.* Ch VII.)

We know that none of these realities will ever be altered or surpassed, since we await no new Public Revelation. God has rendered the foundation *singular* and *immovable*, and He has done this to inspire us to devote ourselves wholeheartedly to building upon it without puzzlement over what the building's footprint will ultimately include. How misguided, therefore, are those who, like children afraid of a thunderstorm, treat the Deposit of Faith as a desk to crawl beneath and hide under! With Public Revelation being complete, we now know *that* we know *what* we know about God and His plan. We have our battle orders, and we are certain of the victory. This should inspire us to boldly engage in the fight, not demoralize us to retreat to realms of comfort and apparent safety.

> "Brothers and sisters: You are God's building. According to the grace of God given to me, like a wise master builder I laid a foundation, and another is building upon it. But each one must be careful how he builds upon it, for no one can lay a foundation other than the one that is there, namely, Jesus Christ." –1 Corinthians 3:9-11
>
> "O God, who from living and chosen stones prepare an eternal dwelling for your majesty, increase in your Church the spirit of grace you have bestowed, **so that by new growth your faithful people may build up the heavenly Jerusalem**." –Collect for the Feast of the Dedication of the Lateran Basilica. Roman Missal.

Though each era in the history of the Church has a special task assigned to it, the fundamental approach of Spirit-led growth described above is the one adopted by all the saints, none of whom were deluded by the allure of "primitivism."

Against Primitivism

> "This tradition which comes from the Apostles develops in the Church with the help of the Holy Spirit. For there is a growth in the understanding of the realities and the words which have been handed down ... For as the centuries succeed one another, the Church constantly moves forward toward the fullness of divine truth until the words of God reach their complete fulfillment in her." –*Dei Verbum*, §8

For victims of the error of Primitivism, the truth will be surprising to hear: Church history is the theater of Providentially orchestrated growth toward the goal of God's Will being accomplished on earth as in Heaven—not the diabolical descent toward the fate of supreme misery reigning, whereupon the Second Coming finally arrives to put the world out of its misery.

The base premise in the falsehood that is Primitivism holds that in each successive generation throughout Church history, Christianity *as such* merely deteriorated spiritually. From this it follows, the Primitivists say, that the best we can do is eliminate all development which Sacred Tradition has graced the Church with these two thousand years, and endeavor to make everything about the Faith look exactly as it did in the first century.

The truth, indeed, is to be found in the exact opposite of Primitivism's insistence that we reject the growth that God Himself has given the Church in her Sacred Tradition. For although it may be the case that we will always admire the heroism of the *early Christians themselves* from a position of relative inferiority, this reverence does not involve denouncing the development seen *in Christianity* since its early days. The proper understanding of Sacred Tradition's growth does not hold that *the average Christian* becomes holier and holier as history progresses; therefore, presenting 1st-Century Christians' heroic virtue as an argument in support of Primitivism would be a red herring. The proper understanding, rather, is that—despite the failures of many of her members—the Church *herself* is the Bride of Christ, and the Bridegroom Himself cannot fail to bring about what He has promised in His beloved. As Pope Benedict XVI teaches:

> There are views that see the entire history of the Church in the second millennium as a gradual decline. Some see this decline as having already begun immediately after the New Testament. In fact, "*Opera Christi non deficiunt, sed proficiunt*": **Christ's works do not go backwards but forwards.** What would the Church be

> without the new spirituality of the Cistercians, the Franciscans and the Dominicans, the spirituality of St. Teresa of Avila and St. John of the Cross and so forth? This affirmation applies today too: "*Opera Christi non deficiunt, sed proficiunt*", they move forward. (General Audience. March 10, 2010)

From this ever forward-moving nature of God's work in the Church, it follows that, even if sin and error of all forms are observed to become more grave and widespread over a certain duration of time within the ranks of those who belong—nominally, at least—to the Church, God nevertheless remains the Architect of History, and He never fails to increase His work in the sanctification of the Church *as the mystical Body of Christ*, purifying her more and more in preparation for the Heavenly wedding feast to commence at the end of time.

This reality is not obscured by the corruption that may exist within the Church's own hierarchy. Clergymen are also mere members of the Church, and no amount of sin committed within their ranks can prevent God from increasing the holiness of the Church *as such*. For the holiness of the Church *as a mystical body* is not some ephemeral notion which is sufficiently amorphous that the proponents of spiritual or theological fads may claim it for their own ends. The holiness of the Church, rather, is a concrete and observable reality: what is seen in the lives and teachings of the *saints*.

> Faced with this mystery, we are greatly helped not only by theological investigation but also by **that great heritage which is the "lived theology" of the saints.** (Pope St. John Paul II. *Novo Millennio Ineunte*, §27)

Our duty, therefore, is to observe what God has already brought about in the *lived theology of the saints*. As we engage in this inquiry throughout the forthcoming pages, we will see that this Divine task above all consists in the accomplishment of His Will on earth as in Heaven.

Before we do so, however, it bears emphasizing that rejecting Primitivism does not mean welcoming Modernism. For we know that "*we have received not the spirit of the world, but the Spirit which is from God, that we might understand the gifts bestowed on us by God,*" (1 Corinthians 2:12) that "*the god of this world has blinded the minds of the unbelievers, to keep them from seeing the light of the gospel of the glory of Christ...*" (2 Corinthians 4:4), and, finally, that worldly ways must be left behind by the followers of Christ, for " *... you formerly walked according to the course of this world, according to the prince of the power of* *the air, of the spirit that is now working in the sons of disobedience."* (Ephesians 2:2)

Neglecting these teachings, Modernism (repeatedly condemned by the Church's Magisterium) is guilty of confusing the *unholy* spirit—the very spirit *of the world* that Scripture condemns—with the Holy Spirit Himself. Accordingly, Modernists[26] pretend that the various heresies and sins which arise are themselves willed by God by the mere fact that they are popular. They succumb to this diabolical trap because, instead of looking to the *saints* to ascertain what the Spirit is bringing about in the Church, Modernists look to worldly sources.[27] If Modernism and Primitivism are opposite vices, then love of Sacred Tradition is the "golden mean virtue" standing between them. We will abide in this virtue if we look to the right places to ascertain what the Holy Spirit is doing in the Church and if we are careful to avoid all heresy (especially those condemned under the umbrella of Modernism).

In sum, if we wish to appreciate the greatest realities of the Holy Spirit's work in the last two thousand years of His continual guiding influence, we must presuppose—as an absolute certainty—that *the development of the Church's Sacred Tradition in her saints is no mere accident.* We must, rather, regard as a *given* God's closeness to us; we must accept as *settled* the fact that He always has been close to us, that He is leading us by the hand, and that He is doing so with a purpose. This purpose, as we will see, is found in the Greatest Prayer's supreme eleven words with which we are now well acquainted.

---

[26] Too many examples of the Modernist view of the present theme exist to here list, but we should note that Church history's growth towards God's ultimate plan is in no way a Leibnizian, Hegelian, or Darwinian reality. In these latter erroneous theories and their offshoots, there is—among many other fatal flaws—a failure to differentiate between God's permissive Will and His ordained Will. Accordingly, these theories impel one to regard whatever he reads in the news or the history books as an intrinsic good merely because it happened, when in fact God allows evils only so that good can come about from them: goods which, though *enabled* by the evils which preceded them, do not *contain* any of the evils within their own substance. Ascertaining God's Will in Sacred Tradition is not a matter of merely explicating whatever trend is evident in the pages of a history book, as is the strategy of those who take the erroneous view of history. It is, rather, a matter of prayerfully studying what God Himself has been at work in bringing about through what He has inspired in the souls in whom His grace most powerfully dwells—i.e., as we have said, in the lives and teachings of the saints.

[27] Whether the openly worldly or the false prophets in the Church—the wolves in sheep's clothing—who wrap the lies of the prince of this world in the language of "tolerance, equality, acceptance, and compassion."

The Fathers of the Church: Divinization. The Seed Watered

> "Constituted in a state of holiness, man was destined to be fully 'divinized' by God in glory. Seduced by the devil, he wanted to 'be like God', but 'without God, before God, and not in accordance with God.'"–*Catechism of the Catholic Church* (§398)

Although Scripture exalts the Will of God—the *Fiat,* the third petition of the Our Father—as its own supreme principle, what this means for us is not laid out in great detail within the pages of the Bible. As with many of the most consequential Scriptural realities (*e.g., Our Lady's mediation of grace, Purgatory, the centrality of the Eucharist and Confession, etc.*), Providence would have it that only the seed was to be given within the body of Public Revelation, whereas the watering and the growth of that seed was left to Sacred Tradition.[28]

> "In His manifestation of truth God does not proceed by violence but by conviction, **gradually integrating truth up to its fullness**."–St. Gregory of Nazianzus, Father of the Church

Such is their inexhaustible glory, that the development of the Church's understanding of the depth and breadth of the words, "*Thy Will be done on earth as it is in Heaven,*" took many centuries to accomplish. This development will continue until the end of time, for even upon the commencement of the Era that we will discuss in Part Five, growth will only accelerate still more—not diminish. Indeed, "once" the Kingdom comes to earth, we will still pray for it to "*come!*" (Matthew 6:10), because until we arrive at the Kingdom's definitive perfection in Heaven, it can always come *more* fully on earth.

Although this work of plumbing the depths of the Our Father's third petition and thereby rendering more explicit what already existed in Public Revelation is an effort that finds its greatest exposition in a certain recent private revelation (which we will discuss in Part Four), that revelation was not introduced in a vacuum, nor was it placed like a crown floating in the air. Quite the opposite, it was given to the Church with such perfect timing that its revelation can only be

---

[28] For example, no single theologian could by himself deduce all the Marian Dogmas and prayerfully happen upon all the glories enjoyed by Our Lady. Organic Sacred Tradition, therefore, was indispensable for this process of developing a more complete Mariology which, though present, was only a small seed in Public Revelation. Many centuries of efforts were needed; efforts all prodded on by the grace of the Holy Spirit, Who knew exactly what He was doing the whole time; efforts by saints and mystics, Popes and private revelations, theologians and philosophers, priests and lay people.

compared to the crescendo of a classical masterpiece; one which, though comprising many centuries, is impeccable in its composition.

Within this masterpiece, we can see the entire development of the Church's Sacred Tradition as a Divinely guided step-by-step construction of the very Sanctity of the Divine Will that was God's purpose from the beginning. But many developments, on top of the foundation in Scripture, were needed before the bestowal of the crown. The first of these developments[29] is seen in the teachings of the Fathers of the Church on the "divinization (or deification) of man."

Although most of the New Testament's content does not directly concern itself with what could be plausibly considered a direct treatment of this theme, the Fathers of the Church, moved by the Holy Spirit, nevertheless realized—from the shining *seeds* of this truth contained in Scripture—that the fundamental, essential call of the Christian is not merely to be delivered from damnation, to be virtuous, to do good things, or to have a "personal relationship" with Jesus; rather, the fundamental call of the Christian is far higher—*it is to become like God*; which is what it means to be "divinized" or "deified." Dr. Scott Hahn, in his foreword to *Called to be the Children of God: The Catholic Theology of Human Deification*, laments that this teaching is neglected by many Christians. He writes:

> Jesus saves us from sin and death. **Rescue from sin and death is indeed a wonderful thing—but the salvation won for us by Jesus Christ is incomparably greater...**

This observation should in no way detract from the immense importance, which cannot possibly be overstated, of the Redemption and of the application of its graces to individuals for their salvation. Redemption remains the foundation, and the Church Fathers affirmed this fact; however, they also knew that Redemption was the

---

[29] *Divinization* was indeed a true *development* in the Church's holiness, not a mere cautious commentary on Scripture undertaken with Primitivist presuppositions. Consider that in terms of their length in relation to the whole, only a minuscule fraction of the New Testament's verses could be plausibly taken as a direct exhortation to pursue "divinization;" that is, the loftiest levels of the spiritual life and the most exalted types of sanctity which render the soul itself Godlike. Almost the entire content of the New Testament's twenty-seven books relays what Jesus did externally via His human nature, what the Apostles did in their travels, what Christian Faith and Morals consists in, how Christianity fulfills Judaism, denunciations of apostasy, idolatry, and other sins, and prophecy. Vital as all this content is, the preponderance of such themes says nothing about their standing relative to the theme of divinization. Spiritual value cannot be calculated by adding up verses. If it could be, then the Old Testament would be far superior to the New Testament, the details of the Ark of the Covenant's construction would be more important than the Ten Commandments of *the* Covenant itself, and the preaching of the Apostles would surpass in importance the preaching of Jesus Himself.

beginning, not the end, of the spiritual life. The "end," or *purpose*, of the spiritual life is better relayed by "The Great Exchange," about which the *Catechism of the Catholic Church* teaches, **"God was made man that we might be made God."** (§460)

This bold teaching comes to us first and most explicitly from St. Athanasius, whom many will recall as the great Father and Doctor of the Church who heroically defended the Divinity of Christ against the onslaught of the Arian heresy. Sadly, however, his mysticism is often forgotten. The Catechism's emphasis on this quote from Athanasius should remind us—as we turn to his intercession and example to confront the various crises of orthodoxy in the Church today—to not lose sight of the entire purpose of the Christological orthodoxy which he fought for; namely, that we too become "other Christs."

Teachings on divinization are a constant theme for the Fathers of the Church; therefore, we can be certain that these admonitions are essential to Christianity, although we can only sample a few here:

> **St. Augustine**: "Of [Christ's] own will he was born for us today, in time, so that he could lead us to his Father's eternity. God became man so that man might become God." (Office of Readings. Saturday before Epiphany)
> **St. Gregory of Nazianzus:** "[God] continues to wear the Body which He assumed, **until He make me God by the power of His Incarnation**." (*Oration* 30. Paragraph XIV)
> **St. Irenaeus:** "The Word of God, our Lord Jesus Christ, who did, through His transcendent love, become what we are, **that He might bring us to be even what He is Himself**." (*Against Heresies*. V)
> **St. Clement of Alexandria: "The Word of God became man, that thou mayest learn from man how man may become God**." (*Exhortation to the Heathen*. Chapter 1)
> **St. Gregory of Nyssa: "By this communion with Deity mankind might at the same time be deified, for this end it is** that, by dispensation of His grace, He disseminates Himself in every believer through that flesh, whose substance comes from bread and wine, blending Himself with the bodies of believers..." (*The Great Catechism*. Part III. Chapter 37)

These exhortations, even among Patristic teachings in general, exist in a league of their own. For while each theme discussed by the Fathers is important and must be taken seriously, their insistence upon divinization was not about this or that *aspect* of the Christian's mission, but rather encompassed the *essence* of *the Christian mission itself.* In a word, divinization was not "an opinion" of the Fathers; it was, rather, *the passion* of the Fathers. We will not dwell here on seeking to demonstrate the uniqueness of deification among the Fathers' teachings; a plethora of easily accessible treatises from contemporary Patristics scholars has already proven it well. In just one of these treatises, we find a helpful insight regarding the theologian who may have been the most towering of all the Patristics scholars of the 20th Century, Hans Urs von Balthasar:

> **According to Balthasar, divinization is ... the most basic and fundamental question of all religious, existential, and philosophical thought** ...[it] has a "structural significance" as **the basic question ... of the relationship between God and the world**, the infinite and the finite, the one and the many.[30]

The author of the piece above points out that if Balthasar did not focus as much specific attention on divinization as one might have expected, this was in fact only because he regarded it as *so* broad a matter as to encompass *all* questions relating to God and man.

Church teaching also affirms divinization's centrality. The same paragraph from the Catechism quoted earlier answers that most vital of Christian questions—*"Why Did the Word Become Flesh?"*—by teaching:

> The Word became flesh to make us "partakers of the divine nature": "For **this is why the Word became man**, and the Son of God became the Son of man: so that man, by entering into communion with the Word and thus receiving divine sonship, might become a son of God." "For the Son of God became man **so that we might become God**." "The only-begotten Son of God, wanting to make us sharers in his divinity, assumed our nature, so that he, made man, might make men gods." (§460)

Here, the Catechism quotes Scripture (2 Peter 1:4), St. Irenaeus, St. Athanasius (both of whom are Fathers of the Church), and St. Thomas Aquinas, respectively. Each quote included affirms the *reality* of divinization, and the nature of this section in the Catechism is a testimony to the *primacy* of divinization. For we cannot imagine a question more essential to the Faith than the one which asks why the Incarnation itself—the greatest event in history—happened; nevertheless, *divinization* is that simple question's straightforward answer.

We will not, however, find extensive content within the writings of the Fathers that gives a detailed illumination of precisely how

---

[30] Jonathan Martin Ciraulo. *Mystical Doctrines of Deification. Case Studies in the Christian Tradition*. Contemporary Theological Explorations in Mysticism. Routledge. 2019. Chapter 12.

divinization is best attained in the spiritual life of a Christian, just what a "divinized" life looks like, and what this means for ordinary Christians. In this realm, the Fathers of the Church were victorious in their God-given mission by insisting upon divinization and defining it. The task of further illuminating the details of divinization's pursuit (what scholars have referred to as "**The shift from an ontological concept of divinization to one focused primarily on a union of wills**"[31]) was being saved by the Holy Spirit for the next era of Sacred Tradition's development. But before bringing about that era, the bridges necessary to pass on to it had to be constructed.

The Bridges: Maximus and Bernard

> "Surely [God's] creatures ought to conform themselves, as much as they can, to His will ... in all things we should seek only to do His will... even as we pray every day: *'Thy will be done on earth as it is in heaven'* ... To reach this state is to become godlike."
>
> –St. Bernard of Clairvaux

Perhaps the most profound of the Patristic reflections on the theme of divinization comes from one of the later Fathers of the Church, St. Maximus the Confessor. Dr. Normal Russel insists that Maximus' "teaching on deification represents **the true climax of the patristic tradition.**"[32] Pope St. John Paul II, well known for his insistence that the Church "breathe with both lungs" (that is, appreciate Eastern and Western Sacred Tradition), referred to Maximus as a "bridge" between the Church's East and West, and one whose charisms "must" be relied on for the new evangelization.[33] Later, Pope Benedict XVI summarized the "fundamental" theme of Maximus' teaching within an address whose value cannot be overstated:

> St. Maximus tells us that, and we know that this is true, Adam (and we ourselves are Adam) thought that the "no" was the peak of freedom ...[but] the height of freedom is the "yes", in conformity with God's will. It is only in the "yes" that man truly becomes himself; only in the great openness of the "yes", **in the unification of his will with the divine**, that man becomes immensely open, becomes "divine" ... it is in the "yes" that he becomes free; and this is the drama of Gethsemane: *not my will but yours.* **It is**

---

[31] Ibid.

[32] *The Doctrine of Deification in the Greek Patristic Tradition*. Oxford University Press. 2004. Introduction.

[33] Pope St. John Paul II. Address to the Greek Orthodox Delegation sent by H.B. Christodoulos. March 11, 2002

> **by transferring the human will to the divine will that the real person is born**... This, in a few brief words, is **the fundamental point of what St. Maximus wanted to say and here we see that the whole human being is truly at issue; the entire question of our life lies here.**[34]

Here, Benedict rightly insists, Maximus' *fundamental* point is communicated to us in one single theme—notwithstanding the enormous breadth of the latter's teachings.[35] Herein, too, the Pope equally well claims, lies the *entire* question of our life! And this question's resolution is found in transferring of the *human will to the Divine Will*, only whereafter "**the real person is born**." Could more consequential teachings even be imagined? Moreover, in the saint's own words, we find the teaching that—on Christ's example—*all that matters* is the accomplishment of the Divine Will:

> The human will [of Christ] is wholly deified, in its agreement with the divine will itself ... **[Christ] shows that all that matters is a perfect verification of the will of the Father**, in his saying as a human ... *Not mine, but your will be done*, by this giving himself **as a type and example of setting aside our own will by the perfect fulfilment of the divine**... (St. Maximus)[36]

Maximus' emphasis on the themes of both *divinization* and *will* establishes his role as a bridge between East and West *and* as a bridge to the next era of the Holy Spirit's work of sanctifying the Church.

For while the Eastern (Greek) Church Fathers are renowned for their teachings on divinization (although the theme is certainly not absent from the Western [Latin] Fathers[37]), there was—before Maximus—little to be found within their teachings that emphasized the centrality of *will* as the means of divinization's accomplishment. Even the very concept of "will" was largely foreign to ancient Greek thought and to early Greek Christian writers.[38] However, for Sacred Tradition's great developments of sanctification to progress, a theological and spiritual synthesis of the greatest insights into divinization *and* will was needed. With Maximus, it was provided.

---

34 Pope Benedict XVI. General Audience on St. Maximus the Confessor, Father of the Church. June 25th, 2008

35 Maximus is considered one of the greatest of the Eastern Patristic theologians and he wrote and taught prolifically.

36 Maximus the Confessor to Marinus. Oposcule 7. 80D. Cited in *Maximus the Confessor*, by Andrew Louth. Page 185.

37 See, for example, Dr. Jared Ortiz's recent work: *Deification in the Latin Patristic Tradition*. Catholic University Press. 2019.

38 Cf. Ian McFarland. *The Theology of the Will. The Oxford Handbook of Maximus the Confessor*. March 2015. 2.

But another lane was still needed in the construction of this "bridge to the next era" in the Holy Spirit's plan for the Church; one which would provide a greater and more profound exposition—within the context of divinization—of the virtue of charity, the importance of Marian devotion, and the accessibility of sanctity and mysticism to all. This exposition was given by St. Bernard of Clairvaux, Doctor of the Church and *"last of the Fathers, but certainly not inferior to the earlier ones."*[39]

As recently as the year 1953, Venerable Pope Pius XII, who used the title above for Bernard and thereby settled his status as a bridge between eras in the Church's Sacred Tradition, dedicated an entire Encyclical to extolling this saint's contributions to this tradition. Entitled *Doctor Mellifluus* and promulgated on the Feast of Pentecost, the encyclical teaches that *"perhaps no one"* had ever spoken "more excellently, more profoundly, or more earnestly" on Divine Charity than Bernard (cf. §17). The Pope even went so far as to say that "[Bernard] was in nothing inferior to the great apostles ... [he is] a mainstay of the Catholic Church." (§1) As we can see, understanding the designs of the Church's Spirit-led growth over the centuries requires discovering the fundamental contribution of St. Bernard of Clairvaux.[40]

Bernard, like the Church Fathers before him, spoke of the deification of man, but he specified—furthering Maximus' insight—that it consists not only in a "perfect verification" between the human will and Divine Will, but rather in a veritable *transformation* and *transmutation* of the human will *into* the Divine Will; a transformation itself based on the love of God, enabled by the mediation of the Blessed Virgin Mary, and within the reach of ordinary Christians, for whom the mystical life is indeed a genuine calling. Thus we see, in one extraordinary saint, an entire era's worth of spiritual developments! In his greatest work, *On Loving God*, we read:

> Surely [God's] creatures ought to conform themselves, as much as they can, to His will ... in all things we should seek only to do His will ... even as we pray every day: *'Thy will be done on earth as it is in heaven'* (Matt. 6.10) ... To reach this state is to become godlike. As a drop of water poured into wine loses itself, and takes

---

[39] Quoted in *Doctor Mellifluus*. Encyclical of Pope Pius XII. (St. Bernard was born in the year 1090, therefore despite his informal title, he did not technically rank among the Fathers of the Church, although his teachings rival their influence.)

[40] This very task was given borderline eschatological importance in the Encyclical under consideration, wherein Pius XII also implied that heeding the writings of Bernard is important for *bringing about an Era of Peace to the world.* (cf. §14,15)

> the color and savor of wine... **so in the saints all human affections melt away by some unspeakable transmutation into the will of God.** For how could God be all in all, if anything merely human remained in man? (Chapter X)

To "become godlike" is what the Church Fathers admonished, but here Bernard insists that becoming so consists in "*transmutation* into the *will* of God," itself a consequence of man *escaping* the "**intolerable weight of his own self-will**." (Ibid.) These few words accurately describe the predisposition for receiving the "Gift of Living in the Divine Will," which is the ultimate aim of the spiritual development found within the Church's Sacred Tradition, and which we will discuss explicitly in a later chapter. But even now, we see the Divine Architect of Church history already inspiring this saint to allude to it a full 800 years before its explicit description in private revelation.[41]

Just as St. Bernard built upon the Fathers, so the Doctors of the Church who followed Bernard built upon him. These Doctors will be our focus in the next chapter, but first, one more danger must be addressed, as another brand of Primitivist temptations may assault some who read Bernard's teachings.

Another More Subtle Primitivist Trap

> "... Even if Revelation is already complete, it has not been made completely explicit; it remains for Christian faith gradually to grasp its full significance over the course of the centuries."
>
> –*Catechism of the Catholic Church*, §66

Although it may seem that the perils of Primitivism have now been successfully averted, we must in fact remain on guard against them. For sadly, each era of Church history can count *modified*-Primitivists among the ranks of its most zealous devotees. They may have rejected the downright Primitivism we discussed earlier, but they apply its errors to their own favorite time of Church history, and they

[41] Bernard's novel insights, however, do not end here; we mustn't fail to honor his teachings on the Blessed Virgin Mary. The Mariological doctrine of Bernard is equally essential in forming the "bridge" to the era of Sacred Tradition that we will consider in the next section, since a recognition of whom one finds the quintessence of human divinization within is necessary for its undertaking, just as a familiarity with the "state of the art" is necessary for any craftsman to master his own craft. In divinization – that is, in the task of sanctification in the spiritual life – this quintessence is found only in the Blessed Virgin Mary. Of Our Lady, St. Bernard teaches, **"It is the will of God that we should have nothing which has not passed through the hands of Mary."** (*Doctor Mellifluus*, §30) Amazingly, Bernard here espouses the doctrine of Our Lady's universal mediation – that is, her office as Mediatrix of All Grace- long before it had been specifically formulated.

proceed to insist (in so many words) that the present call of the Christian consists in nothing more than turning back the theological and spiritual clock—if not to 70 A.D.—, perhaps to 700 A.D. or 1300 A.D. We must, however, reject Primitivism in *all* its forms, since God will continue to grant growth in holiness to the mystical body of Christ *until the end of time*.

For example, some scholars today who rightly promote a "ressourcement" (a "return to the sources"—particularly by a heightened focus on the Church Fathers), have only succumbed to mitigated primitivism applied to the Patristic era by supposing that this return should also entail a rejection of the Church's positive developments *since* that time. Cardinal Ratzinger shrewdly denounced this tendency. After acknowledging that "the Church of the first millennium knew nothing of tabernacles," he lamented those who, from this valid premise, wrongly conclude that we should go so far as to promote the:

> ... canonization of the early days and romanticism about the first century. Transubstantiation ... the adoration of the Lord in the Blessed Sacrament, eucharistic devotions with monstrance and processions—all these things, it is alleged, are medieval errors, errors from which we must once and for all take our leave. "The Eucharistic Gifts are for eating, not for looking at"—**these and similar slogans are all too familiar. The glib way such statements are made is quite astonishing**...[42]

Here we see that in implicitly rejecting the fact that God did not cease to give growth to the Church's holiness *after* the age of the Fathers (e.g., in the era of medieval Scholastic Theology), some of the advocates of this *ressourcement* erred so grievously that they incurred not only the rebuke above, but also the condemnation of Pope Pius XII in the encyclical *Humani Generis*. (cf. §16-18) The Pope's rebuke was motivated by the fact that some advocates of *ressourcement* had essentially regarded the Holy Spirit as inoperative throughout the entire Scholastic era of Sacred Tradition's development. Yet some who feel vindicated by this very encyclical will only find themselves condemned by another encyclical from the same Pope if they, hypocritically, insist that whatever development followed the *Scholastic* era must be left aside! For it was also the deeply traditional Pius XII who taught, in the encyclical *Divino Afflante Spiritu*:

---

[42] *The Spirit of the Liturgy*. Chapter 4.

> **All moreover should abhor that intemperate zeal which imagines that whatever is new should for that very reason be opposed or suspected.** (§47)

Instead of introducing yet another brand of mitigated Primitivism and incurring yet another Papal condemnation, therefore, let us simply renounce this heresy entirely. Without doing so, we will not be prepared to learn from those whom we will discuss next: the great saints, writers, and Doctors of the Church from the 17th to 19th centuries. For they—in a few points—departed from some of the scholastics (including Aquinas[43]) who preceded them. These Doctors do so only rarely, with great caution, and with the utmost reverence for the Scholastics. But *they do so precisely because the Holy Spirit moved them to do so*, for it was their task—not the task of the Scholastics (whose Divine mission, though also extremely important, was different[44])—to bring about the next great development in the Church's spiritual Sacred Tradition. Their task was to present new teachings on the heights of sanctity to which God calls His children, and the principal means (uniformity with the Divine Will) by which this sanctity is attained. In the next chapter, we will see their astounding doctrine.

> "I dwelt in the apostles, and they did not experience My presence in the way that you do. ... **I will bestow on [souls] even greater graces there than on the saints of centuries past**." (Jesus to Bl. Angela of Foligno, 14th-Century Franciscan mystic.)
> [Bl. Angela:] "[Jesus] promised to give to His new friends, if He finds them, **greater graces than He gave to the ancients.**"[45]

---

[43] A personal note is here necessary: I am a Thomist, therefore none need worry that what follows is presented with anything but the utmost regard for Aquinas and the philosophical and theological system of Thomism which he inspired. Even though I depart from a very small selection of his opinions, I regard Aquinas as the greatest philosopher and theologian who ever lived, and his teachings remain the framework and lens with which I approach these realms in general.

[44] In my opinion, God did not primarily give the Scholastics the mission of providing the next development of Sacred Tradition's spiritual teachings on the great sanctity of the Divine Will. The Scholastics' Divine mission, rather, seems to consist in their prodigious refinement, systematization, and defense of Catholic moral and dogmatic theology as well as philosophy—a contribution that was itself needed for many reasons (e.g., the counter-reformation, the development of modern seminary education and catechesis, a refutation of modernism before it existed, etc.) I am in no way seeking to diminish the enormously important contribution of the Scholastics by not giving them a chapter here; I merely do not see them as the principal exponents of Sacred Tradition's paradigms of exalted sanctity.

[45] Quoted by Fr. John Aririntero in *The Mystical Evolution in the Development and Vitality of the Church*. TAN Publishing. Footnote 88.

5. The Doctors: The Supreme Principle of Christianity

"Among the true children of our Savior, every one shall forsake his own will, and shall have only one Master Will, dominant and universal, which shall animate, govern and direct all souls, all hearts and all wills ... so that the will of Christians and the Will of Our Lord may be but one single will."
–St. Francis de Sales.[46]

The pioneering teachings of St. Bernard on Divine love enabled the saints and Doctors who followed him to describe the very divinization exalted by the Church Fathers with more precision. These towering figures of the spiritual life in the Middle Ages and Early Modern period referred to divinization's goal as a *mystical marriage.*[47] (Also referred to as "transforming union," the pinnacle of the third stage of the spiritual life, the Unitive Way.) This teaching received its most famous exposition in the works of the 16th Century Doctors of the Church, St. John of the Cross (*Ascent of Mount Carmel, Dark Night of the Soul*) and St. Teresa of Ávila (*The Interior Castle, The Way of Perfection*). Nevertheless, although mystical marriage was elucidated by their treatises, it was not an entirely new concept they introduced; for example, St. Catherine of Siena experienced it hundreds of years before their time.

---

[46] *Treatise on the Love of God.* Chapter VII

[47] I will not go into great depth here regarding their teachings on this subject, as my purpose in this chapter is to, more precisely, trace the development of the singularly exalted paradigm of Sacred Tradition's spiritual growth – union with God's Will. It is not my intent to present a comprehensive summary of the teachings on the spiritual life in general (which is what any attempt at a catechesis on mystical marriage would quickly become). I must also acknowledge that readers who are well versed in certain writings on mystical marriage may be confused as to why I am including it here as a *development* of the Church's Sacred Tradition regarding the heights of sanctity, instead of the *pinnacle* of the same. Although this matter will be dealt with in detail in Part Three, for now it will be sufficient to note that mystical marriage – though often regarded as the supreme state of earthly sanctity – in fact clearly calls for something higher still (consider that the analogy it employs- marriage – exists not for its own sake, but for the sake of fruitfulness in childbearing), and the very Doctors of this era of Church history openly taught that *Heavenly* sanctity is higher than spiritual marriage. Jesus has revealed explicitly to approved mystics of the 20th Century (e.g., St. Faustina and Blessed Conchita) that this *Heavenly* holiness is now available on earth.

Beginning with this mystic, then, let us journey through some of the most important teachings from several of the greatest teachers who have graced over 500 years of Sacred Tradition's development regarding the most important theme within it: *the accomplishment of God's Will on earth as in Heaven, through the complete union of the human will with the Divine Will.*

St. Catherine of Siena (b. 1347), a Dominican mystic who died at only 33 years of age but was nevertheless declared a Doctor of the Church (the second woman to be so declared), provided teachings on the divinization of the human soul. In summarizing them, Fr. Andrew Hofer, O.P., writes:

> Just as a maid becomes an empress through marital union with the emperor, so a creature becomes deified through a union with God made possible by the Passion of Christ ... The will, now completely transformed by God's love, has no selfishness in it, but is completely divinized.[48]

In her *Dialogue,* St. Catherine teaches that these divinized souls "... keep nothing at all, not a bit of their own will ... They have been made one with [God] and [God] with them."

St. Catherine of Genoa (b. 1447) was an Italian mystic, wife, noblewoman, and zealous helper of the poor. Her interior life was so profoundly permeated by Divine revelations and miraculous phenomena that the old *Catholic Encyclopedia* describes it by saying it can scarcely even be "called a life in the ordinary sense." These revelations she received from Jesus, moreover, were so impeccable that the Church pronounced they "**contained doctrine that would be enough, in itself, to prove her sanctity**."[49] (Her writings also had a powerful influence on St. Francis de Sales; a connection which will become evident when we consider that Church Doctor shortly.) Jesus Himself revealed to the saint what our life's *maxim* should *always* be:

> My daughter, observe these three rules, namely: never say *I will* or *I will not*. Never say *mine,* but always *ours*. Never excuse yourself, but always accuse yourself. **When you repeat the 'Our Father' take always for your maxim, *Fiat voluntas tua,* that is, may his will be done in everything** that may happen to you, whether good or ill; **from the 'Hail Mary' take the word Jesus,**[50] and may it be implanted in your heart, and it will be a sweet guide and

---

[48] *Called to be the Children of God*. Chapter 5.

[49] Old *Catholic Encyclopedia*. St. Catherine of Genoa.

[50] Recall, from Part One, our considerations of the parallel supremacy of the "Fiat Voluntas Tua" among the petitions of the Our Father and the pronunciation of the name, "Jesus," among the elements of the Hail Mary.

> shield to you in all the necessities of life."[51]

In Catherine's own words, we read the following exhortations:

> **As Adam opposed his own will to the Divine Will, so we must seek to have the Will of God as our only object, and by it to have our own disposed and annihilated.**[52] And as we cannot by ourselves discover our own evil inclinations, and our secret self-love, nor possibly annihilate our own self-will, it is very useful to subject our will to that of some other creature, and to do its bidding for the love of God. And the more we so subject ourselves for that divine love, so much the more shall we emancipate ourselves from that evil plague of our self-will which is so subtle and hidden within us...[53]

As with all the saints and mystics we are discussing, St. Catherine's impact was essential to God's overarching plan, and yet another later Church Doctor noted the profound influence this mystic had upon him:

> **The Lord recommended** to St. Catherine of Genoa, every time she said the Our Father, to **pay particular attention to these words: "Thy will be done," and to beg for the grace to fulfill the Will of God as perfectly as the Saints in heaven**. Let this be our practice also, and we shall certainly become saints. May the divine will be loved and praised! (St. Alphonsus Liguori, *Uniformity With God's Will.* Final paragraph.)

St. Teresa of Ávila (b. 1515), Doctor of the Church, held a uniquely exalted position among the Church's spiritual teachers. Teresa is especially regarded for emphasizing the value of contemplative prayer, but the saint insists that *even perfect contemplation* consists in none other than the *Fiat*; it is found in saying, simply, "Thy Will be done":

> **[In] perfect contemplation**... we do nothing on our part: we neither labour, nor negotiate at all, nor is more requisite, for **all else disturbs and hinders us, except saying: "Thy will be done."** May Your will, O Lord!, be fulfilled in me in whatever way You shall please... do me the favour to give me Your Kingdom, that I

---

[51] *The Life and Doctrine of St. Catherine of Genoa.* New York Christian Press Association Publishing Co. 1907. Chapter VI.

[52] As we will discuss in more depth later, references like these (whether in the writings of the saints of Sacred Tradition or in 20th-Century private revelations) should be understood as exhortations to "annihilate" the *independent operation* of the human self-will, *not* as exhortations to—like advocated for in some Eastern religions—seek to extinguish its substance, and *not* to—like advocated for by the Quietist heretics—seek to render it entirely passive.

[53] *The Life and Doctrine of St. Catherine of Genoa.* Ch XII

> may be able to accomplish Your will, since [Jesus] asked it of You for me; dispose of me as one entirely Yours, according to Your will. O my sisters! How powerful is this gift! ... it transforms us into Himself, and unites the Creator with the creature ... what can we pay, who, as I have said, have nothing to give but what we receive? We can however ... perfectly resign ourselves to His will. All else is a hindrance ... One caution I give you, not to think of reaching this degree by your own strength or diligence, for it is vain: even if you had devotion, you will remain cold, **but only say with humility and simplicity which obtain everything—"Thy will be done."** (*The Way of Perfection*. Chapter VI)

St. John of the Cross (b. 1542), known as "the Mystical Doctor," whose importance is on par with that of his mentor above (St. Teresa), provided a wealth of teachings on the spiritual life. Nevertheless, John also located the essence of all his teachings in a theme no reader will now be surprised to see; he did not hesitate to tell us clearly that the "entire matter" of the mysticism he so profoundly expounded upon is summed up in one principle:

> **The entire matter** of reaching union with God consists in purging the will of its appetites and emotions so that **from a human and lowly will it may be changed into the divine will**, made identical with the will of God. (*Ascent of Mt Carmel. Book III*, Ch. 16, §3)

St. Mary Magdalen de' Pazzi (b. 1566) was an Italian Carmelite nun, an extraordinary mystic, and a miracle worker who provided deeply influential teachings on the spiritual life. The old *Catholic Encyclopedia* entry on her life says the saint's teachings are "more frequently quoted by spiritual writers than those even of St. Teresa [of Ávila]." Like St. Catherine of Siena, she "bore the Bark of Peter on her shoulders"[54] by serving as a victim soul. These graces, however, did not require anything esoteric for their actualization, but only the mere mention of the *Fiat*:

> So great was the love and tenderness which St. Mary Magdalen di Pazzi entertained for the Divine will, that at the mere mention of it, she would be lost in an ocean of spiritual joy, and sometimes rapt into ecstasies ... it was her joy and glory to do [God's] will, not that He should do hers ... she once said: "... I would prefer having no gift at all except that of leaving all my will and all my desires in God, to having any gift through desire and will. Yes, yes, *in me sint, Deus, vota tua, et non vota mea*—Thy will, not mine,

[54] Fr. Juan Gutierrez Gonzalez. *Priests of Christ*. Introduction.

be done."[55]

St. Francis de Sales (b. 1567) was a French Bishop and Doctor of the Church whose contributions to Sacred Tradition's teachings on sanctification are unrivaled. Due to the magnitude of these contributions, however, we will dedicate a section to de Sales after covering several other writers.

Pierre de Bérulle (b. 1575) was a Cardinal, founder of the French Congregation of the Oratory, and a deeply influential spiritual writer. Theological scholars have recently explained that Berulle's teachings foreshadow what we will discuss in a later chapter; namely, "doing all your acts in the Divine Will":

> Bérulle takes the daring position that, because divinity and humanity coexist in the Word, all the states of the interior of **Jesus' human life have been divinized and made available to those who conform themselves to Him**, thus enabling humankind to be divinized. The process of conformity is explicitly Pauline and must take place **through a profound adherence of the will to the divine Will.**[56] According to [Bérulle], in fact, the possession of God happens through knowledge of his will, and knowledge of the divine will is carried out in the **renunciation of self will.**[57]

Bérulle, unsurprisingly, came under unfair attack for these true (though bold) teachings, but St. Louis de Montfort himself, in his famous treatise entitled *True Devotion to Mary*, came to Berulle's defense (§162). As Bérulle taught, and as we will see in more detail in a later chapter, Jesus *divinized* human acts through His earthly life, and what He accomplished remains open for us to claim. This is precisely what we do through receiving "*the Gift of Living in the Divine Will,*" and then doing our own acts in His Will, but Bérulle here anticipates the theme centuries before its explication in 20th-Century private revelation.

St. John Eudes (b. 1601) was a French priest who founded multiple congregations, zealously promoted devotion to the Sacred Hearts, and was strongly critical of Jansenism (the heresy that essentially minimized the Divine Mercy). Regarding St. John Eudes' spiritual teachings, theologian Dr. Michon Matthiesen writes:

> Mutual indwelling [of Christ and Christian] indicates the actual continuation of Jesus' holy life in his followers. Eudes points to several other New Testament passages (for example, Col 3:3-4; Eph 2:5; 2 Cor 4:10-11; Gal 2:20; 2 Thess 2:11-12) that insist upon

---

[55] *A Year with the Saints.* (New York: P.J. Kennedy & Sons, 1891).

[56] W. M. Wright. *The Blackwell Companion to Christian Mysticism.* 2012 P. 445

[57] Jean-Yves Lacoste. *Routledge Encyclopedia of Christian Theology.* 2004. P. 202

> this intimacy between Christ and his disciples: this scriptural witness leaves believers no choice but to conclude that "**Jesus Christ should be living in us and that we should live only in him... that our life should be a continuation and expression of his life.**" In fact, we have "no right" to live any other life on earth but his. In short, the baptized Christian should aim for nothing short of being "other Jesus Christs on earth". This "basic truth" of Christianity reflects the will of Jesus, whose union to us makes such an existence possible...[58]

Here again we see a saint insisting on a veritable "Living in the Divine Will," wherein Christ continues to carry out *His very own life* within those who hand their self-wills over to the Divine Will. The *Blackwell Companion to Christian Mysticism* reports of Eudes:

> Eudes' spirituality was heart-centered. He combined Berulle's mystical Christocentrism with [a] spirit of devotion ... to live in constant intimacy with Jesus and his mother Mary, the unity of whose hearts he insisted on... He taught that Mary's heart... was perfectly conjoined to that of her son. **As exemplar of the human person, Mary shows the way in which divinization takes place**: loving incorporation into the mystery of the Christ life...[59]

The pinnacle of Christian sanctification could not be reached until Sacred Tradition had sufficiently developed its Mariological dimension: recognizing Mary as the *example par excellence* of sanctity, and acknowledging that this is a position she holds not merely for the sake of our admiration and praise, *but also for the sake of our consecration and imitation*; which, if undertaken wholeheartedly, truly can generate Mary's own type of holiness in our souls!

While the Church's understanding of this consecration needed more time to develop, that process itself was made possible by St. John Eudes, who insisted that devotion to each Sacred Heart (that is, the Sacred Heart of Jesus and the Immaculate Heart of Mary—for the latter, although not Divine, is indeed also sacred) was inseparable from the other. Rightly, therefore, did Pope St. Pius X declare Eudes the "father, doctor, and apostle of the liturgical [devotion] of the Sacred Hearts." Another priest born in the same century, however, is even more renowned for his Mariological contribution to this development, and to him we now turn.

St. Louis de Montfort (b. 1673) was a French priest who is best known as the father of modern Marian Consecration. He taught that

---

58 *Called to be the Children of God*. Chapter 8.

59 *Blackwell Companion to Christian Mysticism*. Page. 446

by consecrating ourselves to Our Lady, we do not merely strive to imitate her, but can actually receive her graces, which themselves exist on account of the perfect union of her will with the Divine Will of her Son:

> [Mary] gives her whole self, and gives it in an unspeakable manner, to him who gives all to her. **She causes him to be engulfed in the abyss of her graces. She adorns him with her merits**; she supports him with her power; she illuminates him with her light; she inflames him with her love; she communicates to him her virtues... (*True Devotion to Mary*, §144)

Pope St. John Paul II even took de Montfort's insistence that we be *totally Christ's by being totally Mary's* ("Totus Tuus") as his Papal Motto. But since de Montfort's contribution is so important, we will dedicate a section within this chapter to Marian Consecration as he understood it, and will now proceed to the next pivotal teacher of Divine Will spirituality.

Jean Pierre de Caussade (b. 1675) was a French Jesuit priest who is universally revered as one of the giants of Catholic spirituality. Dr. Jeff Mirus wrote the following about Fr. Caussade's book, *Abandonment to Divine Providence*:

> Fr. de Caussade's work is one of the **great classics of spiritual direction, holding a place in Catholic spiritual literature which is about as high as one can go** without having been canonized and declared a doctor of the Church ... Catholic spiritual directors around the world have been recommending the book regularly now for some two hundred and fifty years. It has stood the test of time. There are some concepts which, under whatever name, are **fundamental to the spiritual life.**[60]

This Catholic scholar is correct in insisting that Caussade's *Abandonment to Divine Providence* is such an important work of Catholic spirituality that its main exhortation—which we will consider in a moment—is "*fundamental* to the spiritual life." Caussade's book is nevertheless known to sometimes cause consternation in beginners who stumble upon it, for they understandably wonder if the astonishing magnitude of his teachings are orthodox. One such person contacted the Eternal Word Television Network with precisely this concern, and was given the following response from one of their theologians, Dr. David Gregson: "*Abandonment to Divine Providence* is a

---

[60] catholicculture.org/commentary/otc.cfm?id=879.

spiritual classic, and Jean Pierre de Caussade's orthodoxy is unimpeachable."[61] Turning to Caussade's book itself, we see both a profound summary *and furthering* of the greatest themes of Christian sanctification given up to his own day:

> **The true philosopher's stone is submission to the will of God,** which changes into divine gold all occupations, troubles, and sufferings... O my God! **how much I long to be the missionary of Your holy will, and to teach all men that there is nothing more easy, more attainable, more within reach**, and in the power of everyone, than sanctity ... Oh! All you that read this, it will cost you no more than to do what you are doing, to suffer what you are suffering, only act and suffer in a holy manner. It is the heart that must be changed. **When I say heart, I mean will. Sanctity, then, consists in willing all that God wills for us. Yes! Sanctity of heart is a simple "fiat," a conformity of will with the will of God**. (§ IX)

This is no isolated teaching of Caussade. It was *his life's mission*. In an introduction to this book, Dom Arnold, OSB, writes:

> The "Abandonment to Divine Providence" ... is a trusting, childlike, peaceful abandonment to the guidance of grace, and of the Holy Spirit: an unquestioning and undoubting submission to the holy will of God in all things that may befall us, be they due to the action of man, or to the direct permission of God. **To Fr. de Caussade, abandonment to God, the "Ita Pater" of our Divine Lord, the "Fiat" of our Blessed Lady, is the shortest, surest, and easiest way to holiness and peace**.

Regarding the teachings of both Caussade and St. Thérèse of Lisieux two centuries later, Dr. Matthiesen explains:

> Both of these later figures discover the **possibility of deification in loving abandonment to the providential will of the Father**. De Caussade and Thérèse understand that this abandonment—simple and complete—means that Jesus Christ becomes the source of action within the believer ... Thérèse speaks of God entirely taking over one's desire, will, and actions. For both of these spiritual writers, the universality of their spiritual teaching—its hidden, sacrificial way—epitomizes the *vive Jesus* [Live Jesus] ... De Caussade puts it this way: "God desires to be the unique cause of all that is holy in us, so all that comes from us is very little. In God's sight there can be nothing great in us—with one exception: our total receptivity to his will." ... **This surrender [to**

[61] ewtn.com/v/experts/showmessage.asp?number=481328.

> **the Divine Will] thus becomes a kind of perpetual state, one that shares in Jesus' continual *fiat voluntas tua* (thy will be done)** ... the will does not recognize the act as its own—which is, in fact, the ideal, for then it is **God acting through the human will without resistance of any kind**. At this point, what God wills and what the believer desires is one. **When such a unity of wills obtains, the believer is participating not only in God's design, but in God's life** ... De Caussade eloquently articulates the vive Jesus and Eudes' firm assertion that Christians continue in their daily lives that holy and divine life of Jesus. His particular contribution is to locate this participation in **a union (by way of surrender) of the human will to the divine will.**[62]

In a word, Caussade admonishes us to *"Live Jesus"* by the total surrender of the self-will to the Divine Will, which itself must be an echo of the perfect *Fiat* of Jesus and Mary, so that we not only *participate* in the Divine Nature, but even *possess* the Divine Life as our own life! (Not by nature, but by grace.) I suspect that readers are beginning to sense a pattern. Indeed, we see, in the greatest paradigms of Sacred Tradition's development, an astounding *continuity* and *ascendancy*.

At this point, we have arrived at so close a description of what God would bring about in the 20th Century mystics that we are scarcely even speaking of "preparation" any longer. Already we can see that the Holy Spirit ensured that everything was accomplished to prepare the way for the Gift of Living in the Divine Will, so that, upon its revelation, no honest observer could criticize it as an artificial or disjointed development at odds with a hermeneutic of continuity.

Yet, we still are not done. God's "Final Preparation" for the Gift—a certain extraordinary nun by the name of Thérèse—would not be born until the century after Caussade's death, and a contemporary of Caussade, whom we will consider next, taught similar things—while also providing novel developments of his own—*only to be canonized and then declared a Doctor of the Church*! The contributions of the three Doctors whom we will now turn to are so powerful that each requires a section of his or her own.

---

[62] *Called to be the Children of God.* Chapter 8.

St. Alphonsus Liguori

> "Take care always to keep yourself united to the will of God in all contrarieties. *Fiat voluntas tua*! [Thy will be done!] These are the words that have made all the saints."
>
> –St. Alphonsus Liguori

St. Alphonsus Liguori (b. 1696) was an Italian bishop, theologian, and a Doctor of the Church. A prolific writer, an ardent devotee of the Blessed Virgin, and a masterful spiritual guide, he was also despised by the Jansenists. The expert in spiritual theology, Fr. Jordan Aumann, wrote that "**Like no other theologian of his time, St. Alphonsus made the traditional doctrine on the spiritual life practical and popular**..."[63]

St. Alphonsus presents beautiful, practical, and powerful expositions on the spiritual life centered on the Divine Will; therefore, it is unsurprising that he succeeded in making this supreme sanctity popular to a degree that no one else had up to that point. The saint dedicated one of his greatest works to this very theme, entitling it *Uniformity With God's Will*. In this work, he begins by reminding us that the essence of our Faith is nothing other than the Will of God:

> Perfection is founded entirely on the love of God: "Charity is the bond of perfection;" and **perfect love of God means the complete union of our will with God's**: "The principal effect of love is so to unite the wills of those who love each other as to make them will the same things." It follows then, that the more one unites his will with the divine will, the greater will be his love of God. **Mortification, meditation, receiving Holy Communion, acts of fraternal charity are all certainly pleasing to God—but only when they are in accordance with his will ...** The greatest glory we can give to God is to do his will in everything. Our Redeemer came on earth to glorify his heavenly Father and to teach us by his example how to do the same ... Our Lord frequently declared that he had come on earth not to do his own will, but solely that of his Father: "I came down from heaven, not to do my own will, but the will of him that sent me." ... Furthermore, he said he would recognize as his brother, him who would do his will: "Whosoever shall do the will of my Father who is in heaven, he is my brother."

In one paragraph, St. Alphonsus captures the essence of Parts One and Two of this book! He locates the single and supreme principle of

[63] Jordan Aumann. *Christian Spirituality in the Catholic Tradition*. P. 215

a Christian's life in the Divine Will, and he traces this supremacy back to Jesus' example in the Gospels themselves. Alphonsus then moves on to demonstrate that this is not some entirely new insight, but was, in fact, the essence of the lives of the saints even up to his own day, for it finds its impetus in *the greatest petition of the Greatest Prayer*:

> **To do God's will—this was the goal upon which the saints constantly fixed their gaze**. They were fully persuaded that in this consists the entire perfection of the soul... "Those who give themselves to prayer," says St. Teresa, "should concentrate solely on this: the conformity of their wills with the divine will. They should be convinced that this constitutes their highest perfection..." During our sojourn in this world, we should learn from the saints now in heaven, how to love God. The pure and perfect love of God they enjoy there, consists in uniting themselves perfectly to his will ... **Our Lord himself teaches us to ask to do the will of God on earth as the saints do it in heaven: "Thy will be done on earth as it is in heaven**."

Having insisted upon the primacy of the Will of God, Alphonsus moves on to extol its extraordinary power in the life of a Christian who unites himself completely with God's Will:

> **A single act of uniformity with the divine will suffices to make a saint** ... [This is] absolutely true—because he who gives his will to God, gives him everything. He who gives his goods in alms, his blood in scourgings, his food in fasting, gives God what he has. But he who gives God his will, gives himself, gives everything he is ... St. Augustine's comment is: "There is nothing more pleasing we can offer God than to say to him: 'Possess thyself of us'." We cannot offer God anything more pleasing than to say: Take us, Lord, we give thee our entire will ... **Let us not only strive to conform ourselves**, but also to unite ourselves to whatever dispositions God makes of us. **Conformity signifies that we join our wills to the will of God. Uniformity means more—it means that we make one will of God's will and ours,** so that we will only what God wills; that God's will alone, is our will. This is the summit of perfection and to it we should always aspire; this should be **the goal of all our works, desires, meditations and prayers** ... Mary [is] the most perfect of all the saints because she most perfectly embraced the divine will.

Two major developments are evident in this passage: first, Alphonsus' teaching that with the Divine Will, a single act of uniformity "suffices to make a saint;" second, his teaching that this *uniformity* with the Divine Will to which we are called is even higher than *conformity* with the same. These are truly new insights, and the Church has confirmed them as authentic by his elevation to the status of *Doctor.* These teachings rise above earlier theologians' opinions that a saint can *only* be made through an arduous and lengthy process, and that the sanctity of the human will is limited in scope to the *imitation* of the Divine Will (conformity) and cannot on earth rise to the higher level of *merging with* the Divine Will (union).

From these and many other developments imparted by St. Alphonsus to the Church's Sacred Tradition, we can see just how indispensable he was in preparing the way for the great Sanctity of Living in the Divine Will, to be explicitly revealed 100 years after his death. The intervening century, however, saw the arrival of the Final Preparation: the spirituality of St. Thérèse of Lisieux. Before covering her contribution, we must first discuss the astounding teachings of still another Doctor of the Church who preceded St. Alphonsus Liguori, and who, Pope Benedict XVI noted, paved the way for Thérèse.

St. Francis de Sales

> "It is almost unbelievable with what vigor and constancy he defended the cause of Jesus Christ."
> –Pope Pius XI on St. Francis de Sales

St. Francis de Sales (b. 1567) was a French bishop and, doubtless, one of the greatest Doctors of the Church. He is often aptly described as the best teacher on the spiritual life for the laity, for he insisted upon the need for—and ability of—all Christians to reach the loftiest heights of holiness, and he gave unequaled insights into how ordinary people could attain it. Like Bernard of Clairvaux, de Sales is among the few saints who are so important that entire Papal Encyclicals have been dedicated to extolling their teachings long after their deaths. In 1923, Pope Pius XI promulgated *Rerum Omnium Pertubationem,* dedicated to de Sales. A paragraph found within it illustrates beautifully that this spirituality of total submission to the Divine Will does not in the least lead one to a Quietist[64] or passive life:

> **It is almost unbelievable with what vigor and constancy [de Sales] defended the cause of Jesus Christ** ... he was known to have traveled through deep valleys and to have climbed steep mountains. ... he never gave up the struggle; when threatened he

[64] "Quietism" is a heresy which, though in few ways deceptively resembles Divine Will spirituality, is in fact starkly opposed to it. More on this matter can be found in the Appendices.

> only renewed his efforts. He was often put out of lodgings, at which times he passed the night asleep on the snow under the canopy of heaven ... At no time did he ever lose his mental poise or his spirit of kindness toward these ungrateful hearers. It was by such means as these that he finally overcame the resistance of his most formidable adversaries. (§8)

Upon reading this, none will fear that regarding uniformity with the Divine Will as the supreme principle of the spiritual life in any way diminishes the extreme importance of all the other principles and practices associated with sanctification (growth in virtue, frequenting the sacraments, constant prayer, good works, orthodoxy, etc.). Focus on the centrality of the Divine Will can only strengthen these things in the life of any Christian. In de Sales—who was as absorbed by this singular, supreme principle as anyone—we see an evangelist whose zeal in all the matters of the Faith is "almost unbelievable" even to Popes—who are anything but unacquainted with the lives of the saints and are not easily surprised by descriptions of heroic virtue!

As important as St. Francis' example, however, were his teachings, to which we now turn our attention. Pope Benedict XVI, speaking on de Sales' book, *Treatise on the Love of God* (which he insisted was the saint's main work), taught that:

> Francis found peace in the radical and liberating love of God... he simply loved God and abandoned himself to his goodness. And this was to be the secret of his life which would shine out in his main work: *The Treatise on the Love of God*... **In an intensely flourishing season of mysticism, *The Treatise on the Love of God* was a true and proper summa** ... [in it] we find a profound meditation on the human will and the description of its flowing, passing and dying in order to live in complete surrender not only to God's will but also to what pleases him... we rediscover traces precisely of [de Sales] at the origin of many contemporary paths of pedagogy and spirituality; without him neither St. John Bosco nor the heroic "Little Way" of St. Thérèse of Lisieux would have come into being.[65]

In referring to this work of de Sales as a "summa" of a "flourishing **season** of mysticism," Benedict XVI makes an extraordinary claim. He indicates that we find—summarized within the pages of this work—the most important themes of the Church's spiritual Sacred Tradition leading up to its composition. More than a summary of what already existed, Benedict continues, this same Treatise made possible some of

---

[65] Benedict XVI. General Audience. March 2, 2011.

the most important developments that occurred long *after* de Sales' own lifetime; even the spirituality of St. Thérèse of Lisieux herself! Moreover, Benedict places this exalted treatise's own most important theme in none other than its meditation on the nature of sanctification as consisting in the human will completely surrendering to God's Will.

At this point, I suspect no doubt remains that *the paradigm and principle* of Christian sanctification—the most important theme of Sacred Tradition's Spirit-led growth over the centuries—is indeed the Our Father's third petition; the *Fiat*; the total uniformity of the human will with the Divine Will *on earth as in Heaven*. Let us see how St. Francis puts it:

> The soul that loves God is **so transformed into the divine will**, that it merits rather to be called, God's will, than to be called, obedient and subject to his will ... **among the true children of our Savior, every one shall forsake his own will, and shall have only one master-will, dominant and universal, which shall animate, govern and direct all souls, all hearts and all wills: and the name of honor amongst Christians shall be no other than God's will in them, a will which shall rule over all wills, and transform them all into itself; so that the will of Christians and the will of Our Lord may be but one single will.** This was perfectly verified in the primitive Church ... the singularly one heart and soul of true Christians, [is] no other thing than the will of God. Life, says the Psalmist, is in the will of God, not only because our temporal life depends on the divine pleasure, but also because our spiritual life consists in the execution of it, by which God lives and reigns in us, making us live and subsist in him ... Yes, we are in this world not to do our own will, but the will of thy goodness which has placed us here. It was written of thee, O Saviour of my soul, that thou didst the will of thy Eternal Father, and by the first act of the will of thy human soul, at the instant of thy conception, thou didst lovingly embrace this law of the divine will ... **Ah! who will give my soul the grace of having no will save the will of her God!** (Ch. VIII)

This remarkable passage from de Sales' main work exemplifies not only the type of spirituality we have been tracing the development of throughout this book, but also alludes to the universal reign of the sanctity here described! For indeed, the time will come when the Lord's Prayer is fulfilled universally; when, as de Sales says above, "*every one shall forsake his own will, and shall have only one master-will, dominant and universal.*" Discussing in detail this reign of the Divine

Will—the Era of Peace—will have to wait for Part Five, however.

Given that we have already seen—in a 17th Century Doctor of the Church—many of the boldest teachings we will cover in Parts Three and Four (e.g., those given by Jesus to Blessed Conchita and the Servant of God Luisa Piccarreta), it may be surprising to hear that God is still not, with de Sales, done preparing the way for those revelations. But the Holy Spirit is incomprehensibly diligent, and He still had one preparation left. Before turning to her—The Final Preparation, St. Thérèse of Lisieux—let us address one last thing: The Catalyst.

The Catalyst: Marian Consecration

> "Almighty God and his holy Mother are to raise up great saints who will surpass in holiness most other saints as much as the cedars of Lebanon tower above little shrubs" –St. Louis de Montfort

Marian devotion is both a preparation and a catalyst for the "Gift of Living in the Divine Will;" that is, it paved the way for that Gift while it also even now serves as *a dimension of* that supreme sanctity itself. For in Marian devotion's own pinnacle, Marian *Consecration*, we find an impetus for the greatest holiness possible to explode throughout the Church. As we will see in the following chapters, there is a "New and Divine Holiness"—spoken of by Pope St. John Paul II and relayed by the 20th Century mystics—which takes as its model the holiness of the Blessed Virgin Mary herself. To be sure, no (authentic) mystic claims that we ourselves can ever equal Our Lady, much less surpass her: she, and she alone, will ever remain the rightful claimant to her singular titles (e.g., Mother of God, Mediatrix, Immaculate Conception), and even the greatest saints beneath her will always be small in comparison to her.

Nevertheless, through Marian Consecration, we dare to unite ourselves so closely and completely to Our Lady as to render our own her very virtues and graces, and the completion and fulfillment of this process is none other than "Living in the Divine Will," wherein the same *type* of holiness that Our Lady enjoys becomes ours as well. As we have already seen, this was alluded to by St. Louis de Montfort, but as we will later see, it was taught explicitly by St. Maximilian Kolbe. And although he could not predict the time at which it would occur, de Montfort knew that when this spirituality spread sufficiently, it would form the greatest saints of the end of the present era and usher in a New Era, so much so that he wrote:

> **Almighty God and his holy Mother are to raise up great saints who will surpass in holiness most other saints as much as the cedars of Lebanon tower above little shrubs** ... They will be exceptionally devoted to the Blessed Virgin. Illumined by her light, strengthened by her food, guided by her spirit ... Mary has produced, together with the Holy Ghost, the greatest thing which has been or ever will be—a God-man; and she will consequently produce the greatest saints that there will be ... They shall be great and exalted before God in sanctity... with the humility of their heel, in union with Mary, **they shall crush the head of the devil and cause Jesus Christ to triumph**. (*True Devotion to Mary* §46-48)

The unfolding of that prophecy is happening before our eyes among the living saints of the Church, and it consists in precisely what we are now discussing. To the Final Preparation for that unfolding, we shall now turn.

The Final Preparation: St. Thérèse of Lisieux

> "In Heaven, God will do all I desire, because on earth I have never done my own will..." "Holiness consists simply in doing God's Will, and being just what God wants us to be..."
> –St. Thérèse of Lisieux

We now have arrived at the humble nun who is "the Greatest Saint of Modern Times," according to Pope Pius X; the one who is sure to cause a "spiritual revolution," according to Pope Pius XI. That is, St. Thérèse of Lisieux, Doctor of the Church, born in 1873.

Here we have something amazing and unprecedented in the ability of her "Little Way" to inspire and console countless ordinary Christians, and to help them recognize that the heights of sanctity described by the saints and writers we have already covered (and many more like them) are *truly* within reach of *everyone*. Others had affirmed this truth before Thérèse, but she succeeded in inflaming her readers' confidence in a way that none before her had.

In her autobiography, *Story of a Soul*, Thérèse wrote extensively on *littleness* and insisted that, far from impeding the supreme heights of sanctity, it is *the very key* to the same. As we will see in a forthcoming chapter, it is precisely this littleness which is among the principal prerequisites for the "Gift of Living in the Divine Will," and it is due to Thérèse's emphasis on this theme that we find, in her, God's final preparation for the great Gift of that Sanctity which He would soon reveal to the 20th Century mystics who will be covered in the next part of this book.

Indeed, before revealing the Gift of Living in the Divine Will to another soul resembling Thérèse in the "greatness of her littleness," God chose not to allow any doubt whatsoever to remain among the Faithful regarding who, exactly, is "eligible" for it. He chose to allow no fear to linger in the minds of those rightly zealous for Catholic orthodoxy as to what it takes to receive it. *All* are eligible for it, and one need only be *little* to receive it. It is through St. Thérèse of Lisieux, her swift canonization, and her being declared a Doctor of the Church[66] that the Holy Spirit settled these truths within Sacred Tradition, and thus accomplished the Final Preparation for His Final Effort.

Thérèse also focused on the Divine Will as the supreme principle of the spiritual life (*littleness* is not the end—purpose—of the spiritual life, but the *means*), and she did not hesitate to insist upon the mode of holiness we see described in earlier writers like St. Francis de Sales and St. Alphonsus Liguori. In her own words, we read:

> **My heart is full of the Will of Jesus**. Ah, if my soul were not already filled with His Will, if it had to be filled by the feelings of joy and sadness which follow each other so quickly, it would be a tide of very bitter sorrow. But these alternatives do nothing but brush across my soul. I always remain in a profound peace which nothing can trouble ... **I only will what He wills; it is what He does that I love ... I acknowledge that it took me a long time to bring myself to this degree of abandonment**. (*Story of a Soul.* Epilogue: A Victim of Divine Love)

The words of Thérèse relayed above are contained in the Epilogue of her autobiography, which was compiled posthumously by the Prioress of her convent. Within its pages, the Prioress explained that "by this trial [of illness which Thérèse was enduring], the Divine Master wished to put **the finishing touches to her purification.**" In other words, Thérèse was here summarizing the most important lessons of her life, and she was truly providing a simple synopsis of the spiritual teachings with which she had earlier filled many pages.

And what does this summary consist of? *Willing only what God Wills*. Even more, being "*filled* with His Will." Thérèse acknowledges that attaining this supreme state took her a very long time, and, as we know she was ever *growing* in sanctity until death, we can thus conclude that even in the spirituality of the Little Flower, union with the Will of God is the supreme principle.

---

[66] Pope St. John Paul II declared her a Doctor of the Church in 1997. She was the youngest person ever so declared.

A great link exists between Thérèse and the mystic we will begin covering soon. In the official Church-sanctioned biography of the Servant of God Luisa Piccarreta, *The Sun of My Will*, published by the Vatican in 2015, we read:

> Luisa has a great devotion to [St. Thérèse], who teaches with her life the trusting abandonment into God's hands and a "new" way of uniting with him ... When the first translation of her "Story of a Soul," ... it becomes understood that everyone, not just priests and nuns, can live a mystical life built on the awareness of a love that is already present in the heart of every person created in the image of God. But this mystical life is to be expressed by each person in the way most appropriate to the life one leads. That way, many **people learn that they can always be united to God, even in their daily tasks, through the union of will. So often mothers who go running to Luisa for advice end up hearing the same thing!** (Page 30)

It is no accident that Luisa was deeply devoted to Thérèse (long before the latter's canonization); for indeed, as we have seen, Thérèse's *Little Way* is the necessary preparation for what Jesus would tell Luisa. Nor does the Providential orchestration end there. Luisa herself was commanded, under obedience to her Bishop-appointed priest-spiritual directors, to begin writing down the revelations that Jesus gave to her in February 1899. This was a mere six months after *Story of a Soul* was first published (although, further demonstrating the Providential orchestration of these events, it was before the book was published in Italy!). In an obedience identical to that of Thérèse's own (who had likewise been ordered to write her autobiography), Luisa commenced. *God wastes no time and with Him there are no coincidences.*

6. A Summary of Two Millennia of Preparations

"The redeemer of man, Jesus Christ, is the centre of the universe and of history ... And in her turn the Church, in spite of all the weaknesses that are part of her human history, does not cease to follow him who said: 'The hour is coming, and now is, when the true worshippers will worship the Father in spirit and truth...' (John 4:23)"
–Pope St. John Paul II

We have undertaken an extraordinary task in the first two parts of this book—summarizing, in less than one hundred pages, the heart of the New Testament as well as two millennia of the most important developments *of the most important aspect* of Sacred Tradition's God-given growth. Before proceeding to Part Three, let us review a summary of this summary.

***

Two thousand years ago, the One Who created the Universe entered into the very world He made. This God-made-man, Our Lord Jesus Christ, taught and commanded us to pray only one prayer—the Our Father, the Greatest Prayer—and the supreme petition of this prayer is indisputably the plea that *God's Will be done on earth as it is in Heaven.* (Matthew 6:10)

This supplication—which can also be called the *Fiat*—is the supreme principle of Public Revelation itself. By the *Fiat* was Creation called into existence. By the *Fiat* was Redemption commenced with the Virgin Mary's abandonment to the Divine Will, whereupon the greatest event within history, the Incarnation, was precipitated. By the *Fiat* Jesus teaches all of us, by example, how we are to live: "Not my will, but Thine be done." (Luke 22:42). Though the verses are relatively few, their consequences stand immeasurable, for the greatest developments of the Millennia to follow would, above all, be dominated by striving after the accomplishment of God's Will on earth as in Heaven.

Indeed, this supreme principle of Public Revelation remained the supreme principle of Sacred Tradition. The Fathers of the Church all insisted upon our divinization—not as one optional task of many, but as the fundamental call and essence of Christianity itself. This process of divinization was eventually described—especially by St. Maximus and St. Bernard, who provided its greatest exposition—as *the union of the human will with the Divine Will.* The saints and Doctors of the Church who followed them (especially St. Francis de Sales and St. Alphonsus Liguori) continued to develop this theme with teachings of ever greater exaltation, breadth, and depth. They insisted that *everything* in life and Faith is contained within the total surrender of the human will to the Divine Will. Moreover, they commandingly taught that this surrender, if undertaken wholeheartedly, can result in a real *union* of wills. Once firmly established, this spiritual theology was ready to have the final preparation bestowed upon it by God through the teachings of St. Thérèse of Lisieux. This "spiritual revolution" (cf. Pope Pius XI) existed to convince everyone that this great sanctity is for all, not a mere few; and that attaining it is achieved by littleness, not apparent greatness. Mariology, likewise proceeding step by step throughout the centuries of Sacred Tradition's growth, attained its maturity at the same time, wherein it was finally rightly taught that Our Lady is the perfect mirror of the Holy Spirit, that she is the quintessence of our call to divinization, and that the type of perfect union between her will and the Divine Will of her Son can likewise define our own wills' union with His—if only we totally consecrate ourselves to her.

These paragraphs describe the essential work of God throughout 1,900 years of preparing the way for the fruition of His ultimate plan: that, upon the dawn of the Third Millennium, His Will be done on earth as it is done in Heaven.

Why so many preparations?

> "[The Church is] a reality pervaded by the presence of God and, consequently, of such a nature that it always admits of new and deeper explorations of itself." –Pope St. Paul VI[67]

After reading of the extraordinary nearly two-thousand-year-long journey of preparatory Divine inspirations evident in Church history and summarized within the preceding chapters, one would be forgiven for asking, *"Why such an ordeal? Why couldn't God have just inspired all these teachings—from the Fathers up to St. Thérèse and everything in between—to come about right away, so that we could have arrived at this point long ago? Better yet, why didn't Jesus just say it all Himself in the Gospel?"*

The answer is simple: even the unfathomable Divine Intervention that is the Incarnation and Redemption—and the bestowal of the

---

[67] Address at the inauguration of the 2nd session of Vatican II

whole content of Public Revelation in general—did not change the fact that God always operates in an organic way; that is, *step by step.* To explicitly reveal everything that we now know about the implications of those loftiest of all words, "*Thy Will be done on earth as it is in Heaven,*" within the New Testament or at the beginning of Church history would have been artificial; like trying to teach Calculus to a student just beginning Algebra. Such a student could be forced, by a teacher only eager to boast of his own talent, to memorize the definition of a definite integral, but this would not enable the student to do Calculus.

Indeed, the whole essence of Calculus is contained, seminally, within Algebra itself and no new analogous "public revelation" is needed to progress from one to the other. But much time and effort *are* needed to gradually render more explicit what was only subtle from the start. Therefore, much growth of the Church *as a whole Mystical Body*—in the life and teachings of her saints, that is—was needed; just as much more growth was needed before the Church was likewise ready for the Marian Dogmas. God, being the very best of teachers, only causes the Church to proceed from one understanding to the next when the time is right.

In a word, although 2,000 years ago was truly the *fullness of time,* the time was not yet ripe to reveal the Sanctity of Living in the Divine Will in all its clarity and invite the nascent Church into it—but only to reveal its beginnings. And even though they are beginnings, we have seen that what they point to is in no way unclear. Realizing this, the greatest minds and the greatest saints in the history of the Church undertook what we traced out within the preceding chapters.

The theater of this eschatological and Divine conquest, Church history, is neither a mere waiting room for Heaven, nor a mere epilogue affixed to the Salvation History which preceded it. On the contrary, *Salvation History was the prologue to Church history,* which itself grows towards its Penultimate Destiny of likeness to Heaven, by virtue of the Divine Will being fulfilled on earth. If, neglecting these facts, we approach Church history with a diminished perspective of the exaltation of its mission, then Pope Benedict XVI admonishes us:

> What is our attitude with regard to the Church's experiences? ... is it an attitude full of love and open to the mystery of **those who know—through faith—that they can trace in the history of the Church those signs of God's love and the great works of salvation wrought by him**?... "History has a hidden content... that of God's works which constitute in time the authentic reality concealed behind the appearances..." (Address. June 13th, 2007)

At some point, one must simply stop asking "but why not this other way?", and instead acknowledge that God knows exactly what He is doing. Above all, God has inspired loftier and loftier claims, from the mouths of those most exalted by the Church, in describing what He Wills of us; not only in Heaven, but also here and now on this earth. And although the greatness of the claims rises ever higher, God gives more and more hints as to the point at which these claims will converge—for, in masterful artistry, it is precisely the point at which they all find their beginning: *Thy Will be done on earth as it is in Heaven.* As the Angelic Doctor declared, *all things find their perfection in returning to their origin.*

The mastery displayed in the process—incarnate within 2,000 years of Sacred Tradition's growth—that we can now observe is infinitely beyond the ingenuity of any human mind to generate. The Holy Spirit's guidance of the Church throughout her Sacred History has not been accidental or random. He has, rather, *formed* Sacred Tradition with a *goal* in mind, and everything He has inspired in the growth of this Tradition contributes to it. St. John Henry Newman describes this process that takes place throughout the Church's development as follows:

> Each argument is brought for an immediate purpose; minds develop step by step; without looking behind them or anticipating their goal ... **Afterwards, however, this logical character which the whole wears becomes a test that the process has been a true development,** not a perversion or corruption, from its evident naturalness; and in some cases from the gravity, distinctness, precision, and majesty of its advance, and the harmony of its proportions, like [a plant's] tall growth, and graceful branching, and rich foliage... *(Essay on the Development of Christian Doctrine*)

Although we have considered the analogy of a student of mathematics, an even better one is employed here by Cardinal Newman. This saint was a powerful advocate for both orthodoxy and for openness to organic development, which he here compares to the maturation of a plant. Just as a plant's growth, especially when viewed in retrospect, conveys a "logical character which the whole wears," so too does all legitimate development in the Church give evidence of its authenticity through the "majesty of its advance." Nowhere else do we observe such an astounding degree of these virtues, extolled by Newman, of "majesty, harmony, grace, and proportionality" as we see in the growth of Sacred Tradition's supreme paradigm of sanctity: the union of the human will with the Divine Will.

And while a plant's organic growth precludes ruptures (here analogous to the "evolution of dogmas," modernism, etc.), which we could compare to grafting[68] one plant on another, it does not preclude great leaps in glory. In other words, *it does not preclude the bearing of fruit or the blooming of a flower*.

Though astonishing to witness, fruit-bearing and flower-blooming is an eventuality that is not only fully harmonious with the principles of organic growth, but, even more, is the very epitome and quintessence of the same. It satisfies each of the seven criteria Newman gives for legitimate development.[69] The bloom of the fruit-bearing flower will surprise one who thought he was only observing the linear and entirely predictable growth of a blade of grass. But how lamentable it would be for this observer to turn his surprise into a denunciation of the flower! What we must ask ourselves, then, is simple: *If we are to compare the Church's Sacred Tradition to a plant, do we suppose that the Holy Spirit would render it more like a lowly blade of grass, or would He influence its growth to more resemble a breathtaking rose?*

Everything in Sacred Tradition has been—utterly perfectly and beautifully—leading up to this development on the sanctity of the Divine Will, which we will presently consider. But this can only be recognized by the humble. To suppose that one must choose between, on the one hand, openness to the Holy Spirit's work in the Church and, on the other hand, complete Catholic orthodoxy and reverence for Sacred Tradition, is a false dichotomy. The saints always had both virtues, and we should imitate their example.

---

[68] In Romans 11, St. Paul uses the grafting analogy with respect to Christianity itself in relation to Judaism. Indeed, analogous "grafting" *is* there acceptable since Christianity *is* a new Public Revelation—not a mere development of Judaism. However, that will never again be true, since Public Revelation is now complete, and the Age of the Catholic Church will persist until the end of time.

[69] Preservation of Type, Continuity of Principles, Power of Assimilation, Logical Sequence, Anticipation of Future, Conservative Action upon Past, and Chronic Vigor

Part Three: The Crown of Sanctity: The "New and Divine Holiness" of 20th-Century Mysticism

"[St. Hannibal di Francia saw] the means God himself had provided to bring about that 'new and divine' holiness with which the Holy Spirit wishes to enrich Christians at the dawn of the third millennium, in order to 'make Christ the heart of the world.'"
–Pope St. John Paul II

7. The Next Phase: God's Final Effort

"We are incontestably in a new era of spirituality"
–Fr. Marie Michel Philipon. (1978)

We have just completed our journey through one thousand nine hundred years of the Holy Spirit's guiding influence of sanctifying the Mystical Body of Christ through the teachings of the Church's Fathers and Doctors, and of her saints and sages. Through these holy men and women, God Himself developed the central and supreme paradigm of Sacred Tradition's maturation: the sanctity of union with the Divine Will in accordance with the Our Father's third petition.

Nevertheless, these great spiritual masters, lofty as their teachings were, could not describe precisely how this perfect and complete union they so desired and exalted in their writings goes about happening. How can the human will really be fused with the Divine Will? What effects does this fusion – this *living in* – entail? What else does it teach us? What do we "do" with this Gift? What can be said of the relation of the Divine Will to Creation and Redemption? What exactly does this mean for our lives? What exactly does this mean for the *world*? They knew that this union with the Divine Will was both necessary and was the supreme principle of the spiritual life, but they could not give all the answers to these questions and similar ones.

For two reasons, this is no mark against them. First, what they did teach on this matter is impeccable and groundbreaking—capable of creating great saints both then *and now*. Second, their teachings were orchestrated by Providence for their own sake (in edifying their immediate hearers), indeed, but also as preparations for what would come *after* the Holy Spirit completed the work that He was doing through them.

The works of God are always both intrinsically valuable and preparatory for something more—since stagnation is never His Will. The Eucharist, for example, is both the "source" *and* the "summit of the Christian life." (Catechism, §1324) In other words, the Blessed Sacrament is both that for which we long for its own sake (summit) and is itself a preparation (source) for the Heavenly Wedding Feast it anticipates, *as well as* an inexhaustible treasury of graces for the accomplishment of God's Will in our temporal lives. The same is true with the Divine Will's exposition in Sacred Tradition: it greatly sanctified those fortunate enough to be blessed with knowing these teachings in earlier centuries, and it also served as a preparation for its own culmination in the Gift of Living in the Divine Will, to be revealed as soon as the time was ripe. As the ripened fruit is now ready to be picked, let us consider the new strategy God has used for doing so.

> "During this earthly existence the spiritual edifice is continually increasing not only in grandeur and magnificence, but also in splendors of virtue and sanctity. Here alone is the reason for our passing existence. The Church still remains and withstands all persecutions because it must progress and be perfected completely and especially in sanctity. For that did Jesus Christ establish His Church ... it is necessary that the Church finish her course ... that the number and perfection of all her members be completed, that all should be transformed in the same divine image from glory to glory; and that all should be sanctified ... much is yet lacking for the complete fulfillment of the prophecies concerning the general effusion of the gifts of the Spirit." -Fr. Arintero, O.P.[70]

[70] *The Mystical Evolution in the Development and Vitality of the Church Volume II*. Appendix. *Imprimatur* 1951.

The New Strategy

> "The mystics are the great representatives of this lived theology of the saints. They transmit to the whole Church their profound knowledge of the Mystery of God the Trinity, of the God known and loved in Jesus Christ by means of the great work of his Love which is the Redemption of man." –Fr. François-Marie Léthel[71]

The next phase of God's effort required a new strategy. While up to this point it was fitting for the Holy Spirit to inspire gradual growth, over the course of centuries of Sacred Tradition, regarding the Church's understanding of the sanctity of the Divine Will, it would not be likewise fitting for the astounding claims found in the 20th-Century mystics—on the "New and Divine Holiness" of the *Gift of Living in the Divine Will*—to be presented through anything but a direct Divine (private) revelation.

The same dynamic is observed with the Divine Mercy. It was fitting for the Church's Sacred Tradition to grow, through the human (though Divinely motivated) contributions of the saints, in its exaltation of this greatest of God's attributes. Accordingly, great Doctors of the Church like St. Alphonsus Liguori masterfully refuted the heresy of Jansenism, and in so doing they contributed to Sacred Tradition's understanding of just how extraordinary God's Mercy really is. But it would not be fitting for anything other than a direct Divine revelation to make claims of the tremendous magnitude found in St. Faustina's Divine Mercy revelations. Instead—and as usual with His greatest works—the Almighty chose an ordinary, lowly virgin as the instrument through which He entrusted revelations to the Church and the world.[72]

In the present considerations on the great sanctity of union with the Divine Will, all the preparations have been made. The astounding teachings of St. Thérèse of Lisieux were the capstone of these efforts; serving the same role as the highest stone placed in a Romanesque

---

[71] Fr. François is a Vatican theology professor, a Carmelite, and a Papal Preacher.

[72] Mariology's growth follows a similar pattern. While it was fitting for its theme to develop over the course of centuries of Sacred Tradition, even to the point of culminating in the teachings on Marian Consecration given by St. Louis de Montfort, it would not be fitting for one—even a saint as great as he—to boldly demand that the Holy Father, along with all the Bishops of the world, consecrate Russia to the Immaculate Heart of Mary, and that all souls should undertake the First Saturday Devotion and add an extra prayer at the end of each decade of the Holy Rosary. The magnitude of these exhortations clearly merited a direct Heavenly intervention. Hence, the revelations of Our Lady of Fatima.

arch bridge. Placing the final stone makes the entire bridge structurally solid and ready to be used at once for its originally intended purpose of facilitating travel between the two points it connects: in this case, the Divine Will and the human will—Heaven and earth.

How fitting, therefore, that having carefully set the capstone in place, God promptly got to work in *using* the bridge. Indeed, He immediately began *directly revealing* to the world what He had spent thousands of years preparing for. He began revealing *the* crown and completion of all sanctity—the Gift of Living in the Divine Will, as found in many 20th-Century private revelations, above all those to the Servant of God Luisa Piccarreta.

Before looking at the revelations themselves, however, some background information is in order on the nature of private revelation, for it is often misunderstood.

On Private Revelation in General

> "Right from the beginning of my ministry in St. Peter's See in Rome, I consider this message [the private revelations to St. Faustina on the Divine Mercy] my special task. Providence has assigned it to me in the present situation of man, the Church and the world. It could be said that precisely this situation assigned that message to me as my task before God."
>
> –Pope St. John Paul II.[73]

The first thing to be understood about private revelation is precisely what its very name implies: it is not *Public* Revelation. As the *Catechism of the Catholic Church* teaches:

> ... no new public revelation is to be expected before the glorious manifestation of our Lord Jesus Christ." Yet **even if Revelation is already complete, it has not been made completely explicit[74];**

---

[73] Pope John Paul II, Angelus Address. November 22nd, 1981.

[74] Here we must consider that rendering explicit what is only embryonic in Public Revelation is an enormous mission which counts among its tasks the most grandiose conquests in Church History. Analogously, the study of Geometry is none other than rendering explicit what already exists seminally within a mere five simple postulates. Nevertheless, this undertaking produces thousands of truths that each flow from these mere five postulates and with which one can construct a magnificent cathedral, traverse oceans, and predict astronomical phenomena. Imagine how absurd it would be to downplay the importance of the derivation of these Geometrical theorems because they "merely render explicit what is already contained in the postulates." Now, the Faith is infinitely beyond mathematics, therefore the task of rendering explicit what is only embryonic in Public Revelation is an even greater task than in Geometry.

> **it remains for Christian faith gradually to grasp its full significance over the course of the centuries**. Throughout the ages, there have been so-called "private" revelations, some of which have been recognized by the authority of the Church. They do not belong, however, to the deposit of faith. It is not their role to improve or complete Christ's definitive Revelation, but to help live more fully by it in a certain period of history. **Guided by the magisterium of the Church, the *sensus fidelium* knows how to discern and welcome in these revelations whatever constitutes an authentic call of Christ** or his saints to the Church. Christian faith cannot accept "revelations" that claim to surpass or correct the Revelation of which Christ is the fulfillment, as is the case in certain non-Christian religions and also in certain recent sects which base themselves on such "revelations." (§66-67)

We must always heed these teachings of the Catechism when dealing with private revelation; both those which exalt private revelation and testify to its great importance, and those which describe its boundaries. We will consider the former in a moment; first, let us settle the indispensability of the latter.

Public Revelation *alone* demands the assent of supernatural Catholic Faith from all people (cf. Pope Benedict XIV's 18th-Century treatise, *Heroic Virtue*.)[75] Public Revelation alone is the unquestionable and inerrant foundation for our Faith until the end of time. Any claim of any alleged private revelation must, therefore, *always* be understood through the lens of Public Revelation, and any claim of any alleged private revelation must be rejected if—implicitly or explicitly—it contradicts any teaching contained within Public Revelation. Furthermore, Public Revelation was already rendered complete upon the death of the Apostle John, and it may neither be added to nor subtracted from at any time, for any reason, by anyone.

But that is where the limitations on private revelation end. Moving forward, therefore, we must dedicate some pages to addressing the lukewarmness towards private revelation that has spread within some sectors of the Church. Before doing so, however, I hasten to add that the admonitions which follow likely do not apply to those

[75] Note: even *supernatural* Faith in a private revelation could, however, be required of the seer himself or herself who received it. Some have employed Benedict XIV's point to pretend that only the actual seers themselves can ever have any obligation *of any sort* in private revelation. The forthcoming sections correct that notion. As one can see, I am openly acknowledging that *supernatural Faith* is only universally demanded for Public Revelation, therefore presenting this fact as if it were a rebuttal of anything in this chapter, regarding the importance of private revelation, would be a straw man.

who have bothered to read this book thus far! For they are more directed towards those who would immediately throw a book like this in their ever-ready "burn pile." But the following sections are included here to equip you for those situations, bound to arise, wherein another Catholic castigates you for caring about private revelation.

Nor is my intention to lay a heavy burden upon anyone's shoulders by making them feel guilty about refraining from concerning themselves with a message they do not feel comfortable about. Private revelation must indeed be judged by its fruits, and there is a subjective dimension to that judgment which flows from each individual assessing the degree of peace (or lack thereof) in his soul when he reads their messages. It is not my place, nor anyone else's place, to question that assessment. So please be at peace, and do not ever fear that your salvation may be lost simply because you do not feel ready for, or comfortable with, any given private revelation—no matter how zealously I or anyone else may promote one! If you love Christ and heed those truths of His which constitute Public Revelation's Deposit of Faith, then you will be with Him forever. It is that simple.

Now, essential as it is to remain ever grounded in these truths regarding the supremacy of Public Revelation and the fact that it alone is a universal, objective necessity for salvation, it is also essential to avoid drawing conclusions from them which, like the following, are mistaken: *"The Deposit of Faith alone is enough! We have Scripture, Tradition, and Magisterium; anything else is a distraction. Catholics may always regard any private revelation however they please, and they should always feel free to ignore or even reject any such revelation."* Indeed, each of those three statements, though drawing from truths, only do so fallaciously.

First, because the Foundation (the Deposit of Faith)—though necessary, unchangeable, and final—is not "sufficient" in an unqualified sense ("Sola Scriptura" teaching is heretical for many reasons, not only because it rejects Magisterium!). Second, because the Word of God itself implores us to remain open to the Holy Spirit, for He—even *after* the age of Public Revelation—"leads us to **all** truth" (John 16:13), including those truths that are not rendered fully explicit within the pages of the inerrant Word of God.[76] Finally, because no person is ever free to reject the Holy Spirit or to contradict his own conscience; indeed, one's conscience always compels him to believe certain truths and do certain things which are not themselves strictly

[76] Hence the Catechism's own teaching, quoted earlier, that Public Revelation is most affirmatively *not* yet "completely explicit;" and its implication that private revelation is indispensable to that explication.

required by the Faith, and private revelation is well within the reach of conscience. As the Catechism also teaches:

> **In all he says and does, man is obliged to follow faithfully what he knows to be just and right.** (§1778)

The Church does not say *"only in those matters that the Catholic Church formally teaches are true must man follow faithfully what he knows to be just and right;"* but rather, that he must do so *always and everywhere.* We must never erroneously conflate "not required *as* a matter of Catholic Faith" with "never possibly an obligation of any sort *for any Catholic.*" For the latter is not only taught nowhere by the Church, but is in fact—here and elsewhere—expressly repudiated by her.

Admittedly, rejecting a true but extra-Magisterial claim will not constitute formal heresy. But one may licitly respond, *"So what?"* Formal heresy is just one of many ways to harm oneself and others. Another is by neglecting God's Will even as it is expressed outside the strict boundaries of Public Revelation. For, as we shall presently see, *not only* Public Revelation is necessary, *not only* Public Revelation is urgent, and *not only* Public Revelation can make tremendous claims.

We should begin with a concrete example: the Rosary. Every pontiff in recent memory has begged Catholics to pray the Rosary. Every saint who spoke of it encouraged it, with this encouragement growing ever more fervent over the centuries until it became a veritable insistence. The only Fatima seer who survived to adulthood, the Servant of God Sr. Lucia, went so far as to say, "**All people of good will can, and must say the Rosary every day**."[77]

Yet, it is "just another private revelation!" We should always remember, therefore, that whatever we categorically say about private revelation, we also say about the Rosary, which itself is—in a real sense—*necessary,* and which has an eschatological importance that is difficult to overstate. The mere fact that the Rosary is not a *universal and objective necessity for salvation* does not suggest it isn't *necessary* for other reasons.[78]

The need for private revelation was embedded into the Faith

---

[77] National Catholic Register. "Fatima's Sister Lucia Explains Why the Daily Rosary is a 'Must'" November 19, 2017. Joseph Pronechen, Citing *"Fatima in Lucia's own words, volume 1"*

[78] Moreover, whatever one says about private revelation categorically, he also says of devotion to the Sacred and Immaculate Hearts, the Miraculous Medal, the Brown Scapular, the Divine Mercy (e.g., the Image, the Chaplet, the Feast), Our Lady of Guadalupe (and Fatima, Lourdes, etc.), and on the list goes. Furthermore, while the Eucharist and Confession are obviously not the results of private revelations, the way we rightly approach them today (e.g., emphasizing the importance of daily Communion, frequent confession, Eucharistic adoration, etc.) was largely inspired by private revelation.

from the beginning. We are told in Scripture that *"he who prophesies edifies the church,"* (1 Corinthians 14) and such prophecy is a form of private revelation. Moreover, these extraordinary charisms of the Holy Spirit, of which prophecy is one, exist not for one's own sanctification, but rather for the sanctification of the entire Church. As the Catechism teaches:

> Charisms are to be accepted with gratitude by the person who receives them **and by all members of the Church as well**. They are a wonderfully rich grace for the apostolic vitality and for the holiness of the entire Body of Christ... (§799-800)

To assert that only faith in the Deposit of Faith ultimately matters is to present a slightly Catholicized version of the Protestant "Faith Alone" (*Sola Fide*) heresy. Catholic teaching, of course, rejects this idea. Consider what the Catechism teaches, quoting St. John of the Cross: "**At the evening of our lives, we will be judged by our love**." (§1022) Love of God and love of neighbor are the standards of our judgment, not simply faith in the Deposit of Faith. Let us, therefore, treat God as a loving Father Who is always next to us, not an indifferent master who imparts orders and then leaves us alone for 2,000 years. Let us rekindle in our hearts the holy excitement that proceeds from this proper approach to our loving Father; an approach which does not exclude a passion for seeking out those occasions wherein Heaven directly intervenes into earthly affairs. Let us heed the wisdom of Pope Benedict XVI, who taught:

> The shepherds made haste. Holy curiosity and holy joy impelled them. In our case, it is probably not very often that we make haste for the things of God. God does not feature among the things that require haste. The things of God can wait, we think and we say. And yet he is the most important thing, ultimately the one truly important thing. **Why should we not also be moved by curiosity to see more closely and to know what God has said to us?** At this hour, let us ask him to touch our hearts with the holy curiosity and the holy joy of the shepherds, and thus let us go over joyfully to Bethlehem, to the Lord who today once more comes to meet us. (Christmas Eve Homily, 2012)

In a word, our calling is to become saints. Submitting to the contents of Public Revelation may enable one to pass Catechism class, but it is only the very beginning of the mission of sanctification. Accordingly, our own fathers in the Faith had precisely this holy curiosity that Benedict recommends, and the glorious history of the Catholic Church advises a radically different response than the "whatever floats your boat" approach to private revelation. For it is a story in which the drama of whether Catholics respond faithfully to genuine private revelations determines the course of history—the requests at Fatima, the message to St. Faustina, the requests of Jesus for the Sacred Heart devotion, the requests of Our Lady of Guadalupe through St. Juan Diego, etc.

Whoever is tempted to regard private revelation as "unnecessary" should ask himself: Would God have taken no offense if the seventy thousand who witnessed the Miracle of the Sun at Fatima turned their backs on that "unapproved private revelation," by calling it "just a distraction from the Sacraments"? Would St. Faustina's spiritual director have committed no injustice if he ignored or opposed the promulgation of the Divine Mercy message instead of helping it, saying to himself, "this is extraneous and what we already have with the Sacred Heart devotion is enough"? Would Bishop Zumaragga have been safe in the Will of God by ignoring St. Juan Diego coming to him with the request of Our Lady of Guadalupe to have a church built, supposing that his own Diocesan expansion plan was better? Did not King Louis XIV's failure to respond to the Sacred Heart requests of Jesus through St. Margaret Mary spell disaster for France?

Though each revelation mentioned above is now fully Church approved, none of them had already enjoyed full approval at the time Heaven called for the corresponding response to each, and this brings us to our next point on private revelation.

"Unapproved" Private Revelation can be Important

> "The Marian dimension of the Church precedes the Petrine."
> –*Catechism of the Catholic Church*, §773

Someone may concede that private revelation can be important, but still refuse to heed any except those bearing so-called "full approval." But the approach which ignores all private revelations unless, or until, they are "fully approved" has likewise already been rendered irrational by the facts of Church history, as we see explained in the following anthology recently published on Mariology:

> Can an obedient member of the Catholic Church make a personal assent of belief regarding a reported revelation before the Church, local or universal, has made an official statement about its authenticity? The answer, based on the **Church's repeated precedent**, is in the affirmative ... Practically speaking, **it is oftentimes only after the faithful begin to pilgrimage privately to**

> **reported apparition sites that the local Church initiates its authoritative evaluation.** The beatification of Fatima visionaries Jacinta and Francisco Marto in 2000 by John Paul II further illustrates the legitimacy of the faithful personally accepting a private revelation as authentic before the Church's official decision.[79]

While "Is this approved?" is certainly an important question, it is not the *most* important question. Condemned private revelations, indeed, should not be promoted, for the Church should always be obeyed. But ignoring any private revelation that is not yet "fully approved" is no more reasonable than ignoring the advice or teachings of any person who is not yet canonized. Each now-approved revelation was once unapproved, and its contents did not magically become Heaven-sent upon receiving Ecclesiastical approbation. Whatever value and urgency exist in any approved revelation also existed in the same revelation's pre-approval days.

Each example listed previously testifies to this fact, but the case of Our Lady of Kibeho is especially relevant. In this approved apparition, the Virgin Mary came to warn the people of Rwanda of an impending disaster that would entail *rivers of blood*, and to instruct them on how to avert it. Twelve years later, the Rwandan genocide occurred, in which one million innocent people were slaughtered by their own neighbors. As Rwandan Genocide survivor and Apostle of Christian forgiveness, Immaculée Ilibagiza, explains in her book *If Only We Had Listened*:

> [The revelation of Our Lady of Kibeho was] a prophetic warning from the Virgin Mary that if Rwandans did not cleanse their hearts of hatred and fill their souls with God's love, evil would win out and a genocide would sweep across the land. **Sadly, the Virgin's warning went unheeded and in 1994, Our Lady's prediction became reality**: the terrible Rwandan genocide unfolded exactly as she prophesized. (Page XV)

Though now an approved apparition, Kibeho's full approval only came in 2001, which was years after the genocide it sought to prevent took place. If, despite its not yet "fully approved" status, enough people had been willing to believe that apparition—on account of the verifications of authenticity it enjoyed—a million innocent lives could have been spared. Wisely, therefore, does the Church acknowledge, "**The Marian dimension of the Church precedes the Petrine**..." (*Catechism of the Catholic Church*, §773)

---

[79] *Mariology: A Guide for Priests, Deacons, Seminarians, and Consecrated Persons.* Mark Miravalle. Page 840.

Private Revelation Can Make Great Claims

"You will prepare the world for My final coming."
–Jesus to St. Faustina (*Diary*, §429)

Another mistaken notion holds that private revelation may be important to a limited extent, and even necessary in a certain sense, but still cannot make claims that are too lofty, and instead may only sit quietly in a corner and make occasional polite suggestions about a few pious devotional practices. Based on an elementary misreading of the Catechism's text which teaches that no private revelation may claim to "**improve or complete ... surpass or correct**" Public Revelation (§67), the notion above draws a fallacious conclusion, contained nowhere in the Magisterium, that "no private revelation may *make claims which surpass anything in* Public Revelation." But the Catechism does not imply that no private revelation may ever *speak of* matters of the greatest possible import. Approved revelations to many canonized saints, for example, speak much about Heaven—a far more important thing than is spoken of in many portions of Scripture and Magisterium, for the latter have no choice but to often concern themselves with relatively smaller matters when circumstances demand doing so (e.g., St. Paul's request, in 2 Timothy 4:13, that his cloak left with Carpus be returned!)

Here, the Catechism only declares that private revelation may not claim to *itself* constitute an improvement, completion, surpassing or correcting the Public Revelation.[80] But there is nothing to preclude even the *greatest* claims being made *within* a private revelation, so

---

[80] Analogously, no other Bishop may claim to himself surpass the Bishop of Rome's (the Pope's) authority. So long as, however, a Bishop respects this distinction, there is nothing to prevent a Bishop's own teaching from perhaps even exceeding, in some cases, the magnitude of the preaching of the Pope himself. Few, I suspect, deny that the importance of the teachings of St. Augustine, Bishop of Hippo, Father and Doctor of the Church, exceeds even that of Pope Zosimus (who reigned during Augustine's life). Clearly, if Zosimus were to have authoritatively contradicted Augustine, then in those matters we would be forced to side with the Pope, with respect to the superiority of his office. But Augustine never claimed superiority to the Pope, nor did he ever formally contradict the latter's Magisterium; therefore, no problem exists with regarding Augustine as bearing a greater importance. (Augustine did, however, once correct a non-authoritative erroneous statement of Zosimus regarding Pelagianism; clearly, the analogy here breaks down, as *no* private revelation may *ever* speak against *anything* in Public Revelation.) Similarly, no one can deny that it was Bishop Athanasius' preaching against Arianism that proved superior to that of the reigning Pontiffs (Liberius and Damasus I), notwithstanding the latter's superior authority. Finally, could anyone deny that Our Lady of Fatima and the revelations on the Divine Mercy are more consequential than the 33-day pontificate of John Paul I?

long as first, these claims themselves are in accord with Catholic orthodoxy, and second, the texts providing the claims do not propose to *themselves enjoy* superiority to Public Revelation.[81]

Unfortunately, many examples can be given of supposed "revelations" that *do* claim to improve, complete, surpass, or correct Public Revelation, in contradiction of this norm, hence we can see the great importance of its inclusion within the Catechism and the wisdom of the authors of this text. From the multitudes of them, we will consider here only three; one selected from each primary category (Catholic, Christian, and non-Christian) of illicit "revelations": the Koran, the Book of Mormon, and the claims of the "Army of Mary." In each of these cases, we see a "revelation" which ostensibly respects the validity of the one true Public Revelation, but in fact attempts to dispute either its inerrancy, finality, or supremacy.

The Koran claims that the Bible is basically true but became largely corrupted, that the Koran is actually the final public revelation, and that the Koran corrects the Bible's "corruptions." The Book of Mormon does not claim to correct the Bible, but does claim to be a new public revelation, capable of adding to the very foundation of the Christian Faith, and serving as a lens through which to understand the Bible. The 20th-Century "Catholic" movement, the "Army of Mary,"[82] was based on false "private revelations" which, though pretending to respect the inerrancy of Public Revelation and not proposing to correct it, do claim to improve and complete it: for example, these false revelations claimed that the New Testament's revelation of the Holy Trinity was true, but only *part* of the Truth: they heretically taught that God really was a "Quinternity" of five persons in one Divine Nature.

In each of these cases (and there are many more like them), we find an example of an alleged revelation claiming to *itself* "surpass or correct" Public Revelation. But so long as Public Revelation's superior authority is respected and orthodoxy is maintained, nowhere does the

---

[81] The latter limitation is essential because even when no clear contradictions between what is explicitly stated in two texts exist, there are nevertheless often a multitude of ways a given passage can be interpreted. When interpreting multiple texts in order to ascertain what we should do and believe, whichever text is superior is the one that must always give the lens through which the text in the inferior must be understood. Therefore, it is utterly essential that no private revelation ever claim equality, much less superiority, to Public Revelation—even if no blatant contradictions between them exist.

[82] Also known as the "Community of the Lady of All Nations," this sect was founded in 1971 in Canada and eventually claimed many thousands of members. It has since been condemned and its members excommunicated.

Church place any limits on the magnitude of the claims which a private revelation may make.[83] The Church, however, has gone further than simply not condemning the existence of tremendous claims in private revelation; it has affirmatively rebuffed the placement of limitations on the significance of private revelation's claims through the immense degree of approval and exaltation given to St. Faustina's revelations.

Faustina's revelations make the most tremendous claims one can imagine. Within the saint's Diary, we see: the insistence that her revelations constitute *the* very preparation of the *world* for the Coming of Christ (§429); the demand for the institution of a new Liturgical Feast (Divine Mercy Sunday; §570); the insistence upon the veneration a particular image (the Divine Mercy Image; §49) — a veneration which ensures that the soul who undertakes it "shall not perish" (Ibid.); the clear revelation of a *New and Divine Holiness* (as we will see in the upcoming chapters); and even the offer of an absolute promise, unprecedented in all Church history, that the faithful undertaking of its requests will result in complete remission of all sin *and* punishment — a veritable second Baptism, for it does not entail the same requirements as a plenary indulgence (§300, §699).

None of these extraordinary, unprecedented claims prevented the Church from giving these private revelations the highest possible levels of approval (though, like other revelations we will discuss, these claims did cause St. Faustina's writings to spend some time condemned, on the Index of Forbidden Books!). It is especially the wisdom of Pope St. John Paul II which we can thank for this approval, therefore, we should consider what his teaching and example — and that of others of the modern era — tell us about private revelation in general.

Great Saints and Minds on Private Revelation

> "One cannot lead a life of faith with public revelations alone."
> –Bishop Paul Kim

Pope St. John Paul II, justly referred to by many as "John Paul the Great," gives us the example *par excellence* of the proper approach to private revelation. When speaking about his Encyclical *Dives in*

---

[83] Considerations of one case — the compatibility of Jesus' revelations to the Servant of God Luisa Piccarreta with Catholic Teaching on the nature of Public vs. private revelation — can be found in the Appendices.

Misericordia (which was inspired by his reading of St. Faustina's Divine Mercy Diary), he disclosed:

> Right from the beginning of my ministry in St. Peter's See in Rome, I consider this message ["Divine Mercy"] my special task. Providence has assigned it to me in the present situation of man, the Church and the world. It could be said that **precisely this situation assigned that message to me as my task before God**.[84]

Here we see this great and saintly Pope bluntly stating that the entire purpose of his Pontificate was a private revelation! Not only that, but a private revelation given to a mystic who, upon his elevation to the Papacy, had not even been declared Venerable.[85] This apparent deficiency, however, did not stop the Pope from regarding Jesus' revelations to her as his own "special task" which constituted his mission "right from the beginning" of his Pontificate.

When faced with this stunning example, how could we—who are nothing compared to him—fear dedicating parts of our lives to private revelation if that is what God has called us to do? Were we to thus fear, we would be like poor misers afraid to invest a few dollars in a noble cause when a wise millionaire living next door sells all his possessions to invest his entire fortune in the same thing.

It is not Pope St. John Paul II alone in whom we see the proper approach to private revelation exemplified. We see this approach of not only openness to private revelation, but also zeal for it, in all the saints of the Church. As the dismissive approach to private revelation is a uniquely postmodern phenomenon (peruse the treatises of the saints of old, and you will frequently find them deferring to the direct Heavenly insights given to other holy people—canonized or not, approved or not), there is no need to review examples from the older saints here, but it is helpful to consider the approach of some other holy souls who lived in the 20th Century.

Mother Teresa of Calcutta, among the greatest saints of the 20th Century, was also one of the most well-known supporters of the apparitions at Medjugorje.[86]

St. Padre Pio was among the greatest mystics of the Church's entire history. He had great zeal for private revelation, and his willingness even to endorse and promote unapproved private revelations

---

[84] Pope John Paul II, Angelus Address to Collevalenza. November 22nd, 1981.

[85] It was also John Paul II who, years earlier as Karol Wojtyla, had initiated Faustina's cause

[86] Mark Miravalle. *Is Medjugorje Real? Facts and First-hand Accounts.* 2008.

was widely known. In addition to strongly supporting Luisa Piccarreta[87] (though her revelations did already enjoy many approvals by that time), he was a believer of the apparitions at Garabandal.[88] Of course, St. Pio ran up against extraordinary opposition from some members of the Church hierarchy; for a time, he was even censured by Rome. An overly cautious person would have seen this as a reason to *not* be like the saint: that is, to avoid all the "risks" involved with private revelation. But "risk avoidance" is not a saint-making motto.

Mother Angelica, the holy foundress of EWTN (The Eternal Word Television Network), was one of the greatest evangelists of the 20th Century. She was also one of the most wholehearted and zealous promoters of private revelation in the Catholic world, even dedicating her first appearance on her own television network to discussing private revelation on The Warning, or the "Illumination of Conscience."

Father René Laurentin was a giant of the Catholic world of the 20th Century. The author of over 100 books, he is cited and mentioned dozens of times in the authoritative *New Catholic Encyclopedia*, and Pope Benedict XVI named him a Prelate of His Holiness in 2009. Fr. Laurentin, however, lamented the state of the modern Church with respect to private revelation, forthrightly assessing the secularistic and skeptical rationalism that now dominates in too many Catholic circles. He said that, given this climate, *not even the apparitions at Lourdes would be approved by the Church today!* Regarding the work of another contemporary theologian, Fr. Edward O'Connor, Fr. Laurentin himself wrote:

> Edward O'Connor, former professor at the University of Notre Dame, is **a classic theologian, open to apparitions** and their discernment. He knows how to recognize false visionaries, and defend those who have been discredited unjustly by the mistakes that commonly occur in this domain ... we are grateful to Father O'Connor for having resolved the paradoxical contradictions between the spiritual phenomenon of apparitions and the canonical repression which sometimes broke out against the visionaries. (*Listen to My Prophets*. Preface.)

Turning our attention to Fr. O'Connor, this theologian writes:

> Being cautious and discreet does not mean being closed-minded.

---

[87] Cf. *The Sun of My Will*. The Official Vatican Biography of the Servant of God Luisa Piccarreta. www.SunOfMyWill.com

[88]https://www.ewtn.com/expert/answers/garabandal.htm

> **Visions, apparitions and messages from God, while always being extraordinary, are a normal part of the Christian life. They are much more abundant than is generally recognized.** Pope John Paul II himself declared: "The Church is mission! Today she also needs 'prophets' who can reawaken in the communities faith in the revealing Word of God, who is rich in mercy"[89]

Bishop Paul Tchang-Ryeol Kim wrote the following in a Pastoral letter to his flock:

> **Our age is indeed an age of private revelations**. However ... disturbing remarks are now being heard within the Church... words of apprehension are being uttered by most of the shepherds. Such apprehension, however, is groundless, caused by lack of proper understanding of private revelations ... false revelations unavoidably have been occurring also, causing confusion. However, should we throw away money because there is counterfeit money? Because there are false private revelations, should we frown upon and ignore private revelations and inspirations themselves? All of the devotional movements and apostolates such as the Eucharistic devotion, the devotion to the Sacred Heart of Jesus, the devotion to the Immaculate Heart of Mary, the Stations of the Cross, the rosary, novena devotions, ... Third Orders of the Franciscans, of St. Vincent, of St. Damian, etc. could not have started in the Church without private revelations ... **One cannot lead a life of faith with public revelations alone.** That is because the life of faith is a living communion with God. A church that only has organization, dogmas and theology would be a cold, lifeless organization ... **This is the very reason why our Church has untiringly defended the need for and the important role of private revelations** by both explanations and actions despite the persistently recurring false private revelations and their harmful effects.[90]

Let us heed this bishop's plea, and put an end to the miserly approach to Heaven which is little more than Deism dressed in pious looking attire and which, in response to any Heavenly invitation, hastens only to the accumulation of excuses to justify apathy. (cf. Luke 14:16-24)

---

[89] *Listen to My Prophets*. xii (Fr. Edward O'Connor was indeed an authority on these matters, and it is noteworthy that, of the many books he wrote, he only published one entirely dedicated to a particular private revelation: *Living in the Divine Will*, published in 2014, in which he defended and explained Luisa's revelations. It was his last work.)

[90] Pastoral Letter by His Excellency Paul Tchang-Ryeol Kim, Bishop of the Cheju Diocese, Korea. Easter Sunday. 1999

We must instead return to the sincere and simple response when an alleged revelation comes about; namely, *"Is this true or not?"*

In the modern world (and sadly in the modern Church which is far too influenced by it), wherein the Dictatorship of Relativism reigns supreme, that question—the only question that ultimately matters—is, at the same time, the systematically ignored one. Let us, therefore, reject Relativism in *all* its forms. Let us remember that, ultimately, a simple question confronts us when dealing with any alleged revelation: *"Is this from God?"* If good Catholic discernment yields an answer in the affirmative, then we should not presume that God will be pleased by quibbles, apathy, or tepidity.

A Word of Comfort and Caution

> "Jesus Christ is the same yesterday and today and for ever. Be not led away by diverse and strange teachings." –Hebrews 13:8,9

Now that we have settled that private revelations deserve a glorious place in our lives as Catholics, we conclude by reiterating that they are never universal and objective necessities for salvation, and no follower of Christ should ever allow his peace to be disturbed if he—simply and sincerely—does not feel prepared to approach any given one among their ranks, no matter how lofty. There are, of course, an enormous number of private revelations in existence. Practically speaking, therefore, only heeding a small fraction of them will be possible for any one person, which itself necessitates passing over most. In the appendices, we will address why this fact should not cause anyone to ignore the revelation which features most prominently in this book, but for now I merely wish to focus on the importance of maintaining the proper attitude towards private revelation in general. All I have sought to accomplish with the preceding sections is the refutation of knee-jerk reactions of apathy, lukewarmness, or even coldness that dominate in too many circles of Catholicism today with respect to private revelation. All I have wished to do is reject that lamentable attitude which regards "safety first" as the ultimate norm of life—since *"God's love first"* must instead always be our axiom. But I most definitely do not want to push anyone into the opposite extreme, as that too is unacceptable.

Therefore, we must conclude with a word on the dangers that arise with private revelation. Indeed, we must always remain prudent. We should have a disposition of openness to private revelation, *not* a by-default presumption of its validity, and certainly not a willingness to contradict Church teachings because of an alleged "revelation." Finally, a particularly careful (perhaps even initially skeptical) approach is called for with respect to *living* putative seers—it is especially after death that a person's true nature becomes apparent through the legacy of fruits (or lack thereof) left in his or her wake.

Just as many glibly dismiss private revelation, so, too, many err in the opposite extreme, and readily go head over heels in following anyone who claims to have any sort of supernatural insight. Furthermore, they approach private revelation without ensuring that *Catholic orthodoxy* is the unquestionable standard of all their discernment. This is a deeply problematic demeanor, and, in some circles, it is growing rapidly. The problem is particularly acute among those with an inordinate desire to know the details of future events, and among those who crave immediate, simplistic solutions to all their temporal problems and conundrums, instead of bearing their crosses (including the cross of not immediately having all the answers to the various confusing matters dominating political, societal, and ecclesial discourse) with complete resignation and trust in God.

The problem is grave because there are *many* false private revelations, and their true nature is not always at first obvious. Recently, supposed seers have provided an extraordinary number of false prophecies and false revelations. But perhaps the greatest damage we find in their aftermath is the eliciting of a cynical approach to private revelation which exists in some Catholic circles today. It should, however, surprise no one that the devil misses no opportunity; that, seeing the incredible outpouring of God's grace through the explosion of private revelation of the modern era, he has taken it upon himself to inspire many false apparitions and messages to stifle this outpouring of grace. But, as Bishop Kim said, we mustn't "throw out the baby with the bathwater." Thankfully, we are well equipped to throw out only the filthy bathwater here, as the Church has given us norms for discernment.

In 1978, the Congregation for the Doctrine of Faith promulgated a document entitled "*Norms regarding the manner of proceeding in the discernment of presumed apparitions or revelations*." The document itself is short and worth reading, but the essence of its criteria is summed up as follows.

Criteria in support of validity: psychological equilibrium, honesty, rectitude of moral life, docility towards Ecclesiastical Authority, normal regimen of faith continued following the apparition, theology and spirituality free of error, and spiritual fruit (e.g., conversion, charity). The last item—the document instructs—is to be given "special regard."

Criteria against validity: Doctrinal errors attributed to (that is, allegedly said by) God or a saint, evidence of a search for profit connected to the revelation, grave sins associated with the events of the revelation on the part of the seer or followers, and psychological disorder or psychopathic tendencies.

As we can see, this discernment is not "rocket science." While it must be undertaken with care and diligence, the direction that it leads us in must not be indefinitely put in doubt by epistemological scrupulosity. In other words, we must not forever come up with rationalizations to pretend that we do not know what we do in fact know full well. When an alleged private revelation has been scrutinized by the Church, and 1) The messages have been found to be orthodox, 2) The seer has been found to be spiritually, morally, and psychologically stable, 3) The seer has been found to be sincere, pure, and obedient, and 4) The fruits of the messages are good and enduring; then we must simply unclench the fist, bend the knee, and acknowledge the finger of God in what is transpiring.

This duty becomes even more imperative when clear evidence of miracles and other supernatural verifications of authenticity exist, and it becomes extreme when decades have passed since the seer's death with all these verifications only growing in their testimony to the seer's authenticity. Each major mystic and private revelation included in Parts Three and Four of this book passes all the criteria above with flying colors, thus they warrant no incredulity.

In order, however, to ensure that even the most temperamentally-skeptical souls will have no difficulty seeing the truth in what this book exists to introduce—*the New and Divine Holiness that is the Gift of Living in the Divine Will, in fulfillment of the Our Father prayer*—we will begin our journey through these private revelations with two mystics whose authenticity is beyond evident: Saint Faustina Kowalska and Blessed Conchita (Concepción Cabrera de Armida).

8. Faustina and Conchita: The New Era of Spirituality

"The words [John Paul II] pronounced ... were as a synthesis of his Magisterium, evidencing that devotion to Divine Mercy is not a secondary devotion, but an integral dimension of a Christian's faith and prayer."
–Pope Benedict XVI

Great and exalted indeed is the sanctity of union with the Divine Will that is described by the saints and Doctors of the Church up to St. Thérèse of Lisieux. But in the revelations of the 20th-Century mystics, we see something new and higher still.

When considering these messages from Jesus, we are no longer in the era of preparation, but of completion. The great Dominican theologian, Fr. Marie Michel Philipon, saw this clearly when explaining the revelations of Blessed Conchita Cabrera de Armida His observations, however, apply just as validly to Faustina's; for in 1978, summarizing the message Jesus entrusted to Conchita beginning with her 1906 reception of "Mystical Incarnation," he wrote: **"We are incontestably in a new era of spirituality."**[91]

St. Faustina's verifications of authenticity—too numerous to list here, but easy for anyone to verify—assure us that we can be completely confident in her revelations. And a New Era of Spirituality is truly revealed therein; a new holiness of the highest possible type. As we read in her Diary, *Divine Mercy in My Soul*:

> The soul receiving this **unprecedented grace of union with God** cannot say that it sees God face to face, because even here there is a very thin veil of faith, but so very thin that the soul can say that it sees God and talks with Him. It is "divinized." God allows the soul to know how much He loves it, and the soul sees that **better and holier souls than itself have not received this grace. Therefore, it is filled with holy amazement**, which maintains it in deep humility, and it steeps itself in its own nothingness and holy astonishment. (§771)

We begin with this Diary quote for two reasons: first, not only the greatness but also the *newness* of this supreme gift of grace is made

[91] Fr. Marie Michel Philipon. *Conchita: A Mother's Spiritual Diary*. Conclusion

clear (Faustina insists it is "unprecedented"); second, in it we see addressed the very question some people have when first hearing of this: "*How could I, unworthy as I am, receive a Gift of sanctity that is so much greater than what was received by the saints of days past who dwarf me in virtue?*"

Faustina, however, acknowledges that "better and holier souls" have not been given the Gift. Wisely, she reacts with gratitude and humility, instead of snubbing the offer and thereby giving offense to the One Who made it. The answer to the concern, therefore, is simple: *it is a gift!*[92] We don't deserve it. But it is offered to us, nevertheless.

This understanding is the one we must have as we continue to learn about the New and Divine Holiness; the fulfillment of the Our Father prayer—Living in the Divine Will *on earth, as the saints and angels do in Heaven*, and which, moving forward, we will refer to simply as "the Gift." It is pure gratuity on the part of God, not something we have managed to merit or individually work our way up to. We ought, therefore, not to be scandalized that God "saves the best wine for last" (cf. John 2:10). Instead, we ought to, with Faustina, be "filled with holy amazement," and not fret over the fact that we do not deserve this privilege.

The Human Will's "Transconsecration"

> "O Divine Will, You are the delight of my heart, the food of my soul, the light of my intellect, the omnipotent strength of my will; for when I unite myself with Your will, O Lord, **Your power works through me and *takes the place* of my feeble will.**"
>
> –St. Faustina (*Diary*, §650)

The great spiritual masters who wrote before the 20th Century taught well on the need to submit one's human will so entirely to the Divine Will that they eventually so resemble each other as to appear one. But in the teaching above, St. Faustina says that God Himself "*takes the place of*" her human will—indicating an *absorption* of her will by God's initiative (though not without her own active consent). This

---

92 The New and Divine Holiness—if you receive it—does not make *you* better than others. It simply gives you a greater gift than they received without changing the fact that you may be less deserving of it than those who did not receive it *merely because they lived before its time*. Analogously, consider that St. Joseph is the greatest saint to have ever lived besides the Blessed Virgin Mary (*Quamquam Pluries* §3). But not even he was given the great gift of the Eucharist, since he died before the Blessed Sacrament's Institution. The early Christians were not greater than St. Joseph, but they did receive a greater gift than he did in receiving the Eucharist. This matter is dealt with in more detail in the Appendices.

is greater than a oneness that results from a lengthy process of seeking *conformity*, directed at hopefully someday attaining *uniformity*.[93] This absorption means that it is no longer Faustina's own self-will animating her acts, but is rather the Divine Will doing so—a *Divine Substitution*.

Relatedly—and earlier still in her Diary—St. Faustina describes a profound turning point in her life. While at the convent, she was asked by Jesus to give her consent to become a victim soul. A profound exchange follows:

> I said, "Do with me as You please. I subject myself to Your will. **As of today, Your holy will shall be my nourishment**" ... I was [then] extraordinarily **fused with God** ... A great mystery took place during that adoration, a mystery between the Lord and myself ... And the Lord said to me, 'You are the delight of My Heart; from today on, every one of your acts, even the very smallest, will be a delight to My eyes, whatever you do.' At that moment I felt **transconsecrated**. **My earthly body was the same, but my soul was different; God was now living in it with the totality of His delight.** This is not a feeling, but a conscious reality that nothing can obscure. (§136-137)

"Transconsecration" is not a word one will often hear, but it is a wonderful name for the Gift of Living in the Divine Will! By using this word (and it appears she may have been the first), St. Faustina dares to say that what occurs within the host during the Mass has, in a sense (though not an identical one), occurred within her soul as well. Jesus' words to Faustina elsewhere in the Diary reveal just how this Transconsecration of the self into a Living Host transpires—by "living exclusively by the will of God," itself made possible by "absolutely cancelling" the self-will:

> [Jesus says:] "**Host pleasing to My Father,** know, My daughter, that the entire Holy Trinity finds Its special delight in you, because **you live exclusively by the will of God**. No sacrifice can compare with this." (§955)

How exactly this status as a true "Host" (a *living Eucharist*) came about in Faustina's soul is described earlier in her diary when, during a retreat, Jesus told her:

---

[93] Admittedly, St. Alphonsus did preempt this theme in Faustina by insisting that a "single act of uniformity with the Divine Will can make a saint," but Faustina takes this teaching much farther.

> **You will cancel out your will absolutely in this retreat** and, instead, My complete will shall be accomplished in you. [*On the following page in her diary a large "X" appears, and these words of Faustina are seen:*] **"From today on, my own will does not exist."** (§374)

Even if relatively small in number, passages like these in Faustina's Diary more than compensate for in their enormous weight, for they describe the most important moments in her spiritual life and therefore deserve our most resolute attention. Jesus is using these passages to communicate to us *all* what He is asking of us *after* we have accepted the Divine Mercy—the quantitatively predominant theme of her revelations. For as important as accepting and venerating the Divine Mercy is, this step is only the first in the realization of God's Will for our lives. (*Proclaiming* the Divine Mercy, however, always remains essential for all souls, even if they have arrived at the point where accepting it and trusting it are second nature; indeed, whoever receives the Gift will be inflamed with a burning desire to proclaim Jesus' Mercy to everyone.) The completion of this realization is found in the Gift.

In this point, let us defer to a true apostle of Divine Mercy whose expertise in and devotion to the matter is beyond question: the esteemed priest, biochemist, and monk, Fr. George Kosicki. This great priest wrote a small but powerful book, *Be Holy! The Legacy of John Paul the Great; A "Living Eucharist,"* which is strongly endorsed by at least three Cardinals, including the late Cardinal George of Chicago. Fr. Benedict Groeschel, summarizing Kosicki's message in the book's Preface, wrote: "Fr. Kosicki has identified the **principal themes of the writings of St. Faustina as trust, thanksgiving, 'being a living Eucharist'**, and, what she calls, "a bit of good will." In the book, Fr. Kosicki explains:

> **Pope John Paul II recently wrote of a "'new and divine' holiness** with which the Holy Spirit wishes to enrich Christians at the dawn of the third millennium ... to make Christ the heart of the world" ... The new and eternal holiness is a maturing of the holiness of Jesus revealed in the Gospels. **It is living the fullness of the Lord's Prayer**—His kingdom come—that the Lord reign in our hearts now by the Holy Spirit to the glory of God the Father"—**that His will be done on earth now as it is in heaven** ... **We [live the fullness of the Our Father] by becoming holy through the Holy Spirit and by doing and living in God's will on earth as in heaven** ... We are to become a living presence of Jesus radiating His love and mercy as we live in and by His will.

> And by praying "Give us this day our daily bread" we are asking for the grace we need to be a living presence of Jesus on earth—a "Living Eucharist." (Chapter 12)

Fr. Kosicki rightly insists that becoming a Living Eucharist is a *principal* theme of Faustina's revelations, and he connects this reality to both the "New and Divine" holiness extolled by Pope St. John Paul II (a teaching we will consider in depth in Part Four) and the fulfillment of the Our Father prayer itself!

Faustina's phrase referred to above by Fr. Groeschel appears in the following passage from the Diary:

> **How very easy it is to become holy**; all that is needed is a bit of good will. If Jesus sees this little bit of good will in the soul, He hurries to give himself to the soul... [who] **can very soon attain the highest holiness possible for a creature here on earth**. God is very generous and does not deny His grace to anyone. Indeed He gives more than what we ask of Him. (§291)

The phrases—namely, "all that is needed," "very soon," and "highest possible"—should give us great pause. As we now know, St. Faustina understood that Jesus had revealed to her a new sanctity of unprecedented exaltation—her Diary makes it clear in entries written before this one. Faustina, therefore, knew exactly what she was asserting: this very sanctity—this "New and Divine Holiness"—could be attained by a soul *quickly*, and that its attainment was *easy* if only we have good will. That is to say, if only we have the willingness to hand over our self-wills to God and ask that His Will alone be totally fulfilled in us.

The previous section's conclusion settled the need to respond, like Faustina, with "holy amazement" at this Gift being offered to us. Presently, we must conclude by affirming the *ease* with which this Gift can be received. Otherwise, we will become discouraged upon gaining knowledge of just how astonishing this Gift is—and that discouragement would only be a temptation from the devil. The truth is that the greatest holiness possible is *easy*—or, rather, it is only as hard as we insist upon making it by how stubbornly we choose to cling to the self-will.

Beyond Mystical Marriage

> "My beloved child, delight of My Heart, your words are dearer and more pleasing to me than the angelic chorus... [your] smallest act of virtue has unlimited value in My eyes because of your great love for Me. **In a soul that lives on My love alone, I reign as in heaven ...** rest a moment near My Heart and taste of the love in which you will delight for all eternity." –Jesus to St. Faustina (*Diary*, §1489)

What we see above is not alone in Faustina's Diary in relaying that the holiness of Heaven is now available on earth; Faustina also writes that "The veils of mystery hinder me not at all; **I love You as do Your chosen ones in heaven**," (§1324) and later still, "**I live Your divine life as do the elect in heaven**..." (§1393)

There is no unorthodoxy in this claim, because (as we saw in her Diary, §771), Faustina holds that this new grace she describes does not entail the Beatific Vision (i.e., "seeing God face to face"); a distinction whose ramifications will be discussed at greater length in the following chapter. But the *life and holiness* of Heaven is the Divine Will, and perfect union with it—Faustina insists—defines her own sanctity even as a pilgrim on earth.

This Heavenly sanctity is precisely what St. John of the Cross referred to as the supreme holiness *possible* (the "perfect state of glory"),[94] superior even to mystical marriage. What, then, is new about this teaching revealed to Faustina? Not what is possible in *absolute* terms, but rather what is possible *on earth*. Until the 20th Century, mystical marriage was considered the highest possible *earthly* sanctity. As the old *Catholic Encyclopedia*, published in the very beginning of the 20th Century, says in its entry on mystical marriage:

> The term mystical marriage is employed by St. Teresa and St. John of the Cross to designate that mystical union with God which is **the most exalted condition attainable by the soul in this life**.

Although great theologians of the past have indeed speculated that our sanctity on earth is limited to mystical marriage, the Church has never taught this. The most relevant Magisterium is perhaps found in Pope John XXII's condemnation (in the year 1329) of 28 propositions taught by Meister Eckhart, and Pope Innocent XI's condemnation (in the year 1687) of 43 propositions taught by Miguel de Molinos (and

94 Cf. *The Living Flame of Love*. Stanza 1, §14

other so-called "Quietists"), which do indeed curtail what some mistaken writers wished to claim about the nature of a human soul's sanctity, but none of these propositions are taught by any of the mystics cited in this book. Those interested in the theological details can find them addressed in the Appendices, but for the present purposes, it will suffice to point out that we see a stunning convergence:

1) Theologians have always held that there is indeed a sanctity higher even than mystical marriage.
2) They have usually supposed, however, that this higher sanctity is only possible in Heaven.
3) Notwithstanding the popularity of that opinion, the Church has never presented it as Doctrine.
4) Those theologians who tried to advocate for an earthly sanctity higher than mystical marriage, before the 20th Century, fell into heresy.
5) Upon the start of the 20th Century, however, we began to see an explosion of mysticism (Faustina is joined by an army of contemporaries making the same claims) now teaching that this higher sanctity is available on earth—and the Church has not merely refrained from condemning teachings; but has, rather, *strongly endorsed* them and the mystics and revelations providing them.

Here, yet again, we are confronted with an unavoidable but extraordinary conclusion regarding the work of the Holy Spirit in the Church. *Something new and enormous is happening*. There really is, as Pope St. John Paul II said, a "New and Divine Holiness" available to us. We really are, as Fr. Marie Philipon said, "*incontestably* in a new era of spirituality." One thousand nine hundred years of preparation have not been in vain. *The World's Penultimate Destiny,* built on the foundation of the highest holiness possible, is now in motion, and nothing can stop it.

The fourth point listed above may appear to detract from the reality we are highlighting. In fact, it only affirms the same. Recall that the entire theme of Part Three of this book is the direct action of God Himself in inspiring private revelations which testify to this new holiness. Related to this premise is the fact that God alone can reveal a new holiness, and that He began doing so *as soon* as the time was ripe for its announcement (after the dissemination of the teachings of St. Thérèse of Lisieux). This premise, therefore, is only strengthened by observing the downfall of those who, *before* that time, sought to preemptively arrogate God's sovereign mission. Heresy always results whenever one tries to get *ahead* of the Holy Spirit instead of *following* Him, and those who advocated expressly for a higher sanctity than mystical marriage—*before the time of* that new sanctity—did just that.

It bears emphasis that it was *not* merely the case that Meister Eckhart, Miguel de Molinos, or others like them, were "ahead of their time." They deserve no such praise. Quite the contrary, they taught heresy, and thereby did great damage to the Church. The heresies they taught then are still heresies today, and always will be heresies. The writings of the 20th-Century mystics do *not* seek to baptize or rehabilitate these errors. These private revelations, rather, express the very truths to which the heresies are parasitic; they express the orthodox understanding of the same themes that the heresies promote fraudulently.[95]

In even greater clarity than He conveyed to St. Faustina, however, Jesus assures Conchita that this New Holiness He now wishes to give us surpasses even mystical marriage, and thus unquestionably constitutes a New Era for the Church and the world. To Blessed Conchita, then, we must turn our attention.

Blessed Conchita: The Greatest Holiness Attainable by All

> "See what love the Father has given us, that we should be called children of God; and so we are." –I John 3:I

To Concepción Cabrera de Armida—now known as *Blessed* Conchita (she died in 1937 and was Beatified in 2019)—the Gift is revealed in unmistakable clarity. Not only are her writings astounding, however; so is her example: a Mexican wife and mother to 9 children, Conchita's own life demonstrates that this holiness is for everyone, no matter their vocation. The theologian commissioned by the Church to examine all of Conchita's writings during her cause of Beatification

[95] This connection will not concern anyone who is acquainted with the history of heresies. Such a person knows that *all* heresies cleave to some orthodox truth, and that the distinction between the truth and the heresy which deforms it is often subtle. The Church's greatest masters of the spiritual life whom we discussed in Part Two were, for example, regularly calumniated as "Quietists" by perhaps well-meaning but confused theologians whose efforts did great damage to the Church. Truly good theologians, on the other hand, work with scalpels and not hammers. While Pharisees are ever prepared to scream "anathema!" at any teaching in which they can identify any mere relationship with any heresy, this approach would have every canonized mystic in the history of the Church condemned; not only the Saints, Blesseds, Venerables, and Servants of God we are considering in this book who proclaimed the New and Divine Holiness. Further discussion of potential objections, however, will be saved for the appendices.

wrote that her "doctrine is completely sound and Catholic," but went on to offer a rare admission for a scholar in his position:

> I must confess that when I read these pages I received great spiritual benefit and **often felt enveloped by a holy fear, as if by the presence of God who was speaking.**[96]

When someone, so experienced with reading spiritual treatises as a theologian appointed by the Church to scrutinize a mystic's cause, speaks so profoundly about a given work, we can rest assured that something Divine is at play, and we can rest doubly assured of the same when the mystic herself is later beatified.

Conchita produced thousands of pages of writings, and their predominant theme teaches that there is a new sanctity, available for the asking, which far surpasses the greatest possible sanctity of the previous era. Confirming this analysis are the works of Father Marie-Michel Philipon, already quoted. A towering theologian whose writings are cited multiple times in the *New Catholic Encyclopedia,* and who proved the prophetic nature of his intuitions by advocating for St. Elizabeth of the Trinity's daring spirituality before she was even declared a Servant of God, Fr. Philipon sums up Conchita's spirituality in the following passage:

> A theologian must above all pose this question to himself: "What then did God intend to bring about through His humble servant [Conchita] for the benefit of His entire Church?" ***The greatest degree of Holiness is attainable for everyone ...*** The most sublime mystical graces described by spiritual masters are not privileges confined to souls consecrated to God, [in] priestly and religious life. They are offered to all Christians no matter what their state of life. It seems that God wanted to give us through Conchita living historical proof of this truth ... The Lord Himself has announced to her that she would be a model wife and mother, but that her mission would extend far beyond to make shine the sanctifying might of Christ and of the Holy Spirit in all states of life ... ***We are incontestably in a new era of spirituality.***[97]

Fr. Philipon has left no room for doubt or confusion: a new holiness is upon us. It is the *greatest* holiness possible, and it is offered to *all.*

---

[96] Juan Gutierrez Gonzales, M.Sp.S. *Priests of Christ*. Theological Introduction.
[97] Fr. Marie-Michel Philipon. *Conchita: A Mother's Spiritual Diary*. Conclusion.

The Mystical Incarnation: the Grace of Graces

> My soul empty of all else, I [Conchita] received [Jesus] in Communion ... [Jesus said to me:] "Here I am, I want to incarnate Myself mystically in your heart ..." [Conchita responds:] **"Would it be, my Jesus, Spiritual marriage?" [Jesus says:] "Much more than that... it is the grace of incarnating Me,** of living and growing in your soul, never to leave it, to possess you and to be possessed by you as in one and the same substance ... in a compenetration which cannot be comprehended: **it is the grace of graces ... It is a union of the same nature as that of the union of heaven, except that in paradise the veil which conceals the Divinity disappears** ... For you [will now] **keep ever in your soul my real and effective presence.**"
>
> –A dialogue between Jesus and Bl. Conchita[98]

Described above is the climactic moment of Conchita's entire life. During this event, Jesus reveals that the grace He gave Conchita (and which, as we will shortly see, He offers to us all) is much more than mystical (spiritual) marriage. It is, rather, the very same holiness of the blessed in Heaven. I must reiterate that one may search all the approved mystical revelations and spiritual treatises of the entire history of the Church, before the 20th Century, and he will not find these assertions anywhere. But now, as we have arrived at the "New Era of Spirituality," we see these assertions incessantly repeated, approved, and exalted by the Church!

Theologian Monsignor Arthur Calkins confirms that this great grace of the "Mystical Incarnation," which Jesus tells Conchita is equivalent to the holiness of Heaven and to His *real* presence in the soul, was the entire aim of Conchita's life:

> **The great crowning grace of her life, received on March 25, 1906, [was] known as the "mystical incarnation."** The late Bishop Joseph J. Madera strove to explain this extraordinary grace in this way: "The mystical incarnation may be compared to the indwelling of Jesus in Mary from the moment of His conception in her womb ... [but] even though God grants extraordinary graces to chosen souls, what he confers on them is **eventually intended for the up-building of the entire Body of Christ."** [Monsignor Calkins continues:] Although Conchita received this extraordinary grace in 1906, **she would effectively spend the rest of her life trying to fathom what had been done in her and**

98 Ibid. Pages 57-58.

how to respond to it.[99]

In various passages, Conchita herself explains that this Mystical Incarnation—this "grace of graces"—is accomplished by virtue of the will:

> [Jesus] clothed Himself in humanity out of love for the Father and humankind **in order to realize one will of love on earth** ... In the soul the will is the mover which directs it to heaven or hell. In the will, a power of the soul, God is reflected, and the germ of the divine exists in it... This will, united to the divine will, glorifies God and brings about eternal happiness ... I never want to have my own will any more and every day, at each moment, I will lose myself in His adorable will and love it. To love the divine will is to love Jesus, to be united to Him, to enter His Heart, to live His life. What else did Jesus accomplish on earth if not His Father's will, loving until death on the Cross? Was not His dominant passion to please His beloved Father? (*Priests of Christ*. Retreat Day 2. October 15, 1935) **I desire to sacrifice my own will to the Father in order to live only by His will ... I will be a nothing that expects everything from the All** (*Under the Gaze of the Father*. Introduction)

Fully aware of the newness and incomprehensible magnitude of this Gift, Conchita had at times thought that receiving it would be impossible. She even wrote the following admission and resolution, almost thirty years after first receiving the Gift:

> My God, my God! Is it still possible to doubt, to stop, and not to want to look directly at that grace, to evade it? **Should I not cry over all these years I had kept the grace in the closet because it seemed to me impossible?** Bishop Ruiz, Fr. Ipiña, and other **priests assured me that the grace was new but certain**. And I still had doubts? But then came my director, and he drew back the veil, and overcame my fears. I promised to fully accept the grace with gratitude... **Here I am, my Jesus. May it be done to me according to Your word.** Let's turn the page of my life and forget my ingratitude.[100]

---

[99] Arthur Calkins. Missio Magazine. "The Venerable Conchita (Concepción Cabrera de Armida)—Part 1"

[100] Martinez, Luis; de Armida, Concepción. *Under the Gaze of the Father*. 2011. Third Day of the Retreat: October 16, 1935.

Just as true humility is the key to the realization of God's Will, so, too, a false humility destroys it. Archbishop Martinez (the spiritual director mentioned above, and later himself declared a Servant of God) gently scolded Conchita for this very reason, saying:

> For a long time now you have been conscious of the mystical incarnation, **after having forgotten it because of exaggerated humility.** But it is not enough just to be conscious of it; it is necessary to live it fully.[101]

Now, despite this soft rebuke, Conchita certainly deserves our sympathy: the Gift was revealed to her when it was almost entirely unknown! But we, who have the benefit of countless approved mystical revelations relaying this Gift (not to mention Conchita's own Beatification), ought neither doubt it nor hesitate to pursue it.

The Partaking of Mary's Own Graces

> "**[Mary], more than anyone else, wants to share her own graces**... she knows that the mystical incarnation is the most suitable way to be transformed into Me ... Certainly, she cannot bring about in priests[102] the real Incarnation of the Divine Word, which she alone experienced, but she can bring about the faithful and effective reflection of that same Incarnation, **mystically accomplished... [which is] no less real just because [it is] mystical.**"
>
> –Jesus to Blessed Conchita[103]

In the message above, Jesus assures Conchita that the Gift of sanctity which both He and His mother ardently desire to give the faithful is not a literal Incarnation—that is the Blessed Virgin's privilege alone—but a mystical one. But it is "**no less real.**" This distinction is also a recurring theme of 20th-Century mysticism, wherein we are told of the ability to now bear the *real life* of Jesus in our souls. That is, we can now carry in our souls a degree of reality of His presence through this unprecedented grace—a grace even greater than what

---

[101] Ibid. Day 4.

[102] While many of Jesus' revelations to Conchita focus on the transformation of priests through the Gift (indeed particularly urgent and important), He also told her, "**All that I want to do in souls, I want to do first in many of My priests** ..." (Concepción Cabrera de Armida. *Priests of Christ*. Society of Saint Paul, 2015. *imprimatur*. Page 326.) Accordingly, we can be sure that this message, and the many others like it, though given in the context of priestly renewal, also apply to all the Faithful.

[103] *Under the Gaze of the Father*. Page 39

was described by the saints of earlier times, since it is now not "only" mystical, but mystical *and* real.

Until this point, speaking of a *mystical* presence as opposed to a *real* presence was often used as a way to mitigate the enormity of the claim. For example, it has been said that Jesus is really and truly present in the Blessed Sacrament (as indeed He is!), but "only" mystically present in the souls of the faithful who form the Body of Christ which is the Church. When referring to the Gift, however, this *mitigation* no longer exists while proffering the same distinction.

Do not misunderstand: the distinction itself remains! (Contrary to the errors of Eckhart.) Important aspects of this distinction will be covered shortly. Nevertheless, what was previously described as "only" a mystical presence (which I place in quotes because it is quite wrong to in any way diminish the unfathomable glory of the mystical presence of Christ in the saints before the 20th Century!) can now become a *type* of *real* presence. To understand why will require us to soon turn our attention to some subtle theological matters. Now that the fundamental nature of the Gift has been made clear through the revelations of Jesus to St. Faustina and Blessed Conchita, we must do the precise work of laying down the proper orthodox understanding of what we have just discovered.

But first, one more teaching from Blessed Conchita must be included, and its wisdom will succeed in anchoring all readers in the traditional, orthodox, Catholic truth—the truth which will persist until the end of time—of the matter at hand, even if they struggle to meticulously follow each detail of the next chapter.

In sum, Conchita tells us in light of her revelations, the Gift *changes* nothing; it only *builds*, ever more gloriously, on what we as Catholics already know, believe, and practice. It does not exclude anything that Catholics have always associated with sanctification; instead, it makes all these practices and beliefs even *more* resplendent and thus even *more* important than in the days preceding the availability of the Gift:

> God's will is a bouquet which is made up of all virtues practiced in an ordinary manner or in a perfect state. **His will divinizes them and makes them shine with splendor in His presence. It gives to each a new value** on the divine scale and, in the purified soul, it vests them with a special color pleasing to the Holy Spirit. This total and perfect submission to the most holy will of its God and Lord is the greatest of all the virtues a soul can possess. **This**

> **sublime virtue implies the integral practice of all the other virtues... it is the culminating point.**[104]

The Gift is, in sum, *the Crown and Completion of all Sanctity.* A crown does not replace that upon which it is bestowed. It fits perfectly and beautifully upon what is already there.

---

104 Concepción Cabrera de Armida. *Priests of Christ.* Page 117

9. The Theology of the New and Divine Holiness

"It is by transferring the human will to the divine will that the real person is born."–Pope Benedict XVI

The orthodox understanding as to the nature of this new grace requires distinctions which make it clear that what we are confronted with is not some Eastern Pagan notion of the annihilation (or "extinguishing") of self. Neither is it some Eckhartian theory of transubstantiation of the self in a manner indistinguishable from the Blessed Sacrament, nor a Quietist heresy which insists upon the total passivity of the will, nor some Millenarian fantasy of enjoying on earth that which is absolutely reserved for Heaven.

These distinctions will make it equally clear, on the other hand, that this Grace is not merely another way of referring to the same graces spoken of and received by the saints throughout Church history. To understand these distinctions, we will enumerate various degrees of the presence of God, in ascending greatness:[105]

1. His presence in all things through His Omnipresence – in ascending order of greatness from inanimate matter, to plants, to animals, to His Revelation (Scripture).
2. His presence in all human beings by virtue of their creation in His Image (no hierarchy can be given here, since *all* humans are made *only* in the Divine Image, and all are of equal – intrinsic and infinite – dignity).
3. His presence in the *actual* graces of His various interventions annexed to the undertaking of His Will (e.g., repenting before absolution, non-Christians obeying the Commandments; generally, the graces available to the Old Testament saints after the Fall of Adam[106]).

---

[105] With this list, I am not proposing to exhaustively describe the various degrees of God's presence and grace, as that would require a treatise of its own – I only wish to provide enough of a framework for considering the distinctions that follow, though this framework certainly leaves out distinctions that are essential for other considerations.

[106] This, however, is not to claim that sanctifying grace was non-existent or impossible to acquire after the Fall and before Christianity.

4. His mystical presence through *sanctifying* grace, now available *ex opere operato*[107] (as opposed to only extraordinarily; i.e., through perfect contrition or perfect love) upon the institution of the Sacraments by Christ, which allows the soul to live "with God"[108] and please God[109]; including—in ascending order of greatness:
   a. Those just embarking upon or moving towards the path of sanctification (i.e., beginning the "Purgative Way").
   b. Those engaged in sanctification (proceeding from the Purgative, to the Illuminative, and eventually to the Unitive Way).
   c. Those who have reached the pinnacle of "pre-20th-Century holiness" (the mystical marriage of the "Unitive Way").
5. The *type* of Real Presence He has in the Blessed Sacrament; the type of presence in the Blessed Virgin's soul, the souls of the Blessed, and in prelapsarian Adam and Eve; including:
   a. The *replacement* of one substance by another substance (i.e., the Blessed Sacrament).
   b. The *animation* of one substance by another substance (based primarily on will; i.e., the Mystical Incarnation, being a "Living Host," and receiving the Gift of Living in the Divine Will).
   c. The *beatification* of one substance[110] by another substance (based primarily on intellect; i.e., the Beatific Vision of Heaven).

Perhaps more than with any other question, theologians wrestle with the intricate details of the nature of Divine grace, but my aim here is not to delve into these controversies, much less resolve them. Instead, we need only employ these few themes listed above, which are already clear enough in Catholic thought.

Surely, a new Era of Grace was commenced on earth upon the birth of Christianity; the readily available degree of God's presence in souls was elevated from the third step listed above to the fourth step. Within this fourth step, the Holy Spirit motivated the great spiritual masters of Sacred Tradition to progress the Church's "lived theology," step by step, to the point where it almost touched the fifth step. (A journey we traced out in Part Two of this book.) Moreover, the fifth

---

107 "From the work performed"; that is, from the mere objective fact that the Sacrament was validly administered—notwithstanding imperfection on the part of the minister and/or recipient of the Sacrament, so long as a baseline subjective disposition exists (for example, at least imperfect contrition and the will to amend for absolution).

108 *Catechism of the Catholic Church*, §2000

109 Ibid. §2024

110 Persons are "substances"—individual substances of a rational nature, to be precise. In Heaven, the Divine Persons beatify all the created persons (angels and saints) by virtue of bestowing upon them the direct vision of Their Essence without medium.

and highest form of God's presence—His Real Presence—was given to the Church immediately, in the Blessed Sacrament.

At that time, however, Christ's *Real Presence* was not offered to souls,[111] but was restricted to the Eucharist, in which Christians have always had the unfathomable privilege of *access to* God's Real Presence as an inexhaustible source of grace. Presently, however, this *type* of presence (*Real Presence*) is now offered to souls through the Gift.

As we can see from the list above, this grace—this new and highest possible degree of God's presence—although it enjoys the same *reality* of presence as does the Blessed Sacrament, is nevertheless markedly different. Both, indeed, are found within the fifth and highest level, but 5a) and 5b) are quite distinct. Only the Blessed Sacrament has its substance *replaced* entirely by another substance: the substance of bread ceases to exist, and is replaced with the Body, Blood, Soul, and Divinity of Christ. *This is never the case* with the Gift of Living in the Divine Will; the New and Divine Holiness. Whoever receives this holiness is just as much himself as he was before receiving it, and his substance (his existence as an individual person) does not in any way cease to be. This is why we worship the Eucharist (it is God, not bread), but would never worship someone who had the Mystical Incarnation—the latter would always be idolatrous, as the creature remains a creature despite his reception of the *grace of graces*. For it is still a grace—that is, an *accident* that *inheres* in the *substance* of his soul.[112]

Instead, the recipient of this new grace has his soul's independent *operation* replaced by the Divine Will itself, and therein lies the *reality* of the Divine presence; a presence which previously was only mystical, through sanctifying grace, when the soul's operations were *guided and informed* by the Divine Will, but are now *animated* by the same. The soul with this grace becomes *animated by another principle superior to itself*. No longer animated by the self-will, the soul becomes animated by the Divine Will, and the type of presence of God that this entails is no less real than the type of presence of God in the Blessed Sacrament. (This way of life, therefore, is the very opposite of the Heresy of Quietism—discussed in the appendices—which advocates for the radical passivity of the human soul, and the human will in

---

[111] Except for the Blessed Virgin, who enjoyed God's *Real Presence* in her soul from the moment of her own Immaculate Conception.

[112] Philosophically, an "accident inheres in a substance" because "accidents" (e.g., color, quantity) do not have independent existences, whereas substances (e.g., water, a tree, a dog, a person, a person's soul) do, and these substances can be described by virtue of their accidents that "inhere" within them.

particular; for we are here speaking of an even *more* active will, though one animated by a distinct, supernatural principle.)

While it would be abhorrent for a human's *substance to be replaced* by another substance (as this would entail the person's annihilation—which is precisely what some Eastern Pagan religions and philosophies advocate for), it is not only unproblematic for a human's *operation to be animated* by God, but—quite the contrary—it is precisely therein that man becomes truly free, definitively fulfills the loftiest dimension of his sacred calling ingrained in his nature, and enjoys the full actualization of all the potencies with which God created him. In a word, Living in the Divine Will is *man fully alive*.

Twentieth Century mystical revelations are known to refer to this *animation* as the Divine Will itself assuming the same relation with the human soul as the human soul already has with the human body. This, I believe, is the most helpful analogy of the countless ones offered by the mystics, so we should delve further into it.

Your material body is certainly no less truly a material body merely because it is being animated by the immaterial faculties (intellect, will) of your soul. Here, your soul does not deprive your body of its "freedom," nor is your body any the worse for enjoying a spiritual principle—far more exalted than its own material existence—as the very thing that animates its own operation. Similarly, your soul—when animated by a principle (the Divine Will) which is infinitely more exalted than even its own spiritual existence[113]—is no less so what it essentially was (free, active, individual, etc.) before it enjoyed this Grace.

Alternatively, imagine a person who, due to some unfortunate illness or injury, needs an "iron lung" to breathe. Though a blessing for those whose condition calls for such an intervention, it is of course an unfortunate situation, since it is generally below the body's nobility to have its operations animated by a principle inferior to itself (all technology is inferior to the human body's natural functioning by Divine design). It is far greater for the body's own inner principles to govern its operations (here, for its own diaphragm to cause its lungs to inhale and exhale due to a motion that arises interiorly, instead of being applied externally).

---

[113] Although intellect, memory, and will are spiritual faculties of the soul, and we also rightly say that "God is spirit" (John 4:24), it is nevertheless true that God is spirit in an infinitely higher sense than an angel or a human soul is spirit. We are essentially speaking analogously in referring to God as spirit and to the soul as spirit; therefore it remains true that God's existence is on a level as high above the human spirit as the human spirit is above matter (or, rather, the distance is even greater: it is infinite).

Good as it is when the body animates itself (or, to be more precise, is animated by the *sensitive* faculties of the soul), it is not the greatest thing the body can do. It is more impressive still when the body undertakes some activity which the *immaterial* faculties of the soul directs. No one pays money to sit in a stadium and watch athletes breathe, but they will often pay far too much to watch something more impressive: the expertise involved in playing a sport.

Here, the body is still just as much a body as when it is merely breathing, but its actions are elevated to a far greater dignity, for it is undertaking the motions that a spiritual soul animates within it. It is actually incarnating the activity of intellect and will—powers shared by the angels themselves—instead of only doing that which even animals can do.

Clearly, therefore, a person's body is most truly a *human* body when it hands over its operations to a principle categorically above its own realm of existence—that is, when its own material actions are animated by a spiritual reality. But what about a human *soul*? Here too, we can analogously demarcate three distinct degrees of operation:

First, the soul is in something akin to an iron lung when it submits to direction from below its own dignity: e.g., when it follows the passions, pride, or the temptations of demons.

Second, the soul is doing something much better when it directs itself correctly in accordance with its own powers: that is, when, intellectually discovering God's Will (whether in the universal moral law itself or in those details of God's Will specific to a person's own life) it exercises the virtues in order to strive as much as possible to conform to it. Herein lies actual graces and "ordinary" sanctifying graces. Here, the soul is doing something analogous to bodily breathing.

Third, the soul has only arrived at its ultimate destiny when it is not merely governing itself in accordance with its own proper inner principles, but is even allowing itself to be animated by another principle beyond itself: *the Divine Will*. Only thus is the soul doing something analogous to what the body does when playing a sport (or undertaking any other skilled activity at the spiritual soul's deliberate direction—singing, building, conversing, creating art, etc.), and only then is the soul fully achieving what it was originally designed for.

In a word, the mystics tell us that the universe was created to house man, but man was created to house God. Our bodies truly house God Himself for 15 minutes after receiving Communion, but He desires to be with us—in a way that, though not physical, is no less real—24 hours a day, in our souls. Hence, the Mystical Incarnation. Hence, the call to be *Living* Hosts. Hence, the Gift of Living in the Divine Will.

"Living Hosts" vs. the Blessed Sacrament

The call of Jesus (through the 20th-Century mystics) for us to become "Living Hosts" requires understanding more distinctions between it and the Eucharist itself. For another great exaltation enjoyed solely by the Blessed Sacrament is the *certainty* we always have in the Transubstantiation. The bread *always* becomes the Body of Christ when the words of institution are pronounced by a priest. Not so with the Gift—which has no *ex opere operato* formula attached to its bestowal, and instead depends upon the potential recipient's will (which God alone can see).

Moreover, the Blessed Sacrament is *purely* Christ—with no admixture of anything else inferior. On the other hand, even a soul who receives the Gift of being a "Living Host" may well retain plenty of his own imperfections that need purification. This is so because the Gift, *even if and when* successfully received by a soul, entails not a *cessation* of the soul's striving to grow in the spiritual life, but rather an *acceleration* of the same effort. Since being a "Living Host" is not a prize for the perfect, but is rather a Gift that God freely gives to anyone disposed for and desirous of it, what follows is that even souls who truly have this Gift may have much room to grow in virtue, in prayer, in apostolate, etc.

Finally, even within the Gift, there is an infinite amount of space to accommodate an entirely unique calling for all people; each of whom will merit a varying degree of exaltation. Indeed, no two people with the Gift will appear identical, since the reality of hierarchy and variety in God's works certainly applies to all souls who will become "Living Hosts." On the other hand, every single particle of every Sacred Host of the Eucharist that ever has been or ever will be consecrated is identical in its exaltation: the highest possible exaltation. For each such particle is none other than God Himself. This remains true whether consecrated by a priest mired in mortal sin, or by the holiest priest on earth; whether consecrated by the Pope himself, or by a newly ordained Diocesan priest.

Two people, on the other hand, who both have received the Grace of being Living Hosts, may be worlds apart in the degree of their sanctity. While even the "lowest" of the Living Hosts is the recipient of so much grace as to astonish Heaven and earth on the Day of Judgment, there may yet be another Living Host—perhaps even in his own parish!—who towers above him like a mountain above a grain of sand. But even the greater of these two will himself be a very small thing when compared to the ultimate Living Host: the Blessed Virgin Mary.

Despite all these distinctions, one may be inclined to ask: *"Which, then, is "greater:" the Blessed Sacrament, or a "Living Host"; that is, a soul who has received this New and Divine Holiness?"*

Such a question cannot be answered any more straightforwardly than the question *"which is greater: a truckload of bricks, or five miles?"* The Eucharist itself is a substance, the Gift of becoming a "Living Host" is a grace; and grace (philosophically and theologically speaking) is an "accident"—meaning it is a quality that *inheres* in a substance; not a substance itself. Therefore, we can only answer this question with yet more distinctions!

Regarding the intrinsic nature of the substance of the Eucharist, it is beyond question that nothing can be greater, for in this sense the Eucharist is, quite simply, *God.*

There are, however, two ways in which something may legitimately be said to be "greater" than the Eucharist. The first way is on the part of the *subjective effect on the recipient*. For example, if one is in a state of mortal sin and is not perfectly contrite (but is indeed imperfectly contrite),[114] then the Sacrament of Reconciliation would be far greater *for him* than the Eucharist. The Eucharist would only serve to increase his condemnation (cf. 1 Corinthians 11:29), whereas Confession would restore him to Sanctifying Grace.

The second way a thing may be "greater" than the Eucharist is if the same reality of its substance (Christ's Real Presence), dwells underneath accidents that correspond more fittingly to the substance than in the case of the Eucharist. The Eucharist is the sole example in the universe of a disconnect between the substance of a thing and its accidents. This disconnect enables Christ's true, substantial[115] presence to remain with us always (cf. Matthew 28:20), for it is only thanks to the lowliness of the accidents that we can even now bear His Thrice Holy Presence. However, it is inherently imperfect for accidents to be so poorly conformed to the substance which underlies them, and this

---

[114] Cf. *Catechism of the Catholic Church,* § 1453.

[115] Although it is true that Christ is not in the Eucharist by way of *quantitative extension in space,* He nevertheless is physically present in the Eucharist inasmuch as He is literally substantially present, and the substantial presence of a thing which has physicality necessarily implies that same physicality present at least *qualitatively.* In my opinion, therefore, it is indeed accurate to say that Christ is physically present in the Eucharist.

is why the Sacrament of the Eucharist will cease to exist upon the consummation of the world, when we are ready to see God face to face. If the Eucharist, in its current form, was as great a reality as is even possible, then our entrance into Heaven would be an evil, for it would directly cause, in our lives, the cessation of the greatest possible good. Such an assertion of course would be absurd. Heaven is something we eagerly await with unbounded joy, not something we dread because the Sacraments (including the Eucharist) will not exist there!

Likewise, the Incarnation of the Word is in this sense identical to the Eucharist. At the Annunciation, Mary's womb was changed from an empty vessel to a tabernacle for the eternal, infinite, almighty God. At the consecration, the priest's hands go from holding a piece of bread to holding the eternal, infinite, almighty God. But we rightly say that the Incarnation was greater still than the consecration we witnessed at Mass this morning. We say this for many reasons. First, the Incarnation was preceded by the greatest act of Faith in history: the *Fiat* of the Blessed Virgin. Secondly, in the Incarnation, the Second Person of the Blessed Trinity assumed a human nature—which is more pleasing to Him than the accidents of mere bread and wine.

In a similar way, Jesus reveals to the 20th-Century mystics that He deems it, in a certain sense, even greater to actualize His *real* life in the *soul* of a human creature than in the accidents of bread and wine; accidents which, though they never rebel, also cannot themselves please Him. Bread needn't be prepared to receive the Real Presence of Christ; hence the institution of the Sacrament of the Eucharist immediately upon the birth of the Church. The mystical body of Christ, however, needed much preparation; hence the 1,900 years of effort in this regard which we traced in Part Two.

***

Enough has now been said about the distinction between the Blessed Sacrament and the human who receives the Gift (5a and 5b in the previous section's list). But what about 5c? That is, how is the Gift different from Heaven itself? This is the final question we must address before returning to the writings of the mystics themselves.

The New and Divine Holiness vs. Heaven

It is correctly said that, "we don't get to Heaven until we get to Heaven," but as with all tautologies, any number of inferences can be supposed to follow from them, and most of the inferences that tend to arise from this particular truism are mistaken.

Here, the most important thing to remember is that—in terms of the *degree of reality* of God's presence and the *type of holiness* this entails—*there is no difference between Heaven and having the Gift on earth.* This is why the 20th-Century mystics are repeatedly told, by Jesus Himself, that this New and Divine Holiness *is* the life of Heaven, now available on earth. In brief, it is the fulfillment of the Our Father prayer!

But the truism above certainly has its correct interpretations. The Gift does not *beatify* us on earth; that can only happen in Heaven, when we see God face to face. This lack is no loss of merit, grace, or Divine Presence on our part. Quite the contrary, the fact that we still have the veil means that we can still gain merit for Heaven; the fact that we can still suffer means that we can please God even more than does a soul in Heaven, since we can now enjoy the same holiness while nevertheless suffering and offering it all to Christ. But as the Gift does not bestow the Beatific Vision upon us, whatever flows only from the Beatific Vision itself cannot be said to be had by a soul on earth who has the Gift, and attaining any such benefits will have to wait for Heaven.

Specifically, sin remains possible with the Gift, since ontological confirmation in grace (and the concomitant absolute impossibility of ever committing any sin) is an effect solely of the Beatific Vision. Suffering, death, and corruption of mortal remains likewise remain despite the Gift. Faith remains necessary, since we still do not see God Himself with the Gift. Many other differences exist between a soul with the Gift and a soul in Heaven, but so long as we remember that nothing which is absolutely reserved for the Beatific Vision itself will be given along with the Gift (neither now nor during the Era of Peace), then enough has been said.

***

Readers must forgive the lengthiness and technicality of the preceding expositions: it is extremely important, as we move forward, to correctly understand the distinctions between three paradigms of the fifth and highest level of God's presence (His Real Presence). Without that understanding, we will either fail to recognize the true nature of this Gift being offered to us (which will hamper our ability to receive it), or, worse, we will fall into heresy. Far more could be said, but there is no need to explain everything here. All will be well if we simply remember that *the New and Divine Holiness does not change a single Church teaching*. Keep your Catechism handy and remember that everything it teaches still applies (to be sure, none of the mystics considered in this book contradict any Church teachings; the risk lies only in *bad interpretations* of these mystics), therefore you should always consult it when seeking to properly understand the nature of the Gift. And not only do all these teachings still apply, but even more so we must remember to respect the principle that *they* give the lens through which the mystical revelations which describe the Gift are to be understood—*not vice versa.*

Now that this proper understanding has been laid out, we are ready to delve more deeply into the nature of the Gift. Before turning to Luisa in Part Four, we will first review a number of other 20th-Century mystics more briefly (though I heartily recommend exploring the great depth of writings of all the mystics who follow).

And although limitations of space require brevity, even the small excerpts that follow will succeed in demonstrating that the *New and Divine Holiness* is real and is exactly what it sounds like: an unprecedented gift of sanctity that elevates us to the highest possible level of holiness, even while still a pilgrim on earth.

10. Other 20th-Century Mystics

"Come over me so that in my soul there is an incarnation of the Word so that I might be for Him an extra-added humanity" –St. Elizabeth of the Trinity

Saint Faustina and Blessed Conchita are joined by an army of souls whom Jesus has also chosen to be heralds of this new gift of sanctity that He ardently desires to bestow upon the Faithful. Before taking Part Four to focus our attention on the primary herald of this Gift, let us review here the teachings of some of these great souls.

St. Elizabeth of the Trinity: Personal Possession of the Trinity

> "A soul who lives in union with God does nothing that is not supernatural"–St. Elizabeth of the Trinity

A French Carmelite mystic who died in 1906 and was canonized in 2016, St. Elizabeth of the Trinity entrusted profound spiritual meditations to the Church which refer to the Gift. Employing themes of becoming a living host, living in God, becoming another humanity of Christ, personally possessing the Trinity, and receiving an incarnation of the Word into one's soul, Elizabeth calls us to take the definitive step in sanctification. Theologian Dr. Anthony Lilles (who wrote his dissertation on Elizabeth of the Trinity) explains:

> When [Elizabeth's] prayer evokes "My God, My Three," **she invites us to take personal possession of the Trinity** ... [which] not only sets the soul apart and makes it holy, but it glorifies the Father and even extends the saving work of Christ in the world. She called this "the praise of Glory" and understood this to be her great vocation. By canonizing Elizabeth of the Trinity, the Church has ... validated her mission ...[116]

Here, too, we see intimations of something new and glorious; a real sort of personal *possession* (by grace) of the Trinity, surpassing the mere "participation" spoken of in earlier saints' writings. The "praise of Glory," mentioned above by Dr. Lilles, is perhaps the notion for

[116] Dr. Anthony Lilles. "Elizabeth of the Trinity: A Saint for Our Time." National Catholic Register. October 16, 2016.

which St. Elizabeth is best known. The saint defines it simply as follows: "**A praise of glory is a soul that lives in God...**"[117] The arrangement of the nouns surrounding the preposition is not accidental—by being a "praise of Glory" it is not only the case that God lives in us (which is the nature of sanctifying grace), but that *we live in God* (which is the nature of the New and Divine Holiness). For indeed, "**So often we say that God dwells in us, but it is better to say that we dwell in him**."[118] If anyone were to regard this as "just another" ordinary admonition to holiness, Elizabeth's greatest piece—her prayer *O my God, Trinity Whom I adore* (written November 21, 1904) corrects him:

> O my God, Trinity whom I adore, help me to forget myself entirely, and establish me in You, calm and quiet as though my soul were already in eternity... clothe me with Yourself, to identify my soul with every movement of Your Soul, to drown me, invade me, **substitute Yourself for me, so that my life may be nothing more than an effusion of Your life** ... O consuming Fire, Spirit of love, **come over me so that in my soul there is an incarnation of the Word so that I might be for Him an extra-added humanity** in whom He can renew all His mystery.[119]

St. Elizabeth's reference to an "incarnation" in one's soul was a frequent theme of her mysticism. As theologian Fr. Conrad de Meester, O.C.D., writes: "In her Christmas poems, Elizabeth loved to evoke **'the new incarnation' in us ... 'a birth no longer in the crib, but in my soul, in our souls...'**"[120] While the reiteration of the theme of becoming "another humanity" of Christ, through an "incarnation, as it were" (that is, a *mystical* incarnation), is one we have already seen in Blessed Conchita, St. Elizabeth also adds weight and additional insight to the notion of being a "Living Host." In her letters, Elizabeth repeatedly speaks of the total transformation of the soul into Christ, and she also goes so far as to expressly request, of priests, that they *consecrate her, in the host itself,* as they said Mass! In at least three letters she wrote, she made the same request we see here:

> **At Mass, when you consecrate the host in which Jesus becomes incarnate, would you also consecrate your little child to All-Powerful Love, so that He may transform her "into a praise of**

[117] St. Elizabeth of the Trinity. *Heaven in Faith*. Tenth Day. §43

[118] *Gaudete et Exsultate*. §51. March 19th, 2018

[119] Sr. Giovanna Della Croce, O.C.D. *Elizabeth of the Trinity: A Life of Praise to God*. 2016. Chapter 2.

[120] *The Complete Works of Elizabeth of the Trinity*. Volume 1. ICS Publications. 2014. Annotation 27.

glory." (L 256 to Canon Angles. December 1905)[121]

When filling out paperwork upon joining the convent, Elizabeth was required to write down what name she wished to be given in Heaven. Her answer was three words: "Will of God."[122] Nor did Elizabeth hesitate, years after joining the convent, to assert straightforwardly what the very union that defined all her pious expressions considered above consisted in: the human will being **"entirely lost in the will of God, and since this is what creates union**, it can cry out: 'I live no longer I, but Christ lives in me.'"[123] The famous theologian, Fr. Hans Urs Von Balthasar, studied the mysticism of St. Elizabeth extensively, and wrote that her mysticism above all insists that:

> **The human will has to be 'enclosed' in the will of God**, for otherwise it remains without focus or direction. [as St. Elizabeth wrote:] **'Our will only becomes free when we enclose it in the will of God.'**[124]

While the expositions of the New and Divine Holiness, in all their astounding depth and breadth, can become overwhelming rather quickly, we should always remind ourselves that the essence of this Gift—no matter how it is expressed—is perfectly simple: the Divine Will. One needn't be a theologian or an expert in mysticism to achieve this New Holiness; one need only be willing to say, with all his heart, *Fiat*!

Blessed Dina Bélanger: The Holiness of Heaven on Earth

> "This grace... is the state of the elect in heaven, yet I, in bodily form, am still on earth"–Blessed Dina Bélanger

A Canadian nun who died in 1929 and was beatified alongside Duns Scotus by Pope St. John Paul II in 1993, Blessed Dina Bélanger received revelations on an extraordinary grace referred to as "Divine Substitution." In his homily at her Beatification Mass, John Paul said she *"actualized in her life celestial gifts that awaken our admiration,"* made specific reference to her *"high degree of intimacy with God,"* mentioned

[121] *The Complete Works of Elizabeth of the Trinity*. Volume 2. ICS Publications. 2014. We also see the same request in Letter 225 to Canon Angles, March 1905, and Letter 244 to Abbe Chevignard, October 1905.

[122] Cf. Claire Dwyer. *Between Two Words: This Present Paradise, Part 10*. SpiritualDirection.com.

[123] Letter 224 to Madame Angles. March 1905.

[124] Hugh Owen. *New and Divine*. Page 77

the *"life of the Most Holy Trinity in her,"* and even singled out for praise her "**desire to correspond fully to the Divine Will.**"[125]

In Blessed Dina's revelations, Jesus confirms what He said to St. Faustina and Blessed Conchita, telling her that this new grace is so great that its recipients will "not possess Him any more completely in Heaven."[126] Within these revelations, Jesus also said:

> **I wish to deify you in the same manner that I united my Humanity to my Divinity in the Incarnation** ... The degree of holiness that I desire for you is my own Holiness, in its infinite plenitude, the Holiness of My Father realized in you by Me.[127]

Explaining these graces in her own words, Bl. Dina writes:

> This grace which the Trinity of my God grants me with so much love is a foretaste of my participation in the divine life; I say a foretaste, because **it is the state of the elect in heaven, yet I, in bodily form, am still on earth...**[Now] my soul can dwell in heaven, live there without any backward glance toward earth, and yet continue to animate my material being ... My union with the Heart of Jesus has been like his Real Presence after holy communion, while the consecrated Host is still with me.[128] [Jesus] gave me His spirit in place of my own; His judgment so that I might appreciate things, happenings, people in the way He wished. After that, **He replaced my will with His own**; then I felt a great strength which urged me on towards good and compelled me to refuse Him nothing.[129]

St. Maximilian Kolbe: Merging of Wills with the Immaculata

> "...changed into her, transubstantiated into her, that she alone remains, so that we may be as much hers as she is God's..."
> –St. Maximilian Kolbe

Most often revered as a heroic martyr of charity—having been killed in 1941 at the infamous concentration camp at Auschwitz, after he willingly volunteered himself to take the place of another man—

---

125 John Paul II. Beatification Homily. March 20, 1993.

126 Rev. Joseph Iannuzzi. *The Splendor of Creation*. Ch. 3

127 Quoted in *Listen to My Prophets*. Fr. Edward O'Connor. P. 134.

128 *The Autobiography of Dina Bélanger*, translated by Mary St. Stephen, R.J.M. (Sillery: Religious of Jesus and Mary, 3rd edition, 1997), P. 219. (February 22, 1925). Cited in *New and Divine* by Hugh Owen.

129 "A Sister of Mary." *I will think of Everything. You, think only of loving Me: The Ceaseless Act of Love*. 2016. Chapter 9.

St. Maximilian Kolbe was struck by Our Lady's words at Lourdes, "I *am the* Immaculate Conception." He realized that this was no grammatical mistake, but that these words revealed something essential about Mary herself: that she is not merely a person who happened to be conceived without original sin; much more so, she *is the* Immaculate Conception herself, and truly a mirror of the *Uncreated* Immaculate Conception, Who is none other than the Holy Spirit. And although a perfect reflection derives all its reality from the thing being reflected, there is nevertheless no dissimilarity between the two.

Fr. Kolbe furthermore realized that Mary is simply the *Created* Immaculate Conception—the perfect creature contained within the mind of God before the dawn of time, destined before all ages to be the Mother of the Word—before mankind was even created, much less fallen and in need of salvation. But Kolbe did not stop there; he insisted that through Mary, this reality of union with God must essentially define our sanctity as well. Accordingly, he wrote:

> We are hers without limits, most perfectly hers; we are, as it were, herself... may she herself think, speak, and act through us. We want to belong to such an extent to the Immaculate that not only nothing else remains in us that isn't hers, but that we become, as it were, annihilated in her, changed into her, **transubstantiated into her, that she alone remains, so that we may be as much hers as she is God's** ... What a magnificent mission! ... Divinizing man to the God-Man through the Mother of the God-Man.[130]

Here, St. Maximilian reaps the fruit of the tree which St. Louis de Montfort planted centuries earlier. He teaches that the ultimate purpose of Marian consecration is not only to be totally devoted *to* her, but rather, to "*become* her," with the only differences being somewhat superficial; or in other words (and to continue with the "transubstantiation" teaching), the differences are mere accidents; we become "veils" for Mary's holiness (which, as we will see, is simply the Divine Will) as bread and wine become veils for Christ's literal presence upon their Consecration. While we of course cannot use the term "transubstantiation" here in the same exact way we use it in reference to the Blessed Sacrament, we also cannot write this teaching off as mere exaggeration or hyperbole, either. The great Marian theologian, Fr. Fehlner, describes the teaching of Fr. Kolbe as indeed endorsing a radical transformation of the self through Marian Consecration:

> [Kolbe explains that Mary's union with God is] so intimate that

---

[130] Letter #508. to Fr. Antonio Vivoda.

> the whole being and person of the Immaculate is permeated through and through by that characteristic of the Spirit ... of Father and Son as to be herself **"transubstantiated" into the Holy Spirit and to share his name' ...** far from being the dangerous formula some see in it, it is an original, yet deeply traditional insight of St. Maximilian... **Being [Mary's] property [Kolbe] defines as our being annihilated in Her, changed into Her, transubstantiated into Her, so as it were to be Her**... Another word to describe this promotion of the cause of the Immaculate is **marianization, or the Fiat**, which with that of the Creator effects the recreation or new creation.[131]

Once we consider the magnitude of St. Maximilian Kolbe's contribution, we must concur with Fr. Fehlner's assessment that Kolbe's teachings, while "traditional" (remaining perfectly grounded in what is fundamental to Marian Consecration and orthodox Catholic theology in general), are also indisputably "original." The saint's claims are so great that we are, in fact, dealing with something so new that it can only be called yet another description of the Gift. They surpass anything one will find described in any of the pre-20th-Century treatises on Marian Consecration (which, at most, insist upon a strong *moral* bond between Our Lady and the one being consecrated to her); yet Kolbe unabashedly and repeatedly insists upon a far deeper transformation. This is the proper form for Marian Consecration to assume in the era of the New and Divine Holiness. Moreover, in a letter to a fellow brother of his order, Fr. Kolbe describes how this transformation comes about; by *merging* our wills with Mary's (and thus the Divine):

> To annihilate oneself and become her. **The essential component of such a transformation consists in conforming, in merging, in uniting our will with hers. Undoubtedly, her Will is fully joined to the Will of God; therefore, we need but unite our will to hers**, so that, through her, we unite ourselves to God ... Let us not lose our sense of peace if feeling grows "cold." Here it is **a matter of will and of will only.**[132]

Unlike the mystics already discussed, Fr. Kolbe was also a theologian. He wrote extensively and often gave precise, dogmatic detail in his expositions. For him to bluntly relay what the "essence" of Marian Consecration—the *passion of his life*—consists in is quite significant;

---

[131] Fr. Peter Fehlner. *St. Maximilian Kolbe: Martyr of Charity–Pneumatologist*

[132] Letter 579. To a Cleric of the Mariological Section of the MI Circle, Krakow. April 18, 1934

yet he readily does so. He says it is in none other than a *merging of wills*. A perfectly sound suggestion, we should add, when it pertains to the *only* creature who always lived perfectly in the Divine Will of God. As Kolbe points out:

> [The Immaculata is the holiest creature because] **one's degree of perfection depends on the union of one's will to the Will of God... not even for an instant did her will move away from the Will of God**. She has belonged always and freely to God. In her there takes place the miracle of God's union with creation.[133]

As the entire purpose of Marian Consecration is to merge our wills with the Will of God by means of the Virgin Mary, it follows that the Will of God is the supreme principle of the spiritual life. In keeping with this, St. Maximilian taught that all devotions, no matter how good and holy, merely "**are designed to help us carry out that Will of God**."[134]

Servant of God Luis Martinez: Transformation into Christ

> "With divine light [the saints] see in the divine will the good of God, which is their own good, and with all the impetuosity of love, with all the vehemence of the Spirit's motion, they give themselves up to that will... only **[the Holy Spirit] can bring us to know the Father and teach us to love Him, by transforming us into Jesus.**"
> –Servant of God Archbishop Luis Martinez

We have already happened upon the words of this holy Mexican prelate several times; in his profound teachings on the Our Father and the Divine Will in general, and in his capacity as spiritual director to Blessed Conchita. But he was also a mystic in his own right, and he expressed the Gift with clarity and in his own words. A philosopher, theologian, and poet who died in 1956, the Servant of God Archbishop Luis Martinez was, more than other mystics, aware of the various quibbles that some academics in the Church levied against the New and Divine Holiness. His response to them was simple:

> If one could only understand the possession of the Holy Spirit in the transformed soul! **Some consider the expression "transformation into Jesus" excessive because they do not understand**

[133] *The Writings of St. Maximilian Kolbe*. Volume 1. Nerbini International. 2016. Chapter 12. 1.b.

[134] Ibid. Letter 643 to Br. Mateusz. October 10, 1935

> **spiritual realities.** If the Spirit who moved Jesus and inspired His life is the same Spirit who moves and guides souls, why is it excessive to say that souls become the reflection of Jesus and their lives the image of His life?[135]

Lest there be any doubt as to exactly what notion he was defending, we can see that the archbishop's teachings were no less bold and no less new than those of his spiritual directee, Blessed Conchita. He taught:

> The mystical incarnation is the intimate and **perfect transformation of the soul... which transforms and divinizes [it], which fuses the soul with God ...[136] The mystical incarnation ... encompasses all the graces and wonders of God**, just as the sun's ray contains all the colors of the spectrum.[137]

Here, the Servant of God equates the Gift (the Mystical Incarnation) with the *fusion* of the soul with God; asserting that it is not just "a" grace, but is rather *the* grace which "**encompasses all**" graces. Indeed, "The Grace of All Graces" is a fitting name for the Gift. More explicitly still, however, he locates this Grace in the will:

> ...The essence of holiness, love and wisdom is to offer oneself to the divine will ...[The supreme art is] experiencing the fullness of the beauty, the unspeakable harmony of God's will being done in the universe. ...**If the mystical incarnation is the sharing in the fruitfulness of the Father, then the putting into practice and development of this outstanding grace should be losing oneself in His adorable will**. ... Creation, history and the Church have a center, a key and a meaning: Jesus Crucified. To love God's will is to love Jesus, to be united to Him, to enter into the depths of His mystery.[138]

The archbishop also emphasizes that this grace must not remain sterile; it is given to a soul in order that Jesus may be given to still other souls:

> Upon pouring Himself out in the soul by the mystical incarnation, the Holy Spirit not only makes it Jesus, but also communicates spiritual fruitfulness to it, so that the soul may give Jesus to other souls.[139]

---

[135] Martinez, Luis; de Armida, Concepción. *Under the Gaze of the Father*. St. Paul's/Alba House. 2011. Day 4 of the Retreat: October 17, 1935.

[136] Ibid. Retreat of November 7, 1935. Cited in Introduction.

[137] Ibid. Day 4. October 17, 1935

[138] Ibid. Day 3. October 16, 1935

[139] Ibid. Day 10. October 23, 1935.

In short, the Gift is the single most powerful way to evangelize, and with this power comes enormous responsibility. "To whom much is given, much will be expected." (Luke 12:48) When the Blessed Virgin herself received the Real Presence of Jesus into her womb at the Annunciation, she at once brought Him to her cousin Elizabeth; not merely to pay a visit, but to become a channel of grace for others. We, likewise, after striving for the Gift, must ensure that we only increase our zeal for proclaiming Jesus to the world. We will be more successful than ever before in doing so, as it will be Him speaking through us. As *Living Hosts,* we will simply be His veil.

St. Thérèse of Lisieux: The "Spiritual Revolution"

> "I don't see very well what more I shall possess in heaven than here on earth" –St. Thérèse

Worry not if you are now experiencing déjà vu—we did already discuss (in Part Two) this great saint as "The Final Preparation" for the Gift of Living in the Divine Will. Why, then, is she included here among the mystics whose writings described the Gift *itself*? The answer is that the Little Flower is unique; despite the brevity of her 24-year-long life, she spanned the time of *preparation* for the Gift and the time *of the Gift itself*. More significant than the calendar years of her birth and death, however, is the fact that in her mysticism, we see not only the final preparations for the New Era of spirituality, but also—in her later teachings—direct references to that new spirituality. Therefore, just as St. Maximus and St. Bernard served as bridges to a new era of spirituality in the Church's Sacred Tradition, so Thérèse—with feet placed firmly in the spiritualities of two eras—did the same for the final era.

While we have already discussed the power of her Little Way in serving as the Final Preparation, theologian Dr. Matthiesen explains those themes in Therese's spirituality which exemplify the Gift of Living in the Divine Will:

> **Thérèse petitions to be so transformed by Jesus' divine substance in the Eucharist that she might ascend to the very Furnace of Love in the Trinity.** It is the work of divinization to lift up and consume the soul, but Thérèse avers that such divine operation is effective only in one who becomes nothing: the smaller one is, the wider the vessel one presents to God to fill with himself. Abandonment of the self, **abandonment of the will to God's desire, should be the Christian's only "compass"**. Such abnegation allows God to be working through the soul so that every act

> is love ... **Thérèse, in a manner more strikingly direct than Francis de Sales and John Eudes, teaches that the believer who lovingly makes herself nothing before the will of God does indeed become a continuation of the life of Christ and a daring sharer in his divine powers.** The divine and prodigal excess of the Father finds a receptacle in the soul's abandonment.[140]

Like St. Francis de Sales—whom, we recall, Pope Benedict XVI regarded as essential to the development of Thérèse's own spirituality—Thérèse confirmed the great difference between merely *doing* God's Will and being in true *union* with His Will. In her autobiography, she relays that,

> The other day I came across this striking passage: "To be resigned and to be united to the will of God are not the same; there is the same difference between them as that which exists between union and unity; in union there are still two, in unity there is but one."[141] (III. January, 1889)

Although this entry in her autobiography is included well before her death, we later find her own words affirming that the sentiments expressed therein, which "struck" Thérèse earlier, grew in her own soul and became a veritable exposition of the Gift in her last days. (The passage above is from 8 months before God first gave the Gift to Luisa, thus initiating on earth the Age of the Gift and rendering it available to all.) Soon before her death, she told a sister:

> **I don't see very well what more I shall possess in heaven than here on earth ... of course in heaven I shall see the good Lord, but when it comes to being with Him, I already have this entirely**. (*Story of a Soul. Epilogue*: A Victim of Divine Love.)

Here, Thérèse says the same thing that so many of the other 20th-Century mystics did: the degree of God's presence her soul enjoys is identical to that of the Blessed in Heaven, with the only difference being the absence of the *sight* of God (i.e., the Beatific Vision). As Fr. François Jamart explains, regarding this last period of her life:

> So great was this abandonment that ... the will of God, and the ardent desire to love Him, were her only aspirations. Moreover, suffering had become so sweet to her, that she no longer suffered but felt she was the happiest of creatures. She said she knew from experience that the kingdom of God is within us and that **Jesus Himself, hidden at the bottom of her heart, was acting in her in**

---

140 *Called to be the Children of God.* Chapter 8.

141 Thérèse was here quoting a contemporary Russian mystic, Sophie Swetchine.

a mysterious way.[142]

This "mysterious way" in which Jesus dwelt in Thérèse's heart was no doubt the Gift of Living in the Divine Will. It may even be the case that the very first exposition of this Gift, as it became known to the world, came through the writings and sayings of St. Thérèse! How well, therefore, we can now comprehend the prophecy of Pope Pius XI, who insisted that this little but great saint would cause a "**spiritual revolution**." That is *precisely* what began immediately after the publication of her writings, and it is none other than the revolution against the "prince of this world," the devil, by means of the greatest weapon: the Gift of Living in the Divine Will, which will take the world back from him and claim it again for the Reign of Christ the King.

Still More Mystics

> "It is no longer I who live, but Christ who lives in me."
> –Galatians 2:20

Many living seers are currently receiving private revelations similar to those we have just seen. For the sake of preserving a particularly high degree of confidence in the authenticity of what we will review, however, our present considerations will remain restricted to those seers for whom sufficient time has passed since their deaths to conclude that their legacy of holiness will likely remain unmarred.[143]

Servant of God Sr. Mary of the Holy Trinity, a Poor Clare nun who died in 1942, received the following messages from Jesus:

> [I desire a] **will fused in My Will,** a spirit so devoid of selfishness that My Spirit can take possession of it, and reign there as King... My little daughter, **I live in souls as I lived on earth**... And the most favored souls? Oh, there are many! They are those whom I call to join Me in the **Apostolate of My Eucharistic Life**... If every soul would take these words to heart, each fulfilling her destined role**, then the glory of God would be visible upon earth!** If each soul thus made that portion of the light which has been entrusted to her 'shine before men,' the House of Light, which is **the**

---

[142] *Complete Spiritual Doctrine of St. Therese of Lisieux*. Hauraki Publishing. 2017. Chapter XIII.

[143] This is not at all to imply that living seers should be ignored; only that, in the present inquiry, consulting their messages is not necessary for conveying the facts this section exists for the sake of.

> **Church, would become irresistibly resplendent.**[144]

Servant of God Sr. Josefa Menendez, a nun who died in 1923, received revelations from Jesus which were endorsed by the very Cardinal who would later become Pope Pius XII, and in which we see the following:

> Submit yourself wholeheartedly to the Will of your Beloved. Let Me do with you what I like, and not what you desire. You ought so to **conform yourself to Me that My Will in you becomes your own,** by total submission to My good pleasure. You have given over to Me all your rights by the vow of obedience. Would that souls understood that never are they more free than when they have thus given themselves up to Me, and that never am I more inclined to grant their desires than when they are ready to do My Will in everything ... Josefa ... **My will is yours, your will is Mine. I shall be master of your thoughts, or your words, and of your actions. If you have nothing, I will provide everything for you. I will live in you** ... (*The Way of Divine Love*. Book III. Chapter X)

Gabrielle Bossis was a French lay woman, nurse, playwright, actress, and mystic who died in 1950. Her revelations, contained in the book *He and I* (bearing an *Imprimatur*), include the following words from Jesus:

> "**Repeat this often: 'Father, may Your will be done. May Your will be done.'** Can you imagine a world where God's will is done everywhere?" (December 7, 1937) "Never stop asking that the Spirit of holiness, the Holy Spirit, may come and take possession of you... **Live for the Host like another host ...** Make Christ your whole life." (October 1, 1937) [Gabrielle:] *After Communion. I was saying the Lord's Prayer* [and Jesus said:] "What other prayer could equal the one I composed myself?" (April 24, 1939) "**I want to indwell your very being.** I'll live you. I am Life. Life itself. **So don't have any other will than Mine**, the will of My Father, and you will be rewarded on the final day." (June 26,1939) "Ask Me for every grace. Don't ever think *'That's impossible. He couldn't give me that.'*" (April 17, 1938) "**Pray for bigger things ... Pray for My kingdom to come everywhere**." (December 22, 1939) [Gabrielle:] *"Lord, of what is love for God made?"* [Jesus:] "The will." (May 1940). "... although it may seem strange to you, there is grace that I cannot give unless you ask Me for it... since I never impose on

---

[144] Fr. Alain Marie Duboin, *The Life and Message of Sr. Mary of the Holy Trinity*. TAN Publishing. 1987. Part 2, Ch 3.

you, you must invite Me; you must make Me act with you. **In this way I live My life again on earth**... just imagine what it would be like if at this moment all the people on the earth let Me live in them by grace. What a spectacle for heaven!" (October 11, 1940) "Remember this; as one lives so one dies. If, during these moments that divide you from death, **your heart is full of Me; if zeal for My kingdom consumes it...** death will find you like that and you will pass on with a thought of love." [Gabrielle:] "*Help me to live from now on as I shall live in heaven; I mean, in my soul.*" [Jesus:] "But this is the reason why I lived—just in order to be the Life of your life." (February 26, 1941) **"Merge with Me** by saying: 'It is You who pray in me. It is You doing the work as I work. It is You speaking when I speak.'" (March 24, 1942)

Servant of God Cora Evans was an American lay woman, mother, and mystic who died in 1957 and whose cause for Beatification was approved by the Vatican in 2012. She received revelations from Jesus on the "Mystical Humanity of Christ" in souls, writing that "**by loaning Jesus my humanity for him to govern as well as dwell within would make my life a living prayer, for he was life, living life within me...**"[145] In Cora's revelations, we read the following messages from Jesus and Mary:

[The Blessed Virgin:] "[Veronica's] veil is the symbol of individual souls, souls **coming so close to Jesus in His Humanity that His image is impressed upon their souls**, never to be effaced... they are then a priceless living relic, as it were, living on earth doing His will in the love of unity..." (September 25, 1947)[146] [Jesus:] "I am giving My friends this gift through you, better to establish My kingdom of love within souls ... The greater knowledge of My kingdom in souls is but another step towards the Golden Age. Golden, because souls in sanctifying grace will resemble the light of the golden sun and in that golden kingdom, I may personally dwell if I am invited. For I have said, 'The kingdom of God is within you.' Through this **knowledge many souls will loan me their bodies, and in this way they actually become My Mystical Humanity. My borrowed Humanity, My other Humanity, and in them I relive My life on earth as I did after**

[145] *Our Sunday Visitor*. "Cora Evans: Mystic, wife and mother. Monterey diocese backs sainthood cause of woman who proclaimed 'Mystical Humanity of Christ,'" Jim Graves. July 26, 2017.

[146] *Cora Evans: Selected Writings. Excerpts from a Servant of God*. The Mystical Humanity of Christ Publishing. San Mateo. 2016. Page 32.

> **the Resurrection,** and in them I cause a beautiful transfiguration." (May 27, 1947)[147]

Blessed Elżbieta Róża Czacka was a Polish nun who died in 1961 and was Beatified in September 2021. The foundress of the Franciscan Sisters Servants of the Cross and a mystic, she expressed the reality of a theme we will discuss later, "doing our acts in the Divine Will," wherein Jesus Himself truly does, in us, whatever we ourselves are doing. She described:

> ... the experience of being out-of-yet-still-in her body...[and] the **domination of the will over other human powers**... she became aware of how, in prayer, **Jesus prays through us**. In praying the Divine Office [she writes], "... the Lord Jesus gave me to understand, that in the Church's prayers it is the Lord Jesus Himself who represents the human race and that **all who say those prayers should be so united with the Lord Jesus as to be the Lord Jesus' lips**, and the Lord Jesus praying that Office with their lips..."[148]

Servant of God Vera Grita was an Italian mystic and Salesian cooperator who died in 1969. In May 2021, the Vatican authorized the cause for her Beatification. Father François Marie Léthel wrote that Grita was given a "**truly prophetic message for the Church** of today and tomorrow." She authored a work entitled *The Living Tabernacles*, bearing a *nihil obstat*, within which Jesus said to her (referring to "her" in the third person, and likewise issuing this call to all the Faithful):

> I am already a living tabernacle in this soul and she does not realize it. She must realize it because **I want her to assent to My eucharistic presence in her soul.** Have you not already given your soul to Me completely? **Wherefore I, Jesus, am the Master of your soul. And the Master is free to give as much as he likes... If souls learned to at least seek Me in humility... they would discover My human-divine real presence: Me, Jesus**... Behold, I will return to the world, I will return in the midst of souls to speak to them, to draw closer to them, to address them directly until the veils fall and they recognize Me in every brother... Prepare the [Living] Tabernacles for this gift so that from this mystical union My coming in your midst may be revealed to the good ... **My Will will be done on earth as in heaven.**[149]

---

[147] Ibid. Page 105 (From *Golden Detachment of the Soul.*)

[148] John Grondelski "'Through the Cross to Heaven': The Life of Blessed Elżbieta Róża Czacka." National Catholic Register. September 13, 2021.

[149] Fr. Joseph Iannuzzi. *The Splendor of Creation*. Ch. 2.

While we have already been seeing allusions to this very theme, what exists in Vera Grita's messages is more explicit still: *Christ is coming soon*. Not in the flesh (which will only happen at the end of time) to command the General Resurrection and Last Judgment, but *in grace* to commence the fulfillment of the Our Father over the entire world. This prophecy, in fact, is yet another avenue of the Gift's exposition in 20th-Century mysticism, which leads us to our next point.

Prophets of the Reign of the Divine Will

> "[During Mass,] I renewed the resolution to direct my whole life to fulfilling the divine Will … The moment of the Consecration arrived; as I raised the Sacred Host … some words of Scripture came to my mind, with extraordinary force and clarity: *et si exaltatus fuero a terra, omnia traham ad meipsum* [And I, if I be lifted up from the earth, will draw all things to myself.] (John 12:32) … And I saw Our Lord triumphant, drawing all things to Himself."
>
> –St. Josemaría Escrivá[150]

There are many mystics who—though they did not provide new names for or detailed expositions of the New and Divine Holiness—received messages from Heaven clearly indicating that the Our Father prayer *will* be fulfilled in the truest and fullest sense. It is, therefore, right for us to number them among the ranks of those to whom Jesus and Mary gave knowledge of this Gift. For regardless of whether one provides advanced mystical descriptions of the Gift, its essence is contained within the *total* fulfillment of the Lord's Prayer. It is not surprising, therefore, that along with mystical expositions like those we have already covered, the dawn of the 20th Century also saw an explosion of prophecies and teachings, from the most authoritative voices, testifying to the literal and complete fulfillment of the Our Father's third petition; an insistence one only saw occasionally before the 1900s. In Part Five, we will discuss some of these prophets, which even include Popes in the capacity of their Magisterial teachings.

The final individual we will consider in this Chapter is very special. Even if not a "mystic" in the common sense of the word, Fr. Walter Ciszek gives a personal testimony and an associated wealth of

---

150 *The Way: St. Josemaría Escrivá Complete Works*. First Part. Ch. 13. §301. The saint described this experience as life-changing, even calling it "**supernatural**." Biographers describe it as remaining "**engraved in his soul forever… it sank in deeply and configured his conception of the Christian existence**." (Ibid.)

teachings that are no less powerful in relaying the essence of the Gift than are the writings of anyone we have already discussed.

Servant of God Fr. Walter Ciszek

> "That the sole purpose of man's life on earth is to do the will of God, contains in it riches and resources enough for a lifetime."
> –Fr. Ciszek

Servant of God Fr. Walter Ciszek was a Polish-American Jesuit priest who died in 1984. During World War II, he infiltrated the USSR to offer clandestine ministry to the faithful while working as a logger for cover. Eventually discovered, Fr. Ciszek was arrested, tortured, and imprisoned. What followed were 23 years spent enduring the most severe hardships, until, in 1963, President John F. Kennedy was able to negotiate his release (only one month before the latter's assassination). Fifteen years of Fr. Ciszek's exile were spent in the infamous Siberian Gulag, where:

> Conditions ... were horrific. Prisoners were starved and overworked, poorly housed and poorly clothed. Perhaps one and a half million of them died in the push to industrialize the frozen wasteland. **Yet in this nightmare realm, Fr. Ciszek knew the joy of bringing Christ to his fellow prisoners** ... though it cost him. He was punished with assignments to the dirtiest work. He shoveled coal for fifteen hours straight, hauled logs out of a frozen river, crawled through dangerous mine tunnels, and dug sewer trenches with a pickaxe in subzero temperatures.[151]

One wonders how such composure was possible under these extreme circumstances. In one book he authored, entitled *He Leadeth Me*, Fr. Ciszek provides the answer while writing about the sudden and complete "conversion experience" he had while imprisoned. This experience of "blinding light" followed the darkest of his days; wherein, under extreme duress from being starved, beaten, drugged, and kept for months in solitary confinement, he signed a rigged confession to being a spy. After this mistake—humiliated in body, mind, and spirit—God intervened in the form of an epiphany which, from the moment it entered Fr. Ciszek's soul, radically changed his life forever and enabled the very joy and heroism described above despite the worst conditions imaginable.

---

151 "The Priest Who Died Three Times." By Louise Perrotta. *The Word Among Us*. April/May 2010 issue.

The change consisted in nothing other than a leap from merely seeking *conformity* to the Divine Will to actually *living* in the Divine Will. The former—which, as a priest, he had always rightly sought after—consisted in "learning to discover God's will in every situation and then in bending every effort to do what must be done." But truly living in His Will was much more. It was, according to the Servant of God:

> ... a complete gift of self, [with] nothing held back... once understood, it seemed so simple. I was amazed it had taken me so long in terms of time and of suffering to learn this truth... I had talked of finding and doing [God's] will, but never in the sense of totally giving up my own will... I could never find it in me, before, to give up self completely... [that moment] was at once a death and a resurrection... **like every grace, it was a free gift of God ... I chose, consciously and willingly, to abandon myself to God's will,** to let go completely of every last reservation. I knew I was crossing a boundary I had always hesitated and feared to cross before. Yet this time I chose to cross it... across that threshold I had been afraid to cross, things suddenly seemed so very simple. **There was but a single vision, God, who was all in all; there was but one will that directed all things, God's will**. (Ch. 7)

Fr. Ciszek is not merely giving another admonition to resign oneself to God's Will; he insists that this sublime revelation was about more than *conformity*, writing, **"It was not just conformity to the will of God**... I can only call it a conversion experience, and I can only tell you frankly that my life was changed from that moment on." (Ibid.) Moreover, he was convinced that this recognition was not merely for him; it was a message that he had a Divine duty to announce to the world for the coming of the Kingdom of God *on earth*:

> **My life was to do the will of God, as the prayer our Savior taught us put it quite simply, "on earth as in heaven." ... This simple truth, that the sole purpose of man's life on earth is to do the will of God, contains in it riches and resources enough for a lifetime.** Once you have learned to live with it uppermost in mind, to see each day and each day's activities in its light, it becomes more than a source of eternal salvation; it becomes a source of joy and happiness here on earth. The notion that **the human will, when united with the divine will, can play a part in Christ's work of redeeming all mankind** is overpowering. The wonder of God's grace transforming worthless human actions into efficient means for **spreading the kingdom of God here on earth** astounds the mind ... (Chapter 12) The kingdom of

> God, reintroduced among men by the Incarnation of Christ—who came to set us a most perfect example of a man totally dedicated in all things and at all times to the will of the Father—cannot and **will not be established until all men live each day of their lives according to his example.** (Chapter 17)

In the epilogue to this spiritual memoir which bears the message that God entrusted to him for the world, and written a decade after his release, Fr. Ciszek concludes by saying:

> **For all my apologies, therefore, I am not ashamed of what I have written here—simple as some may find it. The terrible thing about all divine truth, indeed, is its simplicity ...** And yet how curious it is that this very simplicity makes them so unacceptable to the wise and the proud and the sophisticated of this world.

This is the simple wisdom of the Servant of God Fr. Walter Ciszek. He exhorts us in the most elementary but unforgettable terms to dedicate ourselves entirely to *Living* in the Divine Will. Moreover, his practical mysticism, forged into the depths of his soul from years spent laboring under the most extreme and grueling conditions, can sometimes be more helpful than the literal mysticism of the other saintly souls already discussed.

He did not see and describe the Gift in ornate terms originating from extravagant inner mystical ecstasies—terms like "mystical marriage," or "Mystical Incarnation," or "Divine substitution," or "personal possession of the Trinity," or anything of the sort. Rather, he saw it and described it in the coal he shoveled out of mines in negative forty-degree weather in the Arctic Circle. He saw it in the logs he hauled out of icy waters with his own hands. He saw it in the pain he endured during his many sleepless 72-hour-straight stretches of work and apostolate. Above all, he saw it in the people to whom he ministered and the sacraments he administered to them.

Surely, the teachings of the more "literal" mystics are also necessary, but Fr. Ciszek brings us back to the utter simplicity of it all: *the Will of God*. Total, absolute, unreserved handing over of the self-will to the Divine Will is the single human act which surpasses all the intellectual knowledge—of mysticism or of anything else—that one could possibly attain. If some of the mystics we have already covered are like the loquacious and florid Solomon in his *Song of Songs*, then Fr. Ciszek is like the iron-willed and flint-faced Job, who sums it all up in a few pithy verses:

> "Naked I came from my mother's womb, and naked shall I return; the Lord gave, and the Lord has taken away; blessed be the name of the Lord." (Job 1:21) "Though he slay me, yet will I trust in him." (Job 13:15)

Perhaps some claim they "cannot relate" to the mystics. While it is true that this statement misses the point (we needn't "relate" to the mystics—we need only heed the call that Jesus gives to the world in His messages to them; a call sometimes embedded in much surplus content), I nevertheless hope that even those people will heed the wisdom of this great priest. We can all—and should all—be like Fr. Ciszek. For it is not God's Will that we presently all be literal mystics or converse sensibly with Jesus, but it *is* His Will that we all receive this Gift of Living in the Divine Will which, in so many words, Fr. Ciszek is begging us to receive.

***

Now that we have completed our journey through brief glances at the main themes of several 20th-Century mystics, some more general observations are in order on the nature of what we have observed, in this same century, due to the Gift that their mysticism reveals.

The Gift's Collateral Damage to the Devil's Kingdom

> Pray as I taught you in the Our Father: ... If you say to me truly: "Thy will be done" ... I will intervene with all my omnipotence, and I will resolve the most difficult situations...You see evil growing instead of weakening? Do not worry. Close your eyes and say to me with faith: "Thy will be done, You take care of it." I say to you that I will take care of it, and that I will intervene as does a doctor and I will accomplish miracles when they are needed."
> –Jesus to the Servant of God Fr. Dolindo Ruotolo (†1970)

The 20th Century was an extraordinary time. While placing one's focus on the news would tempt anyone to despair, focusing on the movements of the Holy Spirit could only overwhelm a faithful observer with joy at what they portend. For if it is true that the Gift of Living in the Divine Will is the highest sanctity possible, and that it became available upon the dawn of the 20th Century, then we would only expect to see a surge of *effects* of this grace in proportion to its own promulgation, even if many remained unaware of the explicit knowledge of the grace itself.

This surge is, indeed, exactly what we have seen. Time would fail me if I were to provide a spiritual history of the 20th Century, so I will instead only mention the sudden explosion of the Universal Call to Holiness; Marian Consecration; daily reception of Holy Communion; the reception of Communion by younger Communicants than ever before; Perpetual Adoration; Apparitions of Jesus and Mary across the world as never before in history; incredibly saintly Popes (especially the two who opened and closed the century—Pius X and John Paul II, respectively[152]) who, like never before in Papal History, evangelized the world; renewed emphasis on Sacred Scripture; renewed emphasis on the Church Fathers; cognizance of, devotion to, and openness to, the outpouring of the Gifts of the Holy Spirit; unheard-of evangelization efforts (e.g., Legion of Mary, EWTN); sanctification of work (e.g., Opus Dei); the incredible spread and impact of the Divine Mercy devotion; increased focus on the Rosary and St. Joseph; the incredible work done and astounding fruits borne in the pro-life movement; the birth of new religious orders to revive neglected charisms (e.g., Franciscan orders dedicated to renewing the charisms of Francis himself); the birth of great lay-movements in the Church (e.g., Apostolate for Family Consecration, the Charismatic Movement, Militia of the Immaculata, the World Apostolate of Fatima); the growth of Eucharistic Congresses and other major events dedicated to sanctification (e.g., World Youth Days); insistence upon and fighting for the Reign of Christ the King (especially incited by Pius XI's 1925 encyclical *Quas Primas*), etc.

How easy it is to be so overcome by the evil in the world that we forget what glorious things God has been doing! Any non-catatonic observer could not help but ask, in awe, "*What is going on!?*"

The answer is simple—it is what we have been discussing these last chapters—a *New and Divine Holiness is upon the Church*, and we are seeing the repercussions of this sanctity being lived by some souls who *shine like lights* in this perverse generation (cf. Philippians 2:15). But we have only seen the very beginning of these repercussions. If we wish to see unleashed the full power of the Gift, then we can no longer remain content with the *explicit* knowledge of it being known by so few. For as we live in the Age of the Gift, extraordinary souls can always receive it—but once we add explicit knowledge of the Gift into the equation, even "ordinary" souls can receive it. When that happens, everything will be radically transformed.

---

[152] Although a similarly great pope, Leo XII, reigned at the turn of the century itself, Pius X was elected only three years later, and it was especially his teaching which set the Pontifical tone for the following decades.

Of course, all of this was and is responded to by the devil's own counterattack. God gives a new Gift, and the devil unleashes the "new age." We see modernism invading seminaries and parishes; abuses seeping into Liturgies; vocations plummeting; heresy and mortal sin running rampant among the ranks of those putatively within the Church (and none of this is even to mention how deep into evil the secular world has recently been plunged). Sadly, this list could be extended for many pages. But the glory of one saintly soul (whether canonized or not) far outweighs the darkness of a thousand sinners, therefore quantitative measures of the dynamics of the 20th Century will always fail to capture the essence of what God was at work accomplishing. These measures only succeed in discovering the coal, filth, and pressure that existed, but if only we peer more deeply into the apparent disarray, we see revealed the formation of a breathtaking diamond. Jesus always knew He would bless the world with the greatest private revelations precisely when its sinfulness had reached the summit, and He will ensure—with our cooperation—that even this redounds to His greater glory and our own good.

> "With Mary, and in communion with the new saints, let us also implore the miracle of a new Pentecost for the Church. For the humanity of our time let us ask an abundance of the gifts of the Holy Spirit. Come Holy Spirit, enkindle the hearts of your faithful! Help us to spread the fire of your love in the world. Amen!"
> -Pope St. John Paul II. Homily. May 19, 2002.

11. God's Final Effort: Divine Mercy and Divine Will

"And I will grant my two witnesses power..."
–Revelation 11:3

There is so much more that could be said in summarizing the 20th-Century mystics, but I will leave that for you to explore elsewhere. The preceding excerpts from those astounding revelations suffice to prepare us for what lies ahead. Thankfully, the brevity of our consideration of such an enormous topic as this will prove no detriment: comprehensive knowledge of an entire era of mysticism is not necessary for us to undertake the Divine mission now before us. I have provided the glimpses in the preceding sections only to bolster your faith in the main thrust of what we must understand and to share small pieces of advice to help in receiving the Gift, not to imply there is a rigorous academic prerequisite for what follows.

While each mystic and topic here discussed is monumentally important, the Gift of which they speak is nevertheless far and away best expressed by the simple message of the *one* mystic we will cover in Part Four. She, the Servant of God Luisa Piccarreta, is *the* secretary, chosen by Jesus Himself, for the mission of the fulfillment of the Our Father prayer. It is His words to her—He repeatedly insists—which will above all enable souls to Live in His Will, and also call down the reign of His Will on earth. Though I cannot strongly enough encourage diving into these writings and devoting yourself to reading them, it nevertheless remains true that if you are even cursorily acquainted with their main thrust (and you will be in the course of a few short pages in Part Four), then you are already prepared to receive the Gift and promote it.

Despite this silver bullet of His, God never runs out of other ammunition, and each round has its purpose. As His ultimate desire is the reign of His Will in souls, I have no doubt that He will continue to inspire even *more* mystics to relay this Gift to us, and that even more 20th-Century mysticism which has already relayed it will continue to be discovered. We should not be surprised by this. The time for the Gift is truly upon us! The time began upon Jesus' first giving the Gift to Luisa in 1889 and revealing it in her writings in 1899. After that point, the door was opened, and there was nothing to prevent Jesus from revealing and giving the Gift to extraordinary souls. Whether or not these souls are (or were) aware of Luisa's revelations, Jesus has given (and will give) an understanding of the Gift in the terms best suited to their own individual understandings, background, and human subjectivity. Each way the Gift is expressed will prove effective in captivating certain souls, therefore each exposition has its place.

However, I am equally certain that each will eventually point us back to His words to Luisa. This is a simple corollary to the fact that Heaven never contradicts itself, and Heaven has already given an unsurpassably definitive status to Jesus' words to Luisa. You needn't, therefore, ever feel overwhelmed by the already enormous and continually growing amount of mysticism relaying this Gift—*if you are aware of the Gift as relayed by Jesus to Luisa, then you are already, fully successfully, heeding your call to receive it!*

Luisa's definitive status as the Secretary of the Divine Will is not my interpretation. I am merely submitting to the words of Jesus Himself that He has used in the various mystical revelations of the 20th Century. Only with one other mystic has Jesus used the superlative and singular approach that He has with Luisa: namely, St. Faustina. In the latter's diary, we read:

> When I became aware of God's great plans for me, I was frightened at their greatness and felt myself quite incapable of fulfilling them ... **I soon recognized it was not true humility, but rather a great temptation from the devil** ... I heard these words spoken distinctly and forcefully within my soul**, You will prepare the world for My final coming.** These words moved me deeply, and although I pretended not to hear them, I understood them very well and had no doubt about them. (§429)

Similarly, no one who has read Luisa's revelations denies that, within their pages, Jesus repeatedly bestows singular exaltation upon them, and continually refers to them as *the* very revelations which God has chosen to be *the* instrument for *the* fulfillment of the Our Father. We will see this displayed in the next chapters; for now it is enough to point out that St. Hannibal di Francia was certainly convinced the revelations enjoyed this status (even though he died a decade before the revelations ended; years that provided continued proofs of the same reality). For he was honest enough to recognize they either *did* stand so exalted, or they were utterly and thoroughly false—and he was wise enough to realize that the latter explanation was impossible.

What, then, are we left with? *Two Witnesses*. Two humble virgins, lowly in the eyes of the world but exalted before God, through whom Christ is undertaking His Final assault against the prince of this world, to cast him back into the abyss and prepare the way for His universal Reign, in grace, before the end of time. The reason for the necessity of *two* witnesses, both definitive in their own right, is what we will address next.

Salvation and Sanctification: The Tasks of the Two Witnesses

> "May your holy gifts, O Lord, we pray, give us life by making us new, and, by sanctifying us, lead us to things eternal."
> –Prayer after Communion. 4th Week of Lent. Roman Missal.

There is no contradiction between the finality and supremacy seen in St. Faustina and Luisa, since although their content greatly overlaps, their particular missions are distinct. These two missions coincide with the two things which we know are, above all else, ultimately willed by God: *salvation* and *sanctification*. For we know that God wills "all men to be saved," (1 Timothy 2:4) and that "this is the will of God, your sanctification." (1 Thessalonian 4:3) Even reason alone, when contemplating the nothingness of all that pertains to earth by virtue of its temporary nature, can easily conclude that ultimately, only two things matter: *getting to* Heaven (salvation), and building up as much treasure there as possible (sanctification).

Immediately after teaching the Our Father, Jesus reiterates the finality and supremacy of these two themes; first, emphasizing the need to do what is indispensable to attain salvation: *forgive*. "... if you forgive men their trespasses, your heavenly Father also will forgive you ..." (Matthew 6:14) Then, He exhorts us to not merely arrive at, but also to *glorify* our eternal home:

> ... that your fasting may not be seen by men but by your Father who is in secret; and **your Father who sees in secret will reward you**... **Lay up for yourselves treasures in heaven**, where neither moth nor rust consumes and where thieves do not break in and steal. (Matthew 6:18,20)

This Divine pairing is summed up beautifully in the prayer of the Liturgy of Good Friday, wherein we beseech the Almighty for our salvation (abolishment of death by being conformed to Christ) as the precursor to our sanctification (attaining the "image of the man of Heaven"):

> O God, who **by the Passion of Christ your Son, our Lord, abolished the death** inherited from ancient sin by every succeeding generation, grant that just as, being conformed to him, we have borne by the law of nature the image of the man of earth, **so by the sanctification of grace we may bear the image of the man of**

> **heaven**. Through Christ our Lord. (Roman Missal. Passion of the Lord.)

Just as the groundbreaking revelations on the Divine Mercy given by Jesus to St. Faustina constitute God's final effort of *salvation*, so His revelations on the Divine Will given to the Servant of God Luisa Piccarreta constitute God's final effort of *sanctification*. Salvation is the foundation for sanctification; therefore, it is Providential that, following not only the order of the Gospel verses above, but also the same pattern we see displayed in all of God's works, Faustina's revelations from Jesus became widely known first.[153] Ultimately, however—as we discussed at length in Part One—God desires not merely that we accept His mercy, but that we accept His very Own life as our life and become like Himself as much as is possible for a creature.

Thus we proceed first from justice to mercy, and then from mercy to justice. That is, first, in receiving forgiveness and salvation, we progress from being under God's justice to being under His mercy. Then, once we are in God's grace, we seek to rise to reclaim the *justice* of original holiness through the Gift.[154] We have already seen that Faustina's revelations regularly allude to this sanctity of living in the Divine Will, but it has been left to Luisa's revelations to be the primary herald of this Gift which justice requires God return to the world before its conclusion. From that justice, however, we must then become channels of Divine Mercy to the whole world; hence, I am convinced, Jesus' efforts through both Faustina and Luisa remain the two prongs of God's Final Effort in the world; *not* that we "move from" Faustina to Luisa.

The Trinity Itself is reflected in this threefold progression from Justice to Mercy, from Mercy to Justice, and again from Justice to (proclaiming) Mercy. For God creates, redeems, and sanctifies—whereas our souls are "recreated" by receiving mercy, "glorified" by receiving sanctification, and *only then* can truly become vessels for the entire world's redemption in a new outpouring of the Holy Spirit—a New Pentecost to "renew the face of the earth." In Part One, I promised that diving more deeply than ever before into the very center of the

---

[153] Luisa's revelations, however, were *received* before (and during) Faustina's; here, too, the pattern of the Gospel is followed, as in Jesus' remarks after teaching the Our Father, He first emphasizes salvation, then sanctification - but within the Our Father itself, that which especially pertains to sanctification (the third petition) is revealed first, and then what especially pertains to salvation (forgiving others) is revealed.

[154] Do not misunderstand; we never "graduate from" Divine Mercy, as we will always need it until ontological confirmation in grace in Heaven; rather, we build on it in our spiritual growth.

Our Father would enable us to cooperate most powerfully with the Holy Spirit to effect this renewal. Now, we are prepared to do precisely that.

I conclude by sharing an opinion and a personal testimony. I believe that Jesus speaks to many more souls than is commonly known. I have conversed with a number of hidden seers and mystics, and they have told me that before they had any knowledge of Luisa's writings, Jesus was essentially telling them the same thing as is relayed therein. Some went so far as to make a stunning admission to me: even though they were already conversing with Jesus sensibly, it was nevertheless by *merely reading* His words to Luisa that their spiritual lives drastically improved.

Sit and ponder that for a moment. *Bona fide* mystics and seers themselves, extraordinarily blessed as they are by Jesus' direct words spoken to them, are exposed to something far greater just by reading some ink on a page—the words of Jesus to Luisa—a task anyone can accomplish, from the mystic monk to the pragmatic businessman, and everyone in between.

You can, and will, succeed in joining the Almighty's ultimate effort to fulfill the Our Father prayer if only you read on and see what He has revealed to Luisa regarding this fulfillment. All are called to join this army, not only those who have enough time to bury themselves in mystical literature. For although delving into these revelations can easily fill a lifetime, knowing enough about their essence to receive the Gift which they convey and hasten its universal reign takes only minutes. Let us, therefore, without any further delay, turn our attention to Jesus' revelations on the Divine Will.

Part Four: The Servant of God Luisa Piccarreta: the Gift of Living in the Divine Will

"The world will be full of Luisa. The Third Millennium will see her light."
–St. Padre Pio

12. The Divine Mission of St. Hannibal di Francia

"[St. Hannibal saw] the means God himself had provided to bring about that 'new and divine' holiness with which the Holy Spirit wishes to enrich Christians at the dawn of the third millennium, in order to 'make Christ the heart of the world.'"–Pope St. John Paul II[155]

In the Year of Our Lord 2004, Pope St. John Paul II canonized a certain priest. This priest had dedicated the last decades of his life to a certain mission. This mission consisted of the private revelations of Jesus to a certain mystic. This mystic was a lowly virgin whom this priest had spiritually directed upon being appointed to do so by the Archbishop. And the messages Jesus entrusted to this mystic contain the most extraordinary news one can possibly imagine.

As you will have surmised, the saint is Hannibal di Francia, the mystic is the Servant of God Luisa Piccarreta, and the mission is the fulfillment of the Our Father prayer – first, in individual souls, then, across the entire world. It is a mission not only relayed in *but also made possible by* sharing knowledge of Jesus' messages to Luisa.

Before proceeding to consider this news, therefore, we should recall that not once in the history of the Church has a canonized saint's

155 Address of Pope John Paul II to the Rogationist Fathers. § 6. May 16, 1997.

life mission been later proven fraudulent. To suppose that such a scenario is even possible is to overlook the Church's indefectibility by misunderstanding the nature of what canonization assures us.[156] If the Church might possibly canonize someone who in his life, above all else, promoted a spiritually destructive message, then canonization is useless. But canonization is *not* useless! Therefore, if we find that a canonized saint's life mission consisted in nothing other than *the* fulfillment of *the very thing* that every Christian has been asking for (in the Our Father)—more passionately and repeatedly than any other plea—then we would be, for lack of a better term, quite insane to not want to learn about this mission. Preferring sanity, we proceed with this chapter.

> **Father Di Francia is so convinced of the importance and benefit of [Luisa's] writings** that he decides to publish [*the Hours of the Passion*] in 1915 ...with a *nihil obstat* and *imprimatur*. The text will be expanded and re-edited the same year and then again in 1917 and 1925. **His enthusiasm for the text is so great that in 1915 he sends a copy to the archbishops and bishops with a circular letter attached in which he asks it be made more widely known**. He does this, he says, because the person who has written it is "**a chosen soul who ... enjoys great union with God** ... These pages seem inspired..." (*The Sun of My Will*. Official Biography of Luisa, published by the Vatican. 2016. Page 109)

[156] Many canonized saints clearly had done unfortunate things with their lives for a time, but then had conversion experiences. Such saints were of course canonized for what *followed* these experiences, not what preceded them. Here, by "life mission," I am referring to what the saint *primarily dedicated* himself or herself to *during their years of Heroic Virtue* and which motivated the canonization itself (note that canonizations do not merely infallibly assure us that the person is in Heaven, but also infallibly declare that he or she lived Heroic Virtue). While Heroic Virtue does not imply utter perfection or inerrancy, it is certainly incompatible with dedicating the last decades of one's life to promoting fraud! If the surety of this norm is ever in doubt, it is only so with those who were canonized as martyrs, since different criteria apply to those processes; this, however, does not apply to St. Hannibal, as he was not a martyr.

The Man, the Mystic, and the Mission

> "In many ways these revelations [of Jesus to Luisa] open new horizons, not contemplated until now ... one who reads these writings cannot fail to be enamoured with the Will of God, and not feel new strong impulses and a divine commitment to transform all of himself in the Divine Will"
> –St. Hannibal di Francia

St. Hannibal was a prodigious priest, a zealous worker of many apostolates (including starting a school and an orphanage), and an ardent defender and lover of the poor. In his canonization homily, Pope St. John Paul II said that Hannibal had a *"... love for the Lord [that] moved him to dedicate his entire life to the spiritual well-being of others."*[157]

But his truly exceptional qualities were located in his gift for discerning mystical phenomena. From this distinguishing trait of his, we can easily see Providence at work in inspiring Fr. Hannibal to be Luisa's most dedicated director and the most zealous promoter of her revelations. But it is not only that Hannibal, year after year, himself chose to be distinguished by his zeal for this message. Jesus' own words *in Luisa's revelations themselves* also insist on this priest's primacy; both during his life and in the months following his death.[158]

It would have been difficult to find another priest as qualified as he to determine what constitutes an authentic private revelation. He was, firstly, known to be entirely level-headed and prudent in his approach to private revelation in general. He repeatedly and vehemently insisted that they not be treated as infallible decrees, or regarded as equal to Public Revelation, or ever fail to be subject to the Magisterium; he even cautioned against approaching them too credulously! Were there an expert in mysticism to be found anywhere among the clergy who would have been sure to not go unscrupulously falling head-over-heels for a grandiose, though questionable, claim from a private revelation, it would have been Fr. di Francia.[159]

---

[157] Canonization Homily. May 16, 2004.

[158] For example, the message from February 28th, 1928.

[159] One of his many teachings on private revelation, given in a letter to another priest whom St. Hannibal regarded as being too uncritical with private revelation, is as follows. "**Conforming to prudence and sacred accuracy, people cannot deal with private revelations as if they were canonical books or decrees of the Holy See. Even the most enlightened persons, especially women, may be greatly mistaken in the visions, revelations, locutions, and inspiration. More than once the divine operation is restrained by human nature. For instance who could ratify in full all the visions of Emmerich and St. Brigid, which show evident discrepancies? I love very much the private revelations of**

Even more notably, St. Hannibal personally conversed and corresponded with an extraordinary number of saints, blesseds, and mystics, including: Pope St. Pius X, St. Padre Pio, St. John Bosco, Servant of God Mother Mary Nazrena (with whom he co-founded the Daughters of Divine Zeal), Melanie Calvat (the La Salette seer—another of his spiritual directees), St. Luigi Orione, Blessed Ludovico of Casoria, Servant of God Fr. Eustachio Montemurro, Blessed Bartolo Longo, Blessed Giacomo Cusmano, Blessed Paolo Manna, Blessed Guido Maria Conforti, Blessed Rosa Gattorno Custo, and many others. Even Hannibal's own brother, Francesco Di Francia, has now had his cause for canonization introduced and is now "Venerable."

Today, however, St. Hannibal may be most often remembered as the founder of the Rogationists. This religious order undertakes charitable works for—and evangelization of—the poor, and is especially dedicated to praying and working for priestly vocations. Less widely known is the eschatological and superlative mission discussed above, which garnered the greatest place in St. Hannibal's heart and which he *most* earnestly desired to be spread to the whole world. In fact, the saint became so utterly convinced not only of the legitimacy of Luisa's revelations but also of their dire urgency and extreme importance that, towards the end of his life, he completely devoted himself to their proclamation. A mere four months before his death, he provided written testimony to the supreme regard in which he held this mission, despite the numerous apostolates he was engaged in:

> I want you to know that since **I have totally dedicated myself to the great work of the Divine Will**, I practically don't concern myself at all with my institutes.[160]

---

holy persons, but never I accept them in full! ... to consider any expression of the private revelations as dogma or propositions near of faith is always imprudent! The mistakes could amount to thousands. Poulain substantiates this fact with examples of saints we venerate on the altars. It is not surprising because the visions or the news undergoes some modifications while passing through human channels... Aptitudes and dispositions may not be the same: a psychological, moral spiritual, physical event can modify them, hindering the spiritual enlightenment from shining perfectly in the soul. Thus the person is unaware of circumstances, details or propositions, and is mistaken involuntarily. In fact, everything is received through and according to the subject. This is proved by experience, by the mystical theologians, such as St. John of the Cross, St. Teresa, Castrotevere, Poulain, etc. By prudence and reason we cannot accept all the words of revelations as they were propositions near to the faith; still less when they are contrary to the authoritative opinion of renowned writers and to the simple, beneficial devotion of the saints." (*The Father's Soul.* Page 90. Quoted by Fr. Bruno Rampazzo, R.C.J. Pamphlet, "Luisa Piccarreta and Saint Hannibal di Francia")

[160] Letter of St. Hannibal to Luisa Piccarreta, dated February 14th, 1927.

He tirelessly worked to publish, print, disseminate, and approve Luisa's revelations (bestowing nineteen of his own *nihil obstats* upon them[161]). He maintained that they consisted in: "... **a mission so sublime that no other can be compared to it—that is, the triumph of the Divine Will upon the whole earth, in conformity with what is said in the 'Our Father'**[162] and that they "... **must be made known to the world.**"[163] (*And here we should note that any Catholic who has decided to restrict himself to only heeding approved private revelations will indeed find the entire main thrust of Jesus' message to Luisa contained within these nineteen Church-approved volumes.*)[164]

Pope St. John Paul II agreed, for he chose not only to beatify and canonize St. Hannibal, but also to make his own St. Hannibal's belief in the reality of this coming *New and Divine Holiness*. Seven years after beatifying Hannibal, and seven years before canonizing him, John Paul gave the quote we have already seen, in an address to the *Rogationist* order which St. Hannibal founded:

> [St. Hannibal] saw in the "Rogate" the means God himself had provided to bring about that "new and divine" holiness with which the Holy Spirit wishes to enrich Christians at the dawn of the third millennium, in order to "make Christ the heart of the world."[165]

In previous uses of this quote, I did not include the first clause, as we are only now prepared to discuss the meaning of the term "Rogate."

---

[161] A "nihil obstat" is an ecclesiastical assertion that "nothing stands in the way" of a work's publication (which is to say, it contains nothing contrary to Catholic teaching). St. Hannibal was appointed *censor librorum* by the Archbishop to Luisa's writings, hence he was given ecclesial authority to bestow such approbations.

[162] *Hours of the Passion*. Preface.

[163] *The Sun of My Will*. Page 117

[164] Some respond to this by claiming that *nihil obstats* and *imprimaturs* do not themselves constitute affirmative ecclesial declarations that a phenomenon is indeed "supernatural in origin." This is true, but a non sequitur. Revelations of the sort given to Luisa (and St. Faustina and many others) are not of the category that ever receive such declarations, therefore the absence of such a declaration says nothing. Those declarations are generally reserved for the more traditional mode of apparitions (Fatima, Guadalupe, Lourdes, etc.); a mode that is quite distinct from lengthy revelations over the course of years to a particular mystic under spiritual direction. Moreover, those who criticize Luisa's and Faustina's revelations do so by claiming that there is unorthodox content within them. This claim, indeed, is flatly contradicted by the *nihil obstats* and *imprimaturs* which the revelations of both Faustina and Luisa have received—ecclesial approbations which do indeed entail forms of Church approval. Not only, therefore, would it be wrong to claim that Luisa's revelations are "unapproved," it is also misleading to refer to the absence of a declaration of supernatural origin as indicative of anything at all.

[165] Address of Pope John Paul II to the Rogationist Fathers. § 6. May 16, 1997.

Indeed, locating the Gift of Living in the Divine Will within the context of priestly vocations (which is what characterizes the "Rogate") is paradigmatic of the Gift's nature. Jesus repeatedly tells Luisa that this Gift will come to the world *through the ministry of priests*.[166] Moreover, John Paul himself—in this same address—made it clear that he was aware of this dynamic:

> The very prayer of the **"Rogate", source of an original form of apostolic life, is not merely a prayer addressed to God, but a prayer lived in God**: for it is conceived in union with the merciful heart of Christ, motivated by the "sighs" of the Spirit (cf. Rom 8:26) and addressed to the Father, the source of all good. Bl. Annibale Maria Di Francia, docile to the divine Master's teachings and inwardly **guided by the impulse of the Spirit**, highlighted the conditions and characteristics of that prayer which make it an ecclesial work "par excellence", **yielding abundant fruit for the Church and for the world. The first condition is to put the Blessed Eucharist at the centre... It is not without providential coincidence** that 16 May 1897, the date on which 100 years ago the first three young men formed by Bl. Annibale entered the novitiate, was precisely the Fourth Sunday of Easter, "Good Shepherd Sunday". On that same Sunday the Servant of God Paul VI, my venerable Predecessor, established the World Day of Prayer for Vocations. On the occasion of your founder's beatification (7 October 1990), I also wanted to hold up Annibale Maria Di Francia to the Church as **the** "authentic precursor and zealous teacher of the modern pastoral ministry of vocations."

Why—we must ask ourselves—of the countless priests of the modern era (including canonized saints!), would Pope St. John Paul II choose to exalt St. Hannibal di Francia, then only Blessed, as *the* (not "a") "authentic precursor and zealous teacher of the modern pastoral ministry of vocations"?

The answer becomes clear as soon as we meditate on the "New and Divine Holiness" which the Holy Father extols in this same address, and once we consider the context of Hannibal's own life. For no one disputes that Fr. di Francia was the chief apostle of Jesus' revelations to Luisa—revelations which were his life's greatest passion—and their main theme, the Gift of Living in the Divine Will, will be the most important thing for priests of the modern era to mediate to their flocks, in order to "**make Christ the heart of the world.**" That Gift is,

---

[166] e.g., His message to her on January 13th, 1929

and will be, *their mission*; therefore, Pope St. John Paul II gave St. Hannibal this singular primacy and presented him to us as *the* teacher of modern vocations. As Jesus Himself said to Blessed Conchita, another 20th-Century mystic we discussed in Part Three, and whose revelations speak of the Gift and its impending reign:

> **[Priests] can be transubstantiated into Me**, and, even though they will not be gods, they will possess something of God Himself, and they will enter into possession of the Divinity ... This is urgent because the world is decaying, deviating from its goal and is drowning in sensuality and materialism. **Only a holy priest, a priest who is Me, a priest savior, a divinized priest transformed into Me can save it**...if priests are I Myself, if they are transformed into Me, they will have those same prerogatives that I have... they will do amazing things, they will work real miracles of conversion ... **their will will be My Will and that of My Father... Then, as I so profoundly desire, I will come back to the earth through My priest and the face of the earth and hearts will be changed**. It is necessary that this happen and absolutely indispensable in order to evangelize the multitudes once more ... The revival of the world, nations and society will only come about with the transformation of priests into Me. On that day the conflicts that devastate nations will cease ... To this My victory over hell, My triumph and My Church's triumph over the infernal powers is linked.[167]

The simplicity of what now confronts us is exceeded only by its enormity. On that account, let us turn our attention to some items we need to address.

Notes on Luisa's Revelations

In anticipation of the imminent release of the official edition and translation of Luisa's revelations (and the fact that each of the existing ones contain some translation errors which have caused confusion), **no direct quotes from Luisa's private revelations are included within the pages of this book**. Instead, where appropriate, the essence of what is being taught within the revelations will be relayed in a compressed format. A **parenthetical citation will immediately follow, containing the date of the entry (Month/Day/Year) from**

---

167 *Priests of Christ*. Concepción Cabrera de Armida. Society of Saint Paul, 2015. Imprimatur, Domenico Di Raimondo Romo, M.Sp.S. May 30, 2004. (Excerpts from pages 345-353)

Luisa's volumes where the original material and context may be found.

Unfortunately, a lack of theological oversight during the first years wherein access was widely gained to Luisa's volumes (after Cardinal Ratzinger's 1994 nullification of the restrictions placed on them up to that point)—combined with the aforementioned translation issues—enabled the spread of certain bad interpretations of Luisa's revelations: interpretations which are not only at odds with Catholic orthodoxy, but are also unfaithful to the actual text of Jesus' words to Luisa.[168] As a result, Luisa received much deeply mistaken opposition from critics who were exposed to these bad interpretations, but who had little to no understanding of the actual teachings of the recipient of their reproach. Equally unfortunately, these misguided criticisms circulate on the internet to this day. There, they are often mistaken for recent critiques when, in fact, they were published in the last millennium—long before the recent developments nullifying these old criticisms.

Therefore, I here seek to provide the proper understanding of the themes in Luisa's revelations which have at times been misinterpreted; the understanding that enjoys both complete Catholic orthodoxy and fidelity to Jesus' words to Luisa. In this effort, I join my book to many other works published and efforts undertaken in the last 16 years; that is, since the year 2005, when Luisa's diocese rendered a positive judgment on her holiness and orthodoxy, and the Vatican accepted her cause for canonization.

For example (in chronological order), in 2005, *Be Faithful and Attentive* was published by Robert Hart. in 2010, Fr. Robert Young, OFM, began providing what would become many years of talks properly introducing people to Luisa's writings. In 2011, the Benedictines of the Divine Will, a new religious order explicitly dedicated to the spirituality found within Luisa's revelations, was granted formal Ecclesial approval and has since grown and provided a wealth of teachings. In 2012, theologian Fr. Joseph Iannuzzi successfully defended and then published his Doctoral Dissertation, *The Gift of Living in the Divine Will in the Writings of Luisa Piccarreta*, which was unanimously approved by the faculty of the Pontifical Gregorian University in Rome and has received the accolades of dozens of Bishops. In 2013, theologian Stephen Patton's book, *A Guide to the Book of Heaven*, was granted an *imprimatur*. In 2014, theologian and Notre Dame professor, Fr. Edward O'Connor, published his own explanation of

---

[168] Texts which, the competent Ecclesiastical authorities have repeatedly affirmed, are entirely in agreement with Catholic teaching.

Luisa's private revelations: *Living in the Divine Will: the Grace of Luisa Piccarreta.* In 2016, the Vatican's own *Libreria Editrice Vaticana* published *The Sun of My Will,* a biography of the Servant of God—with a preface by Cardinal José Saraiva Martins, Prefect Emeritus of the Congregation for the Causes of Saints—strongly endorsing Luisa and her messages. Also in 2016, Luisa was given her own entry in the Vatican's *Dictionary of Mysticism.* In 2020, well-known EWTN scripture scholar, Frances Hogan, began presenting an abundance of teachings on Luisa's revelations. All these sources (and so many others like them) can be consulted for the proper understanding of the revelations of Jesus to Luisa.

13. Luisa Herself

"The purest virgin, wholly of God, who emerges to be a singular predilection of the Divine Redeemer…"
–St. Hannibal di Francia

(Photo: Luisa with sisters at the convent of the Daughters of the Divine Will sitting with an orphan they cared for.)

March 4th, 1947 marked the Heavenly birthday of a woman who had, on earth, lived what may have appeared to be the most boring life in the history of the world. But, in a Divine irony that only the Holy Spirit could have orchestrated, this ordinary woman, the Servant of God Luisa Piccarreta, *interiorly* had lived the most astounding life imaginable. If the life of an "ordinary" saint is an "interior castle," then the life of Luisa was an interior *continent.*

And what transpired in her interior, under constant ecclesial oversight to ensure its authenticity and orthodoxy, is destined to soon illuminate the whole world.

Luisa was born into the world on Sunday, April 23rd, 1865. It was the Second Sunday of Easter—a day we now celebrate as Divine Mercy Sunday. The day on which, Jesus told St. Faustina, "**all the Divine floodgates through which graces flow are opened.**" (*Diary*, §699). The same day, Luisa's father took her to the parish priest to have her baptized.

Luisa's desire for hiddenness was manifest at the earliest age; as a toddler, her favorite spot was a hollow in a great tree where she would spend hours alone in prayer. She suffered from terrible demonic nightmares as a child, but instead of succumbing to the horror of them, she learned to flee to Jesus for safety. This utter dependence on Christ disposed her, even before she had reached the age of reason, to be the perfect instrument in the hand of God; one who had absolute trust in Him, but no thought for herself. Jesus even insisted that He had chosen Luisa simply because, after searching the whole world, He found her to be the littlest (3/23/1921).

At twelve years of age, Luisa began to hear Jesus speaking to her interiorly. These locutions came in the most precious moments of her life: the moments after receiving Holy Communion. He would instruct her, correct her, and guide her. After a year of these communications, Luisa experienced a life-changing event that invited her to become a victim soul: she received a vision of Jesus below her balcony, carrying His cross, amidst great persecutions from a throng surrounding Him. He then stopped, looked up at her and begged her help. She accepted.

Around this time, her mystical life progressed exponentially; she was soon incapable of keeping down ordinary food, and thus began her lifelong Eucharistic fast—wherein she was miraculously sustained by no food other than her daily reception of Holy Communion. Jesus was training her to live entirely by and in Himself—His Divine Will, and His Body in the Eucharist. Adding to this utter dependency upon God, another mystical phenomenon, seen nowhere else in the entire history of the Church, came to define each of her days: inexplicably, she woke up each morning completely immobilized—rigid "as lead"—incapable of being budged even by a strong person. It was not until a priest came to bless her that, miraculously but like clockwork, she could move. No other saint or mystic has ever been subject to such a radical dependency on the Church and on priests, and this unprecedented sacrifice tells discerning minds that God, in turn, was at work in some task whose glory would be likewise unrivaled.

But this sacrifice brought along with it many other sacrifices and challenges. In the official Church-sanctioned biography of Luisa, entitled *The Sun of My Will* and published by the Vatican in 2016, we read the following:

> The priests who get called in say that her condition is a complete sham; others think that only a beating will put an end to Luisa's nonsense; and there are still others who think that the girl just wants to make herself believe she is a saint or is possessed by demons ... She is thought to be arrogant, a fake, a cheat, someone who wants to grab all the attention for herself. Often, the priests whom her family members approach refuse to go and, even if they do go, they then bitterly reproach her. Once they left her in her rigid state for more than 18 days. Her mother cries. She is mortified. She does not understand ... The fact escapes Luisa that **her dependence on priestly authority has a precise purpose within the church since Jesus manifests His works through His priests.** This is how Luisa spends the next three or four years—subjected to a continual battle ... (Ch. IV) What lingers [even after regaining mobility from a priestly blessing] is a strong revulsion for any kind of food. If sometimes she eats something, when forced by a family member, she brings it all back up again just a few minutes later. This, too, is seen as some form of mischief on her part, so that both her family and other people are after her, scolding her. And yet**, they should be noticing that something unusual is happening—the food she brings back up is whole, fresh and fragrant. But the people around her seem to have a kind of spiritual blindness**. They are not able to take a leap into seeing something miraculous. On the contrary, they keep looking for earthly cures. (Ch. IV)

As we often see in the lives of the mystics, not excepting Luisa, their worst persecutions came from within the Church. It may be difficult for us today, looking back, to understand how such "spiritual blindness" could have existed in those near her during the early years; but this cross was just another sacrifice she offered up for the Coming of the Kingdom, just as the extraordinary and even downright extreme rigor in testing and documented analysis to which she was subject by the Church was allowed by God in order to give us absolute assurance in the authenticity of her mysticism and revelations.[169]

Thankfully, this state of direct opposition from those closest to her did not last for too long; after some years of Luisa's mystical phenomena's continuation, the priests who had been sent by the Church to bless her, say Mass in her room each day (thanks to a special dispensation given by the Pope himself), hear her confessions, and direct her mystical life, no longer were skeptical but instead became Luisa's most ardent supporters and promoters. As we know, the most zealous of all these was St. Hannibal di Francia, and he gave a beautiful description of Luisa in his own words—within which we see the impression Luisa left on this saint who was renowned for his discernment:

> The pious author of *The Hours of the Passion* [one of Luisa's works]... never, for any reason in the world, would have put into writing her intimate and prolonged communications with revered Jesus—communications which have been going on from her tenderest age until today, and are still continuing until who knows when—if Our Lord himself had not repeatedly obliged her to do so, both personally and through holy obedience to her directors, to whom she always surrenders with enormous duress upon herself, and also with great strength and generosity, because her concept of holy obedience would even make her refuse to enter into paradise ... The purest virgin, wholly of God, who emerges to be a singular predilection of the Divine Redeemer, Jesus Our Lord, who century after century, increases ever more the wonders of His love. It seems that **He wanted to form this virgin, whom He calls the littlest one He found on earth, and bereft of any education, into an instrument of a mission so sublime, that is, the triumph of the Divine Will...** (St. Hannibal di Francia. Quoted in *The Sun of My Will*, page 122)

---

[169] Fr. Edward O'Connor wrote of another extraordinary account of spiritual blindness and its resolution: "In 1917, Archbishop Regime, newly appointed to the diocese of Trani, forbade priests to enter Luisa's house or to celebrate Mass there (although this privilege had been granted by Pope Leo XIII and confirmed by Pope Pius X). But as he was signing this decree, the Archbishop was suddenly afflicted by partial paralysis. When the priests who were present came to his aid, he indicated that he wanted to take them to Luisa's house. Supported by two priests, and uttering incomprehensible words, he came to the door. When he entered Luisa's room, she said "Bless me, your Excellency!" The Archbishop raised his hand in blessing, and was instantly cured. He remained for two hours in a secret conversation with Luisa, and thereafter visited her regularly for spiritual conversations. Many vocations, of both men and women, were inspired by Luisa…" *Listen to My Prophets,* Page 60.

Although St. Hannibal was extremely well versed in private revelation and even had unparalleled experience with other living mystics, he did not hesitate to regard Luisa's mission as standing high above those of all others. For her mission—as the saint relayed—is *the* triumph of the Divine Will.

Luisa's Revelations Situated in Her Life

> "All of these events I observed, scrupulously controlled and subjected to careful examination by many doctors and professors of dogmatic, moral, ascetic and mystical theology"
> –Fr. Benedetto Calvi

(Photo: Luisa)

In the year 1898, when Luisa was 34 years old, Fr. Gennaro Di Genarro was assigned as Luisa's confessor. Only one year into this ministry he commanded Luisa, under holy obedience, to write down her revelations from Jesus. So great was her humility that, as we saw above, this was an enormous penance for her; Luisa wanted only to be unknown and hidden. But her obedience being perfect, she began to write.

Fr. De Benedictis came after, as Luisa's next ordinary confessor, and St. Hannibal Maria di Francia was then appointed to be Luisa's *censor librorum* and extraordinary confessor—a role he held until his death in 1927. More than a decade earlier, however, deeply convinced of the necessity of Luisa's revelations, he had been publishing the *Hours of the Passion* (a book of revelations Jesus gave Luisa on the details of His sufferings). Hannibal gave volumes 1-19 of Luisa's diary his *Nihil Obstat* (his own sickness and death prevented him from approving the later volumes) and afterward the Archbishop, Joseph Leo, gave them his *imprimatur*. Fr. Benedetto Calvi was Luisa's final confessor, and he too became a zealous advocate and promoter of Luisa's writings. Fr. Calvi documented an overview of her daily life as follows, wherein we see confirmed yet again the extraordinary graces at work in her life:

> Toward six o'clock in the morning the confessor was beside her small bed. Luisa was found all curled up, crouched over so tightly that when the sister or person of the house—in obedience to the confessor or the Bishop—had to sit her up in bed in her usual position, they could not move her on account of her weight. It seemed as if she were a huge piece of lead ... Only when the confessor, or on certain occasions any priest, imparted to her his blessing by making the sign of the Cross with his thumb on the back of her hand, Luisa's body regained its senses and she began to move ... Throughout the 64 years of being nailed [this figurative terminology likens Luisa's bed to the cross of Christ] to her small bed, Luisa never suffered any bedsores. **Immediately afterwards, there followed the reading of that which Luisa had written during the night concerning the sublime truths on the Divine Will, which was read only by her confessor beside her small bed**. There was yet another extraordinary event. What was her food? Everything she had eaten, after a few hours, came back up completely intact. **All of these events I observed, scrupulously controlled and subjected to careful examination by many doctors and professors of dogmatic, moral, ascetic and mystical theology** ... [Each morning] After having awakened Luisa in the name of holy obedience, the confessor or another priest celebrated Holy Mass in her little room before her bed. Therefore, having received Holy Communion, she would remain there as though in a trance, in ecstasy and in intimate conversation with the Lord for two to three hours...[170]

What Fr. Calvi describes above reminds us that these revelations were written by Luisa *herself*, and that they were then reviewed—carefully and immediately—by her Church-appointed priest spiritual director. In light of this, we can see that Luisa's revelations do not suffer from

[170] Rev Joseph Iannuzzi, Doctoral Thesis. 1.8.

the difficulties of those of some other mystics, who either did not write down the revelations themselves (but rather had them transcribed by another after verbally describing them—a process not always known for accuracy), or who provided revelations independent of careful Ecclesial oversight (an even more potentially dangerous situation).

Moreover, most of Luisa's revelations consist simply in her transcription of the explicitly spoken words of Jesus to her—not in a locution that merely attempts to "recreate on paper" a mystical experience or describe a vision. In this regard, too, Luisa's revelations belong to the most trustworthy category, one which is not prone to the errors of some other mystics who, even if they provide *generally* reliable accounts, may have a particularly heavy degree of human subjectivity intermixed with the legitimately supernatural content.

Finally, there is to this day no doubt regarding what exactly Luisa actually wrote; we possess her original volumes, and scans of these pages are readily accessible. Through this, we see that Luisa's revelations enjoy the highest order of reliability (even aside from the countless verifications of authenticity already discussed and yet to be discussed).

Nevertheless, the supreme nature of the mission entrusted to Luisa meant that she had to be perfectly conformed to the life of Christ. As He was condemned by the ecclesial authorities of his day, she too had to be.

The Index of Forbidden Books

> "Dear Luisa, saints serve for the good of souls, but their suffering knows no bounds." –St. Padre Pio. (Letter to Luisa after the condemnation)

On August 31st, 1938, certain editions of just three of Luisa's works (out of her already finished dozens) were placed on the Index of Forbidden Books, where they were soon joined by St. Faustina's revelations. This placement was promulgated on September 11th of the same year.[171] Immediately after news of the condemnation reached her, Luisa responded with her customary obedience, and wrote a letter to her Bishop, which read in part: "**With humility, I spontaneously and promptly fulfill my duty as a Christian soul, of**

[171] Cf. Acta Apostolica Sedis of 1938. Page 318. Vatican.va.

offering my unconditional, unhesitating, full and absolute submission to the judgment of the Holy Roman Church."[172] Jesus, however, also immediately told Luisa that this trial was necessary in order for her to be better conformed to His Own life; but He promised her also that it would only be temporary (9/18/1938)—a prophecy since fulfilled.

Whoever is concerned by this condemnation must be reminded that the Index of Forbidden Books no longer exists. The Church abrogated it in 1966. One cannot claim that a text on the Index is still condemned unless there is an independent reason to regard it as such. Not only does no such reason exist in Luisa's case, but—as we will see shortly—many developments since the abolition of the Index demonstrate that it was just as mistaken in censuring Luisa as it was in censuring Faustina.[173] One, however, sometimes hears Faustina's placement on the Index being hastily dismissed under the pretense that it was nothing but a procedural misstep, a miscommunication, or a translation issue. In truth, an entire page of the Vatican's annual record of its official acts (the *Acta Apostolica Sedis*) pertains to the prohibition of the Divine Mercy devotion of St. Faustina (page 271 of the 1959 edition). The words of the prohibition itself make it clear that the Supreme Sacred Congregation of the Holy Office *did indeed* carefully examine the "visions and revelations" of St. Faustina. Despite this examination, the Holy Office still forbade any dissemination of the images and *any* of the writings of the Divine Mercy revelations, thereby enacting stronger prohibitions against Faustina than have ever been

---

[172] Cf. *A Guide to the Book of Heaven*. Stephen Patton. 2013. Page 28

[173] As the Church teaches, "... the Index [of Forbidden Books] remains morally binding, in light of the demands of natural law, **in so far as** it admonishes the conscience of Christians to be on guard for those writings that can endanger faith and morals. But, at the same time, **it no longer has the force of ecclesiastical law with the attached censure. In this matter, the Church trusts in the mature conscience of the faithful** ..." (Decree of the Holy Office on the Abolition of the Index of Forbidden Books) In other words, the Index's proscriptions are *only* still binding *in those cases which* the works in question do actually "endanger faith and morals." For such works as these remain the same danger to faith and morals which they were before; they did not magically cease to be dangerous upon the abolition of the Index. But whether or not a work that had been placed on the Index does, in fact, endanger faith and morals is not a question that can be settled by determining whether it was lifted from the index. In Luisa's case, her writings were not looked at again until the 1990s, long after lifting a book from the index was even possible; once the list was abolished, lifting entries from the list also ceased.

enacted against Luisa.[174] As the veteran Vatican journalist, John Allen, points out:

> Officially, the 20-year ban [on Faustina's revelations] is now attributed to misunderstandings created by a faulty Italian translation of the Diary, but **in fact there were serious theological reservations**—Faustina's claim that Jesus had promised a complete remission of sin for certain devotional acts that only the sacraments can offer, for example, or what Vatican evaluators felt to be an excessive focus on Faustina herself.[175]

Clericalism evidently dies hard; even today, some Catholics struggle to accept that the men in the Vatican may sometimes be simply, flat-out, wrong. They ignore that only the *Magisterium* is Divinely protected—not the *juridical* actions of Church employees, irrespective of their rank. Indeed, these juridical actions have not only wrongly condemned Luisa and St. Faustina, but also St. Padre Pio, St. Mary Mackillop, St. Teresa of Ávila, St. Joan of Arc, and many others. While the virtue of obedience surely applies even to ill-advised condemnations *while they are in force* (all these saints always obeyed whatever strictures the Church placed upon them, and we saw that Luisa was no exception), it says nothing about how non-binding past juridical decrees are now to be regarded.

The real reason St. Faustina's revelations were prohibited has little to do with translation issues, even if these were involved. The real reason, rather, is accurately represented by Mr. Allen. As anyone

---

[174] Though this point is essentially irrelevant due to the abrogation of the Index, we should still consider that even when the Index was binding, how its proscriptions applied to Luisa's works was greatly exaggerated by some. As the theologian Stephen Patton pointed out in the year 2000, "**The 1938 condemnation [of some of Luisa's works] had nothing whatsoever to do with Luisa's 36 volume spiritual diary, known as "Book of Heaven," which is her most important work. This work of 40 years, containing the overwhelming weight of her spiritual doctrine on the Divine Will, was never placed on the Index. This is especially significant because in 1938 Vatican officials not only knew about this exhaustive work, they also had the actual, original volumes in the Vatican archives! If they had ever wanted to "condemn" this work of Luisa, that would have been the time. But they didn't. And so, no taint of condemnation has ever been upon the most important thing that Luisa wrote. In fact the official, Church appointed censor, gave the Nihil Obstat to the first 19 volumes of the "Book of Heaven" after examining them intently in their original Italian language over a period of 17 years, prior to his death. The archbishop who appointed this censor gave his handwritten Imprimatur directly on those original manuscripts. Regarding the three books that were placed on the Index in 1938, two of them had several other editions. The condemnation was limited only to the specific editions officially mentioned. Other editions of these same two books have been published with full ecclesiastic approval, even as late as 1997. The third work was a compilation of edited extracts from Luisa's writings, which has never been reprinted.**"

[175] John Allen Jr. "A saint despite Vatican reservations" August 30, 2002.

will recall who has read her diary (*Divine Mercy in My Soul*), St. Faustina's revelations make claims of such an enormous magnitude that whoever was of the "private revelation may only sit quietly in a corner" mindset (discussed in Part Three) would inevitably pounce to condemn them. This is precisely what happened to both Faustina and Luisa.

Knowing that the past condemnation does not impede acknowledging Luisa's authenticity, we will now return to considering her life; or, rather, its holy conclusion.

Luisa's Death

"She died like the saints die."–Fr. Benedetto Calvi

(Photo: Luisa's Funeral. Although, miraculously, her body suffered no rigor mortis, it was equally inexplicably incapable of being laid flat. A special casket was constructed.)

Three months after the condemnation, Luisa finished writing her last volume—the thirty-sixth—and then put down the pen as obediently as she had picked it up forty years earlier. One year later, World War II began. Nine years later, on March 4th, 1947, Luisa breathed her last after speaking her final words, as recorded in her spiritual testament written by Fr. Benedetto Calvi (her confessor at that time):

> Now I die much happier because the Divine Will has consoled me more than ever with Its presence during these final moments of my life. Now I see a long, beautiful and wide road, illuminated by infinite and resplendent suns ... yes, I recognize them: They are the suns of my acts done in the Divine Will. It is the road I must now take; it is the way of my glory to unite me with the immense happiness of the Divine Will. It is my path, it is the path that I will set aside for you, dear father; it is the path that I will save for all those who want to live in the Divine Will. (*The Sun of My Will*. Page 187)

About her death, Father Calvi wrote the following (contained in the Vatican's biography of Luisa, but first published in a parish newspaper in Brooklyn, NY, on April 13th, 1947):

> **Luisa is no longer with us ... she is in heaven** in the immense light of the Divine Will, glorious and triumphant in the glory of the saints ... **She died like the saints die, as a final act in the Divine Will. I am still recovering from the tremendous shock** I experienced from the deeply distressing but sublime impression her last breath made, so I do not know what else to say to those who bombard me with questions, 'A saint has died!' ... We have gained a guardian in heaven. Her body remained rigidly upright, sitting up in bed, but **her limbs completely lacked the rigidity of rigor mortis** so they could be moved in any direction, even all the joints in her fingers; her eyelids were closed but could be opened and **her pupils stayed crystal clear. All of that led to some doubt whether she was really dead, so we had a number of medical examinations** done. Her body was viewed for a good four full days in this state without the slightest sign of decomposition. The entire town and crowds of people from elsewhere came to see her remains out of devotion and admiration, kissing her snow white and pliable hands, placing religious objects on her and jealously preserving them as relics ... Her funeral? ... A real triumph! ... Nobody went to work that day, but everyone without exception took part ... It was an overwhelming display of grief, but also of joy ... even though her eyes were closed, it seemed like she wanted to bless the huge crowd that accompanied her to her final resting place. A truly rare sight, perhaps unparalleled, and whoever had the good fortune to take part will never be able to—and never know how—to express how magnificent it was. (*The Sun of My Will*. Pages 185-186)

Forty-seven years later, with all the condemnations previously discussed nullified, her cause for beatification and canonization was triumphantly opened. Since its opening, it has only seen success after success, and we will, in the next section, focus on reviewing a small portion of these developments.

Luisa's Authenticity

> "Can a tree that produces good fruit be rotten? Jesus Christ answered in his Sermon on the Mount...It is well known that [Luisa] leads a holy life consecrated to God...a virgin who has voluntarily endured being a victim of the passion of her physical and moral suffering for about 60 years with strength and resignation—indeed, with joy." –Fr. Ludwig Beda[176]

Though what has already been said is more than sufficient to demonstrate the authenticity of this mystic and her revelations from Jesus, we should not leave out a brief overview of several other things that testify to Luisa's legitimacy. What follows, therefore, is an assortment of these facts in chronological order; including developments both during her life and since her death.

Pope St. Pius X. When St. Hannibal took Luisa's *Hours of the Passion* to the Holy Father and briefly read from it, he, Pope St. Pius X, said: "*Father, this book should* ***be read while kneeling: it is Jesus Christ who is speaking!***"[177] The Pope proceeded to encourage St. Hannibal to have it printed and promulgated immediately.

Archbishop Joseph Leo. This archbishop gave his *imprimaturs* to twenty sets of Luisa's revelations.

St. Hannibal di Francia. This saint gave 19 of Luisa's works his own *nihil obstat.*[178] (However, as we have already covered St. Hannibal's role in the preceding pages, we will not repeat it here.)

St. Padre Pio. This extraordinary mystic, and Capuchin friar of San Giovanni Rotondo, was known to say to those who came all the way from Corato to see him: "*What have you come here for? You have Luisa, go to her.*"[179] Although these two never met in person, they nevertheless esteemed each other highly. (They corresponded through

---

[176] Letter to the Holy Office. *The Sun of My Will*. Appendix

[177] Bernardino Giuseppe Bucci, OFM. *Luisa Piccarreta, A Collection of Memories* (2000), Ch. 4. Note: As a young boy, Fr. Bucci met Luisa, and she prophesied his priesthood.

[178] *New Catholic Encyclopedia*. 2nd Edition. Volume 5. Page 866.

[179] *Luisa Piccarreta, A Collection of Memories*. Ch. 3

Federico Abresch, a close friend of Padre Pio.[180]) When three of Luisa's writings were condemned, St. Pio even sent her consolation, saying, *"Dear Luisa, saints serve for the good of souls, but their suffering knows no bounds."*[181] The book already quoted, *The Sun of My Will*, dedicates a section to documenting and describing the relationship between Luisa and Padre Pio,[182] and a few excerpts from that section are as follows:

> **There are countless testimonies** beyond these [Federico Abresch and Mrs. Caterina Valentina] that talk about the mutual esteem and faith Luisa and Padre Pio had in each other, perhaps because of the deep similarities in their lives, too ... Padre Pio made the sign of the cross on her head and said, "Yes, by the intercession of Luisa Piccarreta, the Lord has saved [a dying girl]." ... **Even the residents of San Giovanni Rotondo knew how much respect Padre Pio had for Luisa.** Miss Adriana Pallotti recalls that day she asked Padre Pio, her spiritual father, if she was doing the right thing by donating money to have Luisa's books printed. Padre Pio said "yes," and, in fact, rather uncharacteristically, he had her repeat the question, astounding his spiritual daughter to no small degree. The answer again was a clear "yes."

Timeline of events relevant to Luisa's cause, since its opening:

November 20th, 1994: Cardinal Joseph Ratzinger nullified the previous condemnations of Luisa's writings, allowing Luisa's cause to formally open on the Feast of Christ the King of the same year. **February 2nd, 1996:** Pope St. John Paul II permitted the copying of Luisa's original volumes, which up until then had been reserved in the Vatican Archives. **October 7th, 1997**: Pope St. John Paul II beatified Hannibal Di Francia. **June 2nd & December 18th, 1997**: The two Church-appointed theologians submitted their evaluations of Luisa's writings to the Diocesan tribunal, affirming that *nothing* in them is contrary to Catholic Faith or Morals.[183] **December 15th, 2001**: with the

---

180 Unfortunately, some individuals attempt to dispute this fact of Padre Pio's endorsement of Luisa. Their arguments usually stem from a letter allegedly written by a Franciscan at San Giovani Rotondo who implies that, because he himself knows nothing of the correspondence between Luisa and Padre Pio, it could not possibly have happened. The Vatican's biography of Luisa puts this disputation to rest.

181 *Luisa Piccarreta, A Collection of Memories*. Ch. 3.

182 Cf. *The Sun of My Will*, pages 174-175.

183 Rev. Joseph Iannuzzi, Doctoral Dissertation. Approved by the Faculty of the Pontifical Gregorian University, Rome, 2012. Introduction. Excerpt: "Having received a letter of non obstare from the Congregation for the Causes of Saints, on November 20, 1994, Most Reverend Monsignor Carmelo Cassati, Archbishop of Trani presided at the

permission of the diocese, a primary school is opened in Corato named after, and dedicated to, Luisa.[184] **May 16th, 2004**: Pope St. John Paul II canonized Hannibal Di Francia. **October 29th, 2005:** the diocesan tribunal and the Archbishop of Trani, Giovanni Battista Pichierri, rendered a positive judgment on Luisa after examining all of her writings and testimony on her heroic virtue; settling her status as "Servant of God" as no mere procedural step, but rather as an Ecclesiastical Approbation of her holiness and authenticity. **January 31st, 2007:** The Bishops of Puglia petitioned the Congregation for the Causes of Saints in support of the canonization[185]. **June 13th, 2010:** the "Luisa Piccarreta Association—Little Children of the Divine Will" is approved as a public association of the faithful.[186] **April 12th, 2011**: Bishop Luigi Negri approved the Benedictine Daughters of the Divine Will, a religious order explicitly dedicated to Luisa's Divine Will spirituality, and founded by a holy nun from Mother Angelica's order. **November 1st, 2012:** the Archbishop of Trani wrote a formal notice containing a rebuke of those who "*claim [Luisa's] writings contain doctrinal errors,*" noting that such people "scandalize the faithful." This notice furthermore encouraged the spreading of the knowledge of Luisa and her writings.[187] **November 22nd, 2012:** the faculty of the Pontifical Gregorian University in Rome granted unanimous approval to Fr. Joseph Iannuzzi's Doctoral Dissertation (defending and explaining Luisa's revelations), thereby granting its contents ecclesiastical approval authorized by the Holy See. In the following two years, this Dissertation received the accolades of dozens of Catholic bishops.[188] **April 2015**: Maria Margarita Chavez revealed that she was miraculously healed

---

opening of the Cause of Beatification of the Servant of God Luisa Piccarreta and established its Diocesan Tribunal. On December 18, 1997, Rev. Cosimo Reho, professor of dogmatic theology, submitted his theological evaluation of the writings of the Servant of God Luisa Piccarreta to said Diocesan Tribunal in which he affirmed that her writings contain nothing contrary to Catholic faith or morals. His findings concurred with those of Rev. Antonio Resta, Rector of the Pontifical Theological Institute of Southern Italy, who submitted his report to the same Tribunal on June 2, 1997. These two independently commissioned theologians arrived at the same conclusion. On October 29, 2005 Luisa's Cause of Beatification concluded its diocesan iter under the present-day Archbishop of Trani Giovanni Battista Pichierri and, with the collection of testimonies and documents, referred the final decision on her heroic virtues and sanctity to the Congregation for the Causes of Saints."

[184] En.luisapiccarretaofficial.org/news/December-15-2001/195

[185] Cf. *The Sun of My Will*. Page 239

[186] Ibid.

[187] The entire notice can be found in the Appendices of *The Crown of Sanctity*, available for free at www.DSDOConnor.com

[188] Rev. Joseph L. Iannuzzi, Missionaries of the Most Holy Trinity Newsletter (Nov. 2014-May 2015): Page 2.

through the intercession of Luisa eight years earlier; an official diocesan investigation was then initiated. **January 2016**: *The Sun of My Will*, the official biography of Luisa Piccarreta, was published by the Vatican's own official publishing house. Authored by Maria Rosario Del Genio, it contains a preface by Cardinal José Saraiva Martins, Prefect Emeritus of the Congregation for the Causes of Saints, strongly endorsing Luisa and her revelations from Jesus. In this preface, he states that the "Living in the Divine Will" revealed to Luisa *is in fact* "the actual way in which the Son Jesus lived on earth, bringing here with him the life of heaven." (Considering the Cardinal's position, if anyone alive knows what makes a saint and an authentic revelation, it is he who does!) **November 2016:** the Vatican published its own authoritative Dictionary of Mysticism, *Il Nuovo Dizionario di Mistica,* in which Luisa is given her own entry (page 1266). **June 20th, 2017:** The postulator for Luisa's cause, Monsignor Paolo Rizzi, wrote: "I appreciated the work [carried out thus far]... all this constitutes a solid base as a *strong guarantee for a positive outcome* ... the Cause is now at a decisive stage along the path."[189] **November 2018**: Another official Diocesan inquiry into a miraculous healing through Luisa was initiated, this time of a man named Laudir Floriano Waloski in Brazil. **April 23rd, 2019**: The Congregation for the Causes of Saints approved moving the body of Luisa to a more prominent position, next to the high altar, in the church in which she is entombed,[190] St. Maria Greca in Corato. On the same day, Archbishop Leonardo D'Ascenzo of Trani (Luisa's diocese) approved the "Family of the Divine Will" to "promote the spirituality of the Servant of God Luisa Piccarreta as well as the formation and diffusion of the doctrine of the Divine Will."[191] **November 2019**: Bishop Ayo-Maria Atoyebi of Nigeria supported a house of formation for a new religious order (Benedictines of the Lamb of Divine Will) dedicated to Luisa's revelations, writing "... after due examination of its constitution, spirituality and mission I do approve it as a future, authentic institute of religious order. When it is erected as a Public Association it will be of immense benefit to the Church..."[192] The next month, Archbishop Robert J. Carlson of St. Louis encouraged the order's establishment in the United States, and wrote to the order's founder, "**You have my Blessings and Support**

---

[189] https://danieloconnor.files.wordpress.com/2021/11/note.jpg
[190] Luisapiccarretaofficial.org/news
[191] https://en.luisapiccarretaofficial.org/cause
[192] November 27th, 2019, letter of the Bishop Emeritus of the Catholic Diocese of Ilorin to the principal local ordinary.

as we strive courageously in active apostolates to live to the Glory of God in His Divine Will."[193]

Luisa's Fulfilled Prophecies

> "Everything, everything has been predicted [in Luisa's writings] several years before, and everything has come about, and much yet is left to come about."–St. Hannibal di Francia

Imagine set before you a stack of pages relating certain events – pages which you know, with documented proof to bolster your certainty, were written long before the events themselves happened.[194] Imagine that these pages specifically foretell World War II, some of modern history's most devastating earthquakes, some of the 20th Century's most significant events, Globalization, Coronavirus, the abuse crisis in the Church, the canonization of a saint, and much more. You would, no doubt, be utterly awed and would not question for a moment that their author was truly a prophet who received messages from Heaven.

Well, this is no figment of anyone's imagination; this is, rather, exactly what we see with Luisa's revelations, which seem to have more fulfilled prophecies within their pages than any other private revelation in history. Here we will consider just a few. Dive into the writings yourself, and I am sure you will discover more. As St. Hannibal himself said, regarding Luisa's writings:

> There are chapters which foresee divine scourges of earthquakes, wars, fire, cloudbursts, devastation of lands, epidemics, famines and the like. **Everything, everything has been predicted several years before, and everything has come about, and much yet is left to come about**. (*The Hours of the Passion.* Preface.)

World War II. Jesus repeatedly told Luisa about the Second World War long before it began. One example can be found in the January 16th, 1923 message which specifically referred to a *second general turmoil*, with *cities destroyed*. The September 2nd, 1923 message discussed how France, Germany, Italy, and Greece had been ringing war bells, and how only one more was needed to begin *the fight*. The November 16th, 1926 message says that the coming war would involve *more races*

---

[193] Letter from Most Reverend Robert J. Carlson, Archbishop of St. Louis to Sister Mary Ann Ugwueke. December 2, 2019.

[194] Thankfully with Luisa's revelations, this is precisely the case even under the most rigorous scrutiny one could apply; her volumes, in her own handwriting, had been preserved in the world's safest location: the Vatican archives.

and nations than the previous one. The March 31st, 1927 message sees Jesus insisting that the apparent peace agreements were in fact plots for another war that would be even *more extensive* than the prior one. In the August 12th, 1927 message, Jesus lamented that, despite such a terrible war recently occurring, the powerful were already trying to move the whole world to begin an *even more terrible war*.

In the messages from November 16th, 1926, and March 31st, 1927, Jesus also prophesied to Luisa the results of World War II; the unprecedented union of races that would follow in the explosion of international trade and communications. He even said that He in part allowed all the turmoil precisely in order to enable this union, which in turn would allow for the dissemination of the knowledge necessary for the coming of the Kingdom.

Bear in mind that St. Hannibal's conviction of the prophetic nature of Luisa's revelations was formed during the 1920s (he died in 1927), long before the World War II prophecies were vindicated. Imagine how much more certain he would have been if he had lived another twenty years!

Earthquakes and Volcanoes. In the April 17th, 1906 entry in her volumes, Luisa was shown great chastisements; specifically, *earthquakes in three different cities* that were a great distance from each other. *The very next day*, the great San Francisco earthquake struck. According to the USGS (United States Geological Survey), this "ranks as one of the most significant earthquakes of all time," and it remains the deadliest earthquake in American history. Three thousand people were killed and 80% of the city of San Francisco was destroyed. *Four months later*, the 1906 Valparaíso Earthquake occurred in Chile which killed *even more* people than the San Francisco quake. Two years later, the great Messina Earthquake wreaked havoc in Italy on December 28th, 1908. It remains the *worst and deadliest earthquake in European history*. At least 80,000 people were killed (and perhaps up to 200,000), and the cities of Messina and Reggio Calabria were both destroyed. Luisa was also shown this earthquake several hours before it happened in her December 28th, 1908 message—received, as her revelations always were, in the middle of the night, and in which Jesus said there would be an earthquake (the temblor later struck at 5:20 am). On the same page, Luisa wrote that she felt the earthquake *physically* five hours later, at which point Jesus added that more parts of the world would be destroyed by earthquake, water, and war.

Mere days later, in the January 2nd, 1909 message, Jesus revealed that the disasters were anything but over, and that earthquakes *would occur in places where they do not ordinarily happen;* He then showed her *a mass of fire being moved closer to the surface of the earth.* Exactly three weeks after Jesus gave this message to Luisa, the infamous 1909 Borujerd Earthquake struck Iran, killing eight thousand people. Six months later, France—*a region that scarcely ever suffers from any earthquakes*—was struck by what remains to this day the largest earthquake ever recorded in its history: the 1909 Provence earthquake. Within the few decades following this message, hundreds of thousands of people throughout the world died in earthquakes—a scale of earthquake-wrought devastation orders of magnitude beyond anything that had been seen in the world for hundreds of years.

Three years after the message, an astounding event occurred: the 20th Century's largest volcanic eruption (only surpassed in size throughout *all history* by Tambora), which was a full *thirty times* as large as the famous eruption of Mount St. Helens. The truly remarkable thing was that this eruption is said to have "come out of nowhere;" bursting forth from a spot in the ground (accompanied as it was by many simultaneous earthquakes) in Alaska where no volcano had previously existed, in fulfillment of what Luisa was shown three years earlier in the message noted above. This volcano is now fittingly called *Novarupta,* Latin for "newly erupted," but the area was so remote that a scientific expedition to reach the site and examine it took four years after the eruption to complete. Nevertheless, the expeditioners described it as a "modern inferno," saying that it was a "horrifying" sight with tens of thousands of jets of steam roaring from the still burning hot ash (which was up to 700 feet deep), such that it was "one of the most amazing visions ever beheld by mortal eye." Today, the USGS remains stunned by the event due to both it being accompanied by the "extreme seismicity" of fourteen separate earthquakes and due to the dozens of associated phenomena which shattered the then-scientific consensus of the day regarding the operation of volcanoes and earthquakes. But also to this day, scientists admit that the full story of the eruption is not understood, despite being a famous enigma for geologists and perhaps the most rigorously studied eruption in history. It seems the best explanation for the mystery shall remain what Luisa was shown in her vision; that a *mass of fire* was taken by God and *moved towards the surface of the earth.*

The Nature of the 20th Century. Before even two months had passed after the dawn of the 20th Century, Luisa did not hesitate to assert that the new century would become renowned for its pride. (2/19/1900) Looking back, this is an obvious diagnosis, but in the very beginning of the 1900s it was far from apparent that the century then in its infancy would be known above all by the title of the deadliest of sins. For it *seemed* that a period of great prosperity, peace, and progress was in motion and destined to continue. The world was enjoying its 85th consecutive year of *Pax Britannica;* that period of apparent peace with no major wars between the Great Powers during which the unprecedented imperial influence of the British Empire gave stability to much of the world (while of course, as we know now, committing many atrocities). The Congress of Vienna was still in force, and the Napoleonic Wars (the last major European conflicts before World War I) had become scarcely even a memory among the day's centenarians. Amazing new technologies—especially in transportation and communication—were making life easier than it ever had been; opening new opportunities which had never been dreamed of. It seemed that the "public mood" had never been higher. And yet in Luisa's revelations, Jesus indicates that chastisements the likes of which the world had not seen were imminent (7/3/1900), He showed her new machines crushing human bodies and *two* chastisements *in the air* (7/25/1900), and He said that what had been seen in the first decade of the century was *scarcely the beginning* of the chastisements (1/2/1909). In the October 22nd, 1900 message, Luisa also relays how Jesus told her that some of the chastisements He described would occur during her life and some after her death (she died in 1947).

At the time of these messages, military technology had remained similar for many decades. But World War I, fourteen years later, saw the rapid advance of horrendous new weaponry. Luisa was likely shown some of these new weapons in the July 25th message noted above.[195]

Even after World War I, Jesus' messages to Luisa were equally noteworthy regarding the continuation of the evil nature of the century. This, too, is strongly prophetic, because after the end of this so-called "War to End All Wars," many thought lasting peace was finally at hand. Consider what H.G. Wells—the secular world's idea of a "prophet"—said at that time about World War I:

> [This is] a war not of nations, but of mankind. It is a war to exorcise a world-madness and end an age ... It aims at a settlement that shall stop this sort of thing for ever ... **This, the greatest of**

---

195 One also wonders if the *two chastisements in the air* mentioned therein were the atomic bombs dropped on Japan. For this message was given to Luisa exactly 45 years before the eve of the July 26th, 1945 issuance of the Potsdam Declaration, which, with the atomic bombs as its inspiration, promised "prompt and utter destruction" for Japan in the absence of "unconditional surrender."

all wars, is not just another war—it is the last war![196]

But Jesus made it clear to Luisa that this was not so, and not only by the prophecies that foretold World War II. Four *months* after the beginning of World War I (which dragged on for four *years*), Jesus told Luisa that what was then occurring was still nothing, and that more nations would join (11/20/1914). After this message, Italy, Portugal, the U.S., Greece, and other nations all entered the war. In the October 16th, 1918 message—mere weeks before the War's conclusion on Armistice Day—Jesus told Luisa that the nations would gather to form something resembling the Tower of Babel, would revolt, would no longer want kings, and would all be humiliated.

World War I ended the next month, and with the words of Mr. Wells resounding loudly in the ears of all, the League of Nations was soon thereafter triumphantly formed. A historically unprecedented international organization, explicitly established to ensure world peace, was sure—they thought—to succeed in its stated aim. But perhaps it is precisely this reason why Jesus here tells Luisa that it was a mere Tower of Babel. For indeed, it proved itself just that; an opportunity for much babbling, while delivering on none of its promises of the preservation of peace.

Abortion. On the morning of June 9th, 1899, Luisa was suffering as a victim soul to a particularly extreme extent. The brief diary entry from that day likely alludes to the veritable genocide, through abortion, that would begin in the following century. Within the message, Luisa laments that she saw a baby about to be killed before it could even be baptized. She then insists that this is the single sin which *most* cries out to God for vengeance, is a *horrendous dishonesty*, and happens *so very often*. Jesus Himself, however, says little in the diary entry, only speaking to exhort Luisa to unite her sufferings to His. Taking all this together, it seems to be a prophecy of the future regarding the killing of the unborn, not, as Luisa took it to be, a description of the killing of babies during her own time. First, because abortion was not legalized anywhere in the world until 1920 in the USSR. Killing babies before the possibility of baptism was, therefore, most certainly *not* common at the time of this message; on the contrary, it was practically unheard of. Second, because in decrying the act as a *horrendous dishonesty*, Luisa aptly describes the diabolical lie by which abortion is rationalized today (i.e., the line, *"I'm personally opposed to abortion, but it is about a woman's choice and therefore it should be legal"*), but which had never before been heard or entertained. Third, it is difficult to see how

---

[196] H.G. Wells. "The War That Will End War," The Daily News. August 14, 1914

what she described could be the sin that *most* cried out to God for vengeance in 1899, considering how practically non-existent it was; however, for the last 50 years (and perhaps even for the last 100 years) it most certainly has been the sin that most cries out for vengeance. Luisa's revelations are replete with descriptions of various forms of mankind's sinfulness that call down the chastisements; therefore, for these messages to single out *one* sin as *most* crying out for vengeance is extraordinary. Moreover, Jesus' Own words in the message do not confirm the temporal accuracy of Luisa's assessment, adding to the likelihood that He chose to simply let her words stand so that we—reading them today—could realize that, truly, nothing comes close to the sin of abortion in heralding the imminent chastisements.[197]

The 1902 Hague Convention on Divorce. In a series of messages which span the entirety of the year 1902 (e.g., 1/11, 1/12, 2/3, 2/9, 2/24, 12/8, 12/18), Jesus repeatedly laments to Luisa—even in superlative, eschatological terms—about the horror of the efforts to liberalize divorce laws. He called these proceedings worse than war itself, an affront to the Church, and an abomination to God (1/12/1902). The mere acknowledgment of this effort in Luisa's writings is, however, humanly inexplicable; in January of 1902, relatively few—and certainly not ordinary Italian folk like Luisa—were aware of the details of the ongoing "Hague Convention on Private International Law" in the Netherlands, and its documents were not even published until June of that year. The debates on divorce law were in committee phase before that point, and the American experts in the session were fighting for their own nation's divorces to be internationally recognized. Their success would have had massive global ramifications in liberalizing divorce law. These efforts failed in 1902, only to then become a reality in 1969.[198] Jesus told Luisa that this would be the outcome—namely that, thanks to her sacrifices as a victim soul, the law would not pass (2/24/1902); contrary, no doubt, to the expectations of those associated with the effort. But in the same message, Jesus added that once Luisa is taken to Heaven, they would again be capable of resuming their efforts and perhaps succeeding. Tragically, the rest is history. Divorce—extremely rare and legally dif-

---

[197] As I write these words, we are approaching the 50th anniversary of the single most infamous abortion-enabling event in history—the Roe v. Wade U.S. Supreme Court decision—and on account of this fact alone, we should not presume that the Time of Mercy will be extended much longer.)

[198] Arthur T. Von Mehren and Kurt H. Nadelmann. *Family Law Quarterly*. September 1971. Vol. 5. No. 3. Page 306.

ficult during Luisa's entire lifetime—is now fully legal almost everywhere (even the "no fault" variety) and it is, in some nations, how *most* marriages today end. A person reading Jesus' words from 1902 which diagnose the horror of divorce as exceeding even that of war may have regarded them as exaggerated, but today we can easily see how accurate they were. A third World War would not have wrought as much devastation upon society as divorce has in the last several decades. One can also see why Jesus singled out divorce as an affront to the Church; today, the Catholic Church is perhaps the only real bulwark against it.

The Abuse Crisis of the Church. In His revelations to Luisa, Jesus conveyed that the hierarchy of the Church had become so corrupt that the very enemies of the Church were necessary in order to purge and purify her. Indeed, in recent times, it has sometimes been the Church's avowed enemies who did what bishops should have done long before—dealt with the sin and crime of sexual abuse strongly by bringing the perpetrators to justice. Even Pope Benedict XVI openly stated that the uncovering of the abuse crisis has been a *needed purification*, and that some of the secular investigators and journalists have done the right thing in exposing the pervasive evil among so many of the clergy. But Jesus' words to Luisa on this point are a full 100 years before their time. In the May 16th, 1911 message, Jesus responds to Luisa's plea that He confound the enemies of the Church by saying that He will *not* do so, as this would prevent the Church's purging. In the same message, He laments that many with high positions in the Church are dazzled by their power and blunder by protecting the *false virtuous* and oppressing the *true good*. He then grieves over *children* suffering under the weight of injustice, and says that for their sake, He must use His justice, even going so far as to *inducing the secular to rail against* the rot in the Church.

Mussolini's March on Rome. In a prophecy given the day before a certain major historical event took place, Jesus told Luisa that the Italian leaders wanted to *gamble away Rome* in the face of people *coming out from all sides* to storm the city—all under the appearance of sheep, although they are in fact wolves. All of this is contained in the October 27th, 1922 message, and it describes exactly what happened *the next day* when fascist troops under Benito Mussolini entered Rome. Instead of defending the city, the King (Victor Emmanuel III) simply handed power over to the Fascists without conflict; thus, as Jesus said, *they gambled away Rome*, in hopes of placating evil men by so doing. This gamble tragically placed the Vatican State geographically within a political entity being ruled by Fascists—but the King did not care, not seeing Fascism as a threat to his comfortable establishment. Now, Mussolini had indeed threatened to take Rome three days earlier. But this message Luisa received on the 27th of October contains much more than a worry about Rome being taken; rather, it includes a lamentation about Rome being *gambled away,* which only God (and perhaps King Victor) knew would happen. Even the Prime Minister himself (Luigi Facta) assumed this gamble would not happen—proven by his declaration of Martial Law—in order to allow for Rome to be militarily defended against the march (a declaration the King later refused to sign).

Coronavirus. Although the disease's spread in fact began earlier, the first cases of the COVID-19 Pandemic were officially identified in China on December 29th, 2019. *Exactly* 93 years earlier, Luisa described an epidemic that would come as a scourge to almost all nations, even singling out Italy (12/29/1926).[199] Three years before that, she also prophesied contagious diseases that would come, causing people to be carried away to so-called leper hospitals, and causing a *general fright to reign* (6/21/1923). This, of course, is precisely what we have seen with Coronavirus; to be sure, a serious disease for many people, but the fear thereof causing even more damage than the illness itself (especially with respect to the supremely lamentable fact that the Faithful have been barred from the Sacraments like never before in the history of the Church). People have indeed been carried off to *leper hospitals;* that is, forced into quarantines and lockdowns, sometimes even forced into "massive quarantine centers,"[200] all the while having their most basic civil and religious rights violated—just like was done to the lepers in earlier times. Jesus also repeatedly told Luisa that part of the *general uproar* (the chastisements) that will purify the world before the Era will include contagious diseases (e.g., 10/16/1918, 8/19/1910, 5/9/1899, 11/17/1899). Finally, in a vision from July 3rd, 1900, Luisa saw many people dying from contagious diseases and heard Jesus tell her the chastisements already then transpiring were *nothing* compared to what was prepared (7/3/1900). Later that same month, Luisa described a vision wherein she saw *two fires*—one from China, another from Italy—little by little blending

---

[199] Note that this message, having been given in 1926 and speaking of the future, cannot refer to the world's previous major pandemic, the Spanish Flu, which was over in 1920.

[200] *Lessons From Leprosy for Coronavirus: Quarantine and Isolation can Backfire*. NPR. February 7th, 2020.

into one fire (7/30/1900). Coronavirus became a pandemic in precisely this way: coming forth from China and Italy as an apparent trickle until, like wildfire, it dominated the world.[201]

St. Hannibal's Canonization. There are well over a billion Catholics in the world today; presumably, each is striving to be a canonized saint (if only!). Nevertheless, the number of saints who are canonized compared to the number of Catholics who are quite holy and doubtless worthy of the honor is so utterly minimal as to be almost negligible by any statistical standard. And of the many holy people whom Luisa knew—and of the countless people she exhorted to *become* saints—she only referred to one *as* a saint: Fr. Hannibal di Francia. Now, we have all probably referred to some people we know as saints, and time will likely prove all of us wrong (as far as canonization is concerned, that is). But it did not prove Luisa wrong. Fr. Hannibal was indeed canonized 57 years after Luisa's own death; and, not only that, but Jesus also told Luisa that Fr. Hannibal would be the first promoter of the Divine Will to be glorified (despite countless people around Luisa being utterly convicted of her mission and likewise working hard to promote her works). The very day Fr. Hannibal died, Luisa wrote in her volumes (6/1/1927) that she had lost *a saint* (referring to him with that word twice in this entry). Several months after Fr. Hannibal died, Jesus told Luisa that this priest would indeed be glorified when the work of the Divine Will became known, and that his name and memory would be full of splendor (2/28/1928). This, too, is exactly what happened. He was beatified just four years before Luisa's volumes were released (1990) and was canonized in 2004.

***

While all of these fulfilled prophecies are astounding, we should conclude this partial overview of them by recalling what is by far prophesied the most repeatedly and assuredly in Luisa's revelations: the reign of the Divine Will on earth as in Heaven in fulfillment of the Our Father prayer. That is, the *Era of Peace*, which we will consider in Part Five. The assurance of the supernatural origin of these revelations that we attain by considering the already fulfilled prophecies, therefore, should above all inspire certainty in our hearts regarding what has not yet been fulfilled but is guaranteed to be—and will be soon if we do our part.

---

[201] Note: The same message implies a political/revolutionary aspect to the *fire* in question, but this should not rule out the possibility of a double-meaning also referring to an epidemic.

Theology too Deep for Human Origin

> "Who would not be filled with admiration at seeing the marvel of lights and the sublimity of concepts in souls thus enriched by the divine Spirit? ... Whence comes that loftiness of ideas and that elegance and purity of style in souls lacking all human culture? What power of suggestion could infuse in them at one stroke that remarkable Science which they have never studied and those sublime concepts which they have learned from no other person? This is a positive fact against which all human explanations are shattered, however much they may appeal to suggestion, contagion, telepathy, or any other influence which is not supernatural."
>
> –Fr. John Arintero.[202]

When an uneducated lay person who could not possibly have, on her own, generated the concepts displayed in her writings, this itself is a sure sign of Heaven's intervention – and it is precisely what we observe in the case of Luisa. The astonishing degree of spiritual, theological, and even philosophical depth and breadth in her transcriptions of Jesus' words to her is evident from the first volume. As a philosopher myself – and having read countless pages of Plato, Aristotle, Aquinas, Descartes, Leibniz, Boethius, the Stoics, Kant, and so many others – I can readily testify that in none of these exalted human author's works have I found the precision, consistency, depth, and breadth that is evident in Jesus' words to the uneducated, bedridden, unsophisticated Italian laywoman, Luisa Piccarreta. As a recent article in the popular Catholic publication, *Aleteia*, pointed out:

> **With no more than an elementary school education, Luisa composed works of theological depth rivaling great theologians.**[203]

A comprehensive presentation of this depth would amount to none other than re-printing all of Luisa's volumes. Therefore, instead of attempting such comprehensiveness, I will only briefly mention a few scattered points I happen to recall which, although found within her volumes, could not reasonably have arisen from Luisa's own mind.

Free Will and Beatific Vision. Orthodox-minded Catholic theologians still debate whether free will exists for the blessed in Heaven.

---

202 *The Mystical Evolution in the Development and Vitality of the Church Volume II*. Importance of Private Revelations.

203 Bret Thoman, OFS. *A journey to the home of Luisa Piccarreta, the contemplative and mystic*. Aleteia. March 16th, 2021. **Emphasis in original**.

The conundrum is easy to sympathize with: Heaven must mean *absolutely guaranteed safety* for all eternity. This permanent status of one's residence in Heaven must be a metaphysical reality that cannot be undone. Obviously guaranteeing Heavenly safety is not difficult for the Omnipotent God. But would not, some wonder, His granting of this permanence imply that the freedom of our will is annihilated? Wouldn't the will remaining free mean that it might, conceivably at least, someday choose to rebel and thus condemn itself to hell? Jesus tells Luisa that this inference is drawn incorrectly; that, in Heaven, the Blessed still have their free will, but that their Beatitude is so great, their wills are so full of God's goodness, and their intellect so filled with knowledge of God that a truly irresistible force causes them to conform—permanently and perfectly—to the Divine Will. (5/30/1925)

Jesus and Faith. Though some may be scandalized to hear it, it is nevertheless a fact that Jesus had no Faith and no Hope. This is perfectly orthodox and in accord with Church teaching; Faith requires the absence of sight; and Jesus, being God, sees all—even in His human nature, He *saw* Divine Truths so clearly that Faith was not possible. Hope, too, requires not yet possessing that which is hoped for; but Jesus, lacking nothing that a soul in Heaven has, always enjoyed the Beatific Vision from the first moment of His conception, therefore He could not hope for what He already possessed. These teachings are not exactly Catechism 101; in fact, they are almost never touched upon except in advanced Christology graduate courses. Therefore, it is unsurprising to learn that, one day, Luisa prayed to Jesus to make her own faith like His. Innocent and understandable though this prayer was, Jesus did not hesitate to correct her and instruct her that, in fact, He had neither Faith nor Hope. (11/6/1906)

Limits of the Humanity of Jesus. All Christians know that Jesus is both God and man, and that, due to this reality, we rightly worship Him even bodily due to the Hypostatic Union. But the details of more advanced Christological topics are not intuitive and few understand them well. Jesus' words to Luisa nevertheless convey mastery here. When one studies the teachings of St. Thomas Aquinas, for example, he learns that not even the humanity of Christ can completely comprehend the Divinity. This is because perfect knowledge of a thing is none other than the thing itself, and the Divinity itself is infinite, whereas the humanity of Christ—though utterly supreme among all human natures—is nevertheless a created thing (because it began to exist in time). But all created things are in and of themselves finite; intrinsically incapable of containing entirely within themselves the infinite. Jesus conveys this truth to Luisa (10/20/1927) by explaining that not even His Own humanity could enclose within itself the entirety of the Creator's light, since *no created power can exhaust the uncreated power*.

Mariology. Luisa's revelations display a stunning degree of exaltation for Our Lady—even anticipating developments that have only recently become clear to the best of the Church's theologians—while not once straying into realms of unorthodoxy in this exaltation. (Details are addressed in the corresponding Appendix of this book.)

The Number of the Elect. Tragically, it has become fashionable in modern times to pretend that damnation is either non-existent or is reserved only for the occasional Hitler-like figure. But this notion scarcely existed in Luisa's day and, quite the contrary, the prevailing mindset was far too stingy on the question, as a Jansenist tendency continued to exist which minimized the Divine Mercy. This was one reason for the necessity of Jesus' revelations to St. Faustina, in which He promises that He holds absolutely nothing back in the moment of death to save the dying person from hell. St. Faustina, describing these supreme efforts God makes to secure a soul's salvation in its final moment of life, insists that, "**should it show even a flicker of good will, the mercy of God will accomplish the rest,**" and that damnation only results when the soul freely and knowingly rejects even this special "final grace" that is exerted "without any cooperation from the soul" (§1486). Of this grace, Jesus Himself tells the saint, "My omnipotent mercy is active here. Happy the soul that takes advantage of this grace." (Ibid.) Faustina's diary records this exchange in January of 1938. Twenty-eight years earlier, Jesus had explained to Luisa that it is incorrect to infer, from Matthew 7:13-14,[204] that most people are damned. Jesus reminded her that His infinite power can make more people pass through the narrow way than through wideness itself (3/16/1910). Only two months after Faustina wrote the words above, Jesus told Luisa that He makes every effort—*extraordinary industries of love*—in the last moment of life in order to do everything possible to prevent the dying person's escape from salvation, even calling this quest His Own *daily catch,* which He succeeds in so long as He can manage to elicit a single act of contrition from the soul, a result He manages for *all but the most perverse and obstinate* (3/22/1938). Though perhaps tempting for a skeptic, it cannot plausibly be argued that Luisa could have had any access to something St.

[204] "Enter by the narrow gate; for the gate is wide and the way is easy, that leads to destruction, and those who enter by it are many. For the gate is narrow and the way is hard, that leads to life, and those who find it are few."

Faustina wrote a mere two months before, a thousand miles away, in a then-unpublished diary, in another language! Quite the contrary, the uncanny resemblance can only be explained in virtue of the fact that both these revelations derive from the same source: Our Lord Jesus Christ.

No Catholic in the first half of the 20th Century would have supposed she could curry favor in ecclesial circles with messages like these. Therefore, when we see words of such overwhelming mercy promising us that God's goodness is so great that He desires to save as many souls as possible by almost any means necessary, then we can rest assured this is no strategically motivated invention of human art. Similarly, in Luisa's day it was still common for Catholics to murmur when hearing of a person's sudden death without Last Rites, almost assuming that this type of death precludes their salvation. Luisa was not unaffected by this tendency, and therefore was greatly distressed when her own sister was taken by a sudden death. As always, Luisa opened her heart to Jesus, and He gave her the most profound words in response, which assured her that dying without the Sacraments is only cause for concern if one willfully rejects them, and that a sudden death can actually be among the greatest graces, by—for example—preventing extended diabolical attacks against the soul (11/21/1926).

Wisdom in Luisa's Letters

"Here I am, Lord; I come to do your will." –Psalm 40

Unlike the previous section, wherein we saw a theology far too deep and profound—even while preserving impeccable accuracy on the most difficult points—to be of human origin, what we see in her letters, unsurprisingly, is quite different, for it derives from her own thoughts. But what these letters reveal about their author is her possession of a type of wisdom only held by saintly souls, and it testifies to the "normal regimen of a life of faith" which the Church's norms for discerning private revelations (see Part Three) regard as a criterion of authenticity. On this point, the Vatican's biography of Luisa recounts what St. Hannibal himself wrote:

> After all we have mentioned of [Luisa's] long and continuous permanence, rooted to a bed as victim for years and years, experiencing many spiritual and physical sufferings, it might seem that the sight of this unknown virgin would be distressing, like seeing someone on his back with all the signs of the pain endured in the past and of current sufferings and the like. And yet, there

> is something admirable here … nothing, absolutely nothing shows through, nothing of someone afflicted who suffered so much during the night, no appearance of something out of the ordinary or supernatural. On the contrary, **she looks entirely like someone who is healthy, happy and jovial. She talks, chats, laughs when appropriate, but she receives few friends. Sometimes someone with a troubled heart confides in her and asks her for prayers. She listens with kindness, she comforts, but she never goes so far as to act like a prophetess, never a word that might hint at revelations. The great comfort she offers is always one thing—always the same thing—the Divine Will.** (St. Hannibal di Francia. *The Sun of My Will.* Pages 122-123)

Elsewhere in the same biography of Luisa, we read of other people who were deeply touched by her presence:

> Once, a distinguished individual who came to visit her said upon leaving her room, "Luisa possesses an angelic soul! … That heavenly smile and that clear smiling face speak to you of God and they let you catch a glimpse of a tiny corner of paradise. … **In that little room, people forget all about the bothersome things in life; they feel the soul at peace. They forget their quarrels, deceptions, jealousies and they breathe the joy of God's grace.**" ... [Msgr. Luigi D'Oria wrote:] Luisa loved God and others. She could not then be quiet about God, because she wanted God to be known and loved by others … **every conversation, whatever it was about, was illuminated and warmed by God's love. Many people went to her to express their needs—of the spirit and body, drawn by the scent of her union with God. And everyone had, as an answer to their problems, the loving uniformity to the Divine Will**, which not only eases the pain and makes it praiseworthy, it also sheds light on what to do. Those who presented themselves to Luisa in the hopes of finding a fortune-teller were not listened to and were left out. (Pages 63-64)

We cannot go and visit Luisa in Corato as the fortunate people described above could, but we can nevertheless receive the same edification they were blessed with, by virtue of Luisa's letters. Let us, then, look at some of this wisdom that Luisa shared in them.[205]

On Feelings. Luisa knew well how prone people are to focus too much on feelings; supposing that within them is found sanctity.

---

[205] The following excerpts from Luisa's letters are cited and numbered in accordance with the compilation, *Letters of Luisa Piccarreta. The Little Daughter of the Divine Will,* by Marina d'Ariano.

But feelings are not under our control, therefore our holiness (or lack thereof) does not consist in feelings. Luisa wrote:

> Oh, how easily we pay attention to what we feel! **Feeling is not ours, it is not in our power; while Jesus, because He loves us very much, gave us our will into our power,** so that, as we put it on the countertop of the Divine Will, it could turn into divine acts... Therefore, our coldness, the tears not shed, our pains, the involuntary distractions, can ask for the Kingdom of God upon earth. They will be as many sweet pledges in the hands of Jesus, which bind Him to make the Kingdom of the Divine Will come upon earth. Therefore, let us be attentive—let us live as if we had no other life, no other word, but the Divine Will. (*Letter #43 to an unnamed recipient*) Here is the means to sin no more: to be united with Jesus, love Him, and always do His Will. **Don't think about the past,** this harms you a great deal; rather, even today, begin your life with Jesus ... (*Letter #13 to Fr. Bernardo of the Most Holy Hearts from Assisi*) To feel pleasures, imperfections, weaknesses, is not evil. Wanting them is ugly, because **the Lord does not care about what we feel, but about what we want**. (*Letter #120, likely to Federico Abresch*)

On Suffering. Luisa had a special gift for encouraging others in their sufferings. She wrote:

> Therefore, courage, courage. **All other things are left; while sufferings are brought to Heaven, and form our most beautiful throne and never ending glory.** Now I repeat my refrain: continue to promote the Divine Will. (*Letter #18 to Mrs. Constanza Bendetta Pettinelli from Siena*). Together with Jesus, pains change their look, miseries disappear; and from pains, miseries and weaknesses the most beautiful conquests, celestial riches and the strength of God arise, and **the very Angels and Saints envy our lot.** (*Letter #15, to Mrs. Copparo La Scola*). Mortifications, adversities, crosses, come to us veiled and do not let us see the good which they contain; but **peace removes the veil and allows us to recognize the finger of God in our sufferings**... (*Letter #30 to an unnamed religious superior*)

Luisa knew nothing of favoritism and was more than happy to correspond with anyone she could find the time to write to, whether a bishop or a man confined to prison. To one who happened to find himself in the latter circumstance (a Mr. Vincenzo Messina), she wrote (in Letter #35):

> **Never neglect the Rosary to the Celestial Mother**, and if you

can, **be a missionary in the prison**, by making known that the Queen of Heaven wants to visit all the prisoners to give them the gift of the Divine Will.

Even amid the greatest of sufferings—which, for most people, corresponds to the loss of a loved one—Luisa was firm in insisting on peace and trust. To an unnamed recipient, Luisa wrote a letter on August 14th, 1934, containing the following advice:

> It is not good for you to embitter yourself so much over the loss of your beloved son. He is certainly happier now than when he was with you; and if you really loved him, instead of crying, you would rejoice at his happiness. ... **we are just one step away from our dear departed ones; when we least expect it, we will find ourselves together with them**. Therefore, I recommend to you peace, courage and true resignation, and you will see what the Lord will make of you.

Elsewhere, Luisa's advice resembles that of St. Teresa of Calcutta's, who was well known for gently reminding the sickly people she cared for that, in their sufferings, Jesus was kissing them. Similarly, Luisa admonished, **"... think about making yourself a saint. In every pain, give Jesus a kiss, hug Him very tightly, and force Him to let the Kingdom of the Fiat come upon earth**." To Mrs. Mazari, in letter #85, Luisa wrote the following words:

> My good daughter in Jesus Christ, do not get discouraged, never lose trust. What I recommend is that you look at your crosses as many visits from Jesus, Who brings you the life of the Divine Will, to make It reign in you and to give you all His love as food... if you do the Will of God, you will feel a strength in all your sufferings...

On Peace. Perhaps what is seen most often in her letters is the exhortation to peace. Luisa wrote:

> **Three things I recommend to you: firmness in good, perennial peace, filial trust**. Trust will make you live like a little baby in the arms of her mother, and Jesus and the Celestial Mother will take care of all the things you need. They will tell you with facts: "Think about living from Our Will, and We will take care of everything, even the salvation of your brothers." (Letter #12 to Mrs. Antonietta Savorani) If there is peace, there is God. His children are as though kneaded in peace; therefore they are peacemakers, and bearers of peace. Their words, their manners, are never boisterous or sharp, but embalmed with the balm of peace, such as to sweeten the most embittered hearts; so much so, that those who

> are restless feel humiliated and confused in the face of a peaceful soul ... **When the Divine Volition wants to reign in the soul, It first sends Its message of peace. Many times it is about closing one's eyes to little bagatelles, trifles and specks, so as not to lose peace or time; in this manner, the Divine Fiat makes Its own ways in our souls, forming Its throne**. (Letter #36 to Mother Cecilia from Oria) **The storm is always prelude to clear skies**. Therefore, don't lose heart, wait with untiring patience for the hour of God. When it comes, its dominion will put everything into place, and maybe your very enemies will become your friends. (Letter #56, "to a young lady.")

In a fascinating insight from the letter above, Luisa advises that, by refusing to allow peace to reign in our hearts, we *"... let the devil laugh, because if you are not firm and always the same, the enemy will say to you: 'You wanted to do good to others, and you were unable to do it to yourself."* Here, Luisa identifies a common but subtle plague in the spiritual life: failing to love ourselves (in the proper sense of the term) by—in a tragic irony—supposing that our concern for others must render us without peace so long as they are in danger. This is commonly seen in parents who are worried about their straying sons and daughters. Indeed, all such parents should be like St. Monica, praying continually for the conversion of their children. But God's delay in answering these prayers fully and openly must never allow these parents to lose their peace! Luisa knew this well and advised accordingly. She also knew that one of the greatest enemies of peace is the incessant tendency of some to dwell on the past; therefore, she was always firm in insisting that people forget it. In letter #60 (to another unnamed religious), Luisa wrote:

> **As far as wanting to go over the past again—no, because the past has passed in God, and it would be as though stealing His rights, His Own things. If there is something wrong in it, the Lord can let us know with calm**. As far as the future, don't worry about it either, because it is not ours, but belongs to God. **We must obey and make ourselves saints, not for our interest, but for the glory of God.** So, banish every doubt, since doubt, fear and agitation do not come from God, but from the devil; rather, think of loving and doing the Will of God, because with doubts we displease the Lord much more than if we sinned...

Here and elsewhere, Luisa was intent on reminding people not to dwell on their sins, their past, their weaknesses, or their miseries and doubts; but instead to focus on trusting in and loving Jesus. Accordingly, she criticized refraining from receiving Communion when so refraining was unnecessary:

> On the contrary, I tell you that **when you abstain because of fear, you form firewood for Purgatory, and the Communions you do not receive on earth, you will receive with fire in Purgatory, because Jesus burns with love in the Most Holy Sacrament and wants to come into our hearts in order to pour out His flames** ... Oh, how good is Jesus! If we knew Him, we would die enraptured with love ... the doubt that Jesus does not love us very much, saddens Jesus and embitters Him. Love calls for more love. The more we believe He loves us, the more we feel like loving Him; and Jesus, seeing Himself loved, loves us more. Moreover, **when Jesus feels loved, He forgets our sins—and why would we want to lose our minds in remembering them?** (*Letter #49. To a Mother Superior, Sister Maddalena del Moro, from Santa Chiara, Ravello*). And even if in the past [Jesus] was wounded by this creature, He looks at these wounds, smiles and says: "I have conquered her; she is my victory", and He shows her around to all of Heaven to make feast. (*Letter #132 to Federico Abresch*)

Continuing to encourage the frequent reception of Holy Communion, Luisa wrote the following, in letter #100, to "Francesca":

> **I like to hear that you always receive Communion. Never leave it, either out of disturbance, or distress, or fears**. Nothing which is not peace ever comes from God, but always from our enemy, who gains a lot when he sees us disturbed. And we lose true trust; we lose our arms to take refuge in Jesus. Therefore, in order to become saints, nothing is needed but courage, trust and peace, in order to live in the immense sea of the Divine Will.

Although Jesus lavished spiritual gifts on Luisa and she was made aware of their magnitude, she was always conscious of her littleness and her misery. Therefore, Luisa often concluded her own letters by earnestly beseeching the recipients of them to pray for her, insisting that she sincerely needed their prayers. She no longer needs our prayers, but we can surely benefit from hers. Seek her intercession, and you will not be disappointed!

14. Jesus' Message to Luisa

"Let Your Kingdom come! Let Your Will be done on earth as it is in Heaven!"

If all the developments of Sacred Tradition we covered in Part Two of this book are likened to the prophets of the Old Testament, and all the mystics and revelations we covered in Part Three are like the Epistles of Saint Paul, then the revelations of Jesus to Luisa are like the Gospel itself. Do not misunderstand the analogy—Jesus' words to Luisa are *private*, not public, revelations. Nevertheless, they contain the very message which all of Church history has, step by step, led us towards, and they contain the essence and the supreme exposition of the very theme found across the most important mystical texts and private revelations since the dawn of the 20th Century.

The sheer scale of what we are confronted with, therefore, calls for us to begin with an extremely brief exposition of its entire essence in a few short paragraphs, lest anyone be misled into supposing that these revelations are too daunting to approach, or that they are at least not prepared to do so. For I assure you that, whoever you are, such thoughts are simply temptations and nothing more.

Truly, if you merely read the brief section that follows—both believing and heeding the call of Jesus contained within them—then your entire life can be quickly transformed, and the entire world can also be transformed far sooner than anyone could imagine.

The Message in a Nutshell

Jesus, I Trust in You. Thy Will be Done. I give you my will, please give me Yours in return.

At this unique moment in the history of the world, the fitting time has at long last arrived in which God wishes to give us His Own Will—the Gift that contains every imaginable gift—the true Crown and Completion of all Sanctity both in Heaven and on earth. This Gift entails not only the grace to do God's Will perfectly but also the total immersion of your human will within His Will, so that this Divine Will becomes the life principle of your soul even as your soul is the life principle of your body. It is the holiness enjoyed by Adam and Eve before the Fall, by the Blessed in Heaven, and by the Blessed Virgin herself (though none can ever compare to her).

Within this Gift is all love, invincible joy, and perfect peace. Within it is absolute assurance of salvation. Within it is total deliverance from Purgatory. Within it is God's infinite pleasure. Within it is the complete victory of every noble mission in one simple principle. Within it alone is the full realization of man's creation in the Image *and* Likeness of God. Within it is the Culmination of Deification, the fruitfulness of Mystical Marriage, the aspiration of the Unification of Wills, and the essence of Marian Consecration. Within it is the full Triumph of the Immaculate Heart of Mary.

You cannot earn this Gift or merit it—you can only allow God to give it to you. And in exchange for His Divine Will, He asks only that—*in addition to continuing to do everything you are already doing as a Catholic striving after sanctity*—you lovingly and trustingly relinquish the tiny pebble of your own human self-will. Whoever you are, no matter what, it is easy to allow Him to give His Will to you. Simply say with sincerity: **"Jesus, I Trust in You. Thy Will be Done. I give you my will, please give me Yours in return."**

If you strive to converse with Him continually in this manner, always endeavoring to mean those words more and more deeply each time you recite them, then rest assured that He has given you His Will. Although your journey in the Divine Will has only begun, the victory already permeates your every step.

God also wishes to give this Gift to the whole world as soon as possible. Pray unceasingly, therefore, for the Coming of the Kingdom of the Divine Will, by way of which God's Original Design for the world and for mankind will at last be realized. Pray with the joy and confidence that comes from knowing that the arrival of this reign is a guarantee, for it is nothing other than the fruition of the *Fiat Voluntas Tua* of the Our Father, prayed by Jesus Himself, and thus bearing the absolute certainty of being fulfilled. Its arrival is only a question of time; but you can—and now are called to—hasten the arrival of this time.

Entrust yourself completely to Our Lady, who lived more perfectly in the Divine Will than any other creature ever has or ever will, and she, who loves you—her dear child—will ensure that you Live in the Will of her Son. Especially let her sorrows and the Passion of her Son be always before your mind.

Finally, rejoice always in the invincible and continuous peace that will inevitably inundate the soul of anyone who really believes these truths.

Receive the Gift: The Crown of Sanctity

> "For he has made known to us in all wisdom and insight the mystery of his will, according to his purpose which he set forth in Christ as a plan for the fullness of time, to unite all things in him, things in heaven and things on earth." –Ephesians 1:9-10

While it is true that heeding the few preceding paragraphs can succeed in bringing you into the Divine Will, this is only the first step; as long as we live, we are called ever deeper into the great "mystery of His Will" which St. Paul refers to above. While in this book I can scarcely scratch the surface of the mystery, it is nevertheless time for us to begin this effort. Let us, therefore, get to work in considering what is necessary to strengthen our standing in the Divine Will and increase our growth within it.

We have already covered the theology of the Gift in Part Three; the Gift is spoken of by many 20th-Century mystics and the orthodox understanding of it is identical here. I will not, then, be dedicating much focus in the present chapters to such theological explanations. Instead, if any confusion arises at any point in the following pages, simply turn back to Part Three.

"**The greatest obstacles to holiness are discouragement and an exaggerated anxiety**," Jesus revealed to St. Faustina (*Diary* §1488); therefore, we must understand that the task before us is *not* difficult, much less impossible.

The Ease of Living in the Divine Will

> "'Thy will be done' is the essential prayer of the saint; 'my will be done' is the essential demand of the sinner. C.S. Lewis says that 'there are only two kinds of people, in the end: those who say to God, 'Thy will be done' and those to whom God says, in the end, 'Thy will be done.'' By giving us free will, God says to all of us 'Thy will be done,' but only some of us return to Him this compliment."
>
> –Dr. Peter Kreeft[206]

Luisa knew that the sanctity of Living in the Divine Will was and is the greatest sanctity of all – the greatest holiness even *possible* –

---

[206] Peter Kreeft. *Practical Theology: Spiritual Direction from Saint Thomas Aquinas*. P. 194

but she never hesitated to insist that it was for all people, not just for priests or the consecrated. In her letters, she wrote:

> **Do you see, then, how easy it is?** Nor does one have to be a religious to do this. The Sanctity of living in the Divine Will is for all; or rather, to tell the truth, It is for all those who want It. (Letter #19 to Mrs. Antonietta Savorani) Let us be attentive; **it takes nothing but a firm decision of wanting to live in the Holy Will. It is Jesus who wants it**; He will cover us with His Love, hide us within His Light, and will reach the extent of making up for us in all that we are unable to do. (Letter #74 to Mrs. Caterina Valentino from San Giovanni Rotondo)

St. Faustina would agree. Recall that she insisted it was "very easy" to attain the "highest holiness possible" (which, as we even see in Faustina's own revelations, is none other than the Gift of Living in the Divine Will) so long as we have "a bit of good will." (§291) Even the great mystical doctor, St. John of the Cross, who lived before the Age of the Gift, explained that we mustn't be stingy in estimating just who can attain great holiness. He insists, rather, that any soul who has been found faithful, despite the trials of life, can indeed have his own virtue of charity rendered *perfect* in *this* life. (*The Living Flame of Love.* 1.15.3)

Great heroism and extraordinary deeds may well be God's Will for you at times, but neither is required to Live in the Divine Will. On the contrary, and in a beautiful exposition of the Little Way of Thérèse of Lisieux, Luisa wrote:

> With the most tiny things, with trifles, we can form the little stones to give the Divine Fiat the material to build our sanctity. And for this, one attention, one thought, one word left unsaid, one sigh of desire for the Holy Will, is enough. (Letter #81 to Mother Cecelia) More so, since **the Lord does not teach difficult things. What He wants is precisely the little things**, because they are easier to do, and we cannot find an excuse and say: "I could not do it." The little things are always around us, in our hands; while the great ones come rarely. So, we cannot say that sanctity is not for us. (Letter #120)

A victim soul herself, Luisa did not only do small things. She willingly and repeatedly endured the most extreme sufferings in order to save souls, mitigate the chastisements, and console the Sacred Heart of Jesus. Notwithstanding this heroism, Luisa never demanded or expected it of others, but instead wished only that people know how easy it is to Live in the Divine Will if only we desire it. She wrote:

> Do not think it is difficult to obtain this great good; rather, **it is very easy, as long as you want it with a firm decision to live from the Divine Volition [Will]**, converting everything you do into Divine Will. Don't lose heart because of the difficulties and the circumstances of life; they are steps which make us go higher in the Divine Volition. Especially in painful circumstances, dear Jesus takes us by the hand to make us rise higher and achieve beautiful conquests—not human, but divine and of infinite value. As far as weaknesses, miseries and the like, as long as our will is not there, don't worry ... Everything serves His glory and our good in the divine hands of the Fiat. (Letter #44 to Mrs. Mazari from Bari)

Luisa insisted that we focus entirely on the will, and not allow ourselves to be distracted by a navel-gazing contemplation of our own involuntary imperfections. This wisdom of Luisa's was not an opinion she crafted, but a reality frequently attested to in Jesus's revelations to her. He insists that He makes living in His Will *easy* so long as we want it, even to the point of superabounding with such an outpouring of grace that *sacrifice itself* will only cause happiness in a soul who desires His Will. (9/17/1933) Elsewhere, He promises to hold *nothing* back with those who merely *want* to live in the Divine Will; going so far as to present only two things as being necessary: yearning to live in Him, and then *taking the first step*. (5/6/1938) Anyone, absolutely *anyone*, can do that.

While Jesus wants us to live in His Will more than we could ever want it ourselves, the Virgin Mary also desires nothing more for her children than their reception of the Gift. The very last entry (12/28/1938) in the thousands of pages of Luisa's volumes is dedicated to the Blessed Mother, and in the concluding paragraph, Jesus (Who knew this would be the final teaching of the "Book of Heaven," though Luisa did not!) issues the promise that His Mother will raise, on her own lap, all those who desire to live in the Divine Will, to the point of even *making up for everything* they might lack. Could we possibly have more assurance that this is within reach? That this is for *each and every* one of us? Certainly not. Nothing is more imperative, therefore, than banishing the thought that this holiness is too lofty for us to strive after.

The Meaning of Life

> "To be a saint means ... I will renounce my will, my inclinations, my whims and fancies, and make myself a willing slave to the will of God."–St. Teresa of Calcutta

The degree of our reception of the Gift will stand in proportion to our desire for it. As we have settled the fact that receiving the Gift is easy, the next step is knowing that *the Gift is exactly what you have been looking for your entire life*. In the Gift alone is everything you have ever (licitly) wanted. The Gift, in other words, is the meaning of life. We will see, in the following section, that this is true on account of specific promises Jesus gives us regarding the Gift. But before reviewing those promises, let us consider, more generally, why we know—from Faith and reason—that *the Gift is everything*.

All believers know that our *ultimate end*—that which, above all, we hope for and strive to attain—is Heaven. As St. Augustine, in his most famous quotation from his *Confessions*, rightly observes: "Thou hast made us for Thyself, Lord, and our hearts are restless 'till they rest in Thee." Although Heaven is indeed the "meaning of life" inasmuch as this present life is temporary, and what is most pressing regarding it is that we live in such a way that it leads us to eternal life, it does not follow that Heaven *alone* is the meaning of *this* life. Heaven, by definition, is not a part of this life, therefore it would be simply contradictory to assert that this life's meaning is entirely and only found in what this life cannot ever host. Yet, while this life cannot ever host the *Beatific Vision of* Heaven, it *can* host that which is even more important about the life of Heaven: the accomplishment of God's Will. As Pope Benedict taught:

> Every day in the prayer of the Our Father we ask the Lord: "Thy will be done, on earth as it is in heaven" ... **"heaven" is where the will of God is done, [and] "earth" becomes "heaven"**—i.e., the place of the presence of love, of goodness, of truth and of divine beauty—only if on earth the will of God is done. (General Audience. February 1, 2012)

Heaven is our end, but *that fact about Heaven* which most defines our end can now be lived on earth! Philosophically, this is true because the good of any individual thing always consists in the greatest power of that thing being completely dominated by the corresponding power of a being of a higher nature. For example, the "good," or "end," of any musical instrument is to have its musical potency (its own greatest quality) actualized by an expert musician, with the instrument itself providing no impediment to the musician's skill, but rather beautifully incarnating the same. The greatest good of a plant is for its own fruit (the generation of which is its own greatest power) to be consumed and thus incorporated into the "vegetative" powers of the body of a being of a higher order—a sentient creature (man or animal). The greatest good of an animal (though today only attained by some) is likewise for its own greatest faculty, its sentience, to be totally dominated by the *rational* sentience of a higher order creature: a human being, as is observed in the cases of those animals who are well-trained to serve man.

Similarly, the natural end, or good, of man is likewise to have his own greatest faculty—his rational free will—be totally dominated by the corresponding power of *the* Higher Being: the Divine Will of God. In other words, the natural end of man is not only becoming a saint (it is certainly that), but becoming the *greatest* saint possible by receiving the *Crown* of Sanctity, which is none other than the Gift of Living in the Divine Will.

While no serious arguments exist that the body and its passions (or even the soul's memory) is man's greatest faculty, some insist that it is not the will, but rather the intellect, which holds the supremacy in man. Such people, applying this principle, would falsely conclude that the scholar, not the saint, is the pinnacle of humanity. Granted, the intellect enjoys chronological primacy (as the axiom says, "*nothing can be loved unless it is first known*") and must be obeyed *by* the will (what the intellect discovers to be good or true may *never* be licitly rejected by the free will). However, it is nonetheless clearly the will that is, in relation to its sole proper object (love of God), the greatest power of the soul.[207]

It is the will that especially corresponds to the greatest virtue, charity. (1 Corinthians 13:13). It is the will that *chooses whether* to pursue the good after the intellect informs the will of its discovery regarding *what is* good. It is the will that commands the intellect to

---

[207] Note: although usually regarded as positing the superiority of intellect, St. Thomas Aquinas actually agrees on this point, and he insists that the will *is* superior to the intellect as regards the virtue of love of God. (cf. *Summa Theologica*. First Part. Question 82 Article 3.) What Aquinas does not discuss in this Article is the fact that Christians are called to do *everything* as an act of love of God—and from this it follows that, pragmatically speaking at least, the will is superior to the intellect even under Aquinas' own premises. I am not intending to endorse all of Aquinas' philosophical anthropology here, as addressing that matter is outside of the scope of this book, but for now it will suffice to point out that the type of primacy of will I am speaking of in this chapter *is* reconcilable with a Thomist account of intellect and will.

submit to a known truth after the intellect presents it to the will. As Frank Sheed says, "Salvation depends directly upon the will,"[208] not in the intellect. Another axiom teaches that "the corruption of the greatest is the worst," and from this we can conclude that the will must be the greatest among the soul's powers, since no one denies that its own corruption is the worst fate a soul can possibly suffer (as it is even worse to hate God—that is, for the will's disposition toward Him to be corrupted—than it is to hold errors in one's intellect regarding Him). "**All merit lies in the will**," as Jesus Himself said to St. Faustina (*Diary*, §1760), and as life's mission *consists in meriting for Heaven*, it follows that *all of life lies in the will*. Pope Benedict XVI taught, "**the primacy of will sheds light on the fact that God is charity before all else... 'Eternal life is simply the desire as well as the will to love, blessed and perfect**.'"[209] When the angels announced the Incarnation, they proclaimed, "peace to men of good will," (Luke 2:14) not "men of good intellect." Moreover, that the will is below the intellect in *authority* does not detract from its *ontological* primacy; in God's Providential ordering of the universe, it is rarely the case that the greatest glory is found in what holds the greatest authority.[210]

In a word: our rational free will is our greatest faculty. Within it, therefore, is found our life's meaning. The will's greatest possible privilege consists in its complete domination by the Will of God. As the great Thomist, Fr. Garrigou-Lagrange expressed, "**The best thing that one can do with the best of things is to sacrifice it**." When thus sacrificed to God and dominated by His Will, our will loses not one iota of its own existence; but rather becomes animated by a principle infinitely superior to itself. Through this animation, the destiny of man is fulfilled. I repeat: ***to receive the Gift is the meaning of life.*** So let us spare no expense to receive this Gift. Within it is everything; with it we lack nothing. The wisdom of Pope Benedict XVI quoted earlier must here be reiterated:

> The height of freedom is the 'yes,' in conformity with God's will. It is only in the 'yes' that man truly becomes himself; only in the great openness of the 'yes,' in the unification of his will with the divine ... **It is by transferring the human will to the divine will that the real person is born**...

---

[208] *Theology and Sanity*. 1946. Introduction.

[209] Apostolic Letter. October 28, 2008

[210] For example, the Blessed Virgin is greater than both St. Joseph and the Apostle Peter, though both had authority over her; the mother in the family is the true heart of the same, and within her alone is new life generated, notwithstanding the authority of the father as head; and the greatest saints in the Church's history tend to be the lowliest.

The Fullness of Every Blessing

> "For worldly people, the will of God is often a tragic hardship; for imperfect souls, it is a motive for resignation; for saints, it is heaven... With divine light [the saints] see in the divine will the good of God, which is their own good, and with all the impetuosity of love, with all the vehemence of the Spirit's motion, they give themselves up to that will."
>
> –Servant of God Archbishop Luis Martinez[211]

One may be wondering, *what does the Gift of Living in the Divine Will mean for us concretely?* Jesus obliges that same curiosity in His words to Luisa. In fact, much of the thousands of pages of revelations that constitute her volumes consists in describing the Gift, so any attempt at comprehensively summarizing its virtues here would be impossible. Instead, we will keep this section brief and consider only a few tastes of the glories of the Gift.

Jesus promises Luisa that within the Gift, our complete happiness is assured (5/7/1933, 9/21/1931), and that darkness, ugliness, and sin will end in our lives (10/19/1926). He promises that within it is such spiritual strength that no burden can trouble us, and that even suffering becomes easy (7/30/1929).

He promises that with it—and with it alone—can we build up as many treasures in Heaven as possible, (6/8/1931) and thus glorify and adorn our eternal home—for ourselves and for everyone—infinitely more than by any other means. He promises that within it alone are these built-up treasures in Heaven truly invincible and incapable of being lost, no matter what may transpire in our temporal lives after their attainment (3/19/1933). He promises to keep track of and reward *superabundantly* even the smallest acts we undertake with the Gift (3/28/1917).

Jesus promises that, so long as we receive the Gift, our salvation itself is given an invincible anchor, and that even if we have only lived in His Will for a moment on earth, we cannot be lost eternally (4/16/1931).[212] Jesus even promises that, if one were to die after *just*

---

[211] *The Sanctifier*. Chapter XVI

[212] Note: This should not be understood in a Calvinistic way that would render works, conversion, repentance, etc., irrelevant to salvation. Rather, it should be understood like all other promises of salvation in private revelation (e.g., the Brown Scapular, the Nine First Friday devotion) are understood: that is, it should be understood as promising sufficient grace to—should one be so unfortunate to fall into mortal sin in the future—repent before death.

one act done with the Gift—that is, *in His Will*—he would be immediately admitted into Heaven without the need for any time in Purgatory (10/27/1935).

He grants us the grace to transform our past with the Gift—not, of course, altering objective events of the past (a logical absurdity and impossibility)—but by repairing their relation to eternity and allowing them to be spiritually "re-done" (11/3/1936).

With the Gift, Jesus repeatedly promises to turn us into another Jesus, so that our mere presence becomes a Divine encounter for the world (not, of course, because we are ourselves Divine with the Gift, but only on account of the graces received along with it), and that by merely walking, we can transmit superabundant Divine Grace to those we encounter (2/10/1924).

> "[Uniformity with the Divine Will] is the beautiful freedom of the sons of God, and it is worth vastly more than … all the kingdoms in the world. This is the abiding peace which, in the experience of the saints, 'surpasseth all understanding.' ... By uniting themselves to the divine will, the saints have enjoyed paradise by anticipation in this life. ... Our Lord assured his apostles: 'Your joy no man shall take from you ... Your joy shall be full.' He who unites his will to God's experiences a full and lasting joy … since no one can prevent what God wills from happening."
> -St. Alphonsus Liguori

Now that, I hope, all earnestly desire this Gift, let us delve more deeply into what is involved with its reception. To desire the Gift is to desire to live in God. But to want a will other than one's own to *reign* in one's life is to *renounce* one's self-will.[213] This renunciation—also called abnegation, abandonment, or surrender—is what we must consider next.

---

[213] Contrary to the heresy of Quietism (discussed later in the Appendices), Jesus is absolutely not asking for our will or its acts to be extinguished or rendered merely passive. In fact, Luisa's revelations specifically repudiate this notion, and insist that Jesus wants our wills *little* (3/26/1933), that our acts are *embellished* in His Will—not destroyed (9/16/1931), and finally that two wills cannot *reign* in one soul (not that they cannot both *exist*!).

15. Renounce the Self-Will

"The last words of Mary that were spoken in Sacred Scripture were the words of total abandonment to the will of God. 'Whatsoever He shall say to you, that do ye.' As Dante said: 'In His will is our peace.' Love has no other destiny than to obey Christ. Our wills are ours only to give away... the power of filling belongs only to God. Hence all perfect love must end on the note: 'Not my will, but Thine be done, O Lord!'"
–Venerable Archbishop Fulton Sheen.[214]

The renunciation of the self-will necessary for receiving the Gift of Living in the Divine Will is the same renunciation that has always been taught by the spiritual masters. To this end, I recommend the works of St. Francis de Sales, Fr. Caussade, St. Alphonsus Liguori, and St. Thérèse of Lisieux – some of whose teachings are relayed in Part Two of this book. One will be well prepared to receive the Gift by reading not only the quotes included in those chapters, but also the entire works they are taken from (especially Alphonsus' *Uniformity With God's Will*, de Sales' *Treatise on the Love of God*, Caussade's *Abandonment to Divine Providence*, and Thérèse's *Story of a Soul*).

> "**As for self-will, we are forbidden to do our own will.**" –The Rule of St. Benedict. Chapter 7

Since renunciation consists in preferring God's Will to our own, and God's Will is specific to each person's life, this virtue will entail different things for different people. The *fundamentals* of renunciation, however, are identical for all souls, and it would be wrong for us to fail to begin by considering these fundamentals here. Three primary dimensions to renunciation exist that apply equally to everyone alive.

> "For immediately that thou hast given thyself unto God with all thine heart, and hast sought neither this nor that according to thine own will and pleasure, but hast altogether settled thyself in Him, thou shalt find thyself united and at peace; because nothing shall give thee so sweet relish and delight, as the good pleasure of the Divine will. ... Wish always and pray that the will of God be fulfilled in thee. Behold, such a man as this entereth into the

[214] *Go to Heaven. A Spiritual Road Map to Eternity*. Chapter 8.

inheritance of peace and quietness." -*The Imitation of Christ*. Ch. 15 §3, Ch. 23. §3

Three Preliminary Necessities

> "The love story between God and man consists in the very fact that this communion of will increases in a communion of thought and sentiment, and thus our will and God's Will increasingly coincide: God's Will is no longer for me an alien will, something imposed on me from without by the commandments, but it is now my own will based on the realization that God is in fact more deeply present to me than I am to myself."
>
> –Pope Benedict XVI, *Deus Caritas Est* §17

First, we must believe and heed the truths of the Faith both with conviction and supernatural certainty. And the truth is this: There is a God. This God became a man, Jesus Christ. This Jesus founded a Church on Peter alone (cf. Matthew 16:18), to whom He gave authority and keys—keys that have been handed down continuously for 2,000 years to Peter's current successor. Church teaching must *always* be submitted to. If ever confusion arises as to *what* the Church teaches, then abide by the teaching that is clearer. Magisterium cannot contradict Magisterium, and clarity enjoys superiority to ambiguity in Faith and Morals; mere recentness, however, has no special status over age. Pragmatically speaking, we will most effectively achieve this by believing and heeding every single word of the Catechism. There is a reason God decreed that the secretary of His Will (Luisa) lived more subserviently to the authority of the Catholic Church than any other soul in history—incapable of even *moving her body* without the Church's daily intervention. So do not suppose that one can reject a single teaching of the Church and still be prepared to sufficiently renounce the self-will to Live in the Divine Will; that will never happen. Remember that Faith begins as an act of the will; you needn't "feel" like any given Church teaching is true to nevertheless have Faith. You need only command your intellect to submit, and this you can do in full confidence regardless of your feelings, since—in accordance with Christ's direct promise to the Church—it is impossible for Church Teaching to be in error.

Second, we must strive to be rid of all sin. To live a sinful life is to oppose the Divine Will, and it is impossible to live in His Will if we explicitly oppose it through deliberate lifestyles of sin. We must, therefore, examine our consciences carefully. In the Gospel, Jesus' first admonition upon the initiation of His public ministry was simple: "**Repent**, for the Kingdom of Heaven is at hand." (Matthew 4:17) He says the same to us today with even more emphasis, as the total earthly fulfillment of that Kingdom He preached 2,000 years ago is now upon us with immediacy. I cannot include within the pages of this book a lengthy treatment of ridding one's life of sin, but I encourage you to find a good, detailed, traditional, rigorous, and orthodox "Examination of Conscience" (many helpful ones can be found online), prayerfully consider it, and frequent the Sacrament of Confession in accordance with the Holy Spirit's illumination in your soul while doing so. These first two preliminaries can be summarized in seven words: *remain always in a state of grace*. Whatever contradicts such a state must immediately go. Whatever grave sin you are clinging to now—no matter how attached to it you may be, no matter how much you think you cannot live without it, and no matter how much you fear the consequences of being rid of it—is not worth clinging to *one moment* longer. Even if they masquerade as wings, these sins are only chains that bind you, and only your free will (cooperating, of course, with God's grace) can break them.

Third, we must desire and pursue sanctity above all other things. The Gift of Living in the Divine Will is the *Crown* of Sanctity, not a substitution for sanctity. It therefore presupposes the pursuit of "ordinary" sanctity with all the vigor of our ancestors in the Faith. St. Hannibal, the greatest apostle of the Divine Will, insisted upon this foundation, writing: "With [the Gift of Living in the Divine Will,] in order to form Saints who surpass the ones of the past, it is important that the new Saints **possess all the virtues to a heroic degree, just as did the Saints of old**." Pursuing the Gift without "ordinary" sanctity would be like approaching the Sacrament of Holy Matrimony without pursuing what Christian Matrimony holds in common with all marriage: two spouses who love each other, know each other, help each other, etc. Just as good Christian spouses do not forget these virtues of marriage even while focusing on the sacramental dimension of their matrimony, so too one who pursues the Gift must remain just as anchored in—or, rather, *even more* anchored in—ordinary Christian sanctification than those who are unaware of the Gift. Therefore, as we considered some aspects of the glory of the Gift itself in the preceding section, we should now remind ourselves of the glory of Christian sanctification in general, so that we may always desire both it and its crown above all else on this earth.

> **One thing I ask of the Lord, this alone I seek; that I may dwell in the house of the Lord all the days of my life...** (Psalm 27:4)

Love Sanctity Above All Things

> "... all the faithful, whatever their condition or state, are called by the Lord, each in his own way, to that perfect holiness whereby the Father Himself is perfect."
> –*Lumen Gentium.* Dogmatic Constitution on the Church.

Jesus Himself said, "Be perfect, as your heavenly Father is perfect." (Matthew 5:48) Satisfaction with just being a "decent Catholic" never sufficed at any point in the history of the Church, but at this moment it is more impossible than ever to pretend that it could be enough. The "Universal Call to Holiness" has now been expressed in the writings of so many saints as to be an indisputably infallible component of the *Sensus Fidelium*, and has even been elevated to the status of a Magisterial teaching of an Ecumenical Council (Vatican II).

This is not some drab duty foisted upon us by a demanding boss; it is a joyful invitation from those who have succeeded in living life to the fullest, to those of us who have contented ourselves with a life lived in the middle. We must accept it! If only we dedicate ourselves to becoming saints, *everything* else is automatically taken care of. "**There is only one tragedy, ultimately: not to have been a saint**." (Leon Bloy. Quoted in the Apostolic Exhortation, *Gaudete et Exsultate*)

Many things are hard: acquiring advanced degrees, making large sums of money, gaining recognition for ourselves, trying to make people like us, securing our legacy, striving to guarantee our safety and security, acquiring and maintaining possessions, looking for promotions and new jobs, seeking to order all things to our comfort and pleasure, and oh how much we pour ourselves out in the pursuit of all this vanity which seems so pressing and direly important now, and yet the next day is barely even a memory. But avoiding *the only tragedy*—acquiring a veritable invincibility—is comparatively easy. Acquire it! Desire *sanctity* above all else. To do otherwise would be to climb out on a long, feeble, shaky limb in pursuit of a meager copper coin when a shining gold ingot sits directly above you, easily within reach. If only we considered the fact that Judgment Day is speeding towards us like a freight train, we would have no confusion. For on the Day of Judgment, you shall not regret missing out on that copper coin.

> **Indeed I count everything as loss because of the surpassing worth of knowing Christ Jesus my Lord. For his sake I have suffered the loss of all things, and count them as refuse, in order that I may gain Christ.** (Philippians 3:8)

When you find yourself in eternity with Christ and all the saints, the breadth of your joy, your glory, and your closeness to God is no accident: it is decided by, and indeed proceeds from, the holiness you attain to *here and now*. Your last breath, which will in a moment be upon you, coincides with your absolute last chance to acquire any merit for Heaven, wherein no new conquests are made. In building a house, how zealously does one attend to the details of its construction to ensure it is tailored to his needs for the short few decades he will reside in it? And yet, the holiness you will enjoy in Heaven will *never end.* There, the love you now expand your soul to accommodate will be the food you eat, the water you drink, and the splendor of the Kingdom you find yourself in. There, the degree of union with God you *now* arrive at will be the garment you wear forever. "*There*" might be "*here*" for you in a decade, a year, a month, a day, or a minute. There is no time to waste.

> **The kingdom of heaven is like a merchant in search of fine pearls, who, on finding one pearl of great value, went and sold all that he had and bought it**. (Matthew 13:45-46)

Spare no expense. Go all in. Burn any bridge that leads only away from God. Hold nothing back. Put all your eggs in one basket; the only invincible basket: "**Lay up for yourselves treasures in heaven,** where neither moth nor rust consumes and where thieves do not break in and steal." (Matthew 6:20) In this life, you must never allow your focus on sanctity to be distracted for a moment. Desire it always and above all; pursue it always and above all. Living thus will not only bestow enormous blessings on its own account, but will also anchor and advance you in the Gift of Living in the Divine Will.

***

With this desire for sanctity inflamed in our hearts, we can again focus on the renunciation needed for the Gift before formally asking for it.

Renunciation in Crosses

> "If any man would come after me, let him deny himself and take up his cross and follow me." –Matthew 16:24

Renunciation is incredibly simple. It consists in saying, "**Thy will, not mine, be done**" (Matthew 26:39), *and actually meaning it*. One may protest that this appears superficial. It is not.

> **By your words you will be justified, and by your words you**

> **will be condemned**. (Matthew 12:37)

To be sure, our words must be confirmed by works. Thus the necessity of *meaning* what we say when we repeat Our Lord's own prayer in the Garden that the Will of the Father be done. But all of this begins with saying it—time and time again—and always striving to mean it more and more. We are *speaking* creatures, therefore it is especially in our words that spiritual realities are rendered incarnate.

> Death and life are in the power of the tongue, and those who love it will eat its fruits. (Proverbs 18:21)

Do not, therefore, ever fail to constantly repeat these most blessed words on account of scruples that what you are doing is "superficial." Instead, repeat them always, and doing so will help you to *form* all your thoughts and deeds in accordance with the infinite value contained in them. These words are not temporal; spoken by Christ Himself, and serving as the supreme model of our own petition, they contain eternal value:

> Heaven and earth will pass away, but my words will not pass away. (Matthew 24:35)

It is sometimes said that renunciation is only a virtue for those occasions wherein God clearly wills something for us that our nature reviles, but this limitation is mistaken. As we will see in more detail in a later section, Jesus desires that we *continually* hand over our self-wills to Him, regardless of whether doing so appears to us in any given moment to be easy or difficult. The value exists in the love with which we hand over our wills to Him, not in the degree of pain that doing so entails.

Nevertheless, most of us will only advance rapidly in this virtue when we say "God's Will be done" even in something difficult. We should, therefore, now consider the virtue of renunciation in relation to the acceptance of crosses. As all who have read thus far are likely already convinced of and dedicated to the need for sanctity, a cross that is especially important to accept—and what we should consider first—is a cross which, although willed by God, might *appear* at odds with sanctity itself. About such cases, St. Alphonsus instructs:

> Pious souls often fail in this respect by not being resigned to the dispositions of God's holy will. Our sanctification comes fundamentally and essentially from God, not from spiritual directors ... we should receive [with gratitude] whatever crosses God sends us ... "In this life," as St. Teresa used to say, "our lot is not to enjoy God, but to do his holy will." (*Uniformity With God's Will*. Ch. 6)

We mustn't cling to what we "piously" want when circumstances outside of our control have revealed His Will to be otherwise. Instead, in response to anything whatsoever happening in our life that is contrary to our own desires—even holy ones—we must render the words of Job our own second nature, ***"The Lord giveth and the Lord taketh away, blessed be the name of the Lord."***

Expanding our consideration, there is no use protesting that you are within your rights to complain about something on account of your supposition that God did not Will what happened. *If it happened, He did Will it*—whether by virtue of His ordained Will or His permissive Will bears no relevance to the fact that we must resign ourselves. Uncertainty regarding God's Will can only apply to the future, never the past.

> **The workings that befall you receive as good, knowing that apart from God nothing comes to pass.** (*The Didache.* Ch. 3)

Someone else may say, *"but I now find myself in this terrible situation that is a result of my own sinfulness and foolishness, therefore I must lament; to resign myself would be to condone the sin and folly."* This notion, too, is entirely mistaken. Granted, God did not affirmatively will your sin; but He did choose to *allow* it in order to bring about a greater good. Simply repent of it and proceed to trust—blindly and absolutely—that the circumstances which are *now* outside of your control are God's Will for you. "Go and sin no more," (John 8:11), and understand that sin is, in essence, rebellion against God's Will. Do not therefore, heap guilt upon guilt by worrying.

Still another will say, *"but it is possible for this situation to change, so I should not resign to God's Will in it, lest I be guilty of fatalism."* But even this response is itself no less deceived. God's Will is the most active principle that can exist. It is never suspended for a moment, therefore we needn't ever wait for some future victory to find its presence in our lives. We must fight, indeed, for all that we know to be God's Will in the world. But God's Will can—and must—*always* reign in our souls. It must do so even before its reign is actualized outside of us. God has no need for busybody activists who suppose they can advance His causes without being united to Him.

A related concern is that too much renunciation would lead to a sort of weakness masquerading as the virtue of submission to God's Will; a posture of defeatism wherein we give up on our goals once we meet obstacles, supposing that these obstacles "reveal that the goal was not God's Will." This is certainly a legitimate point, as defeats in battles are necessary for victory in war. But the way to avoid this trap is clear: always fight for everything in proportion to—and only in proportion to—the degree of your conviction that the battle is God's Will. When *certain* that some objective is God's Will (as we can be when it comes to, for example, keeping the Commandments, keeping the Faith, staying true to valid vows, and pursuing those things which God has clearly revealed to us personally as being His Will for us), then we must continue to fight for it with every ounce of our strength *no matter what*. In these cases, death would be preferable to defeat. But when we are pursuing some objectively good path which might or might not be God's Will for us and we lack a strong, interior, Spirit-led conviction on the matter, then we must remain aware of the possibility of God's Will being revealed to us, through circumstances, as leading us along some other path. If and when His Will is revealed to us as following another path, then we should not rebel against His guidance, but happily tread it by following the *Fruits* (of the Spirit, that is; a task we will consider next chapter). We can find joy in knowing that everything He has already allowed in our lives was part of a perfect plan, and therefore we must not dwell even one moment on regrets, no matter how lengthily or arduously we walked a path that is no longer His Will for us.

In sum, it is insufficient to only strive to ensure that we are doing good things and are not committing explicit sins, even while living a life primarily dedicated to pursuing and satiating, instead of renouncing, the self-will. Many who might appear virtuous externally, and who seem rather absorbed in objectively good deeds with their lives, will be revealed on Judgment Day to have been driven by nothing but self-interest.

Resignation to God's Will—without which any real sanctity is impossible—is far above this miserly, self-interested approach. Jesus, Who asks us to imitate Himself, did not merely accept the cross upon the Father saying that failing to do so would be sin; rather, Jesus loved the cross, and even tells Luisa that He *rejoiced* upon seeing it presented to Him (7/27/1906). Similarly, a soul in Purgatory once told Luisa that it is easy to know how we are faring in the spiritual life—that we are *only* doing well if we appreciate suffering (1/30/1909)—that is, if we resign ourselves lovingly and willingly to whatever God sends us. And if it—whatever "it" is—is outside our *reasonable* control, then it must be regarded as coming from His hands.

Clearly, love of the cross does not mean physically enjoying pain—that would be a logical contradiction, or at least a twisted and sadistic psychological state (neither of which God asks of us!). Love is an act of the will, not a feeling, and as such, love of the cross is a virtue we can exercise no matter what feelings may exist in our nature upon receiving a cross. Our wills, therefore, should be *trained* in this regard. To be sure, the most important thing here remains to lovingly accept whatever crosses God sends, but it is also important for us to engage in "mortifications" regularly—though with moderation, prudence, and hiddenness. It is not likely we will rise above the self-will if we never make deliberate efforts to deprive it of those things which the human self-will universally tends towards: comfort, pleasure, satisfaction, praise, etc. Therefore, fasting, sacrifice, almsgiving, "extra" prayers, kneeling long and often, depriving ourselves of what we are "in the mood for" or are suddenly craving, choosing the less comfortable or pleasurable of multiple options presented to us, etc., should be regular parts of our spiritual lives.

And while it is true that these efforts and others like them will help us to, as St. Faustina said, "cancel out the self-will" and facilitate our entry into the Divine Will, we mustn't approach them like a self-help program, as if they are merely "spiritual push-ups." We must approach them, rather, with a pure and sincere love of Jesus and a focus on what can be accomplished *through* these things by offering them all up for the conversion of sinners, the salvation and sanctification of souls, the deliverance of the holy souls in Purgatory, the consolation of the Sacred and Immaculate Hearts, the mitigation of the chastisements, and the hastening of the coming of the Kingdom on earth.

All this we can and should do, regardless of how we feel. It is a matter of will, and will is especially rendered incarnate in words, so let us now return to what we began this section with: the need to say, in all things, "*Thy Will, not mine, be done.*"

Instead of leaving this to platitude, however, we should consider some specific examples.

A Renunciation Examen

> "It is certain and of faith that, whatever happens, happens by the Will of God."–St. Alphonsus Liguori.[215]

When something in our own life or in the world goes contrary to our plans—perhaps a sickness, a failure, or a loss—do we complain to God by asking Him, in an accusatory tone, "*Why*?" Jesus tells Luisa that this type of "why?" was created in Hell, first pronounced by a

215 *Uniformity With God's Will*. Ch. 2

demon, and caused the Fall itself (1/20/1909). It is simply not possible to complain by saying "why me!?" while at the same time being in His Will.

When we experience even superficial and small pains, what is our immediate reaction? Upon a bump to the head or after stubbing the toe, does a curse—or any other vain, needless exclamation—immediately exit our mouth, or do we instead immediately offer up this pain (knowing it is a gift)? We must develop a habit of immediate gratitude in response to pain, not immediate exasperation; even so in life's small pains, irritations, temptations, disappointments, etc. First of all, these "small" matters constitute most of life's crosses. Neglecting to approach them rightly will soon have one neglecting to approach *life* rightly. Secondly, Jesus tells Luisa that He is only concerned with the degree of love in our acts, not with the exterior magnitude they seem to carry. Thirdly, our reactions to the small burdens and crosses prepare us to react rightly to the larger ones, which we must consider next.

In life's great tragedies—the death of a loved one or one's own death approaching, being in dire straits financially, the loss of an entire career, betrayal by a close friend or relative, agonizing physical or psychological pains, etc.—do we remain faithful to God and trusting in His plan? Or do we willfully entertain doubts about His goodness and love for us? We are not entitled to a certain period of rebellion against God's Will before submitting to it. Human beings are not balloons, and unruly passions are not quieted by being "vented." We must set our faces like flint, right now, to fall on our knees and with outstretched arms bless God, crying out from the depths of our hearts, "Thy Will be done!" *the very moment* life's next great tragedy comes our way.

In our resignation, do we more resemble Veronica or Simon on the Way of the Cross? Simon's sacrifice, in physical terms, was so much greater than Veronica's. On his own shoulders, he carried so heavy a cross and did so amid horrendous persecution by the crowds and the soldiers. Yet, all Veronica did was hand Jesus a simple cloth and wipe His face. Of the two, Veronica is far more exalted, and one "Veronica" does for God what a thousand "Simons" do not. Our resignation must be like hers—spontaneous and loving (not forced and reluctant), and its value will accordingly be multiplied a thousandfold.

Let us conclude this chapter on Renunciation with a powerful teaching from Venerable Archbishop Fulton Sheen. Resignation and renunciation can be seen as forms of *obedience* to the Divine Will; as such, the holy prelate taught the following:

> Obedience does not mean the execution of orders that are given by a drill sergeant. It springs, rather, from the love of an order, and love of Him who gave it. **The merit of obedience is less in the act than in the love...** Obedience is servility only to those who have not understood the spontaneity of love. Our Lord spent three hours in redeeming, three years in teaching, and thirty years in obeying, in order that a rebellious, proud, and diabolically independent world might learn the value of obedience ... We must do everything within our power to fulfill God's will as it is made known to us by His Mystical Body [Church Teaching], the Commandments and our lawfully constituted superiors, and the duties flowing from our state in life. **Everything that is outside our power, we must abandon and surrender to His Holy Will** ... **God could have prevented any [painful] things ... If He did not, it was for a superior reason. Therefore, say: "God's will be done." ... Every moment comes to you pregnant with a divine purpose**; time being so precious that God deals it out only second by second. Once it leaves your hands and your power to do with it as you please, it plunges into eternity, to remain forever whatever you made it ... surrender yourself to God, and all is yours ... **Cease talking about your pains and aches. Thank God for them ... If you trust in God and surrender to His will, you are always happy**, for "to them that love God, all things work together unto good" (Rom 8:28) ... What matters is not what we are, or what we are doing, but whether we are doing God's will! ... **Rejoice! I say again, rejoice: "Thy will be done on earth as it is in heaven."** (*Go to Heaven*. Chapter 8)

***

Once we desire the Gift of God's Will and have renounced the self-will, we are prepared to formally ask that the Divine Will be made our own. Doubtless, much growth will remain necessary in our lives (and we will cover some aspects of that in the forthcoming "Grow in the Virtues" section), but this growth is necessary as a *co*requisite, not a *pre*requisite, to asking for the Gift of Living in the Divine Will. Please, do not wait until you feel you are perfect to ask for the Gift! Ask *now*.

16. Receive the Gift: Ask and Grow

"Your Father knows what you need before you ask him."
–Matthew 6:8

Asking for the Gift of Living in the Divine Will is as simple as it sounds. There are no magical formulas to be memorized or Gnostic secrets into which one need be initiated. Have we perhaps forgotten that God hears each thing we say, every moment of every day? That He is ever closer to us than our own skin? No special strategies are needed to "reach Him." He is right next to you. Like a child, simply ask Him for what you desire. Jesus lamented to Luisa that there are so many gifts He wants to give us, but because they are not asked for, He holds on to them and waits for someone to ask (3/20/1932). *Just ask!* And be not ashamed if you can sympathize with the Little Flower's sentiments here expressed:

> I have not the courage to look through books for beautiful prayers. I only get a headache because of their number, and besides, one is more lovely than another. Unable therefore to say them all, and lost in choice, I do as children who have not learnt to read – I simply tell Our Lord all that I want, and He always understands. With me prayer is an uplifting of the heart; a glance towards heaven; a cry of gratitude and love, uttered equally in sorrow and in joy. In a word, it is something noble, supernatural, which expands my soul and unites it to God. Sometimes when I am in such a state of spiritual dryness that not a single good thought occurs to me, I say very slowly the "Our Father" or the "Hail Mary," and these prayers suffice to take me out of myself, and wonderfully refresh me. (St. Thérèse of Lisieux)

What matters is not so much *how* you ask, but *that* you ask. What matters is that you do not allow yourself to *forget* to ask. What matters is that you ask *continuously*. Say, as much as you possibly can, "**Jesus, I Trust in You. Thy Will be done. I give you my will, please give me Yours in return.**"

Now, despite how truly simple this matter is, formal vocal prayers can here (as everywhere) be a great help, and these are certainly not lacking in asking for the Gift. I will only share a few here, but there are many beautiful Divine Will prayers to be found.

A prayer for each morning. (A "Prevenient Act"):

> Good morning, Blessed Mother, I love you. Come, help me to offer my first act of the day as an act of love in the Divine Will of

God. Most Holy Trinity, I thank and praise You for this new day. Setting my will in Yours, I affirm I want only to live and act in Your Will, and I set all of my acts of the day in order in You. O Jesus, through, with, and in the Immaculate Heart of Mary, I consecrate and give my will to You in exchange for Your Divine Will. I truly want Your Divine Will to generate Its Divine Life in me this day—to think in all my thoughts, to speak in all my words, and to operate in all my actions for the glory of our Heavenly Father and to fulfill the purpose of Creation. Abandoned in Your arms, my Jesus, I invite all the angels and saints, especially Mary Most Holy, to join in all the Divine Will does in me today, and I am confident that You will not fail to give me the grace to be always faithful and attentive to Your action within me so that my own will dare not interfere with Your freedom to form Your Real Life in me. O my Jesus, I love You with Your own Will and thank You profoundly for the knowledge and Gift of the Divine Will. Amen.

Prayer of Consecration to the Divine Will *(Composed by Luisa at the request of St. Hannibal):*

O adorable and Divine Will, here I am, before the immensity of Your Light, that Your eternal Goodness may open to me the doors, and make me enter into It, to form my life all in You, Divine Will. Therefore, prostrate before Your Light, I, the littlest among all creatures, come, O adorable Will, into the little group of the first children of Your Supreme Fiat. Prostrate in my nothingness, I beseech and implore Your endless Light, that It may invest me and eclipse everything that does not belong to You, in such a way that I may do nothing other than look, comprehend and live in You, Divine Will. It will be my life, the center of my intelligence, the enrapturer of my heart and of my whole being. In this heart the human will will no longer have life; I will banish it forever, and will form the new Eden of peace, of happiness and of love. With It I shall always be happy, I shall have a unique strength, and a sanctity that sanctifies everything and brings everything to God. Here prostrate, I invoke the help of the Sacrosanct Trinity, that They admit me to live in the cloister of the Divine Will, so as to restore in me the original order of Creation, just as the creature was created. Celestial Mother, Sovereign Queen of the Divine Fiat, take me by the hand and enclose me in the Light of the Divine Will. You will be my guide, my tender Mother; you will guard your child, and will teach me to live and to maintain myself in the order and in the bounds of the Divine Will. Celestial Sovereign, to your Heart I entrust my whole being;

I will be the tiny little child of the Divine Will. You will teach me the Divine Will, and I will be attentive in listening to you. You will lay your blue mantle over me, so that the infernal serpent may not dare to penetrate into this Sacred Eden to entice me and make me fall into the maze of the human will. Heart of my highest Good, Jesus, You will give me Your flames, that they may burn me, consume me and nourish me, to form in me the life of the Supreme Will. Saint Joseph, you will be my Protector, the Guardian of my heart, and will keep the keys of my will in your hands. You will keep my heart jealously, and will never give it to me again, that I may be sure never to go out of the Will of God. Guardian Angel, guard me, defend me, help me in everything, so that my Eden may grow flourishing, and be the call of the whole world into the Will of God. Celestial Court, come to my help, and I promise you to live always in the Divine Will. Amen.

Prayer before receiving Communion: "Lord, remove my self-will, and give me Thine in return; that You may receive Yourself in me, and receive perfect and infinite consolation."

Divine Will Missionaries of Mercy prayer. Another means of asking for the Gift of Living in the Divine Will is by way of various apostolates, such as the Divine Will Missionaries of Mercy, wherein we seek the Divine Will in order to proclaim the Divine Mercy. Consider how readily God dispenses grace to those whom He knows will put it at the service of others. When Jesus healed Peter's mother-in-law, she arose to wait on them (Luke 4:39). When He "called to him his twelve disciples and gave them authority," He did so immediately before sending them out, and in order to grant their ministry success (Luke 9:1-2). When He bestowed His Spirit by "breathing upon them," it was to allow them to forgive the sins of others. (John 20:22-23) This is the approach of the Divine Will Missionaries of Mercy:[216] to take the grace received through the Eucharist out into the world and onto the streets after Mass, by way of the Gift of Living in the Divine Will, while wearing a Divine Mercy Image for all to see, praying the Rosary and the Divine Mercy Chaplet, and remaining open to whatever encounters the Holy Spirit may Will to arrange; all an integral part of this apostolate to bring Jesus to others.

Our Lady of the Visitation is the example par excellence of this approach; for she not only lived fully in the Divine Will, but she also, and without any hesitation, took Jesus' Real Presence in her own womb to others. Our Lady tells Luisa that she did this not merely to pay a visit, but because her Immaculate Heart was ablaze with desire

[216] www.DWMoM.org

to bring Jesus to souls.[217] Pope Benedict XVI went so far as to teach that the Visitation was the "**first Eucharistic Procession in history**."[218] Indeed, Living in the Divine Will is not a dispensation from the Christian Mission of proclaiming Christ's Mercy to the world, but is rather an even more powerful demand to engage in it. Luisa herself was shown the faithful being *divinized* by the revelations of Jesus on the Divine Will, enabling them to communicate grace to those around them—*even just by walking*—and furthermore contributing to the full triumph of the Church by doing so! (2/10/1924)

Before setting out, whoever wishes to act as a Divine Will Missionary of Mercy says the following prayer after Mass. I believe it is a powerful means of asking God for the Gift, and it can be modified and adapted to whatever endeavor one undertakes following Mass.

> Most Holy Trinity, You Who now dwell inside my body in all of Your Divinity, nothing is beyond Your power. Therefore I come before You and say *Fiat Voluntas Tua*. I renounce my self-will, and instead promise and desire to do and live in only Your Will. Please preserve the Real Presence of Jesus in the Eucharist within me, so that You may make of me a living Monstrance, that my walk today may be a true Procession through this city's streets. Make of me a Living Host, that all who see me truly gaze upon Your face, and grant me the Gift of Living in the Divine Will, so that Jesus may walk in my walking, speak in my speaking, pray in my praying, and indeed substitute His Divine and Eternal operations for all of my acts, and through me re-do all of the acts of Creation, past, present, and future—in the Will of God, offering them back to the Father with the seal of my Fiat, which I pray may become an echo of Jesus and Mary's perfect Fiat. Dear Jesus, let all of my sufferings serve as atonement for my sins and those of the whole world, and be fused with Yours in Your Passion and console Your Sacred Heart. Let all who see me that lack Faith be as Longinus, and acknowledge You are the Son of God. Let all who see me that lack works be as Dismas, and receive the grace of perfect contrition, hope, and trust. Let all who see me that live in sin be as Magdalene, and amend their ways. Let all who see me that suffer from wounds of spirit be healed of them, and in place of any darkness or despair, be filled with peace and joy, as You preached the good news to the poor. Let all who see the image of Your Mercy that I wear venerate it and therefore receive

[217] Cf. *The Queen of Heaven in the Kingdom of the Divine Will*. Day 20. (Note: These revelations are from the year 1937, but they are essentially additions to the work revealed earlier to Luisa, *The Blessed Virgin Mary in the Kingdom of the Divine Will*)

[218] Address at the Grotto of Our Lady of Lourdes in the Vatican. May 31, 2005.

the promise You entrusted to Faustina, so they may not perish. Let all who see the weapon of Your Mother that I carry receive grace through her intercession, that she may crush the head of the serpent in their lives. Do not restrict these graces to only those few who see me, but let them be extended in the Divine Will to all the friends and family of these, and continue in this manner until they reach the furthest ends of Earth, Heaven, and Purgatory; past, present, and future. I firmly trust and believe that You can do all these things, for I ask them in the name of the Father, and of the Son, and of the Holy Spirit. Amen.

Ask for the Gift in your current spiritual regimen. We mustn't neglect how God has hitherto worked in our lives, for His Will is not to supplant and replace the spiritual practices we have thus far developed as devout Catholics, but rather to build upon them. This said, a key to asking for the Gift will be learning how to integrate it into your current spiritual regimen. Before each ordinary prayer of your day (whether it be the Rosary, Divine Mercy Chaplet, Divine Office, Holy Mass, *Lectio Divina,* or whatever else) you can simply let your intention be known to God that you desire to pray in the Divine Will. For example, your Rosary could begin with, "*In the name of the Father, and of the Son, and of the Holy Spirit. Amen. In the Divine Will, I pray: I believe in God...*" Proceed, then, as you ordinarily would, striving to "practice the presence of God" and pray as if it is truly Jesus Who is praying in you—which is precisely what He promises to those who live in His Will.

Likewise, in the minutes after you receive Holy Communion, beseech Jesus in the Eucharist within you to make the Transubstantiation of the Host you consumed effect the Transconsecration of your very self. Meditate upon the substance inside you—the Real Presence of Jesus—transforming you into Himself, with the accidents of bread and wine, which dissolve, being taken over by your own acts in the Divine Will, which remain. Repeat, with St. Anthony Mary Claret (one of the Patrons of the Divine Will Missionaries of Mercy), "*Lord, by the words of consecration the substance of the bread and wine is converted into the substance of your Body and Blood. All powerful Lord, say over me the word which will change me into You.*"

Ask again if you lose the Gift. Sin—and, more generally, deliberately choosing the self-will in contradiction to the Divine Will—cannot coexist in your soul with the Gift; therefore, if one sins, the Gift departs. Is all then lost for you? Or have you just succumbed to a fate similar to that of Adam's? *Absolutely not.* God never tires of forgiving. We tire of asking for forgiveness. Similarly, God never tires of giving us His Will again, even if we have left it many times. Jesus tells Luisa that one can easily recover the loss of His Will if only he wants it (9/6/1937). We must, therefore, never allow discouragement or anxiety to enter our hearts in the quest to live in the Divine Will. This is always a tactic of the devil, who is incessantly striving to make us forget the infinite mercy of our Loving Father.

In fact, when we begin to falter, Jesus promises Luisa that He only increases the graces He gives us—even *doubling* them (9/5/1938). So whenever we become aware of imperfections in ourselves, we should—far from being discouraged—be affirmatively emboldened to return to Him even more deeply than we ever dwelt in Him before, for we know that new graces are now at our disposal. Indeed, *whenever* we experience a new degree of cognizance of our littleness, misery, weakness, and imperfection, this recognition—even when painful, and even if elicited by an unfortunate fall—is always a great opportunity. For it delivers us from the pride of the Pharisee and inundates us with the grace given to the publican. (cf. Luke 18:9-14)

Any time during the day that you realize you have become self-willed, weak, or even sinful, simply recite a perfect act of contrition, and ask for the Gift again. That's it. You just started your life anew, and you should not think of the past.

> I love you, Jesus, my love above all things, and I repent with my whole heart of having offended you. Never permit me to separate myself from you again, grant that I may love you always, and then do with me what you will. (An Act of Perfect Contrition from St. Alphonsus Liguori)

Of course, the Sacrament of Confession should be frequented, and you should seek absolution as quickly as possible if you have committed a grave sin. But even such falls as these must never discourage us. Jesus' infinite Divine Mercy is absolutely unaffected by our sins, no matter how serious or numerous. Have you sinned gravely for the fourth time in a single day? Just go back to Confession, be assured that you are forgiven, and try yet again to change your ways. It truly is that simple, so do not complicate matters by conjuring up and then entertaining existential crises in your mind. Just keep moving—so long as we do this, Jesus assures Luisa, all will turn out well and we will acquire the virtues we lack.

(Note: Much content from Part Four's remaining sections is taken from *The Crown of History*).

Grow in the Virtues

> "... only by following God's will can we be the light of the world and the salt of the earth! This sublime and demanding reality can only be grasped and lived in a spirit of constant prayer. This is the secret, if we are to enter into and dwell in God's will."
>
> –Pope St. John Paul II[219]

To be continuously anchored in the Gift, we must be virtuous and even strive for perfection in virtue. In the Gospel, however, Christ not only exhorts us to perfection (cf. Matthew 5:48), but also promises that His burden is light, and His yoke is easy. (cf. Matthew 11:30) Jesus likewise tells Luisa that it is false to assert that the path of virtue is difficult. He insists that, quite the contrary, it is very easy for one who *moves*, and only proves difficult for a person who refuses to do so—as by remaining still such a soul feels all the weight of the journey at once (5/15/1905).

Haven't we all found this to be true? When we sit down and dwell upon the difficulties and obstacles that may arise in a task we must undertake, surmounting them appears impossible, and too often we cower in our rooms trembling at the sheer thought. But when we ignore these feelings and simply get to work, we find things proceeding much more smoothly than we would have imagined. Oh, how much we underestimate God! He always inundates us with His grace—making easy anything we need to do in order to carry out His Will, no matter how challenging it appears at first. For, contrary to the errors of Pelagianism, the grace to be virtuous often comes from Divine Intervention, not only as some simple consequence of a studious expertise of the virtues. Therefore, set out! Get to work! Follow your calling. Engage wholeheartedly in your mission and approach your whole *life* as a mission from God—for that is exactly what it is. You know what your mission is. The grace to be virtuous will come amid your faithful undertaking of the Will of God for your life. As Jesus says to Luisa: *move!* (Ibid.)

Nonetheless, with these admonitions being stated and, I hope, remaining on the forefront of your mind, let us briefly consider some important individual virtues for Living in the Divine Will. Truly, the virtues for the Gift are just the virtues that have always been associated with sanctity, thus we have essentially covered this step with the third "Preliminary Necessity" earlier mentioned. Here, I simply wish

---

219 Address of John Paul II to the youth of Rome preparing for World Youth Day. March 21st, 2002. Paragraph 5.

to draw attention to various virtues particularly emphasized by Jesus to Luisa. What follows, therefore, must not be regarded as a comprehensive treatise on virtue—very important things are left out—but only as an assortment of points that one unworthy author wishes to share based on his reading of Luisa's volumes.

Love. Simply put, we mustn't even think about ever allowing a single word or deed to proceed from our wills that is not, in its own way, an act of love (of God, and of neighbor—in that order). Jesus tells Luisa that the virtue of love is on par with the Divine Will itself, that each guarantees the other, and that neither can be had without the other (10/20/1935). He says that charity is the most necessary thing within the soul (10/29/1900), and that love forms the same life as His Will just as heat and light are always inseparable (5/21/1929). Moreover, He teaches that love alone determines the value of a deed—not the objective magnitude of the deed itself (10/16/1906). It is, therefore, impossible to overemphasize the importance of love. "God is love," (1 John 4:8) as Scripture teaches, and, as Jesus conveys in the Gospel, the whole law is summed up in loving God and neighbor (cf. Matthew 22:37-40).

Here are some simple tests to ascertain if we have love. First, our love for God is ascertained by the degree of love we have for the person whom we love least in this world. This is a simple corollary to two Biblical teachings, "he who does not love his brother whom he has seen, cannot love God whom he has not seen" (1 John 4:20), and "you are all brethren." (Matthew 23:8) Second, if we become annoyed, then we do not love. To Luisa, Jesus relays that one who really loves never gets annoyed about anything, but rather uses all that transpires as an opportunity to love more (7/22/1905). Third, if we do not love the poor, then we do not love. Jesus also tells Luisa that a measure of true charity is whether we love the poor (9/2/1908). If Luisa was not bedridden, she would have been a most zealous performer of works of mercy out in the world. Her heart was always breaking for the suffering of others, and she never once failed to offer herself to Jesus to suffer absolutely any pain at all in order to spare others from chastisements, from Purgatory, and above all from damnation. We must be like that—performing works of mercy in accordance with our own circumstances and as much as we can without neglecting the duties of our state in life. If works of mercy do not proceed from our love, then our love is not real. If such works do proceed, but without the tenderness that gives them warmth, then Jesus tells Luisa that they are unacceptable (3/30/1931). Indeed, "God loves a cheerful giver." (2 Corinthians 9:7) Finally, there is only one legitimate inspiration for love of neighbor: *because he bears God's image*. Charity undertaken for other motives is, Jesus tells Luisa, not true charity (9/8/1905).

Let love define your life. If any mystical revelations detract from the virtue of love in your life, then they have only been a waste (and worse). But if you *live* love—that is, if you go about all your days with utterly pure, complete, self-sacrificial love as the absolutely unquestionable form of each and every one of your decisions, thoughts, words, and deeds—then living in the Divine Will will not only be easy, but automatic. If you do not strive to live in this way, then you will never live in the Divine Will.

Humility and Nothingness. As St. Faustina says, humility is "nothing but the truth." (*Diary* §1502) And the truth is that, no matter how seemingly "great" we become, compared to God we are nothing. If only we can recognize that, then receiving the Gift shall prove a smooth path. For we will then forget ourselves (why remember a nothing?), and once we have forgotten ourselves, we have attained the perfection of humility. This need for recognizing our nothingness is neither a Quietistic nor an Eastern esoteric practice; it is, rather, what St. Thérèse of Lisieux repeatedly insisted upon:

> This enlightenment on my nothingness does me more good, in fact, than enlightenment on matters of faith. (*Story of a Soul* Ch. 9)
> It is enough to acknowledge our nothingness, and like children surrender ourselves into the Arms of the Good God. (Letter VI)

Instead of thinking and talking about ourselves, we should live our lives like a tiger in the pursuit of its prey; so fixated upon its mission that a war could be raging on all sides of it and it would scarcely notice. Our mission is the salvation and sanctification of souls, the hastening of the coming of the Kingdom of the Divine Will, and the consolation of our Blessed Lord's Sacred Heart. For us to spend time thinking about and talking about ourselves is more lamentable than a marine who, upon being sent on a mission of utmost importance to help end a war, instead stops for sightseeing in the city into which he was sent. This virtue, of course, does not preclude the need for a nightly examination of conscience (and a particularly careful one before Confession), but it does mean that we should avoid going much beyond that.

To avoid spiritual navel-gazing, we should—if we ever notice our attention wandering inwards—quickly remind ourselves that any and all good within us (no matter how virtuous we become) is entirely thanks to God. Likewise, whenever we are tempted to look down on anyone at all—even if it be something so passing as a brief thought—we must remind ourselves, "there but for the grace of God go I," and proceed to remind ourselves that this person is the image of God; one of His children for whom Christ died.

Attentiveness. God does not waste one second. He understands much better than we do just how incredibly precious this short amount of time is that we spend as pilgrims on earth, and He is always at work molding us into great saints. But this endeavor of His cannot be successful if we refuse to be aware of its execution in *each* of our day's moments. This awareness derives from continual perception of the fact that the circumstances of life which are out of our control are quasi Divine Revelations: they speak to us about what God Wills for us, and if—instead of listening to them—we get caught up in our own ideas about how our days, our life, and even the details of our growth in holiness, should be transpiring, then the Gift may just sail us by. (Fr. Walter Ciszek's teachings, covered in Part Two, are especially powerful on this point.)

God has a much better plan in mind, even for our growth in sanctity, than we ourselves—or any spiritual textbook or spiritual director—could ever conjure up. Despite knowing this, so many people want a "clearer" or "more tangible" path to the goal of sanctity than *the Will of God*. Indeed, there are many clear and tangible *helps* to arrive at the end of sanctity; but not one of them is sanctity itself. Accordingly, many exhibit a multitude of the exterior traits of a great saint even while, in truth, being about as far from this lofty state as possible. As St. Alphonsus teaches:

> **Mortification, meditation, receiving Holy Communion, acts of fraternal charity are all certainly pleasing to God—but only when they are in accordance with his will. When they do not accord with God's will, he not only finds no pleasure in them, but he even rejects them utterly and punishes them.** (*Uniformity With God's Will.* Ch. 1)

Jesus says the same to Luisa. He tells her that, as unspeakably good, glorious, and necessary as these things are, the Devil is nevertheless content with a soul praying, going to Confession, receiving Communion, and doing penances, so long as the soul is not doing God's Will. (9/9/1923) Only God's Will is what the devil ultimately abhors and correspondingly, it is the Divine Will alone—not any specific, exterior, holy thing—that guarantees our sanctification.

This is all to say the Will of God is already perfectly *simple*, therefore it cannot be reduced to anything simpler. And while it may at first be painful to hear that none of the exceedingly *holy things* can guarantee *your holiness* (but that only the Will of God can), this truth should in fact do nothing but allow a great peace to permeate your entire soul; for the Will of God is pure love, and it is always with you. It is never inaccessible; nothing can separate you from it. Through no fault of your own, you may be deprived of the Eucharist, Confession, the ability to perform your preferred works of mercy, etc. But no matter what has transpired thus far with respect to these things, the greatest sanctity is nevertheless knocking at your door this very moment, and always will be—all you need to do is say "yes" to it. *Fiat*. Give everything—*everything*—to God. He will not be outdone in generosity. In fact, you will be inundated with a peace so perfect that none of your prior efforts ever succeeded in giving so much as a morsel of it; the very "peace that surpasses all understanding." (Philippians 4:6) So, let us turn now to Peace as a foundational virtue for the Gift.

Perennial Peace and Trust. Mirroring what He had said earlier to Luisa, Jesus entrusted St. Faustina with the teaching we have already seen: "the greatest obstacles to holiness are discouragement and an exaggerated anxiety." (§1488) Sin, therefore, is not the greatest obstacle to holiness; if it were, then we would all be insane to do anything but find a remote hermitage, utterly devoid of any occasion of sin, and join it. Though indeed a great calling, being a hermit is not the genuine calling of most. In Luisa's letters, what she perhaps exhorted their recipients to most frequently was peace. She knew that the constant temptation in our lives is to deprive ourselves of peace as if this deprivation were somehow called for, when in fact it is always an affront to the goodness of God, Who never desires that we be without it.

> "Above all preserve peace of heart. This is more valuable than any treasure. In order to preserve it there is nothing more useful than renouncing your own will and substituting for it the will of the divine heart. In this way his will can carry out for us whatever contributes to his glory, and we will be happy to be his subjects and to trust entirely in him." -St. Margaret Mary Alacoque

God wants to pour His grace into our lives every moment of every day; we prevent Him by ever preferring anxiety, worry, and fretfulness to peace and trust. Jesus tells Luisa that the souls who shine the most are those with the most trust in His Divine Mercy (4/10/1912), since this trust alone makes Him known for *Who He is* (5/26/1935). He tells her that He will at times tolerate various defects in a soul—even going so far as to hide them from that soul's notice!—in order to not risk eliciting mistrust, since this would be more harmful than any mere defect (9/2/1924). How contrary to God's plan, then, would it be to let our trust in Him wane one iota on account of our own flaws!

> "Do not look forward to the changes and chances of this life with fear. Rather, look to them with full confidence that, as they arise, God to Whom you belong will in His love enable you to profit by them. He has guided you thus far in life. Do you but hold fast to His dear hand, and He will lead you safely through all trials. Whenever you cannot stand, He will carry you lovingly in His arms. Do not look forward to what may happen tomorrow. The same Eternal Father Who takes care of you today will take care of you tomorrow, and every day of your life. Either He will shield you from suffering or He will give you unfailing strength to bear it. Be at peace then, and put aside all useless thoughts, all vain dreads and all anxious imaginations." –Saint Francis de Sales

Discernment. God is not like some referee at a sports game whose only job is to call out fouls or other violations when they occur; He is closer to each of us than our own selves, and what a crime when we treat Him as a mere arbiter! Jesus laments to Luisa that some regard neglecting God's Will as a minor thing (as if, so long as we aren't explicitly sinning, all is well), when in fact it is always evil and causes our own total ruin (4/8/197). What follows, therefore, is the grave importance of trying to discern—so that we may both know and do—the Will of God in all things, instead of erroneously supposing that, so long as we are choosing between morally licit options, God has no Will in the matter. Now, these words of Jesus should not cause in us a sort of paralysis whereby we fear making decisions unless we know with clarity God's Will in a given matter; this clarity is not always His Will. Indeed, on one occasion, Jesus even told Luisa that her *not knowing* His Will about a certain matter *was itself* His Will! The point, rather, is that we must always sincerely *try*—in all things small and great—to both know and do His Will. In this regard, sincerely trying is identical to succeeding, therefore we should never agonize over our lot with words like "*if only* I knew God's Will in this!" If we are honest with ourselves in assessing the sincerity of our attempts, then God's decision to allow us to spend more time in realms of uncertainty regarding the details of His Will can, far from being an impediment to Living in His Will, serve as a powerful means to receiving the Gift. The Faith and Trust in His plan that we can choose to have, even without knowing the details of what this plan portends, is the most meritorious type. We, therefore, must ensure that such times of uncertainty do not cause us to become discouraged, and do not allure us into using them as excuses to do the self-will (for when we do not *know* God's Will for us, we must do what we have discerned to be *most likely* His Will, not suppose that such times are occasions to excuse ourselves from the duty of striving to direct our lives according to the Divine Will!)

I recommend two great helps for proper discernment: *The Spiritual Exercises of Ignatius of Loyola,* and *Finding God's Will for You* by St. Francis de Sales. The principles therein should be employed not only in choosing one's vocation, but also in guiding all of life's decisions. Perhaps the main theme of discernment is *following the fruits*—that is, the Fruits of the Holy Spirit, which, when observed, indicate God's presence and pleasure. These fruits are charity, joy, peace, patience, kindness, goodness, gentleness, generosity, faithfulness, and self-control, and they tend to increase or decrease in one's soul in proportion to whether or not he is doing the Will of God. When we neglect God's Will, we see their opposites arise within us; Jesus tells Luisa that such a soul will feel unhappy and restless (9/6/1937). We ought not, however, be afraid to ask God for signs to indicate His Will for us in those cases wherein doing so is called for (and so long as we do not become superstitious), and when the more ordinary means of discernment are inconclusive.

Here, the first "preliminary step" of living in the Divine Will must be reiterated: successful discernment can only proceed from the foundation of the principles of orthodox Catholic teaching, so we must be sure to never give "discernment" sufficient leeway to contradict these; it never can licitly do so, and when we pretend we can discern our way out of these orthodox principles, we are not discerning at all, but are rather dialoguing with the devil himself, just like Eve in the Garden. Finally, we should note that discernment essentially amounts to hearing (and heeding) the voice of the Holy Spirit within us—but this quiet voice can be drowned out by three things that will destroy discernment: undisciplined flesh, worldly attachments, and constant noise. Eliminating these influences from our lives is key to discernment.

Courage. Along with peace, one of the most prevalent exhortations found in all of Luisa's revelations is Jesus' admonition to the virtue of courage. When God has such great plans at work—and there is no greater plan than this mission of the Divine Will—timidity, fear, and lukewarmness destroy everything. Jesus tells Luisa that a courageous soul accomplishes more in a day than a timid one manages in a year (2/12/1908), and He laments those who are lazy and live a lukewarm life, even as they dare to claim that their sloth is simply due to God giving some, but not others, the grace to become saints (10/20/1916).

Courage, like charity, is not a feeling. It is not a sensation that we are miraculously given before setting ourselves to work. Rather, it is a grace which emboldens our steps when we proceed in accord with God's Will. Do not, therefore, sit idly wondering why you lack the courage to do God's Will; *simply do God's Will*, and trust that you will have the courage to persevere in it. Jesus assures Luisa that He invests such souls with *superabundant* grace and new strength; not *before* they act, but *as* they begin to act (5/15/1938). Jesus admonishes us to be like a soldier who sacrifices himself in battle for the king, not an on-looker who just watches (10/29/1907), and He laments how much a sluggardly *human* prudence[220] often causes Divine works to fail (8/23/1928).

While courage does not consist in the absence of the *feeling* of fear, it does require the absence of deliberately *willed* fear. So, let us now turn to consider the general question of fear.

No Fear of Anything. Jesus tells Luisa that fear of *any* sort is incompatible with His Will, and that we must seek to banish all of it from our lives if we desire to please Him (7/29/1924). Anything but an inconsistent exhortation, this plea from Jesus to Luisa is in perfect harmony with everything else He tells her; throughout the revelations, we see refuted—one by one—every excuse we might give to justify fearfulness.

Are we afraid of Him? He tells Luisa that there is never a need for this—that we should be more afraid of ourselves than of Him, and that *everything* in Him is mercy for us, from our very conception onward! (6/9/1922) Are we afraid of death? Jesus gives Luisa the most consoling possible messages about the moment of death, promising—as He likewise did to St. Faustina—that at this moment He makes every possible, imaginable effort to save the soul from hell, even if the dying person is quite unprepared (11/21/1926, 3/22/1938). Are we afraid of pain? Jesus promises Luisa that, in His Will, no pain may ever enter deeply into our souls—that it remains outside our center—whereas we will always be given more than enough grace to easily endure it (5/10/1928). Are we afraid of the devil? Jesus tells Luisa that Satan is the universe's biggest coward, and that he flees when we resolutely pray (3/25/1908). Are we afraid of the times of trial and tribulation coming upon the world? Jesus promises protection from

---

[220] Jesus greatly extols all the virtues, including prudence, in His revelations to Luisa. But what He condemns here is a pietistical, weak, fearful *rationalization* of neglecting to do great things for God, under the *false* pretense of prudence.

the chastisements for those devoted to His mother (6/6/1935). There is absolutely nothing to be afraid of, therefore we must develop the habit of treating all fears that assail us as what they are: temptations to be prayed away and dismissed, not judicious invitations to be submitted to and appreciated.

Demeanor. With the Gift, Jesus is asking that we be like Him in everything, not only in what is doctrinally defined as a virtue of the highest order. This means that even the more subtle aspects of His life, such as His Own comportment, should be made our own. Although modern ears are accustomed to hearing that their own preferences, temperaments, tastes, eccentricities, routines, and the like, are their own business, and even that they should be catered to, Jesus says the opposite to Luisa. He insists that each thing that we do—even the most apparently mundane—ought to be ordered to the Divine Will and accomplished within the Divine Will, in imitation of Himself. The comprehensiveness of our calling as Christians striving after sanctity—so complete that it covers even comportment and bodily movements—is, however, not a new notion. St. Thomas Aquinas teaches:

> **Outward movements are signs of the inward disposition**, according to Ecclus. 19:27, ... and Ambrose says that "the habit of mind is seen in the gesture of the body ... the body's movement is an index of the soul ... from these things, the man that lies hidden in our hearts is esteemed to be either frivolous, or boastful, or impure, or on the other hand sedate, steady, pure, and free from blemish." (*Summa Theologica*. II-II. Question 168.)

Now, acquiring a demeanor consistent with Living in the Divine Will should not be seen as a prerequisite to asking for the Gift—the placement of the present section *after* asking for the Gift is deliberate! Nor is it primary among our Christian duties (treating it as such would be a form of Pharisaism). But it is something that should be diligently pursued even while striving for the Gift. A few particulars to be especially aware of shall be noted here.

Striving to be like Christ in all things includes striving for *constancy*. We ought, therefore, not be content with a moody, unstable demeanor, or having tastes, intentions, and goals that are constantly changing. Sometimes excitable, other times depressed and irritable. With some people, charitable to the extreme; with others, scarcely willing to listen. Sometimes on fire for the salvation of souls, sometimes caring only for vain, worldly hobbies. Jesus exhorts us to not be so vacillating (6/6/1923). Let us not be giddy or morose, flirtatious or cold, trivial or stern, chatty or shy, sloppy or pretentious, overly informal or uptight, effeminate or machismo. We mustn't be vulgar, temperamental, vain, or superficial. We must, instead, strive to always be dignified and graceful in our comportment. Calm but happy. Serene but joyful. Confident but humble. Of good humor, but with our humor built on a foundation of seriousness, not vice versa. Ready to converse when called for, but preferring a holy silence—Jesus tells Luisa that one who talks much is himself empty of God, and empties others of God with his excessive talking (5/8/1909); a theme He later shared with St. Faustina, saying to her, "I find no rest in [a talkative] soul." (§1008) Faustina herself insisted that a "talkative soul will never attain sanctity." (§477) Christ's demeanor, however, cannot be summarized in a paragraph, so let us ensure we frequently read and meditate upon the Gospel, so as to "put on the Lord Jesus Christ." (Romans 13:14)

Let no one protest that these admonitions deprive us of the ability to "be who we are." Bad habits are *not* "who you are," and no one should be expected to endorse our vices under the pretense of "loving us for who we are." Consider that you will be *most* you in Heaven, and there among the saints, you will certainly have none of those habits you may now feel inclined to defend.[221] St. Josemaría Escrivá put it well in one line: "**Don't say: 'It's the way I'm made... it's my character.' It's your lack of character: Be a man—*esto vir*!**" (*The Way*. Character. #4)

***

At this point, no doubt, we have plenty of virtues to work on! But now that we have our "background" work cut out (not, of course, that virtue is less important than what follows—but virtue comes largely as a consequence of *moving*, as we said in this section's beginning), let us now turn our attention to the *forefront* work: our mission.

---

[221] Likewise, let no one protest that if all were to acquire a Christlike demeanor, the world would be deprived of its diversity. The world has no need of bad character for its full variety any more than a car needs rusty components to function well. Defective demeanors contribute nothing to the world's diversity as ordained by God. Accordingly, Jesus tells Luisa that in the Kingdom of His Divine Will (a reference to Heaven, to those souls even now living in His Will on earth, *and* to the entire earth during the coming Era), though all will be beautiful and holy, each will be so different from the other as to resemble all the varieties of beauty within an exquisite garden—or, rather, as to resemble the beauty of the entire creation itself (5/15/1926). On the other hand, when vices and defective character enter in, individuals become *less* distinguishable.

Grow in Knowledge

> "The Divine Will has such strength that even a single piece of knowledge of It, one word about It, or one action done with It, makes the spirits of darkness feel such torture as to feel their power paralyzed..." –Luisa (Letter #75)

Not in vain did Jesus give Luisa thousands of pages of utterly astounding revelations! Nor did He do so merely that some author might come along one day and write a book summarizing them to dispense all from reading the revelations themselves. No, He revealed these truths to Luisa because He wants them known, read, and understood by all! What I have presented to you within the pages of this book is no *substitute for* Luisa's revelations—it is the opposite: an *invitation into* them!

It is impossible to adequately describe how glorious it is to learn even one additional truth about the Divine Will. Jesus promises that each new truth you learn about His Will as revealed to Luisa gives you more strength to live in the Divine Will, embellishes your eternal home in Heaven, causes all the saints to rejoice, and hastens the coming of the Kingdom. He tells her that by learning about the Divine Will on earth, we even carry new truths to Heaven with us, for the enjoyment of all the Blessed (1/25/1922).

All these promises and so many more like them come with *simply learning one* new truth about the Divine Will! Try to have Luisa's writings always handy and read them regularly (I also highly recommend having an audiobook of them for listening to while driving, doing manual labor, etc.). These promises need not merely be taken on Faith, for the graces are *palpable*. If you are in God's grace and then open Luisa's revelations with the sincere desire to learn the truths therein, you will *feel* yourself being inundated with new graces each time you read (or re-read!) them. Please do not just take my word for it; see for yourself. Your life will be forever changed, and any time you put into reading these revelations will be superabundantly rewarded.

Do the Hours of the Passion

> "The world still has no idea of all that Jesus suffered."
> –St. Faustina. *Diary*, §1054

Beyond her 36 volumes, two revelations of Jesus to Luisa stand out: the *Blessed Virgin Mary in the Kingdom of the Divine Will* (which we will consider in the next section), and the object of our present consideration: the *Hours of the Passion.* This is a short work in which we mystically follow, hour by hour, Jesus and Mary through all the events of His suffering and death. Recall that Pope St. Pius X himself, when presented with these *Hours* by St. Hannibal, said that they should be read "while kneeling," because "it is Jesus Christ who is speaking" in them.

In reading, praying, and meditating upon these *Hours,* we act as victim souls, mystically suffer redemptively with Jesus, and foster our desire to give over our whole lives to Him. Jesus assures Luisa that in undertaking the *Hours of the Passion,* we do far more than simply recall; we enter, rather, into each moment through the power of the Gift itself. We fuse each of our members with Jesus', kissing Him as we strive to endure His Passion with Him in the Divine Will, thus offering Him consolation and assuming the role of quasi-co-redemptrix along with Our Lady, the true Co-Redemptrix. Jesus gave enormous promises to Luisa with these *Hours,* promises that extend to whomever undertakes them. He promised that through them, the saint would become holier still, the tempted would find victory, the ill would find strength, and that, *for each word read,* the salvation of a soul would be granted. He said that an entire city could be spared chastisements if only one soul in it would continually pray these *Hours.* For the next few paragraphs, therefore, I wish only to give you a taste of these *Hours* in hopes that you will be inspired to secure a copy for yourself, dive in head-first, and even consider reading a passage from them each night before bed.

What has always stayed with me from the *Hours* is that Jesus' words in the garden, "If it be possible, let this chalice pass" (Matthew 26:39) were not at all regarding apprehension of physical sufferings. Unspeakably dreadful as the physical pain was, Jesus was about as afraid of them as you would be afraid of getting wet to go and rescue your drowning child from a pool. These words of His referred, rather, to souls that, despite His love, would choose to condemn themselves to hell. For Jesus knew it was possible for the Father to exercise such dominion that He could simply override even the most perverse soul in order to force it into Heaven. But this would contradict the greatest gift with which God endowed the soul—its free will.

Therefore, in the ultimate act of submission to the Divine Will and as a model for us all, Jesus appended His petition with "nevertheless not My Will, but Thine be done," (Mark 14:36) even knowing what He was about to suffer beyond any measure for them. That is the extent of His love; that blood would burst forth from His pores in agony over the loss of His children. It was the damnation of souls that caused Him to sweat blood, and to undergo His most horrible passion there in the garden. Any suffering the soldiers could hope to inflict upon Him with their devices of torture amounted to nothing in comparison; the external passion and pain was minor compared to the internal passion and sorrow as He took upon Himself all the evil that had ever been done or would ever be done. He truly desired to empty out every drop of His blood, to offer every square inch of His flesh for laceration, and to feel every imaginable pain. His burning love knew no bounds, and the more He suffered, the more superabundant grace He won for His beloved creatures.

Because of this, we see throughout His Passion Jesus burning with desire to *suffer more and more*. This desire was not like that of some crazed man obsessed with pain, but rather as one so unspeakably inflamed with love that nothing—not even the greatest sufferings imaginable—could stand in His way of doing everything possible for His children. In the volumes, He tells Luisa that He could have saved mankind with a single teardrop, but had He only done that, His love would have not been content, for it would not have poured itself out entirely (4/16/1933).

This Divine Love Jesus had for His children welled up as a consuming fire within Him and caused *more suffering than the Passion itself*. And whenever He cried out in sorrow, it was not due to the internal or external pain, but due to seeing souls—past, present, and future—utterly refusing Him, hating Him, and choosing hell simply to spurn Him. In the *Hours* we read that He saw these souls as He looked down upon pieces of His Own flesh torn off by the scourging, and it was that sight that caused Him in anguish to cry out. We also read, in the *Hours*, that at the height of agony, at His abandonment upon the cross, Jesus entered into a conversation with these souls *begging* them not to choose hell, begging them to let Him suffer more and more if only they would permit Him to save them.

If it were not for the loss of souls, everything else—all the unheard-of tortures we read about in the *Hours*—would be *nothing* for Jesus. It is only for souls that He thirsts. We, dear friends, can quench that thirst of Jesus. Give Him your soul. Give Him your will. Tell souls about His unfathomable Divine Mercy. Admonish all to trust in His mercy. Remain ever close to Him in His suffering. Offer yourself completely to Him and love Him with all your heart.

Immediately before Jesus' Holy Death, nature itself—horrified at the sight of its Creator so treated—prostrated itself before Jesus as the sun darkened and the earth quaked. Even His persecutors were reduced to silence, as something that no one present (except Our Lady) could have predicted then transpired—He begged forgiveness for those killing Him, and, in that plea, implored forgiveness for all of us who, through sin, contributed to His death. The acts of Jesus on the Cross, being eternal, stand before us now just as truly as they were present two thousand years ago. What He said then, He says now. We, however, must be His hands, His feet, and His voice in the world today: by living in His Will and proclaiming His Mercy.

The description of Jesus' Passion is brutal and difficult; yet, in the *Hours*, the intense love of Jesus is beyond incredible. Throughout these revelations, you will say, along with Luisa, the angels, and the saints, *is such extreme love even possible?* It *is* possible—not for man, but for God. And in Jesus, it is a reality. Never let that reality depart from your mind.

Listen to Your Heavenly Mother

> "... that God's will alone, is our will ... is the summit of perfection and to it we should always aspire ... To this end we should always invoke the aid of our holy patrons, our guardian angels, and above all, of our mother Mary, the most perfect of all the saints because she most perfectly embraced the divine will."
>
> –St. Alphonsus Liguori

As so many great saints—especially in recent times—have discovered, Mary is the key to sanctity. She is the key to her Son, therefore she is the key to her Son's greatest Gift: His Divine Will. Time and time again throughout Luisa's 36 volumes (especially in the very last entry, which we touched on earlier), we see Jesus glorifying His mother, insisting that she is the way to the Gift of His Will, and exhorting our love of and devotion to her. He teaches that she is the terror of all hell (5/19/1931), and that she will not have completed her mission until the Divine Will reigns on earth (5/20/1936). Indeed, Our Lady's mission is not finished. With no less conviction, then, we can say with the Apostles themselves (as they said 2,000 years ago) that we have the Queen of All Creation in our midst who will ensure that the Will of her Son is done. Jesus assures us that His Mother will soon work miracles of such astounding magnitude that the entire earth will be shaken and she will give graces the likes of which have never been seen before (7/14/1935).

In the book of revelations from Our Lady to Luisa, *The Blessed Virgin Mary in the Kingdom of the Divine Will*, our Blessed Mother teaches us lessons on how to live continuously in the Divine Will. This is the real design for the Gift; not that it be a passing thing, but that it define our entire life without the exception of a single moment. While the *Hours of the Passion* cover a 24-hour period, these lessons consist of meditations for each day over the course of a month—namely, the month of May. Each day contains three lessons: one for morning, one for noon, and one for evening. These revelations begin with Mary promising Luisa that she will do *whatever it takes* to form her children in the Divine Will: even if she must go to every family, nation, religious community, etc. We should, therefore, read this book (which can be read any time, not only during the month of May!) aware of the magnitude of this promise; that she will be right next to us no less powerfully than she stands next to the seers who receive apparitions, in order to ensure we live in the Will of her Son. *Learn from Our Lady; follow Our Lady; love Our Lady; be ever consecrated to Our Lady, and you will surely live in the Divine Will.*

Do All Your Acts in the Divine Will

> "Whatever you do, in word or deed, do everything in the name of the Lord Jesus, giving thanks to God the Father through him."
> –Colossians 3:17

Scripture directs us to *"Put on the Lord Jesus Christ."* (Romans 13:14), and with the Gift we can do so in the fullest possible sense. Just as importantly as asking for the Gift, we should always ask Jesus to do with us, through us, and *in* us whatever we are doing at the moment. This is God's plan with the Gift; not that it be passively enjoyed, but that it be employed as the very life principle of all our acts—which, previously merely human, now become divinized.

With the Gift, Jesus is inviting us to have the operation within His Own Self be *always* our *primary* endeavor. Jesus tells Luisa that He re-did each of our lives during His thirty years of hidden life on earth; these "redone" versions of our lives remain suspended in God, awaiting our entrance into the Divine Will to claim their acts for our own by doing all that we do in His Will.

How often do we pause to consider that the Gospel which speaks so beautifully of Our Lord really details only the final three years of His thirty-three-year life on earth? Not often enough! And yet, He easily could have simply come to earth miraculously as a fully-grown man and achieved all He needed to very quickly. Instead, He spent decades doing those things we all must do. This was not in vain. Jesus reveals to Luisa that each element of His entire earthly life was undertaken in order to form a Divine Triumph of each human occupation, and to give each divinized deed to us as a gift (4/16/1933).

While a few of the words here employed may be new, there is nothing strange or esoteric about what we are being invited to do. From the greatest works of Catholic spirituality, we already know that we are called to do everything—that is, to undertake every thought, word, and deed (or, in other words, all of our "acts")—as a prayer. Though encapsulated most succinctly by St. Thérèse of Lisieux's assertion that "to pick up a pin for love can convert a soul," we see this call throughout modern mysticism. One thinks of Thérèse's "Little Way" in general, St. Josemaría Escrivá's spirituality of the sanctification of work, the Servant of God Catherine Doherty's teachings, the message of Fr. Walter Ciszek, and many others. Venerable Archbishop Fulton Sheen summarized this theme well when he taught, in the final words of his famous book, *Your Life is Worth Living*:

> **Every single action in your daily work, whether sweeping the street or teaching classes, can be made a prayer.** Every action is a kind of a blank check that has value only if the name of our Lord is signed to it... The tiny little actions of your daily life, as a mother, father, workman, teacher, nurse, or secretary can be **divinized and sacramentalized provided you bring the divine intention, a prayer of action** to them ... your humdrum routine work-a-day world can be transmuted and changed just on condition that you do it all for the name of Christ. It is not important what you do in this world, but *how* you do it. (Chapter 50)

Here as elsewhere, therefore, we see in Luisa's revelations not so much an entirely new theme, but rather the crown and completion of a work of sanctification that the Holy Spirit was already busy developing within the Church's Sacred Tradition.

Jesus tells Luisa that when we perform our ordinary acts in the Divine Will, they are symbolically like the sun; even if appearing small in themselves (as the sun itself appears in relation to the sky it inhabits), they nevertheless succeed in investing all creation with the light and heat of their splendor. These suns are formed by Jesus truly *doing in us* whatever we are doing. Therefore, as many times as you can remember throughout the day, in whatever you find yourself doing, simply ask Jesus to do it in, with, and through you.

Perhaps for now you can simply choose one specific activity you frequently do: whether changing diapers, hammering in nails, scanning items at a cash register, doing the dishes, or whatever else, and commit to doing it from now on *in the Divine Will*. This can be done easily, by saying or thinking, when beginning the activity, "*Jesus wishes to do ____, therefore we will do ____ together,*" and then proceeding with deliberateness and a spirit of prayer, recollection, and consciousness of God's presence. The more acts you do in the Divine Will, the deeper into it you enter and the more you restore creation.

> **Work itself is not a curse but a sharing in God's own work of creation, a redemptive and redeeming act**, noble of itself and worthy of the best in man—even as it was worthy of God himself. (Fr. Walter Cizsek. *He Leadeth Me.*)
> Making my meditation before the picture of the Curé of Ars, he seemed to say to me with an interior voice: "The secret of my life was that I lived for the moment. I did not say, 'I must pray here for the next hour', but only 'for this moment'. I did not say, 'I have a hundred confessions to hear', but looked upon this one as the first and last. ... By this means I was able always to do everything perfectly, quietly, and in great peace. Try and live this life of the present moment." (Fr. William Doyle)[222]

Doing all our acts in the Divine Will also fulfills the Scriptural admonition to "pray constantly." (1 Thessalonians 5:16-18) Instead of seeing this as a burden, however, we should see this as a joy. The Almighty Creator of the Universe desires to always be in conversation with you! Jesus tells Luisa that He simply cannot resist a soul who undertakes a continuous effort to converse with Him (7/28/1902); therefore, if we find a way to do so, we can be assured that the Gift is ours. So, how can we truly maintain continual prayer when it is simply impossible to always be thumbing our Rosary beads and vocally reciting Hail Mary's? One way is simple: by doing *everything* in God's Will.

Being in continual conversation, not just *during* our acts but *in* our acts, will help us to exercise care, prayerfulness, and upright intentions amid good works instead of letting them degenerate into what Jesus criticizes—merely dry, habitual, reluctant, "check-off-the-box" type, solely external activities (9/6/1905). This does not mean we have to do everything slowly, but it does mean that we must resist the temptation to become like robots—undertaking even our good deeds with an ever-present demeanor of hasty distraction or even agitation, which robs them of value in God's sight.

This mustn't be viewed as "yet another" spiritual practice being asked of us. In truth, it is the opposite. It is a call which acknowledges that few of us are able to spend all day in vocal prayer; that we have many duties required by our state in life which cannot but consume

---

[222] catholicculture.org/commentary/otc.cfm?id=1601

most of our time and attention. We can, however, still "pray constantly" in a deeper sense than always *saying* prayers, by ensuring that everything we do is approached with the intention of doing it through, with, and in Jesus. In so doing, the holiness attained even by a desert-dwelling mystic who truly could spend the entirety of each of his days in vocal prayer can be attained by any ordinary Catholic.

> **Look for the Divine Will in everything, and your being will become continuous prayer, in everything. It is not the words that form prayer, but our union with the Divine Will; and then all is sacred, holy, and prayer within us.** (Luisa Piccarreta. Letter #21 to Sr. Remigia. December 25, 1935)

Our Lady tells Luisa that holiness is found in fulfilling the duties *of the state in life that God has placed one in*; and that marriage, too, is a state in life which is eligible for this supremely exalted sanctity of Living in the Divine Will.[223] By doing our acts in the Divine Will, we can engage in another glorious invitation given to us through Luisa's revelations: *The Rounds*.

Do the Rounds

> "The soul leads all creation to the feet of its God and its Lord, that He may receive homage from every creature"–Blessed Marmion[224]

Just before reciting the *Sanctus* ("Holy, holy, holy…"), one of the most exalted of all the Mass prayers, the Liturgy of the Church proposes to thereby give "**voice to every creature under heaven**." (Eucharistic Prayer IV) It does not merely say that we give "thanks" for them, but rather necessitates that we ourselves truly give them a *voice* with our own Liturgical prayer. Here, again, is another fundamental duty of our Faith, which we find the crown and completion of within Jesus' revelations to Luisa. Indeed, these revelations do not merely invite us to pray for this or that intention, nor do they merely reveal this or that new devotion; they go much further, inviting mankind to reacquire his rightful, original position as both priest and king of creation, thus converting all created things into an explicit act of adoration by "sealing" each one with our own love and adoration of God in the Divine Will.

This understanding of the cosmos, mankind's role within it, and God's plan for it, may sound overwhelming or novel to some, but it

---

[223] Cf. *The Blessed Virgin Mary in the Kingdom of the Divine Will*. Day 16.

[224] *Christ, the Life of the Soul*. 279-80. Quoted in *On Earth as it is in Heaven*. Professor David Meconi, S.J. 2016.

is in fact traditional and orthodox Christian teaching. God is the perfect Author. As such, He does not merely provide an arbitrary setting for His Story (that is, *history* itself); instead, that setting itself is part and parcel to the destiny of the story's protagonists. As Pope Benedict XVI taught:

> God entrusted to man, created in his image and likeness, the mission of unifying the cosmos. And just as Christ unified the human being in himself, **the Creator unified the cosmos in man. He showed us how to unify the cosmos in the communion of Christ and thus truly arrived at a redeemed world** ... Christ indicates that the cosmos must become a liturgy, the glory of God, and that worship is the beginning of true transformation, of the true renewal of the world. (General Audience. June 25th, 2008)

In order for the cosmos—the entire physical universe—to become a liturgy, there must be a priest. And the priest of this cosmic Liturgy is none other than man himself. "**Man is nature's priest**," taught John Scotus Eriugena, one of the greatest Catholic theologians of the early medieval period. In a word, the Liturgy is the model for mankind's approach to *everything*. This is Benedict's earlier teaching in his famous work, *The Spirit of the Liturgy*:

> ... Love-transformed mankind, the divinization of creation and the surrender of all things to God ... is the purpose of the world ... **the goal of worship and the goal of creation as a whole are one and the same—divinization**, a world of freedom and love ... **The cosmos is not a kind of closed building, a stationary container in which history may by chance take place.** It is itself movement, from its one beginning to its one end. In a sense, creation is history. (Chapter 2)

As we can see, this goal is universal in scope. Creation must in a sense be divinized—each element thereof in accordance with its own nature[225]—and the fulfillment of this process requires the action, *in the Divine Will*, of the only being within creation who bears the image and likeness of the Creator Himself.

Therefore, although this cosmic process is exemplified supremely in our current time—the Age of the Church—it also existed in the times of the Old Testament. With the Rounds, we mirror the canticle of Daniel's companions who, when thrown into the fire by Nebuchadnezzar, repeatedly go through all manner of created

---

225 Not, of course, that material things are or may ever be literally Divine (contrary to the errors of Pantheism), but that they may participate, in their proper place—in a quasi-"divinized cosmos" by being set in order by the only spiritual-material being: man.

things—sun and stars, dews and snows, mountains and hills, beasts and cattle, spirits and souls of the righteous—calling upon each to "**bless the Lord, all works of the Lord; praise and exalt him above all forever.**" (Daniel 3) This Old Testament canticle is still in the public prayer of the Church, the Divine Office, the recitation of which is required of all clergy and religious, and recommended for the laity. Although some lament the "repetitiveness" of the passage, such people misunderstand its nature. God's purpose in inspiring these Scriptural verses and in guiding the Church Universal to pray them constantly is not about merely intellectually recognizing the fact that creation mirrors God's Glory. It is, rather, about spiritually *going through* all created things and *acknowledging* the reality of God's Will remaining veiled within Creation. In other words, it is real *work* to be *done* (albeit a work of pure joy), not mere *data* to be *memorized*. The purpose of this work is certainly not motivated by the notion that created things have reason, much less are themselves Divine (Jesus repudiates this notion to Luisa). In fact, it is *precisely because* created things *cannot* explicitly bless God (due to their lack of reason), that it has been left to us humans, the only intelligent incarnate life in the universe, to bless God in and on behalf of all things. Magisterium and Papal Teaching also address this theme. *The Compendium of the Social Doctrine of the Church* teaches:

> Through his corporeality man unites in himself elements of the material world; these 'reach their summit through him, and through him raise their voice in free praise of the Creator' (§128)

Pope St. John Paul II similarly insisted that man does not merely dwell within creation, use it, and benefit from it; but also that, **"God willed that man be the king of creation**."[226] We even see this thread continued at length in the Pope Francis' Encyclical, *Laudato si'*:

> There is a mystical meaning to be found in a leaf, in a mountain trail, in a dewdrop, in a poor person's face ... not because the finite things of this world are really divine, but because the mystic experiences the intimate connection between God and all beings ... Standing awestruck before a mountain, he or she cannot separate this experience from God, and perceives that the interior awe being lived has to be entrusted to the Lord ... Through our worship of God, we are invited to embrace the world on a different plane ... all the creatures of the material universe find their true meaning in the incarnate Word, for the Son of God has incorporated in his person part of the material world, planting in it a seed

[226] General Audience. October 29, 1983

> of definitive transformation ... "when we contemplate with wonder the universe in all its grandeur and beauty, we must praise the whole Trinity." ... **the Trinity has left its mark on all creation. Saint Bonaventure went so far as to say that human beings, before sin, were able to see how each creature "testifies that God is three".** The reflection of the Trinity was there to be recognized in nature "when that book was open to man and our eyes had not yet become darkened" ... it could be readily contemplated if only the human gaze were not so partial, dark and fragile ... [The Pope closes the encyclical with the following prayer:] O Lord, seize us with your power and light, help us to protect all life, **to prepare for a better future, for the coming of your Kingdom** of justice, peace, love and beauty. Praise be to you! Amen. (§233-246)

Perhaps unbeknownst to himself, the Pope is essentially here mirroring Jesus' words to Luisa by showing, in his Magisterium, how to do the Rounds, and is telling us clearly that the Kingdom of God will come upon earth as a result of them!

St. Faustina was keenly aware of the importance of this task of glorifying God on behalf of all creation, writing in her Diary, "I call on the whole universe to glorify Your mercy. Oh, how great is Your goodness, O God!" (§1749) She then went on to write:

> Come, O earth, in all your fine greenery; Come, you too, O fathomless sea. Let your gratitude become a loving song, and sing the greatness of God's mercy. Come, beautiful, radiant sun. Come, bright dawn which precedes it. Join in one hymn, and let your clear voices Sing in one accord God's great mercy. Come, hills and valleys, sighing woods and thickets, Come, lovely flowers of morningtide; Let your unique scent adore and glorify God's mercy. Come, all you lovely things of earth, which man does not cease to wonder at. Come, adore God in your harmony, Glorifying God's inconceivable mercy. (§1750)

This is the rounds! In short: Jesus wishes to find, in our own souls living in His Will, everything that He has done—in Creation, in Redemption, and in Sanctification. How could it be otherwise? The whole meaning of Living in the Divine Will can be relayed by understanding that, by way of this Gift, we are *given by grace* what God possesses by nature; and He certainly possesses within Himself all the works that have come forth from His Creating, Redeeming, and Sanctifying hands.

Jesus tells Luisa that creation and all it contains is like a veil for His Divine Will, and by doing the Rounds, we act to tear open that veil. This task applies not only to earth, plants, animals, etc., but more importantly still to all the deeds He undertook when in the flesh (12/8/1926). In other words, the Gospel is not a mere history lesson. It is a presentation of *living acts* awaiting our own *Fiat*. There is nothing cryptic about responding to this call. Like the Gift itself, the Rounds are operated simply by way of desiring and asking, and we can approach them as an expansion of the same task undertaken above by Daniel's companions in the Old Testament, by St. Faustina in her Diary, and also by St. Francis in his Canticle of the Creatures.

Jesus tells Luisa that, since man is the sole speaking work of God, it has been left to him to speak on behalf of all that cannot speak (2/13/1931). If you simply seek to do this—to make a habit of blessing, thanking, adoring, and glorifying God on behalf of His Will veiled in all things—then you are succeeding in doing the Rounds.[227] In the Rounds, the Divine Will is operative within us, working to subject all creation to God and reorder it in preparation for the Era, setting "**creation free from its slavery to corruption**." (Romans 8:21)

Not only, however, do we accomplish this important work; we also receive so much in return. Jesus tells Luisa that Creation itself is like a book, and doing the Rounds consists in reading that book (7/6/1931); that each created thing is yet another invitation to us to live in the Divine Will, for each contains its own *special delight* which mysteriously achieves this end of *drawing man into God* (6/18/1930). All can palpably discern the reality of these truths for themselves by just walking through a quiet and beautiful place in nature, and they will there find vindicated not only these revelations to Luisa, but also the famous teaching of St. Bernard of Clairvaux:

> **You will find something more in woods than in books. Trees and stones will teach you that which you can never learn from masters.**

Do you feel yourself lacking something—perhaps you know not what? Immerse yourself—even if you can only afford to do so briefly—in the beauty of creation. A simple walk is often all it takes—perhaps in a park, a cemetery, or even just your backyard. Learn from this beautiful Creation. Thank God for it. Bless God in its name. You will quickly find yourself attaining whatever it is you lacked.

---

[227] Consider the Nicene Creed. When praying it at Mass, I have always felt like I am, in spirit, standing before the realities I affirm with my lips; gazing with wonder upon them and relishing the fact that I know of their validity with absolute certainty, impressing my own love and adoration upon them and offering them back to the God Who gave them. This approach to the Creed can inform our approach to the Rounds, in which we spiritually "re-do" all the acts of creation in the Will of God; approaching all that is and all that has transpired as a "Creed" of sorts.

LONG LIVE CHRIST THE KING

17. Proclaim the Kingdom

"Your friends make known, O Lord, the glorious splendor of your kingdom." –Psalm 145

Now that you know some of these most sublime truths of the Divine Will, it is imperative that you not keep them to yourself! To Luisa, Jesus likens those who spread knowledge of this Third Fiat to the very Evangelists who wrote the Gospels. (1/18/1928) There are even ways in which our duty is more exciting and privileged; what they longed for and laid the foundations of, we are now on the cusp of attaining. At what time it is attained, and who shares in its attainment, is dependent upon our response.

What sacrifice, then, is too great to spread this Kingdom of His on earth? What vanity, now clung to, is not worth casting aside for the sake of the reign of His Will? What risk, now feared, is not worth taking to be able to participate in the initiation of the Third Fiat of the Eternal One? Patriarchs, prophets, martyrs, Fathers and Doctors, and yes, even the Angels, envy you for the invitation that God extends freely to you. Take it.

Jesus tells Luisa that if we lived in His Will, it would be impossible for us to not speak of this Gift to others (1/16/1930), that He will give so much grace to those who work to promote the Gift as to astound even the saints in Heaven (2/28/1928), and that if we had even the faintest clue of how glorious what He is preparing for the world actually is, we would sacrifice ourselves to proclaim this message to the world from the rooftops (8/26/1928). He tells Luisa that He desires, with such ardency as to be indescribable, that His Will reign on earth, but that this reign cannot commence until knowledge of it—*through these revelations*—has been spread (5/15/1932).

Therefore, however you can manage to do so, get the word out there—as widely and quickly as you can![228] I recommend introducing

---

[228] You could tell your family and friends, and send them a book on the Divine Will. You could tell your pastor, and ask him if a Divine Will themed event may be held or group started at the parish. You could post about the Divine Will on any social media account you happen to have and otherwise promote it online. You could become a Divine Will Missionary of Mercy (www.DWMoM.org). More ideas can be found at www.ProclaimTheKingdom.com. I will add one more point: there are almost 8 billion people on this planet. Every single one of them needs to hear this message. *There is absolutely no time to waste by pestering and nagging the same people over and over again with this message. Sow the seed, then move on, leaving its growth to God.* For the sad fact remains that many "good Catholics" in the Church today are utterly closed off to the grace of the Holy Spirit. When such people ignore, reject, or even castigate this message, we must simply take Our Lord's admonition to "shake the dust off our feet" instead of wasting time with disputes.

the Divine Will by focusing on what is most essential: *the Our Father prayer*. You could begin by simply relaying that the prayer means exactly what it says, and that Jesus has now revealed—to an approved and absolutely trustworthy Servant of God mystic whose authenticity is beyond question—that the time for the fulfillment of its prophecy and promise has now arrived; *but not without our cooperation*.

> **And Jesus said to him: Let the dead bury their dead: but go thou, and preach the kingdom of God**. (Luke 9:60)

Jesus assures Luisa that the *only* thing needed for His Kingdom to come on earth is souls willing to proclaim it with courage (8/25/1929), and from this it follows that the only reason the Kingdom has *not* yet arrived is because there are insufficient souls engaging in such proclamation. For we must show God that we *want* this Kingdom, in order that His bestowal of it consists in His answering our ardent prayers. Jesus tells Luisa that, in this regard, He is not unlike a leader in this world, who wishes to do what he does in response to his people wanting it (5/30/1928). He moreover says that although the bestowal of the Kingdom will indeed be gratuitous on God's part—not *merited* by us—we nevertheless must cry out for it as a Church just as Israel cried out for the coming of the Messiah (3/26/1933).

Know, too, that in hastening the coming of the Kingdom, you are entering into the most holy and joyous endeavor with the very saints in Heaven. Like good friends competing in a sport, you and they are both endeavoring zealously to see who can do more to hasten the arrival of God's reign on earth. Jesus conveyed to Luisa that the Blessed in Heaven want this reign even more than do the just on earth; due to the latter often being subject to doubts and short-sightedness (5/20/1928). Indeed, the reign of the Divine Will *on earth* will be enjoyed even more *from Heaven* (have we forgotten the Dogma of the Communion of Saints, and that the faithful departed are closer to us than they were even before their deaths?). Therefore, we mustn't ever waste a moment wondering which side of the grave we will see this Era from; we must simply focus entirely on hastening it.

Moreover, we must remember that God wants to give this Kingdom even more than we want to receive it. *It will come*. Banish every doubt, for these will sap you of the energy you need to hasten its coming. Even Luisa herself expressed a doubt about the coming of the Kingdom, and Jesus responded by assuring her that what seems impossible to us is easy to Him, and second, that His Mother will work unheard-of graces and miracles that will *shake the world* in order to ensure that the Kingdom of her Son comes. (7/14/1935) Our Lady herself is imploring the Father for the reign of His Will on earth. The world has already experienced some of these miracles, but we can rest assured that what is coming soon will make what has already transpired look small.[229]

> **Help us to work together for the coming of your Kingdom, until the hour when we stand before you, Saints among the Saints in the halls of heaven**… (Roman Missal. Eucharistic Prayer for Reconciliation I.)

Let Your Cry be Continuous

> "From now on the crown of righteousness awaits me, which the Lord, the just judge, will award to me on that day, and not only to me, but to all who have longed for his appearance."–2 Timothy 4:8

The present world is in many ways a rather miserable place; consequently, there are two kinds of people to be found within it. There are those who are continually irritated, annoyed, anxious, depressed, and even downright furious; and then there are those who have found fleeting relief from such ailments by self-medicating with some psychological or physiological trick they play on themselves—engaging in self-deceit through the "Power of Positive Thinking," practicing self-harm with the abuse of legal or illegal chemical substances, or dedicating themselves with unbounded effort to some vain ambition whose fleeting rewards will scarcely be noticed moments after they have begun.

But, actually, there is a third group of people, and I invite you to join its ranks. These people are honest about the sorry state of the world as it plays out in the details of their own trials, in the grand paradigm-shifts of geopolitics, and everything in-between; they do not pretend these ills are anything other than things to be justly lamented and striven against. Thus, they are as far from the second group described above as a lung doctor is from a cigarette salesman. Despite this honesty, however, they never descend to the antics of those in the first group; for each and every time they are confronted with the sorry state of the world in any of its diverse incarnations, they approach such situations precisely in accordance with what they are: invitations and reminders to engage in battle against the prince of this world—the devil—by imploring God for the coming of the Kingdom, wherein all such sorry things will scarcely be a memory.

[229] Jesus offered this promise even *after* the Miracle of the Sun at Fatima!

Far as they are from the second group, it is equally true that they are about as far from the first group as a U.S. Marine is from an opinionated armchair Twitter activist. One basks in the glory of victory even while still engaged in battle; the other only rants and grows ever more plagued with anxiety.

Remain continually in this third group, and you will succeed in calling down the Kingdom of God upon earth. Has there been another world catastrophe? Or something as minor as another tantrum thrown by a 2-year-old? Always respond—interiorly, at least—"*Lord, let Your Kingdom come.*" Terrorists on the rampage, mass shootings, etc.? Or just obnoxious neighbors at it again with their loud music and arguing? The nations appear to be preparing for World War III? Or is it discord within your family or friendships? Thousands of acres of God's Creation destroyed by a nuclear meltdown? Or, is just the ugliness of litter and billboards presented before your eyes? Are you dreading some great looming trial in your life—a major surgery, an impending death of a loved one; or, are you just feeling subjected to various feelings of depression and anxiety which come with your ordinary life's endeavors?

Respond to all these situations the same way, and never neglect to do so, that your cry may be continuous: *"Lord, let your Kingdom come!"*

Are you in the midst of any personal suffering—great or small? Say always: "Jesus, I Trust in You. Thy Will be Done. I offer this suffering to You for the coming of Your Kingdom." Or, are you blessed to have no particular lamentable thing presenting itself to you in the moment? Then simply pray incessantly—so repeatedly that God Himself cannot bear hearing it from you anymore without granting it—the greatest petition of the Greatest Prayer ever uttered by the lips of man:

> **Thy Will be done on earth as it is in Heaven, Thy Will be done on earth as it is in Heaven, Thy Will be done on earth as it is in Heaven!**

Of course, this continuous cry ought not be restricted to times when a response is needed to various evils you observe. Jesus implores Luisa and us all to ensure that our crying out of the central petition of the Our Father be utterly *continuous* in our lives (5/31/1935). We should harbor as much zeal in crying out for the Kingdom whenever we witness anything good, true, or beautiful as when we experience their opposites; for in the former cases, we are pleading for the universal reign of these noble things we witness. What strikes you each day? The power of the Liturgy?[230] A beautiful sunset? The glory of a small flower? The love of family and good friends? All such things are invitations from God to thank Him, bless Him, glorify Him, and beg Him for the coming of His Kingdom, wherein His goodness, truth, and beauty shall reign supreme on earth—universally and without interruption.

Till the Soil

> "Not enough, therefore, that we seek the kingdom of God: we must also use our best exertions for its attainment."
> –Catechism of the Council of Trent

The reign of the Divine Will shall come on earth as a miraculous, unprecedented, and overwhelming Divine intervention, in response to our ardent prayers for precisely that. Accordingly, it bears no resemblance to erroneous notions like Liberation Theology, Utopianism, Secular Messianism, Progressive Evolutionism, Marxism, and similar false ideologies, each of which—in its own way—supposes that a future golden age may arrive on earth *as a consequence of human effort,* or as a mere natural unfolding of events already in progress. (Millenarianism, on the other hand, is a distinct error, and it is addressed in the appendices.)

But it does not follow from the erroneous nature of these -isms that those who rightly await the *genuine* Era are exempt from doing their part to physically aid its coming! As Padre Pio said, "work as if everything depended upon you, pray as if everything depended on God." Ever cognizant that our efforts will not be the *cause* of the Era, we who long for God's Kingdom on earth should nevertheless be zealous in working to promote and incarnate those goods which will flourish abundantly during its reign. No gardener pretends that his own tilling of the soil is what causes the growth of the plants therein, but this does not inhibit his diligence in so doing. We, too, who await and pray for the Era, should be sure we do not slacken in our evangelization and proclamation of the Divine Mercy, our working for justice and the common good, our fighting for the truth, our insistence upon and promotion of beauty, our involvement in politics, etc.; in a word, our doing all that we can to ensure that when Christ comes in grace to reign as King during the Era, He already as much as possible

---

[230] I especially encourage, at each Mass you attend—as the priest lifts up the Host after Consecration—praying from the very depths of your heart, "**My Lord, and my God! Draw all things to Thyself, oh Lord. Draw all things to Thyself**!" (cf. John 12:32)

finds Himself socially reigning as King through the fruits of our labors even now.

In Jesus' revelations to Luisa, we see anything but a God disinterested in such matters. Quite the contrary, Jesus tells Luisa to intercede for the benefit of those who fight for what is good and true in the world—even in politics (1/12/1902). When once Luisa lamented to Jesus that she only cared about Heaven, not the earth, He responded with a gentle rebuke: *He* cares about earth, therefore we too must care, as our concerns must be His concerns (5/15/1938).

Furthermore, as we will see in this book's following part, Global chastisements the likes of which the world has never seen *will* precede the Era. These chastisements cannot be entirely averted, but the details of their scope, severity, and duration, are not set in stone; therefore, they can be mitigated. This mitigation is especially attained by our imploring the Divine Mercy and promoting the Divine Will, but also by our own labors to accomplish through reform what otherwise will need to be accomplished through suffering. Therefore, *do not bury your talents*. In the Gospel, Jesus has made it clear that neither "but I was tired," nor "but I was afraid," will work as excuses on the Day of Judgment. (cf. Matthew 25:14-30) God expects you to do your part to make this world a better place for the salvation and sanctification of souls.

A final note on tilling the soil: when I speak of this, I am referring to those *external* actions in which we engage in order to better conform the temporal order to the Will of God. Notwithstanding the genuine importance of such endeavors, what far outshines them is that which is undertaken in a hidden and internal way: those deeds done between the soul and God.

On the Day of Judgment it will be revealed that those who achieved the most to save and sanctify souls and usher in the Kingdom were not the great men whose biographies we all know, but those hidden and forgotten ones who always operated in union with God: monks and nuns in monasteries living lives of prayer and sacrifice without ever being thanked, patients suffering in hospitals and nursing homes and offering it all to Christ, ordinary parishioners spending many hours in Eucharistic adoration, humble housewives and menial laborers who do all that they do with love and in the Divine Will.

Till the soil, indeed. But do not become a mere activist who neglects what is internal and hidden for the sake of what is external and recognized by men, for that would be like a soldier snubbing a sword for the sake of a child's toy. Your most powerful weapons will always be those which remain immune from the risk of self-interest and vanity.

***

Let us now begin the final part of this book, wherein we shall learn more about the time of the reign of the Divine Will on earth—the Era of Peace.

> **"Lord, teach me to serve you as you deserve; to give and not to count the cost, to fight and not to heed the wounds, to toil and not to seek for rest, to labor and not to ask for reward, save that of knowing that I do your will."** –St. Ignatius of Loyola

Part Five: The Crown of History: The Era of Peace and the Reign of the Divine Will

"In union with Christ take your stand as suppliants before the Heavenly Father and allow that prayer to rise to Him from your lips again and again...
Thy will be done on earth, as it is in heaven!
Only then shall we be influenced solely by the honor of God and by zeal to give Him greater glory, when we earnestly desire the restoration of His Kingdom—the Kingdom of justice, of love, and of peace—throughout all the world."
-Pope Pius XII. Encyclical, *Fidei Donum*. Easter, 1957

18. Why the Era?

"It culminates in the proclamation of God's sovereignty over human history. Indeed, the Psalm ends with the declaration: 'The Lord will reign for ever' ...we are not left to ourselves, the events of our days are not overshadowed by chaos or fate ..."
–Pope St. John Paul II

Why must a day come when God's Will reigns *over the whole earth*? Is it not enough for us to simply continue trying—bit by bit—to become holier, to evangelize, and to fix a few scattered injustices here and there until Christ comes again in the flesh upon the conclusion of time, to put an end to it all?

Some Christians today still pose these questions. But we can only acquire any real wisdom here by assuming the posture to which

Scripture exhorts us: "**The fear of the Lord is the beginning of wisdom,**" (Proverbs 1:7) and begin by heeding the two very simple answers God has given to those two questions: "Because I said so," and "No." In the following chapters, we will consider the more "satisfying" explanations which Heaven, the Church Fathers, and Magisterium have indeed repeatedly given to those questions. But we begin with the present admonishment because in the absence of this virtue—that is, if we approach what follows with the attitude of jaded modern rationalism which regards any supposed "naivety" as the supreme vice or the attitude of self-assured Pharisaism which is ever ready to see contradictions where none exist and dispense of condemnations upon the slightest suggestion that there may be even more to God's plan for the future of the world than they had in mind—then we will only find ourselves among the very scoffers whom Scripture prophesies for the last days:

> ... Scoffers will come in the last days with scoffing, following their own passions and saying, "Where is the promise of his coming? For ever since the fathers fell asleep, all things have continued as they were from the beginning of creation." (2 Peter 3:3,4)

Let us above all ensure that we never number among those ranks. Let us, instead, *believe God's word*. God has promised that He will reign—He has said so repeatedly, absolutely, and without qualification. We will see this with such clarity in the forthcoming chapters that it will not be lost on anyone whose eyes have traversed their pages. Even so, one may be tempted to first ask, "*But isn't this merely a distraction? Isn't God's reign over the whole earth an unrelated matter to the spirituality of the Divine Will—or to what I must do here and now in order to become the saint I am called to be?*"

The answer to these two questions is also, most emphatically, "No." It is only an individualist fallacy which places a rupture between what the person is called to, and what the world is called to—what it must claim as its *Penultimate Destiny*. If the Gift is real, then the effect of this grace cannot be supposed to be restricted to interiorly renewing the spiritual lives of a few fortunate Catholics. Indeed, what is most important is that we receive this Gift. But whoever supposes that only inner and invisible effects are brought about when Christ comes to a situation ought to read the Gospel. And His coming to individual souls by way of the Gift here and now is preparatory for His Coming to the whole world *in grace* on a day we know not, but which is certainly soon, and which will entail a radical transformation not dissimilar to Lazarus emerging from the tomb at the command of Christ. (cf. John 11:43)

To be sure, individualism's opposite error is equally dangerous—the "collectivism" wherein one forgets that on Judgment Day he will stand before God alone, and ultimately will answer only for his own soul. But our calling here is the same as it is everywhere: avoiding the perversion of error on both extremes, and abiding in the golden mean virtue. The golden-mean truth here consists in our doing everything we can to hasten the coming of the Kingdom on earth, even while always keeping our gaze firmly affixed on Heaven and ensuring that we ourselves become saints; pouring ourselves out like a libation for God's reign over the earth, even while recognizing that we will be judged only by our own life's choices, from which alone our eternal glory is meted out. As Pope Benedict XVI taught, in his encyclical *Spe Salvi*:

> ...Salvation has always been considered a "social" reality. Indeed, the Letter to the Hebrews speaks of a "city" (cf. 11:10, 16; 12:22; 13:14) and therefore of communal salvation. Consistently with this view, sin is understood by the Fathers as the destruction of the unity of the human race, as fragmentation and division … "redemption" appears as the reestablishment of unity, in which we come together once more in a union that begins to take shape in the world community of believers ... This real life, towards which we try to reach out again and again, is linked to a lived union with a "people", and for each individual it can only be attained within this "we". It presupposes that we escape from the prison of our "I", because only in the openness of this universal subject does our gaze open out to the source of joy, to love itself—to God. While this community-oriented vision of the "blessed life" is certainly directed beyond the present world, as such it also has to do with the building up of this world... (§14,15)

The inclusion of the final Part of this book, therefore, is anything but an afterthought; anything but a tangent. It is utterly fundamental for the mission at hand. If we neglect the Divine callings quoted within its pages, then we thereby neglect the Divine Will. If we neglect the Divine Will, how, pray tell, can we *live in* that very thing?

But I would rather leave you with the excitement all the faithful now have a right to; not a sense of yet another burden imposed upon you—for this is anything but a burden. God is inviting us, *today*, to be the protagonists of the greatest mission in history. Our descendants in the times long after our own shall look back upon the day you now see displayed, on the calendar hanging upon your wall, with utter awe and astonishment. Think not, upon reading the Gospel or the Book of Acts, "*Wow! If I were alive then, here is what I would have done!*" Think, rather, "*Wow! I am alive now, here is what I shall do!*"

19. The Dénouement

"We wish to insert ourselves into the 'thanks' of the Lord, and thus truly receive the newness of life and contribute to the 'transubstantiation' of the world so that it might not be a place of death, but of life: a world in which love has conquered death."
–Pope Benedict XVI[231]

The greatest authors all understand that to write a worthy story, they must first place the pen upon the page knowing that, after the story's trial has been endured and conquered, they will return the setting in some manner to where it began. Accordingly, the Greatest Author, God, will not fail to ensure that His Own story—History itself—contains this symmetry between its beginning and ending. Jesus assures Luisa that just as His Will defined the beginning of history, so too its reign *must and will* define the conclusion of the same; since justice itself demands that the end resembles the beginning, and perfect love—which He Himself is—is never content if more remains to be given. (6/16/1928) Since creation began with an effusion of Divine Love, He promises us, through Luisa, that it will close with an effusion of His Love (3/22/1938).

In a later chapter, we will consider deeply—from the more precise perspective of theology and revelation—why and how this is so. But let us now engage in a more common sense reflection upon the structure that history itself has followed, and must follow, in order to see reflected within it the very perfection of its own Divine Architect. For God has not failed—nor *will* He fail—to ensure that His Own story contains each of the five essential elements shared by all great stories.[232] *Once upon a time...*

First, The Exposition: The setting is laid out—*how things ought to be* is made clear. **Second, The Rising Action:** The antagonist enters, the conflict begins, *how things ought to be* becomes distorted, and matters grow ever more serious. **Third, The Climax:** The tides have turned, the main event has transpired, and the protagonist *embarks* upon the path of his eventual victory. **Fourth, The Falling Action:**

---

[231] Reflections on the 65th Anniversary of his Priestly Ordination. June 28, 2016

[232] Cf. "Freytag's Pyramid." Dr. Gustav Freytag. *Technique of the Drama. An Exposition of Dramatic Composition and Art.* 1863. **Note: the following paragraphs are taken from *The Crown of History*. 2019.**

The conflict begins to be resolved; there is much striving—many triumphs, but also failures—it is at once glorious and painful, and though the process has begun, *how things ought to be has* not yet been fully restored. **Fifth, The Dénouement:** Through a "Great Catastrophe," the conflict is resolved. The setting of the beginning is not only restored, but the protagonist is even more blessed than in that Exposition.

Finally, in the very end of the story, there comes the *Happily Ever After*. Now, in the story that is history, God already has led us through the first four elements:

The Exposition. In the Garden of Eden, God showed us His original plan: everything good, everything beautiful, everything perfect. The lion's teeth serving not to tear apart flesh, but rather to glorify God's strength. Man himself living as a being of such glory and holiness as to astonish the angels themselves. The whole earth destined to be filled with people living in perfect peace and harmony with one another and with all creation, each living a long and happy life until his own time came to painlessly depart for his true, *eternal* home: Heaven.

The Rising Action. Beginning with the Fall of Man—by Adam's failure to pass God's simple test of love and the resulting emergence of sin, death, suffering, and ugliness—the world became more and more corrupt; even needing, at one point, to be purged by a universal flood. But God had His chosen people, and within this flock, a remnant never forgot that He had promised the Redeemer. These faithful Israelites, in accordance with their sure and certain hope, always prayed in earnest that the Messiah would come to save mankind.

The Climax. When the fullness of time had arrived, God deigned to create a creature unlike any that had existed before: *the woman* whom He had promised 4,000 years earlier, whose seed would crush the serpent (Genesis 3:15). This woman, reversing Adam's disobedience, gave her *Fiat* to God when He asked permission for her to become His Own true mother. Nine months later, laid in a manger, the Creator of the Universe was worshipped by Kings and shepherds alike. This man, Jesus Christ, founded a Church, willingly handed over His life for our salvation and sanctification, rose from the dead to abolish doubt forever, and ascended to Heaven.

The Falling Action. For 2,000 years, His Gospel has been tirelessly preached and lived in ever-growing nations and numbers. The saints throughout this time have lived this Gospel—often perfectly—

and have both filled the earth with His Love and populated Heaven with their children.

However, great and glorious as the many triumphs of the Church and the saints have been, only a willfully blind man could argue that the Kingdom of God now reigns on earth to the extent that God Wills, and to the extent that God has promised in His prayer of *"Thy Kingdom come, Thy Will be done, on earth as it is in Heaven."* (Matthew 6:10) Some Christians today propose that this fourth element is all the earth will ever see—that in Heaven alone could anyone ever hope to experience the Dénouement. But that is not what Jesus said, and as we will soon see, it is not what Scripture promises, it is not what the Church teaches, it is not what virtually all the Fathers of the Church believed, and it is not what God has spoken to the Church today through the unanimous consensus of His chosen—and proven—prophets. Heaven is our *happily ever after*. But Heaven is not *within* the Story of History—Heaven is the *purpose* of this story and dwells beyond its pages. For the Story of History to be complete, like any story, its *own* pages must contain "The Dénouement."

The Dénouement: You, dear reader, despite the imminence of the "Great Catastrophe" (the chastisements), have nevertheless been blessed to be born in the most exciting part of The Story, for The Dénouement is now being written before your very eyes. It is *the* fulfillment. It is the granting of the greatest petition of the Greatest Prayer ever uttered by the lips of man: the only prayer that Jesus Himself taught us to pray, in which He promised that the Will of the Father would reign on earth just as it reigns in Heaven.

Among Our Lady's many titles, God has now inspired a surprising one to suddenly rise to the top in popular devotion: *Our Lady, Undoer of Knots*. This is anything but accidental. The etymology of the word *Dénouement* comes from the French and Latin words for "untying the knot." For those who can see the Signs of the Times, the message is clear: *the Immaculate Queen is about to undo the knot that was tied in the Garden*.

As this notion that we, who are nothing, are so blessed to be alive at a moment of such cosmic and incomprehensible magnitude, will be almost too much to bear for some, we must dedicate the next section to eliminating the temptation to be scandalized by this astonishing news.

> "The love story between God and man consists in … communion of will ..." -Pope Benedict XVI, *Deus Caritas Est* §17

Be Not Scandalized

"There are more things in Heaven and earth, Horatio, than are dreamt of in your philosophy."–Shakespeare

Some may be perplexed or even offended at the suggestion that they have gone their whole lives as Christians without acknowledging something so basic as what has been described above; something so "obvious" as the assertion that the Our Father means exactly what it says, and that *God will win*—not only beyond history, but also within it. This should discourage no one, however. Let us be reminded that the number of valid understandings and interpretations of a given theme in Sacred Scripture increases in proportion to its importance,[233] and it should not be scandalizing to hear that God would motivate, in the Church, a prophetic understanding which relates to a certain tremendous triumph *in the times proximate to* that Triumph.

As the Roman Catechism (the *Catechism of the Council of Trent*) teaches, this is especially true with the present matter:

> The words, **'kingdom of God,' have a variety of significations, the exposition of each of which will not be found without its advantages**... (Part IV)

The Coming of the Kingdom and the accomplishment of the Divine Will *is certainly* about the Church's ministry, the administration of the Sacraments, the preaching of the Gospel, the conversion of sinners, incremental increases in temporal justice in society, etc. But it is not *only* about these things. To insist upon exclusivity and narrowness in

---

233 Consider, for example, what is meant by the first of the Ten Commandments, "I am the LORD your God: you shall not have strange Gods before me." Countless admonitions are bound up in this single verse. It means that all must worship God and Him alone. It demands possession of all the supernatural virtues (Faith, Hope, and Charity). It forbids placing any person or any thing in God's place, and it condemns atheism, idolatry, superstition, and any form of irreligion. Entire books have been written on what is subtly, but no less truly, contained in this single commandment. If so much is concealed within one verse of the Old Testament, then we can be sure to find an endless treasury of truth within a primary—if not *the* primary—verse of the New Testament. Nor is this dynamic restricted to those cases wherein moral admonitions are extracted from a commandment. What, for example, is taught in the seventh chapter of the Book of Genesis? First, a historical reality: the Great Flood. Also, a prefigurement of Baptism, as the New Testament itself teaches. (cf. 1 Peter 3:21) Likewise, a theological teaching on God's Justice and Mercy is relayed in the Flood narrative—that, although He is always Just, He will preserve the righteous. A moral teaching is also imparted to us on the importance of mankind's cooperation with God's plans for the world; as, instead of commanding Noah to simply wait somewhere safe, He commanded Noah to laboriously construct an Ark. The Flood is likewise the beginning of the covenants between God and man. Much more could be said, and much more has been said.

Scriptural Exegesis is one of the most effective ways of ensuring we close ourselves off to the workings of the Holy Spirit causing grace to run off our souls like water off a rock. This tendency is what we have seen Venerable Pope Pius XII warn against—and which we now must consider the wider context for—when he taught, in his encyclical *Divino Afflante Spiritu*:

> **... all moreover should abhor that intemperate zeal which imagines that whatever is new should for that very reason be opposed or suspected ...** In the immense matter contained in the Sacred Books - legislative, historical, sapiential and **prophetical** - there are but few texts whose sense has been defined by the authority of the Church... **There remain therefore many things, and of the greatest importance**, in the discussion and exposition of which the skill and genius of Catholic commentators may and ought to be freely exercised, so that each may contribute his part to the advantage of all, to the continued progress of the sacred doctrine and to the defense and honor of the Church. (§47)

Nothing, indeed, could be of greater "prophetical" importance than the fulfillment of the Our Father prayer—the coming of the Kingdom and the accomplishment of the Will of God on earth as in Heaven—and no zeal is more "intemperate" and "abhorrent" than one which obstructs God's expressed wishes in that fulfillment.

Now, it is certainly clear—from Scripture, Tradition, and the Magisterium—that the Trinity's mission was at work in Eden itself, when, in the *Protoevangelium* (Genesis 3:15), God promised that the Serpent's head would be crushed. It is likewise clear that the climax of this mission is found in none other than the Paschal Mysteries of the Incarnation; wherein, "Christ accomplished his work of human redemption and of the perfect glorification of God ... in which by dying he has destroyed our death, and by rising restored our life."[234]

Finally, it is clear that the *definitive perfection and enjoyment* of the Kingdom is only found in the Beatific Vision of Heaven; individually, upon one's death; universally, at the end of time, when Christ comes again in the flesh to command the General Resurrection and commence the Last Judgment.

What the Church does not settle—so long as we are careful to always avoid all the errors associated with Millenarianism[235]—is how exactly this greatest petition of the Our Father will be fulfilled on

---

[234] Roman Missal. Universal Norms on the Liturgical Year. §18

[235] This matter is addressed in the Appendices

earth, within time. But we do now have greater insights than ever before into the fact that the fulfillment of this petition, with our cooperation, will soon commence a glorious new Era. And although "new" in one sense, these insights are in a deeper sense as traditional as one could imagine; as perfectly and beautifully harmonious with the Faith as anything could ever be. Church Historian Professor Jacques Cabaud put it well in the following text which begins with a bit of facetiousness:

> *"When we recite the Our Father we petition God for the abolition of life on earth. What a paradox! The creature knows no better way of honoring its Creator than to aspire for the proximate extinction of its own species."* Most of us would find such an interpretation aberrant ... Do [those who teach it] realize, however, that this would imply the concomitant destruction of our world? Are the theologians who deny the possibility of an establishment of the Kingdom of God on earth ... aware that they are thereby excluding the literal interpretation of two demands of the "Our Father"? Is there anybody in his right mind who would say: "*Please Lord, we beg of you, do destroy this world which is unworthy of your divine concern*"? Nobody would be caught expressing himself in this fashion ... Yes, the Our Father in its first half is an eschatological prayer and we should read it in precisely those terms. The Coming of the Kingdom it evokes is good news, not only for the hereafter ... **It will come at the right moment. You should petition for its coming with faith, perseverance and a joyful heart: "Almighty God, 'may thy kingdom come'." This Kingdom is the purpose of Creation.** It should have happened earlier. Original sin delayed its coming but did not preclude it forever.[236]

As essential as it is, therefore, to remain open to orthodox developments in our understandings of Revelation, it is equally essential to ensure these understandings are solidly grounded in Scripture and Sacred Tradition. Examining this harmony, in regards to the Era of Peace, will be our next task.

[236] Jacques Cabaud, *On the End Times*. Chapter 1.

20. The Era in Scripture

"Creation itself will be set free from its bondage to decay..." –Romans 8:21

From the opening to the closing pages of Scripture, we are given promise after promise and prophecy after prophecy regarding a glorious time that will arrive on earth before the conclusion of history. A time of peace and holiness. A time of justice and mercy. A time of harmony and love. A time of restoration of what was lost and a fulfillment of what has been promised.

Only a tiny selection of these Biblical references to the Era can fit within the pages of this book. As we will proceed chronologically, beginning with the Old Testament, we must first refute an ancient heresy which, though vigorously condemned by the Church since the beginning, is popular today among Catholics.

Against Marcion: The Unity of Old and New Testament Prophecy

> "Fear not, little flock, for it is your Father's good pleasure to give you the kingdom." –Luke 12:32

The heresy that is Marcionism rejects Old Testament eschatology and thereby vainly attempts, in one fell swoop, to demolish all the prophecies of the Era in the Bible's first forty-six books. It is, moreover, just one breed of "Progressive Revelation" fallacies; those notions, common in non-Christian religions such as Islam, which allow for later Divine Revelations to contradict what is clearly taught in earlier ones.

Even the modern Catechism condemns Marcionism "vigorously." (§123) In describing Marcion, the heresy's eponymous originator, the *New Catholic Encyclopedia* explains:

> Marcion steadfastly maintained that the Church had been mistaken in retaining the OT [Old Testament] ...[he] was promptly excommunicated; he then gained many disciples among those who found the OT unconvincing or unattractive ... He considered [the "God of the Old Testament"] as legal-minded, offering material rewards ... while the absolutely perfect God, the God of pure love and mercy, was visibly embodied in Jesus ... **Able to see nothing in common between the God of the OT and the God of the NT [New Testament], Marcion concluded that the**

> **Gospel must be dissociated from Judaism and Jewish apocalyptic eschatology**. (*Marcion*. P. 142)

Although Marcion lived in the 2nd Century A.D., his attacks against "Jewish apocalyptic eschatology" proved so enticing that the movement formally continued for another 300 years despite its continued forceful condemnation by the Church. Despite no longer being an organized schism, however, the heresies it initiated still flourish. Indeed, Marcion's heretical teaching will undoubtedly sound familiar to many. The Protestant Reformation was in many ways built upon it; for example, Martin Luther condemned any teaching regarding the Kingdom coming to earth (i.e., a Reign of the Saints), because he classed it a "Judaistic opinion."[237] But Marcionism is also, tragically, resurging in some corners of the Catholic Church today.

In contrast to Marcion's heresies, we know that every prophecy of the Old Testament is a Divinely inspired Public Revelation, and is thereby guaranteed to be fulfilled in accordance with its own wording. This does not mean that every Biblical verse is *intended* literally, but it does mean that we must always revere the clear sense of Scripture and submit to the literal meaning of its words wherever doing so is called for by a faithful exegesis. To reject this reverence and play fast and loose with the Holy Spirit by insisting that every Scriptural verse which clearly speaks of literal blessings on earth is "merely symbolic," is to be radically unfaithful to the Word of God. And it is just one small step short of succumbing entirely to the atheistic approach that empties Scripture of all supernatural content and reduces it to a mere ethical guide.

Lest, however, we only reject Marcionism in name, even while succumbing to its substance elsewhere, we must also address the details of *how* exactly Marcionism goes about seeking to eradicate Public Revelation's infallible insistence, within the Old Testament, that God will reign over the earth. For by whatever name it is called, that view is equally Marcionistic which holds that *all* the prophecies of the Era in the Old Testament are *only* about Heaven, and only "appear" to pertain to earth because ancient Jews "had no understanding of eternal life," and therefore had no way of issuing teachings about it without simply erroneously speaking of temporal blessings. This take on the Old Testament is not only contrary to Catholic dogma on the inerrancy of all Scripture, it is also slander against the ancient Jews, plain and simple.

---

[237] This condemnation even made its way into the *Augsburg Confession,* Article XVII.

Faithful Old Testament Jews who awaited God's Kingdom on earth already knew that there was also a Heaven (see, for example, 2 Maccabees 7), and Jesus, far from claiming to have *revealed* the existence of Heaven, affirmed the opposite; even rebuking the Jewish Sadducees of His day for failing to realize that *their own* Scriptures clearly indicated that Heaven exists (cf. Mark 12). The great 19th-Century theologian and preacher, Fr. Charles Arminjon, put it well in a very special book that, in *Story of a Soul*, St. Thérèse of Lisieux herself called "one of the greatest graces of my life.":

> **Rationalist writers have declared that this belief in the resurrection was not contained in the Old Testament, and that it dates only from the Gospel. Nothing could be more erroneous.** We need only read through the long line of Mosaic tradition, listening to the great voices of the patriarchs and the prophets, to see that they all tremble with joy and hope at the prospect of the promised immortality, and celebrate this new life, which will become theirs beyond the grave, and will have no end. It is said in the book of Exodus, "I am the God of Abraham, the God of Isaac, and the God of Jacob." In St. Matthew, Christ uses this passage to prove to the Jews the truth of the resurrection [cf. Chapter 22] ... **for the saints of the Old Testament, this belief in the resurrection was not only a symbol and a speculative doctrine: it was their fundamental faith, expressed in the marvels and works of their lives.**[238]

Even the ancient Greek philosophers knew there was an afterlife, and they eagerly awaited and prepared for it by living a just life on earth. Each semester, I explain to my undergraduate philosophy students how Socrates (who died in 399 B.C.) logically demonstrates the immortality of the soul and instructs us by both word and example to live our whole lives in preparation for and anticipation of the afterlife. It is quite astonishing that some refuse to accord this same respect for our forefathers in the Faith: the ancient Jews, and even the Old Testament prophets themselves! In knowledge of Divine things, these faithful Israelites towered above the ancient Greek philosophers like a mountain above a grain of sand, whereas the prophets heard God's Own voice and were inspired by His Holy Spirit to inerrantly record its dictates. Indeed, this modernist supposition that (despite such exaltation) they lacked a clear view of eternity, is a great injustice done to our elder brethren in the Faith, and it must be corrected. We can do

---

[238] Charles Arminjon, *The End of the Present World and the Mysteries of the Future Life*. Pages 79-80

so by reminding ourselves that "**All** Scripture is inspired by God," (2 Timothy 3:16) and by proceeding to read again these promises that God has given *us*, in Scripture, through the Old Testament prophets.

Before concluding this section and turning to those prophecies themselves, however, we should note that *even if* Marcionism's heretical premises were valid—premises which hold that the New Testament may overturn what is clearly put forth as permanent (as opposed to merely juridical) in the Old on account of the latter supposedly being capable of error—the conclusion it presents does not follow. In no way did Jesus ever seek to deny the universal ancient Jewish expectation of God's eventual triumph over the earth by the coming of His Kingdom.

Indeed, Marcionists—by whatever name they go by in a given age—are known to claim that the Old Testament prophecies about God's Kingdom coming to earth were "corrected" by Jesus. Now, it is certainly true that Jesus said, while standing before Pilate, "My Kingdom is not of this world," (John 18:36) but it does not follow that His Kingdom would never *come to* this world. According to the Catechism of the Council of Trent:

> Our Lord himself informed Pilate, that his kingdom was not of this world, that is to say, **had not its origin** in this world... (Part IV)

We cannot, therefore, conclude from this Gospel teaching that Christ's Kingdom is never to be *established* on earth. To be sure, the Kingdom of Christ is not something which *comes from* the earth. Rather, "in the tender compassion of our God, **the dawn *from on high* shall break upon us**," (Luke 1:78) and this dawn—this Kingdom of Christ—will come in response to our fervent supplications for its arrival; not as a result of our effort to build it ourselves. Moreover, Jesus' very last words before His departure for Heaven indicate that the Kingdom *will* come to earth, for in the opening verses of the Book of Acts, we read:

> They asked him, "**Lord, will you at this time restore the kingdom to Israel?" He said to them, "It is not for you to know times or seasons ...**" And when he had said this, as they were looking on, he was lifted up, and a cloud took him out of their sight. (Acts 1:6-9)

Our Lord allowed the Apostles' expectation of the coming of the Kingdom on earth to stand in its entirety; He only admonished them that it was not theirs to know the time of its arrival. No faithful reading of Scripture would posit that Jesus, in His final act on earth, would have stood by idly as His very Apostles disclosed that they believed a fundamental error, only to have His sole response to them entail an implicit endorsement of that error! Quite the contrary, this passage must be regarded as just one of the multitudes assuring us of the coming of the Kingdom to "Israel," (that is, to *the Catholic Church*, the *New* Israel, and through it to the whole world), and we must stand in solidarity with the Apostles in our sure and certain hope in its coming.

It is also certainly true that Jesus had to evade those who wished for Him to be a temporal King during His earthly ministry in Jerusalem (cf. John 6:15) and similarly had to correct those who thought the Kingdom of God would be an observable, literal Kingdom. For, "The coming of the kingdom of God cannot be observed..." (Luke 17:20). But Jesus never taught that He would not—*in another way and at another time*—reign as King over the earth; He never implied that we must strictly await the dissolution of the world at the end of time to ever see a more complete reign of God's Kingdom on earth than was already made present by the birth of Christianity.

In contrast, Jesus taught—not only immediately before Ascending to Heaven, but even more centrally and clearly in the Our Father prayer—that He *would* eventually conquer universally and rule the earth by virtue of the reign of the Divine *Will* (but not the observable reign of his physical presence) *on earth as in Heaven*.

Now that Marcionism, its premises, and its corollaries have been addressed, let us proceed with reverence for the Divine Word, and consider just a few of the countless prophecies of the Era of Peace from the Old Testament. Prophecies guaranteed to be fulfilled in their time, and which we can anticipate the realization of with the same certainty with which we await the Second Coming itself.

Old Testament Prophecies: Universal Restoration

> "... until the times of universal restoration, which God hath spoken by the mouth of his holy prophets, from the beginning of the world." –Acts 3:21

As we see from even the Apostle Peter's *New* Testament teaching above, God's promise of worldwide renewal dates to the very earliest of prophecies and continues, with splendor undimmed and surety untouched, into the times of the New and Eternal Covenant. This renewal, ancient Jews always knew, would be brought about by the Anointed One. In keeping with this prophetic knowledge, ancient Judaism was characterized, perhaps more than anything else, by its universal brand of messianism. To be a faithful Jew *was to* faithfully await the coming of the Messiah, whose domain would be worldwide, and who would cause the *whole earth* to become subject to God. As one Christian Biblical scholar explained:

> The "Kingdom of God," internal and external, is the Content and End of all [Old Testament] prophecy, the realization of God's will *on earth*, as in heaven ... **the whole Old Testament administration finds its principle of unity in the prophecy and promise of the "Kingdom of God,"** set up to regulate the individual and national life, and foreshadow the subjection of the world's dominion to the sovereignty of the heavens ... **The whole Old Testament prophecy is already fulfilled in the Person of Christ, but this is a very different thing from saying that it is all fulfilled in the Church, or in the world.** The development is not ended. The death of Christ has, indeed, abolished the old *cultus* [the juridical decrees of the Old Covenant] forever, **but not overturned the prophecies of Israel's rehabilitation** ... **The New Testament presupposes, all the way through, the literal truth of the unfulfilled prophecies of the Old**...[239]

Even though some of the details privately[240] (albeit commonly) involved in this expectation were incorrect (e.g., the supposition that a political conquering king would impose the Mosaic Law upon all people), the expectation itself—of God's Kingdom reigning on earth—was absolutely valid, Divinely inspired, and has no expiration date. We must acknowledge how unfortunate it is that some people today who, though knowing the Law and the Prophets, cannot see that Jesus is the One promised by both. Still, their noble 4,000-year-long persistence in that prophetic expectation nevertheless testifies to the truth of its object. God *will* reign over the whole earth, and that essential tenet of ancient Judaism is a fact.

For as we will now see, the Biblical prophecies themselves explicitly contradict the interpretation which relegates their contents to purely otherworldly or inner realms. For example, some refer to physical blessings on *earth*; others promise events like swords being turned into plowshares and death only at a very old age, etc. Death and swords, of course, will in no way exist in Heaven, and subsequently

---

[239] Rev. Dr. Nathaniel West. *The Hebrew Student*. "Orelli on Old Testament Prophecy." Volume II. January 1883. Page 146. Nota Bene: What this scholar says here is absolutely correct, but elsewhere he strays into unorthodoxy, therefore I do not recommend his works.

[240] That is, those expectations which, though common among Jews, never were put forth within the canonical ancient Jewish Scriptures.

these prophecies cannot refer to our Eternal home. One modern Jewish scholar even confessed his frustration with certain interpreters (even among his fellow Jews) who insist on rejecting the clear sense of Old Testament prophecy. He states:

> **The reinterpretation of the prophetic promises of the Bible to refer to a realm of inwardness**, which **seemed as remote as possible from any contents of these prophecies**, always seemed to the religious thinkers of Judaism to be an illegitimate anticipation of something which could at best be seen as the **interior side of an event basically taking place in the external world**, but could never be cut off from the event itself ... The **history of the Messianic idea in Judaism has run its course within the framework of this idea's never-relinquished demand for fulfillment of its original vision**... [in the prophecies] **hope is turned backwards to the re-establishment of an original state of things** [Eden]... **nourished by a vision of the future**...[241]

You will see this analysis confirmed as you read the selections of the Word of God that follow, each of which makes it impossible to deny that the Holy Spirit has promised a glorious, universal Era of Peace upon the earth.

Before reviewing these prophecies, however, one additional fact must first be reiterated. For, while many of the Old Testament's prophecies we are about to consider speak for themselves, we—as Catholics—know that other prophecies require understanding that the Catholic Church itself *is the New Israel* (see, for example, *Lumen Gentium* §9 and *Mulieris Dignitatem* §20).[242] Unlike those arguments,

---

[241] Gershom Scholem. *The Messianic Idea in Judaism*. 1971.

[242] Nota Bene: In the 19th Century, there was a resurgence of popularity in Millennial interpretations of the Book of Revelation (both perfectly orthodox ones that merely anticipated the coming of the Kingdom of God to earth, and, unfortunately, erroneous Millenarian versions of the same) after several centuries of relative unpopularity. Some of the Millennium's most ardent opponents were Anglican intellectuals who generated caustic attacks at Westminster Abbey and at Cambridge University. There, at the prestigious Hulsean Lectures, one among their ranks (Christopher Wordsworth—an Anglican bishop) delivered the 1848 lecture which, compiled in a book, totals over 500 pages of invective against the Millennium and the Catholic Church. Within these pages he rejects the notion of God's Kingdom on earth precisely because, he insisted, the Roman Catholic Church's reign was itself already the reign of Revelation's "Whore of Babylon," and all that was eschatologically awaited for earth was its ultimate demise at the end of time, with Christ coming again in the flesh to defeat this "Whore." (cf. 1848 Hulsean Lectures. XII) He proceeded to argue, verse by verse, that the Book of Revelation "proves" as a "fact" that the Roman Catholic Church is the Harlot depicted therein. One can, however, easily see their motive; they were too well-read to have any hope of supposing that the Church of England could possibly lay any claim to being "the New Israel"—founded, as it was, only a few

refuted above, which seek to superimpose a meaning upon Scripture in contradiction to its own clear teachings and claim that clearly temporally-oriented prophecies are actually only about Heaven, this acknowledgement of what is meant by "Israel" in no way contradicts what the Old Testament teaches. The Catholic church *truly is* the New Israel—saying so is not a mere figure of speech or employment of hyperbole. When we see Old Testament promises of God's blessings being poured out to an utterly superlative degree upon Israel, this can only be properly understood as referring to the time when God would bless the Catholic Church with her full, worldwide triumph upon earth during the Era of Peace.[243] The outpouring of these prophesied blessings only *began* with the birth of Christianity; in the Era, they will be completed.

> **Genesis:** I will put enmities between thee [the devil] and the woman, and thy seed and her seed: she shall crush thy head, and thou shalt lie in wait for her heel. (Genesis 3) And I will make of you [Abraham] a great nation, and I will bless you, and make your name great, so that you will be a blessing. I will bless those who bless you, and him who curses you I will curse; and by you all the families of the earth shall bless themselves. (Genesis 12)
>
> **Exodus**: ... for all the earth is mine, and you shall be to me a kingdom of priests and a holy nation. (Exodus 19)
>
> **Deuteronomy:** The LORD will open for you His good storehouse, the heavens, to give rain to your land in its season and to bless all the work of your hand. (Deuteronomy 28)
>
> **The Psalms:** The earth shall yield its fruit, for God, our God, has blessed us. (Psalm 67) ... that the mountains may yield their bounty for the people and the hills great abundance…And all kings of the earth shall adore him: all nations shall serve him. (Psalm 72) Let me hear what God the Lord will speak, for he will speak peace to his people, to his saints, to those who turn to him in their hearts. Surely his salvation is at hand for those who fear him, that glory may dwell in our land. Steadfast love and faithfulness will meet; **righteousness and peace will kiss** each other. Faithfulness will spring up from the ground, and righteousness

---

hundred years earlier by an adulterous King. Accordingly, they realized that no Scriptural promise of temporal triumph of *the* Church could possibly refer to *their* Church, and they proceeded to seek to eradicate any hope of such a Triumph ever happening at all, replacing that hope with an *Eschatology of Despair*. To this day, the Era is most viciously attacked by men—including Catholics—formed within this heritage of anti-Catholic Anglican eschatology.

[243] It would of course be absurd to interpret these prophecies as referring only to an outpouring of blessings for a specific nation which, as of this writing, includes only .001% of the world's people.

will look down from the sky. Yea, the Lord will give what is good, and our land will yield its increase. Righteousness will go before him, and make his footsteps a way. (Psalm 85) Then the Lord's name will be declared on Zion, the praise of God in Jerusalem, when all peoples and kingdoms gather to worship the Lord. (Psalm 102)

Isaiah: ... **the light of the moon will be as the light of the sun,** and the light of the sun will be sevenfold, as the light of seven days, **in the day when the Lord binds up the hurt of his people, and heals the wounds inflicted by his blow**. (Isaiah 30) Then will the eyes of the blind be opened, the ears of the deaf be cleared; Then the lame will leap like a stag, then the tongue of the dumb will sing. (Isaiah 35) For the Lord will comfort Zion; he will comfort all her waste places, and **will make her wilderness like Eden,** her desert like the garden of the Lord; joy and gladness will be found in her, thanksgiving and the voice of song. (Isaiah 51) **There shall no more be an infant of days there, nor an old man that shall not fill up his days: for the child shall die a hundred years old** ... They shall not build, and another inhabit; they shall not plant, and another eat: for as the days of a tree, so shall be the days of my people, and the works of their hands shall be of long continuance ... **The wolf and the lamb shall feed together**; the lion and the ox shall eat straw; and dust shall be the serpent's food: they shall not hurt nor kill in all my holy mountain, saith the Lord. (Isaiah 65) From one new moon to another, and from one Sabbath to another, **all mankind shall come to worship before me, says the Lord.** (Isaiah 66)

Jeremiah: At that time, says the Lord, I will be the God of all the tribes of Israel, and they shall be my people ... As **Israel comes forward to be given his rest**, the Lord appears to him from afar: with age-old love I have loved you; so I have kept my mercy toward you. Again I will restore you, and you shall be rebuilt, o virgin Israel ... Yes, a day will come when the watchmen will call out on Mount Ephraim: 'Rise up, let us go to Zion, to the Lord, our God.' But this is the covenant which I will make with the house of Israel after those days, says the Lord**: I will put my law within them, and I will write it upon their hearts; and I will be their God, and they shall be my people**. And no longer shall each man teach his neighbour and each his brother, saying, 'Know the LORD', for they shall all know me, from the least of them to the greatest, says the LORD; for I will forgive their iniquity, and I will remember their sin no more. (Jeremiah 31)

Ezekiel: The cities shall be inhabited and the waste places rebuilt; and I will multiply upon you man and beast; and they shall increase and be fruitful; and I will cause you to be inhabited as in your former times, and will do more good to you than ever before. Then you will know that I am the Lord... And they will say, '**This land that was desolate has become like the garden of Eden**...' (Ezekiel 36)

Daniel: Seventy weeks of years are decreed concerning your people and your holy city, to finish the transgression, **to put an end to sin, and to atone for iniquity, to bring in everlasting righteousness**, to seal both vision and prophet, and to anoint a most holy place. (Daniel 9)

Joel: And it shall come to pass afterward, that I will pour out my spirit on all flesh; your sons and your daughters shall prophesy, your old men shall dream dreams, and your young men shall see visions. Even upon the menservants and maidservants in those days, I will pour out my spirit. (Joel 2)

Amos: "Behold, the days are coming," says the Lord, "when the plowman shall overtake the reaper and the treader of grapes him who sows the seed; **the mountains shall drip sweet wine, and all the hills shall flow with it**." (Amos 9)

Micah: It shall come to pass in the latter days that the mountain of the house of the Lord shall be established as the highest of the mountains, and shall be raised up above the hills; and peoples shall flow to it, and many nations shall come, and say: "Come, let us go up to the mountain of the Lord, to the house of the God of Jacob; that he may teach us his ways and we may walk in his paths." For out of Zion shall go forth the law, and the word of the Lord from Jerusalem. He shall judge between many peoples, and shall decide for strong nations afar off; and **they shall beat their swords into plowshares, and their spears into pruning hooks; nation shall not lift up sword against nation**, neither shall they learn war any more; but they shall sit every man under his vine and under his fig tree, and none shall make them afraid; for the mouth of the Lord of hosts has spoken. (Micah 4)

Habakkuk: For the earth will be filled with the knowledge of the glory of the Lord, as the waters cover the sea. (Habakkuk 2)

Zephaniah: At that time I will change the speech of the peoples to a pure speech, that all of them may call on the name of the Lord and serve him with one accord ... On that day you shall not be put to shame because of the deeds by which you have rebelled against me; for then I will remove from your midst your proudly exultant ones ... **those who are left in Israel; they shall do no wrong and utter no lies, nor shall there be found in their**

mouth a deceitful tongue. For they shall pasture and lie down, and none shall make them afraid ... Sing aloud, O daughter of Zion; shout, O Israel! Rejoice and exult with all your heart, O daughter of Jerusalem! The Lord has taken away the judgments against you, he has cast out your enemies. The King of Israel, the Lord, is in your midst; you shall fear evil no more. (Zephaniah 3)

Haggai: For thus says the Lord of hosts: **Once again, in a little while, I will shake the heavens and the earth** and the sea and the dry land; and I will shake all nations, so that the treasures of all nations shall come in, **and I will fill this house with splendor,** says the Lord of hosts. The silver is mine, and the gold is mine, says the Lord of hosts. The latter splendor of this house shall be greater than the former, says the Lord of hosts; and in this place I will give prosperity, says the Lord of hosts. (Haggai 2)

Zechariah: In those days ten men of every nation, speaking in different tongues, shall take hold, yes, take old of every Jew by the edge of his garment and say, "Let us go with you, for we have heard that God is with you." (Zechariah 8) The weakling among them shall be [strong] like David on that day. (Zechariah 12)

Malachi: Behold, I will send you Elijah the prophet before the great and terrible day of the Lord comes. And **he will turn the hearts of fathers to their children and the hearts of children to their fathers**... (Malachi 4)

New Testament Prophecies: The Coming of Christ in Grace

> "Almighty ever-living God, whose will is to restore all things in your beloved son, the King of the universe, grant, we pray, that the whole creation, set free from slavery, may render your majesty service and ceaselessly proclaim your praise."
> –Collect for the Feast of Christ the King. Roman Missal

The moment Christ initiated His public ministry by proclaiming "**The time is fulfilled, and the Kingdom of God is at hand,**" (Mark 1:15) being a faithful Jew meant becoming a faithful Christian. In the same way, the faithful Jewish anticipation of the reign of God on earth – far from being discarded – was *elevated* to the even greater dignity to a faithful anticipation of the Coming of Christ. This dynamic describes how the Revelation of Jesus always operated in relation to all the most important themes of the Old Testament. Marriage, greatly exalted in Judaism, was elevated even higher: to the level of a

Sacrament. The Commandments, far from abrogated, were rendered more demanding still, as they were perfected by the Beatitudes. The "baptism of repentance" known to the Jews became true Baptism of the Holy Spirit; a Baptism which does not dispose of repentance, but rather renders it the opening act to a life of Sanctifying Grace. Many books have been written explaining how each of the Old Testament's most important realities (or "types") were elevated by Christ in the New Testament's corresponding fulfillments (or "antitypes.") As Pope Benedict XVI taught, "the Jewish understanding of the Bible can prove helpful to Christians for their own understanding and study of the Scriptures," (*Verbum Domini* §41) and the Catechism admonishes us to recognize that none of these pairings detract from the value of what is already clear on its own in the Old Testament:

> ... **the Old Testament retains its own intrinsic value as Revelation** reaffirmed by our Lord himself. Besides, the New Testament has to be read in the light of the Old. Early Christian catechesis made constant use of the Old Testament. (§129)

This pattern, therefore, could not fail to describe what the New Testament did to Judaism's most essential aspect: its *Messianism*. The Old Testament's Messianic expectation of the world one day being totally subject to the reign of God was preserved and assimilated into the sure and certain hope of the glorious coming of Christ in grace to establish His Kingdom. For any Christian, it should be quite telling that not one of the almost eight thousand verses from Matthew 1:1 to Revelation 22:21 contains any indication, implicit or explicit, that any of the Old Testament prophecies which promise immense, universal, and temporal (though eternally oriented) blessings for the earth are no longer to be taken at their face value. Quite the contrary, Christ Himself insisted that everything spoken of in the Old Testament Scriptures would still occur, and that the end will not come before all spoken of by "*the prophets*" therein has transpired:

> Think not that I have come to abolish the law **and the prophets**; I have come not to abolish them but to fulfil them. For truly, I say to you, **till heaven and earth pass away, not an iota, not a dot, will pass from the law until all is accomplished**. (Matthew 5:17-18)[244]

---

[244] Consider that any orthodox-minded Catholic rejects the modernist line which pretends that whenever the New Testament does not explicitly reiterate some moral teaching from the Old, this moral teaching is itself abrogated. (For in truth, only the Old Testament's *juridical* precepts are abrogated.) Such a stance is frequently employed to reject certain

Unfortunately, some Christians fail to see the Era of Peace in the New Testament's repeated promises of the Coming of Christ because they push His coming out of mind by relegating it to only occurring at the very end of time.[245] Thus, they fail to acknowledge His many comings in *grace* before His Second Coming in the *flesh*. Only the latter is rightly regarded as restricted to the world's end, however. As we considered earlier, the more important a theme in Scripture is, the more likely it is to have multiple valid understandings. It certainly is the case with the Kingdom of God itself, and so too it is with that Coming of Christ *which establishes the Kingdom* more fully than ever before. Indeed, if Christianity's founding already constituted the only Coming of the Kingdom that we need concern ourselves with, then the Our Father's petition for it to "come" (Matthew 6:10) is entirely useless, and none should dare accuse Our Lord of teaching a pointless prayer at all, much less as the Church's most substantial one.

Therefore, a fundamental Christian plea—which is even the very exclamation the New Testament itself concludes with—has always been, "Maranatha!" That is: **"Come, Lord Jesus!"** (Revelation 22:20) The Mass itself reminds us of this incessantly: "**His coming in glory we await with unwavering hope**." (Preface V. Roman Missal). This anticipation of Christ's coming was precisely what gave early Christians such heroic zeal, and its absence is what has turned so many modern Christians lukewarm. Therefore, it is today imperative that we reacquire that same anticipation. Reacquiring it would not mean that we thereby hope for the imminent end of time and concomitant destruction of the universe! Perhaps some are understandably uncomfortable with the notion of desiring the world to end in its present lamentable state (with most of its inhabitants anything but prepared to enter eternity) and avoid crying out "*Maranatha*!" because they are unaware of the fact that this is *not* what we are doing by imploring the Lord's Coming. For the Comings of Christ in grace noted above are many. He comes each time someone is baptized, during each consecration and reception of the Eucharist, in each restoration

---

infallible truths pertaining to sexual morality. Similarly, any orthodox-minded Catholic must reject the equally modernist account which discards Old Testament *prophecy* if some of its details are not found specifically reiterated within the New Testament's pages. For just as the New Testament has every right to increase the rigor of the moral precepts contained in the Old (e.g., rendering divorce impermissible) but never dispenses from any of them, so too it has every right to *add* to Old Testament prophecy (and of course *fulfill* it), but it never deletes from it.

[245] This is, indeed, tantamount to excluding Christ's coming from the Christian worldview, since we know that the end of time cannot be imminent, considering how much that is Scripturally guaranteed has obviously not yet happened (e.g., the reign of the Antichrist, the conversion of the Jews, etc.)

of a sinner to grace through Confession, in each time the Gospel is preached and received, in each time His Social Kingship is better established, in each time the Holy Spirit descends into our hearts. And, yes, He will come again in the flesh only at the end of the world to command the Eternal Resurrection and Last Judgment, and He comes fully to each soul immediately after his or her own death as well, during the particular judgment.

But there will also be Christ's spiritual coming to establish His Kingdom more fully upon earth through the reign of the Divine Will. As we will see in the next chapter, the early Church universally expected *this* Coming of Christ in grace. The promise of this Coming contained within itself all the glory of the Old Testament's promises of a restored earth, a glorified "Israel," etc., while at the same time far surpassing them. It is, therefore, only to be expected that the New Testament, instead of merely reiterating what the Old already taught in these prophecies, focused on their own superior context, *the Coming of Christ*:

> Therefore be patient, brethren, until the coming of the Lord. (James 5:7) **Behold, He is coming** with the clouds, and every eye will see Him, even those who pierced Him; and all the tribes of the earth will mourn over Him. (Revelation 1:7) Therefore **be on the alert, for you do not know which day your Lord is coming.** (Matthew 24:42) ... so that you are not lacking in any gift, **awaiting eagerly the revelation of our Lord Jesus Christ** ... (1 Corinthians 1:7) ... looking for the blessed hope and **the appearing of the glory of our great God and Savior, Christ Jesus** ... (Titus 2:13) I solemnly charge you in the presence of God and of Christ Jesus, who is to judge the living and the dead, and **by His appearing and His kingdom**... (2 Timothy 4:1) Therefore do not go on passing judgment before the time, but **wait until the Lord comes** who will both bring to light the things hidden in the darkness... (1 Corinthians 4:5) **When I am lifted up from the earth, I will draw all men to myself**. (John 12:32)

Fulfillment vs. Completion

> Stir up the will of your faithful, we pray, O Lord, that, striving more eagerly to **bring your divine work to fruitful completion**, they may receive in greater measure the healing remedies your kindness bestows.
>
> –Collect for the 34th Week in Ordinary Time. Roman Missal.

The supreme reality of Old Testament prophecy is certainly its Christological dimension. We say in the Mass that "**all the oracles of the prophets foretold him,**" (Preface II of Advent. Roman Missal) and as the Second Vatican Council teaches, "The principal purpose to which the plan of the old covenant was directed was to prepare for the coming of Christ." (*Dei Verbum* §15) Moreover, while these prophecies are *fulfilled in and by* Christ through His Incarnation, Death, and Resurrection; they are not yet entirely fulfilled *in His Church*, who is still in the process of following Christ, her head, towards the completion of the fulfillment.

These Paschal Mysteries, which constitute the very climax of history itself, opened the doors to Heaven and *initiated* the Age of the Church, which in turn would—through two thousand years of additional labors so far—eventually culminate in the union of Heaven and earth through the reign of the Divine Will promised in the Our Father. It is crucial, therefore, that we do not confuse the *initiation*—by which all *is fulfilled in Christ*—with the *completion*—by which all *will be fulfilled in the whole Church*. To be sure, there is no indication in the Bible that we had already seen the latter by the events described therein. No passage anywhere in the New Testament instructs us to regard Christianity itself *as already* received by the world as the *completion* of the fulfillment of the prophecies, but simply the beginning of that fulfillment. The fact was too obvious to be worth presenting as a teaching by the authors of the New Testament, although it was at times mentioned in passing. For example, in the Book of Hebrews, we read:

> Now in putting everything in subjection to him, he left nothing outside his control. **As it is, we do not yet see everything in subjection to him**. (Hebrews 2:8)

As *not* all is yet subject to God—though Scripture repeatedly promises that all *will* be made subject to Him, not only in Heaven but also on earth—we can be certain of a future temporal fulfillment of this promise. We can be sure that, on a day yet to come, *every* knee will bow at the name of Jesus, including all those not only in Heaven, but also "**on earth.**" (Philippians 2:10) The Holy Spirit, through St. Paul assures us that creation awaits not merely its complete dissolution at the end of time—its "ultimate" destiny—wherein we know from St. Peter's second letter that:

> ... **the heavens will pass away with a loud noise, and the elements will be dissolved with fire**, and the earth and the works that are upon it will be burned up... (2 Peter 3:10)

Quite the contrary, Scripture also assures us that *before* the total dissolution of the material universe described above, creation awaits its Penultimate Destiny—its "glorious" deliverance from subjection to the bondage it now suffers from as a result of the Fall:

> **For the creation waits with eager longing** for the revealing of the sons of God; for the creation was subjected to futility, not of its own will but by the will of him who subjected it in hope; because the **creation itself will be set free from its bondage to decay and obtain the glorious liberty of the children of God.** We know that the whole creation has been groaning in travail together until now. (Romans 8:19-22)

This liberation of creation coincides with the fulfillment of the Coming of the Kingdom of God; the reign of the Divine Will on earth as in Heaven; the fulfillment of the Our Father prayer; the Era of Peace. As obvious as it is that we have not yet seen this liberation, it is even more certain that we *will* see it, for Scripture guarantees as much.

The Book of Revelation and the Reign of Saints

> "May the splendor of your glory dawn in our hearts, we pray, almighty God, that all shadows of the night may be scattered and we may be shown to be children of light by the advent of your only Begotten son."
>
> –Collect for Saturday of the 2nd Week of Advent. Roman Missal.

After the Lord's Prayer, one of the New Testament's most commonly quoted prophecies of the Era is contained in the Book of Revelation:

> [An angel] seized the dragon, that ancient serpent, who is the Devil and Satan, and bound him for a thousand years, and threw him into the pit, and shut it and sealed it over him, that he should deceive the nations no more, till the thousand years were ended ... [The saints martyred] came to life, and reigned with Christ a thousand years. And when the thousand years are ended, Satan will be loosed from his prison... (Revelation 20)

What a glorious promise the Book of Revelation here gives us! Although the "thousand years" it speaks of should not be taken as a literal measurement of the Era's duration, this passage nevertheless clearly refers to a "reign of the saints" *on earth*, before the end of time. For only in the later verses of the same passage do we see foretold the Last Judgment *following* this Era: "Then I saw a great white throne and him who sat upon it; from his presence earth and sky fled away, and no place was found for them." (Revelation 20:11) This alludes to the same "dissolution of the elements," noted above, which Scripture reserves for the end of time (2 Peter 3:10).

Now, the "Millenarians" erroneously take this prophecy from the Book of Revelation to indicate that Christ will reign visibly on earth, whereas the passage itself does not speak of Christ physically coming to earth before or during this "thousand year" reign, but after it (cf. Revelation 20:11). (Note: The error of Millenarianism is addressed in the appendices, wherein we will see that its fallacies are unrelated to what is prophesied regarding the Era of Peace.)

It is not reasonable to suppose this passage refers strictly to some time or event that has already transpired, since we have never seen anything remotely resembling a period during which Satan "**deceives the nations no more,**" and whoever thinks otherwise should open any history textbook. Nor have we seen a "**reign of saints**," for the world has, with relatively few exceptions, always remained under the control of men for whom the word "saint" would be the least accurate description. Nor, finally, can this passage refer to Heaven, since that is eternal, whereas the "reign of saints" described here is followed by a brief release of Satan immediately before the very end of the world.

Despite these clear observations, however, it is unfortunately true that many in the Church fail to accord any credit to them, for they are under the impression that a certain highly symbolic, entirely allegorized view of Revelation 20 is the only allowable one, even though the Magisterium has never taught this. Addressing that notion will require a degree of analysis that some may not be interested in, therefore whoever wishes to read it may find it within the appendices. Presently, therefore, we continue following the same pattern we did in Part Two with the Gift itself—tracing out the development of the Church's understanding of the Era beyond Scripture and into the times of the Fathers of the Church.

"**Therefore, a sabbath rest still remains for the people of God.**"
-Hebrews 4:9

POPE ST. PIUS X

PAPAL MOTTO
INSTAURARE OMNIA IN CHRISTO
"TO RESTORE ALL THINGS IN CHRIST"

21. The Fathers and Popes on the Era

"A Kingdom is promised to us upon the earth..."
–Tertullian

Those whom we call Church Fathers are the great and prolific theologians, saints, doctors, mystics, and philosophers of the early Church. Many of them lived close enough to the time of Christ to still have access to trustworthy and direct oral accounts of His Own Divine words, and Christians to this day rightly revere these men as giving the most authoritative teachings on the Faith. The Church Fathers are nearly unanimous in their conviction that the earth's last Millennium, which they generally held to be the third after Christ (and also, therefore, the *seventh* of Creation and correspondingly the "Sabbath Rest" for the Faithful—which we just saw prophesied in the New Testament's Book of Hebrews), would host the coming of the Kingdom of God. Here we will consider only a tiny fraction of their teachings on the matter, with direct quotes from their own writings.

We should first, however, recall that *Millenarianism* is an error, and on some occasions some of the Fathers below may have strayed into it. Therefore, we must always filter their teachings through the Magisterium. But we certainly must never discard a Church Father's entire eschatological contribution on account of a few missteps in need of this purification. The latter approach would leave us with virtually no teachings on any matter from any of the Church Fathers! Therefore, despite the occasional correction we can today easily make on their teachings without detracting from their core, the consensus of the Fathers is clear: Christ's Kingdom *will* come to earth, and its arrival will transform everything.

> **St. John Chrysostom: For He did not at all say, "Thy will be done" in me, or in us, but everywhere on the earth;** so that error may be destroyed, and truth implanted, and all wickedness cast out, and virtue return, and no difference in this respect be henceforth between heaven and earth. "For if this come to pass," saith He, "there will be no difference between things below and above, separated as they are in nature; the earth exhibiting to us another set of angels." (Homily XIX, §7)
>
> **St. Justin Martyr: I and every other orthodox Christian feel certain** that there will be **a** resurrection of the flesh followed by a thousand years in a rebuilt, embellished, and enlarged city of Jerusalem, as was announced by the Prophets Ezekiel, Isaias

and others... **A man among us named John, one of Christ's Apostles, received and foretold** that the followers of Christ would dwell in Jerusalem for a thousand years, and that **afterwards the universal and, in short, everlasting resurrection and judgment would take place.** (*Dialogue with Trypho*. Ch. 30)

Commodianus: The things told of in the law are hastening to their completion. The **Almighty Christ descends to His elect ... the true heavenly people. The son does not die before his father, then; nor do they feel pains in their bodies** ... They who cease depart in ripe years in their bed, fulfilling all the things of the law, and therefore they are protected ... The creation rejoices to see the heavenly people. (*On Christian Discipline* XLII) From heaven will descend the city in the first resurrection; this is what we may tell of such a celestial fabric. We shall arise again to Him, who have been devoted to Him. … They shall come also who overcame cruel martyrdom under Antichrist, and they themselves live for the whole time, and receive blessings because they have suffered evil things … (XLIV) [*In the following Chapter, Commodianus then describes the end of time, to arrive after this Era:*] The whole of nature is converted in flame ... Of the sea nothing remains: it is overcome by the powerful fire. This sky perishes… Another newness of sky and of everlasting earth is arranged. Thence they who deserve it are sent away in a second death, but the righteous are placed in inner dwelling-places. (LV)

St. Victorinus: Wherefore, as I have narrated, **that true Sabbath will be in the seventh millenary of years,** when Christ with His elect shall reign. (*On the Creation of the World*, §5) [*Note: St. Victorinus, though he here taught a "millennial" reign of Christ on earth in the Era, also gives a spiritual understanding of the millennium in his "Commentary on the Apocalypse." Indeed, following St. Victorinus' example, we should not see the two interpretations as opposed, but as complementary.*]

Tertullian: A kingdom is promised to us upon the earth, although **before heaven**, only in another state of existence; inasmuch as it will be after the resurrection for a thousand years in the divinely-built city of Jerusalem... (*Against Marcion*. Book 3. Ch. 25)

St. Irenaeus: The predicted blessing, therefore, belongs unquestionably to the times of the kingdom... when also the creation, having been renovated and set free, shall fructify with an abundance of all kinds of food, from the dew of heaven, and from the fertility of the earth: as the elders who saw **John, the disciple of the Lord, related that they had heard from** him how the Lord used to teach in regard to these times ... (*Against Heresies*. Book V. Ch. 33.)

St. Barnabas: And God made in six days the works of His hands, and made an end on the seventh day, and rested on it, and sanctified it. Attend, my children, to the meaning of this expression, He finished in six days. This implies that the Lord will finish all things in six thousand years, for a day is with Him a thousand years. ... in six thousand years, all things will be finished. And He rested on the seventh day. This means: when **His Son, coming [again], shall destroy the time of the wicked man, and judge the ungodly, and change the sun, and the moon, and the stars, then shall He truly rest on the seventh day** ... when, giving rest to all things, I shall make a **beginning of the eighth day, that is, a beginning of another world**. [*Note: St. Barnabas refers to the Kingdom on earth as the "Seventh Day" and the Kingdom in Heaven – after that temporal "Sabbath Rest" for God's people – the "Eighth Day."*] (*Epistle of Barnabas*. Chapter 15.)

St. Papias: As the elders who saw John the disciple of the Lord remembered that they had heard from him **how the Lord taught in regard to those times,** and said: "The days will come in which vines shall grow, having each ten thousand branches, and in each branch ten thousand twigs, and in each true twig ten thousand shoots, and in every one of the shoots ten thousand clusters, and on every one of the clusters ten thousand grapes, and every grape when pressed will give five-and-twenty metretes of wine. And when any one of the saints shall lay hold of a cluster, another shall cry out, 'I am a better cluster, take me; bless the Lord through me.' "... and that **all animals, feeding then only on the productions of the earth, would become peaceable and harmonious, and be in perfect subjection to man**. (Fragment IV.)

Lactantius: ... beasts shall not be nourished by blood, nor birds by prey; **but all things shall be peaceful and tranquil. Lions and calves shall stand together at the manger**, the wolf shall not carry off the sheep ... These are the things which are spoken of by the prophets as about to happen hereafter: but **I have not considered it necessary to bring forward their testimonies and words, since it would be an endless task**; nor would the limits of my book receive so great a multitude of subjects, since so many with one breath speak similar things; and

> at the same time, lest weariness should be occasioned to the readers if I should heap together things collected and transferred from all. (*Divine Institutes*. Book 7. Ch. 25)

Having already quoted many sources demonstrating his views on a coming of the Kingdom, Lactantius deems it pointless to continue. The task would be so voluminous, he writes, that its results would be "endless." On that same note we now conclude this section, and turn to a deeper consideration of one Church Father in particular.

St. Irenaeus and the Consensus of the Fathers

> "O God, who called the Bishop saint Irenaeus to confirm true doctrine and the peace of the Church, grant, we pray, through his intercession, that, being renewed in faith and charity, we may always be intent on fostering unity and concord."
> –Collect for the Feast of St. Irenaeus

We mustn't forget the explicit insistence, from the Church Father St. Irenaeus (and also St. Justin Martyr), that the reality of the Coming of the Kingdom on earth during its final Millennium is not merely his opinion on how Scripture should be interpreted, but is rather a promise *received from Jesus Himself,* in an oral tradition through the Apostle John. Scripture's own teaching on such traditions must be recalled: "Stand firm and hold to the traditions which you were taught by us, **either by word of mouth or by letter**." (2 Thessalonians 2:15) Indeed, Irenaeus was a disciple of Polycarp, who in turn was a disciple of St. John the Apostle; the bonds were so close that Irenaeus is even sometimes referred to as the "spiritual grandson" of John. When a given prophecy is issued by two Fathers, both saints, as coming directly from Jesus, then we should confidently await its fulfillment on this reason alone.

As of this writing, St. Irenaeus is set to soon be declared a Doctor of the Church; the first such declaration of a Church Father in over a hundred years,[246] which will also give him the extraordinary status as the first *ever* martyr-Doctor. As Fr. John Cush wrote, in a 2019 article explaining the worldwide advocacy of Bishops to have Irenaeus declared a Doctor:

> He is a martyr, and as such, he holds a higher position already than any Doctor of the Church. Irenaeus shed his blood as a wit-

[246] Saint Ephrem the Syrian was declared a Doctor of the Church in 1920

> ness to the Lord and his teachings. In the year A.D. 202, the Emperor Septimus Severus, by imperial decree, ordered the martyrdom of Christians in honor of the 10th anniversary of his ascent to the throne. In the history of the Catholic Church, no one, even if they were great theologians and teachers of the faith, has ever been declared a Doctor of the Church if they were a martyr. Saint Cyprian of Carthage, a martyr and a great teacher of the Catholic faith, is not a declared Doctor of the Church. Saint Ignatius of Antioch, another martyr and a supreme teacher of the faith, is not a declared Doctor of the Church. Saint Justin, the very first true systematic theologian in the Church, is not a Doctor of the Church.[247]

In speaking on this great Church Father's upcoming declaration as a Doctor, however, Pope Francis focused his comments on a particular, overlooked fact about the saint: *the meaning of his name.* As the Pope explained,

> **Saint Irenaeus of Lyons** - whom soon I will willingly declare a Doctor of the Church with the title *Doctor unitatis* - came from the East, exercised his episcopal ministry in the West, and **was a great spiritual and theological bridge between Eastern and Western Christians. His name, Irenaeus, contains the word "peace".** We know that the Lord's peace is not a "negotiated" peace, the fruit of agreements meant to safeguard interests, but a peace that reconciles, that brings together in unity. That is the peace of Jesus.[248]

Discerning hearts who heed Our Lord's admonition to observe the signs of the times (cf. Matthew 16:3) will not fail to conclude what the Holy Spirit is telling the Church, about the Era of Peace, through this forthcoming declaration. Of all the Fathers, it is perhaps Irenaeus who provides the clearest and most forceful teachings on the Era. For he not only insists upon its arrival and relays it to us from the mouth of Our Lord Himself; he also was aware of those who sought to essentially disregard this teaching by considering it to be merely a reference to Heaven or to the Church in its present state, or some non-literal reality, and Irenaeus thoroughly refuted these claims.

Let us, therefore, expand our consideration of his teachings on the coming of the Kingdom of God on earth, trusting that the Holy Spirit has moved the Church to declare Irenaeus a Doctor precisely

---

[247] Father John P. Cush. National Catholic Register. "St. Irenaeus—A Martyr, But Not Yet a Doctor of the Church." December 11, 2019

[248] Address to the Saint Irenaeus joint Orthodox-Catholic working group. Clementine Hall. October 7, 2021

because the time has come to delve more deeply into this passion of his. The following excerpts are taken from his work, *Against Heresies*, Book V:

> **[Christ] will Himself renew the inheritance of the earth**, and will re-organize the mystery of the glory of [His] sons; as David says, "He who has renewed the face of the earth."... **He cannot by any means be understood as drinking of the fruit of the vine when settled down with his [disciples] above in [Heaven]**... for to drink of that which flows from the vine pertains to flesh, and not spirit ... For what are the hundred-fold [rewards] in this word [Luke 18:29-30], the entertainments given to the poor, and the suppers for which a return is made? **These are [to take place] in the times of the kingdom, that is, upon the seventh day** ... **If any one, then, does not accept these things as referring to the appointed kingdom, he must fall into much contradiction and contrariety**... when the creation is restored, all the animals should obey and be in subjection to man, and revert to the food originally given by God (for they had been originally subjected in obedience to Adam), that is, the productions of the earth ... (Book 33) That the whole creation shall, according to God's will, obtain a vast increase, that it may bring forth and sustain fruits such [as we have mentioned], Isaiah declares: "And there shall be upon every high mountain, and upon every prominent hill, water running everywhere in that day..." (Book 34)
> **If, however, any shall endeavour to allegorize [prophecies] of this kind, they shall not be found consistent with themselves in all points, and shall be confuted by the teaching of the very expressions [in question] ... For all these and other words were unquestionably spoken in reference to the resurrection of the just[249], which takes place after the coming of Antichrist**, and the destruction of all nations under his rule; in [the times of] which [resurrection] the righteous shall reign in the earth, waxing stronger by the sight of the Lord: and through Him they shall become accustomed to partake in the glory of God the Father, and shall enjoy in the kingdom ... communion with the holy angels, and union with spiritual beings ... Now all these things being such as they are, **cannot be understood in reference to [Heavenly] matters; for God, it is said, will show to the whole earth that is under heaven your glory. But in the times of the**

[249] The "Resurrection of the Just" is how Irenaeus describes a certain miraculous event before the Era; notice that he is not referring to the *eternal* resurrection at the end of time with this phrase.

> **kingdom, the earth has been called again by Christ [to its pristine condition]... nothing is capable of being allegorized,** but all things are steadfast, and true, and substantial, having been made by God for righteous men's enjoyment. For as it is God truly who raises up man, so also does man truly rise from the dead, and not allegorically, as I have shown repeatedly. And as he rises actually, so also shall he be actually disciplined beforehand for incorruption, and shall go forwards and flourish in the times of the kingdom, in order that he may be capable of receiving the glory of the Father. Then, when all things are made new, he shall truly dwell in the city of God. (Book 35)
>
> **John, therefore, did distinctly foresee the first resurrection of the just**, [Luke 14:14] and the inheritance in the kingdom of the earth; **and what the prophets have prophesied concerning it harmonize [with his vision]. For the Lord also taught these things**, when He promised that He would have the mixed cup new with His disciples in the kingdom. **The apostle, too, has confessed that the creation shall be free from the bondage of corruption**, [so as to pass] into the liberty of the sons of God. (Romans 8:21) And in all these things, and by them all, the same God the Father is manifested, who fashioned man, and gave promise of the inheritance of the earth to the fathers, who brought it (the creature) forth [from bondage] at the resurrection of the just, and fulfils the promises for the kingdom of His Son... (Book 36)[250]

As St. Irenaeus demonstrates, it is simply implausible and even logically contradictory to interpret the promises from Jesus Himself—and from the Apostles, from St. Paul, and from the Old Testament Prophets—as referring to anything other than a glorious Era to come on earth; a "coming of Christ's Kingdom" within history, before the end of time, along with an outpouring of grace and blessings for the whole world. This Church Father is not merely presenting an opinion on how to interpret a single passage in the Book of Revelation; he is, rather, relaying a fundamental conviction from prophecies *throughout* the Old and New Testaments. Even if his take on Revelation 20 were mistaken, this would have no impact on the enduring truth of his conclusion—a conclusion he shares with almost all the other Church Fathers who left treatises on this question.

Thankfully, however, we are not left with the task of interpreting Scripture and the Church Fathers on our own. For we are given

---

[250] Note: In these quotations from Irenaeus, most of the bracketed remarks were in the original text (cf. newadvent.org) and were not added by me.

the Magisterium, whose Divine mandate is to provide the proper interpretation of the Deposit of Faith. This Magisterium has been absolutely clear in proclaiming the Era—particularly so in recent times, as the Church now stands on the cusp of its attainment and the Holy Spirit has moved the Popes to announce its impending arrival.

Papal Magisterium

> "This is our great hope and our petition: 'Your Kingdom come'—a kingdom of peace, justice, and serenity, that will re-establish the original harmony of creation."–Pope St. John Paul II

Beginning especially powerfully in the early 20th Century, Papal Magisterium proclaimed that the Church was nearing its *Final Confrontation* and the corresponding great triumph to follow. These Popes insist that the definitive times of Peace not only *may* come, but *will indeed* come, and that they will not constitute just *any* peace, but rather *the* very Peace of the Kingdom that Christ came from Heaven to penultimately establish on earth.

First, we see the teachings of that great Lion of a Pope, Leo XIII. In his famous mystical vision, he was shown the reign of Satan during the 20th Century; in response he instituted the St. Michael the Archangel prayer, to be said after Mass throughout the world. His teachings, however, prophesied times of peace to follow Satan's reign:

> It will at length be possible that our many wounds be healed ... that **the splendors of peace be renewed, and swords and arms drop from the hand when all men shall acknowledge the empire of Christ** ... (*Annum Sacrum*, §11)

To ensure the reader does not assume these words refer only to the cessation of some specific violent conflict of his day, Pope Leo ends the same paragraph by referring to this renewal *as the reality described by St. Paul,* when the latter wrote that "**Every tongue shall confess that our Lord Jesus Christ is in the glory of God the Father**." (Philippians 2:11)

But it was Pope St. Pius X, following Leo XIII directly, who truly set the stage for the decades that would follow in prophesying the Era. Setting his pontifical motto as "To Restore All Things in Christ," Pius gave his master plan by way of his first encyclical. Entitled *E Supremi* (On the Restoration of All Things in Christ), it teaches:

> When in every city and village the law of the Lord is faithfully observed ... there will certainly be no more need for us to labor

> further to see **all things restored in Christ. Nor is it for the attainment of eternal welfare alone that this will be of service**—it will also contribute largely to temporal welfare and the advantage of human society ... when [piety] is strong and flourishing **'the people will' truly 'sit in the fullness of peace...** May God, "who is rich in mercy", benignly speed **this restoration of the human race in Jesus Christ**... (§14)

The Pope does not here say that all things "might" be restored in Christ, but that they *will* be; not that "some" people will be so restored, but that *the human race* will be. This restoration cannot be anything but a reference to a glorious Era far beyond anything the world has seen since the Fall.

We should also place this teaching of Pius X within the context of his insistence (in the same encyclical, §5) that the Antichrist himself was perhaps already in the world. For it is thereby clear that the Pope is insisting that this glorious Era of Peace is no mere brief period of tranquility *before* the Great Chastisements described in the Book of Revelation. Rather, it consists in a restoration (on earth and within time) that *follows* the defeat of the Antichrist—by a coming, *in grace,* of Christ Himself. (*In the appendices, we address the opinion promoted by some that the Antichrist can only follow the Era.*)

This proclamation of a glorious Era to come was picked up two decades later by Pius XI—its expectation in no way dimmed by the horror of World War I. In his first encyclical, *Ubi Arcano Dei Consilio* ("On the Peace of Christ in the Kingdom of Christ") he prayed that:

> [As Jesus said:] 'And they shall hear my voice, and there shall be one fold and one shepherd.' May God ... **bring to fulfillment His prophecy by transforming this consoling vision of the future into a present reality**. (§63)

Three years later, in his extraordinary proclamation of the Feast of Christ the King—the celebration of which now concludes each Liturgical Year and is among the most exalted feasts—Pius XI taught, within the Encyclical *Quas Primas*:

> When once men recognize, both in private and in public life, that Christ is King, society will at last receive the great blessings of [peace] ... If the kingdom of Christ, then, receives, as it should, all nations under its way, **there seems no reason why we should despair of seeing *that* peace which the King of Peace came to bring on earth.** (§19)

The Holy Father was aware that some were contradicting the clear sense of this encyclical and alleging that its prophecies—of Christ one day reigning on earth as King in an Era of Peace—were nothing more than descriptions of the universality of Christ's reign which He *already* enjoys due to His Omnipotence. Therefore, the Pope was resolute in ensuring that the faithful would not forget or water down what he had taught. Three years after instituting the Feast of Christ the King through the encyclical above, he promulgated another encyclical, *Miserentissimus Redemptor,* wherein he recalled *Quas Primas* and further declared:

> **"Christ must reign" (1 Corinthians xv, 25); "Thy kingdom come" (Matth. vi, 10).** ...We instituted the Feast of Christ the King of All, to be solemnly celebrated throughout the whole Christian world. **Now when we did this, not only did we set in a clear light that supreme sovereignty which Christ holds over the whole universe**, over civil and domestic society, and over individual men, **but at the same time we anticipated the joys of that most auspicious day, whereon the whole world will gladly and willingly render obedience to the most sweet lordship of Christ the King**. (§4,5)

Here, Pius XI is diligent in ensuring that no one could misinterpret his prophecies and teachings; for he insists that a future day *will* come whereupon Christ shall reign over the entire world in a far greater manner than He ever has before.

Shortly thereafter his successor, Venerable Pius XII, both recalled and strengthened Pius XI's prophecy in an encyclical of his own, teaching:

> "May blind spirits ... be illumined by the light of truth and justice," Pius XI asked during the Marian feasts of the Jubilee of the Redemption, "so that those who have gone astray into error may be brought back to the straight path, that a just liberty may be granted the Church everywhere, **and that an era of peace and true prosperity may come upon all the nations.**"[251]

Three months earlier, in an Encyclical promulgated on Easter Sunday, Pius XII declared:

> In union with Christ take your stand as suppliants before the Heavenly Father and allow that prayer to rise to Him from your lips again and again...'... Thy will be done on earth, as it is in heaven!' Only then shall we be influenced solely by the honor of God and by zeal to give Him greater glory, when we **earnestly**

---

[251] *Le Pelerinage de Lourdes*. Encyclical of Pope Pius XII Warning Against Materialism on the Centenary of the Apparitions at Lourdes. July 2, 1957

> **desire the restoration of His Kingdom—the Kingdom of justice, of love, and of peace—throughout all the world.**"[252]

These prophecies, we see, did not end upon the cessation of World War II, as if what had been foretold was thereby achieved. Far from it. The same prophecies were still proclaimed by the two Popes—both canonized saints—who followed this horrible time. Pope St. John XXIII spoke of:

> … **a long-awaited new Pentecost**, which will enrich the Church with new spiritual forces… **a new leap forward in Christ' kingdom in the world**, a new proclamation in an ever deeper and more persuasive way of the joyful news of Redemption; the affirmation of the supreme rights of Almighty God, of human brotherhood in charity, **of the peace promised on earth to men of good will.**[253]
> ... [the] unity of mankind, which is required as a necessary foundation, in order **that the earthly city may be brought to the resemblance of that heavenly city** where truth reigns, charity is the law, and whose extent is eternity. (*Address at the Opening of the Second Vatican Council*)

John XXIII's words speak for themselves—testifying in great clarity to a coming renewal of the world in the most glorious way. After him, Pope St. Paul VI continued on the same theme:

> The unity of the world will be. The dignity of the human person shall be recognized not only formally but effectively. … The relations between peoples will be peaceful, reasonable and fraternal. Neither selfishness, nor arrogance, nor poverty… [shall] **prevent the establishment of a true human order, a common good, a new civilization**. (Paul VI. *Urbi et Orbi Message*. April 4th, 1971)

This "new civilization," wherein the "earthly city may be brought to the resemblance of that heavenly city" was proclaimed more boldly still by Pope St. John Paul II. Up to his death in 2005, John Paul II never abandoned his conviction and his teaching that the Third Millennium would see this glorious new Era dawn. Indeed, these teachings also did not cease upon the Fall of the Berlin Wall, therefore no one could be justified in pretending that it, or related events, fulfilled the "peace" spoken of in the prophecies given before their occurrence—for the "Peace of Christ in the Kingdom of Christ" is not found

---

[252] *Fidei Donum*. April 21, 1957

[253] Patrick de Laubier in *Osservatore Romano*, February 2, 1993 (French edition). Page 8. Quoted in *The Civilization of Love*, by Paul Bouchard. Éditions ACM 2020. Page 148.

merely in the termination of a particular war or the elimination of some particular global threat.

In his early days as a Cardinal, Karol Wojtyła made it clear that the Church was facing its definitive confrontation:

> We are now standing in the face of the greatest historical confrontation humanity has gone through ... **We are now facing the final confrontation** between the Church and the anti-Church, of the Gospel versus the anti-Gospel.[254]

After this bold proclamation, however, he made it equally clear that the Church would enjoy its splendid triumph following this confrontation. As Pope, he taught the following:

> Through your prayers and mine, it is possible to alleviate this tribulation, but it is no longer possible to avert it ... the **tears of this century have prepared the ground for a new springtime** of the human spirit.[255] **After purification through trial and suffering, the dawn of a new era is about to break.**[256] "As the third millennium of the Redemption draws near, **God is preparing a great springtime for Christianity** and we can already see its first signs." (*Redemptoris Missio,* §86)

As we can see from his 1978 teaching (one he never retracted or "clarified"), John Paul was convinced that *the* final confrontation was at hand, and was also convinced that a new springtime would follow, thus refuting any speculation that the "era" he spoke of would be comparable to periods of relative peace already seen on earth. What exactly was the essence of John Paul's vision of the springtime? *That it would consist in the very Kingdom of God on earth*. For he also taught:

> **This is our great hope and our petition: 'Your Kingdom come'—a kingdom of peace, justice, and serenity, that will re-establish the original harmony of creation.**[257]
> A preferential love for Christ means a preference for what Christ loves, a desire to have the same attitude as Christ himself, **a longing to see God's "kingdom come on earth as it is in heaven."**[258]

John Paul made it clear that he saw this new Era, to arrive with the dawn of the Third Millennium, as an outpouring of the "new and

---

[254] *Final speech before departing the U.S.* November 9, 1978
[255] General Audience. January 24, 2001
[256] General Audience. September 10, 2003
[257] General Audience. November 6, 2002
[258] Address. March 10th, 1986

Divine" holiness of Living in the Divine Will. Revisiting a teaching of his from an earlier chapter, we see that he insisted:

> God himself had provided to bring about that **"new and divine" holiness with which the Holy Spirit wishes to enrich Christians at the dawn of the third millennium, in order to "make Christ the heart of the world."**[259]

Furthermore, this Papal expectation has not dimmed in more recent years. In a book entitled *Our Father: Reflections on the Lord's Prayer*, published on the fifth anniversary of his elevation to the Papacy, Pope Francis clearly taught that the coming of the Kingdom of God on earth is a literal reality which will be fulfilled:

> The kingdom of God is here *and* [emphasis in original] the kingdom of God will come ... **the kingdom of God is coming now but at the same time has not yet come completely**. This is how the kingdom of God has already come: Jesus has taken flesh... But at the same time there is also the need to cast the anchor there and to hold on to the cord because **the Kingdom is still coming...**

Elsewhere, Francis referred to the coming Era as the fulfillment of Isaiah's prophecy that "swords shall be beaten into plowshares,"[260] explaining that this Scriptural assurance refers to earth, not Heaven. Years later, in an Angelus Address, he even taught the Kingdom coming to earth will at last effect the accomplishment of God's Will on earth:

> The destruction of the Temple pre-announced by Jesus is the figure not so much of the end [i.e. chronological cessation] of history, as of the end of history [i.e. purpose of history itself] ... This is the **eloquent sign that the Kingdom of God is coming to us, namely, that the realization of the world as God wills it is approaching** ... Faith makes us walk with Jesus on the torturous ways of this world, in the certainty that the force of His Spirit will subdue the forces of evil ...[261]

He even concluded his encyclical, *Laudato si'*, with the following words:

> O Lord, seize us with your power and light, help us to protect all life, **to prepare for a better future, for the coming of your Kingdom of justice, peace, love and beauty**. Praise be to you! Amen.

---

[259] Address to the Rogationist Fathers. May 16, 1997

[260] Pope Francis. Angelus Address. December 1, 2013.

[261] Angelus Address. St. Peter's Square. November 17, 2019

***

In this section, we have seen no fewer than *one hundred nineteen years* of Papal Magisterium consistently, clearly, and repeatedly prophesying and promising a glorious Era of Peace yet to come upon the earth—a veritable coming of the Kingdom of Christ. No grounds exist on which to doubt the validity of a teaching that is so repeated in the Magisterium of several Pontificates over the course of more than a century. But we still must consider the clearest indications of the coming Era: Heaven itself directly assuring us of its arrival in authentic private revelation.

22. The Era in 20th-Century Private Revelation

"In spite of Satan's anger, The Divine Mercy will triumph over the whole world and will be worshiped by all souls." –St. Faustina

Just as an explosion of prophecy preceded the Incarnation itself and grew in both fervor and precision the closer the time came to the Word's arrival in the womb of Mary, so too has the entire Church been inundated with Heaven-sent prophecies during the last century. These revelations foretell the impending close (through great, unprecedented chastisements) of the present sad era, and the subsequent dawn of a new one (equally unprecedented, though in glory). As Fr. Edward O'Connor explains:

> **[Apparitions] of the Blessed Virgin Mary are being reported far more frequently than at any time in the past ...** there were very few during the first ten centuries. After that they increased moderately, reaching 105 in the nineteenth century. But during the twentieth century ... [there were reported] a total of 1,045 apparitions of the Blessed Mother ... (*Listen to my Prophets*. IX)

Although especially forceful and frequent as of late, Heaven-sent prophecies promising the Era have been given throughout the entire history of the Church. Already in 1911, the old *Catholic Encyclopedia* made this clear in its article on *Prophecy*, which sums up the main thrust and overarching themes of 1,900 years of private revelation:

> The more noteworthy of the prophecies bearing upon "latter times" seem to have **one common end**, to announce great calamities impending over mankind**, the triumph of the Church, and the renovation of the world. All the seers agree ... they all promise for the Church a victory more splendid than she has ever achieved here below**. (*Catholic Encyclopedia.* Article on Prophecy.)

This Encyclopedia, which is known for choosing its words carefully, does not in vain describe these prophecies as "**all**" agreeing in the promise of a coming Triumph of the Church that will be greater than "**ever**" before and a concomitant "**renovation of the world**." Therefore, we can be assured that the Era is guaranteed by the *entirety* of Catholic Prophecy which Heaven has blessed the Church with for many centuries. However, since space here is limited and the urgency and prevalence of these prophecies became extreme upon the dawn of the 20th Century, this time period is where we will begin the present consideration.

Our Lady of Fatima

> "In the end,[262] **my Immaculate Heart will triumph**. The Holy Father will consecrate Russia to me, and she shall be converted, and **an era of peace will be granted to the world.**" –Our Lady of Fatima

Three months before working the most astounding public miracle witnessed on earth since Moses lead Israel out of Egypt through the Red Sea (causing, as she did, the sun to dance in the sky before a crowd of 70,000; an event recorded even in the day's secular newspapers), Our Lady entrusted us with the promise above at Fatima.

The prophecy is as clear as it is certain: the Immaculate Queen of the Universe will not be deprived of the right to extend her triumphant reign over the entire earth. A few, however, attempt to argue that this prophecy was already fulfilled simply because of John Paul II's 1984 Consecration of the world to the Immaculate Heart (and because the Soviet Union collapsed and there was not an outright nuclear war). But anyone who supposes that what the world has seen since this prophecy was issued in 1917 is even remotely close to what could be considered "the triumph of the Immaculate Heart" and a worldwide "era of peace," must be exhorted to rise from his existential slumber. Legal abortion ("the greatest destroyer of peace," according to St. Mother Teresa, and which began in Russia only 3 years after this message was given[263]) continues to this day, and has now violently claimed the lives of over a billion innocent children.[264] For those outside the womb, too, the years since 1917 have been by far the bloodiest, cruelest, and most violent years *in the entire history of the world*. We have seen, without respite, relentless genocides, deliberate mass-starvation campaigns, unprecedented persecution of Christians, uninterrupted moral and spiritual decline, and at least *eight hundred* separate wars.

---

[262] This is obviously not a reference to the end of time (the very next sentence renders that interpretation impossible), but refers rather to "the end" of the trials Our Lady had just finished listing in this same message, e.g., "wars and persecutions of the Church." Note also that some translations of this message refer to a "period of peace." The original Portuguese of the message prophesies a "tempo de paz," and whether this is translated as an "era" or a "period" of peace is unimportant.

[263] "Decree on Abortion. People's Commissariat of Health, on the Protection of Women's Health." November 18th, 1920

[264] Cf. Pete Baklinski. "'Greatest genocide in history': Groundbreaking report finds 1 billion abortions in past 100 years." January 25, 2017

It is clear that we have no reason to label any period therein a "period of peace," an "era of peace," or a "Triumph of the Immaculate Heart of Mary." And yet, such a time was promised; therefore it will come. Most faithful souls who read this prophecy immediately recognize what it entails, but as those aforementioned few attempt to dispute that it refers to a yet-to-come glorious Era of Peace, we should acknowledge here the teachings of those most worthy of trust on this matter.

As noted in the preceding chapter, Pope St. John Paul II never abandoned his insistence that, though it had not yet done so, the Era *would* arrive. His successor, Pope Benedict XVI, while celebrating Mass during his apostolic journey to Fatima in 2010, concluded his homily by insisting the Triumph *would* come, but had not yet come:

> **May the seven years which separate us from the centenary of the apparitions hasten the fulfillment of the prophecy of the triumph** of the Immaculate Heart of Mary, to the glory of the Most Holy Trinity.[265]

Cardinal Mario Luigi Ciappi, who was the Theologian of the Pontifical Household to five popes, was an authority on Fatima. Pope St. John Paul II himself gave the cardinal's funeral homily, and in it referred to "[Ciappi's] clear thinking, the soundness of his teaching and his undisputed fidelity to the Apostolic See, as well as his **ability to interpret the signs of the times according to God**..."[266] This Cardinal wrote the following several years *after* the famous 1984 Consecration and fall of the USSR:

> **... A miracle was promised at Fatima. And that miracle will be an era of peace, which has never really been granted before to the world**...[267]

Similarly, John Haffert, one of the world's most respected and prolific promoters of the message of Fatima, wrote:

> The conversion of the world is sure to come. The world will become His by our conversion and His intervention ... The Triumph will be a conversion event that will be so powerful and universal that all will be compelled to praise God... **It will be a historical event of such magnitude that it will make all former moments of glory seem like shadows** ...[268]

[265] Homily of Benedict XVI. Shrine of Our Lady of Fatima. May 13th, 2010.
[266] *Preparation for Total Consecration to Jesus through Mary for Families*. Page 192.
[267] "5 Saturdays, 1 Salvation." Joseph Pronechen. NCRegister.com. Oct 9, 2005
[268] *The Great Event*. Pages 48-49

Blessed Conchita

> "And that we might live no longer for ourselves but for him who died and rose again for us, he sent the Holy Spirit from you, Father, as the first fruits for those who believe, so that, bringing to perfection his work in the world, he might sanctify creation to the full."
>
> –Eucharistic Prayer IV

Blessed Conchita was one of many souls to whom Jesus revealed the Gift of Living in the Divine Will (see Part Three), but she was also given prophecies of the Era. What follows are the words of Jesus to her, wherein we find greater context to what we considered in Part Four:

> May the whole world have recourse to this Holy Spirit since the day of His reign has arrived. This last stage of the world belongs very specially to Him that He be honored and exalted ... **peace will come along with a moral and spiritual reaction, greater than the evil by which the world is tormented... He will come, I will send Him again clearly manifest in His effects, which will astonish the world** and impel the Church to holiness ... I want to return to the world in My priests. **I want to renew the world** of souls by making Myself seen in My priests.[269] **The restoration will be universal, not limited to some places or nations** ... I, who see the future as if it were present, feel that I am already in possession of souls and nations, extending My reign in hearts ... **This world needs to be regenerated, spiritualized and saved**. But the only way to arrive at this end is the transformation of priests into the eternal, pure, holy, and only Priest and Savior, who wants and promises **to return to earth in His priests in order to bring about a new era of salvation and sanctification in the world** ... After so many centuries, which are like a day for Me, I want to perfect this unity in My Church. I want to bring this unity to the very peak of its realization and perfection so that it will give this beloved Church the fullness of its flowering and thus provide souls with a holy means to unify them and bring them to heaven.[270] **I want to come back to the world through My priests. I want to renew the world** of souls by revealing Myself through My priests. I want to give a powerful impulse to My

[269] Fr. Marie-Michel Philipon, O.P. *Conchita: A Mother's Spiritual Diary*.

[270] *Priests of Christ*. Concepción Cabrera de Armida. Society of Saint Paul, 2015. Imprimatur from. Domenico Di Raimondo Romo, M.Sp.S. May 30, 2004. Pages 64-65

> Church, infusing the Holy Spirit into My priests **as in a new Pentecost**... I, the Holy One, want to offer to the Father a triumph in My Church through My holy bishops and priests by **renewing the face of the earth** ... **This is now My ideal: to transform the world** through the perfect transformation of priests into the great High Priest, into the unique Priest from whom all proceed. **The Trinity awaits this profound renewal, and already sees it, feels it, cherishes it and blesses it.**[271] Then all those wills, many haughty, others independent, arrogant and rebellious will finally be united, humiliated and conquered by love ... and they will form only one desire, only one will with Mine, in the Unity of the Trinity. The day when this happens will be a triumph for My beloved Church ...

Blessed Conchita's approved revelations from Jesus focus heavily on Christ's Coming to the earth—a *Second Pentecost*—to establish His Kingdom, *in grace*, through the ministry of priests; a Kingdom which will radically renew the entire world. This is a vitally important point about the Era: it consists not in a sensible reign of Jesus (contra the Millenarian error), but rather in His *Eucharistic* reign on earth, which is itself made possible by the priestly ministry, hence Pope St. John Paul II's insistence on relating the "Rogate" to the "New and Divine Holiness" which will "make Christ the heart of the world" upon the dawn of the third millennium. (See Part Four.)

Still More Prophecies

> "When will all this happen? The divinization of the whole world in her and through [Mary]?" –St. Maximilian Kolbe

St. Faustina (Divine Mercy). St. Faustina, whose revelations have received the highest degree of Church approval and acclamation, wrote the following words in her *Diary*.

> In spite of Satan's anger, **The Divine Mercy will triumph over the whole world** and will be worshiped by all souls. (§1789)

Here, she prophesies a time *on earth* during which there is a triumph of the Faith in all souls alive. For the Last Judgment (the only possible alternative interpretation of this "triumph" about which Faustina speaks) occurs at the definitive end of time and is never referred to as the triumph of *Mercy*; rather, it is always referred to as the time of

---

[271] Ibid. Pages 341-342

Universal and Absolute *Justice*. Earlier, Faustina wrote that she prayed for the "triumph of the Church," (§240) and she desired that this triumph be "hastened." (§1581) She would not have written these things if she did not believe such a triumph was possible and willed by God. Pope St. John Paul II agreed with Faustina, teaching:

> The hour has come when the message of Divine Mercy is able to fill hearts with hope and to become the spark of a new civilization: the civilization of love.[272]

Queen of the Universe (Heede). Beginning in 1937 in Heede, Germany, these apparitions are not only approved by the Church, but also enjoy "undeniable proofs of seriousness and authenticity."[273] Within them, the Virgin Mary appeared to four girls with grave messages. Later, in 1945, Jesus appeared to them with His Own revelations, exhorting obedience to the earlier messages of His mother. (*Note: the following is taken from the International Exhibit on Apparitions created by Blessed Carlo Acutis*). Jesus said in this message:

> I will make myself known to the people. **Every soul will recognize me as their God. I am coming! I am at the door! My love has planned this action before the creation of the world** ... The world lies in dense darkness. This generation would deserve to be wiped out; but I wish to show Myself merciful. The angel of peace will not delay in coming down to earth. I want to heal and save. Over the wounds, which are now bleeding, mercy wins, and justice triumphs ... **May [My faithful] prepare themselves for great things. I am coming Myself and I will manifest my will.** All those who have suffered in these last times, are My martyrs and they prepare the new harvest for the Church... I am coming soon, very soon! The things that will come shall surpass by far what happened. The Mother of God, My Mother, and the Angels will take part in it. Hell by now believes itself certain of victory, but I will take it away ... I am coming, and with me peace shall come. **I will build my Kingdom with a small number of elect. This Kingdom will come suddenly, sooner than what one thinks**. I will make My light shine, which to some will be blessing and to others darkness. Humanity will recognize my love and my power. I will make known my justice and my mercy. My dear children: the hour is drawing near. Pray unceasingly and you will not be confused. I gather My elect. They will converge from every part of the world and they will glorify Me. I am coming!

---

[272] Apostolic Voyage to Poland. Homily of August 18th, 2002

[273] Cf. miraclehunter.com. "Heede, Germany (1937-1940)"

> Blessed are those who are ready, blessed are those who will listen to me.[274]

In addition to the early forms of approval which these apparitions received, they saw Ecclesial endorsements in 1955, 1973, 1977, and 2000.[275] Noteworthy in them is Jesus' insistence that the Era of Peace consists in nothing short of the Kingdom of God on earth by way of His coming to earth in grace.

St. Maximilian Kolbe. St. Maximilian's goal, which motivated his enormous apostolic zeal, was simple: ***"to win the whole world over to the Immaculata."*** This, the saint was utterly convinced, was no fantasy, but a sure and certain hope, and he constantly repeated it. Accordingly, he prophesied:

> [When souls are consecrated to Mary,] Then souls will love the Most Sacred Heart of Jesus as they had never loved Him before, because, like [Mary] ... they will plunge into the mysteries of Love: the Cross and the Eucharist. **Through her, God's Love shall kindle the world, set it on fire, and lead to the 'assumption' of souls through Love**. When will all this happen? The **divinization of the whole world in her and through her**?"[276]

Note that the saint does not ponder "if" this "divinization of the whole world" will happen, but only *when* it will. Kolbe's forerunner in this devotion, St. Louis de Montfort, also knew full well that Marian Consecration's growth would precede the worlds' renewal and help enable Christ's universal triumph, as we reviewed in Part Two.

Fr. Ottavio Michelini. A priest, mystic, and member of the Papal Court of Pope St. Paul VI (one of the highest honors bestowed by a Pope on a living person), Fr. Ottavio received many revelations, documented in the 1976 book entitled *Thou Knowest That I Love Thee*. In this book, we read:

> It will be the Mother, **most holy Mary, who will crush the head of the serpent, thus beginning a new era of peace; it will be the advent of my Kingdom upon earth.** It will be the return of the Holy Ghost for a new Pentecost. Hell will be defeated: my Church will be regenerated: My Kingdom, that is a kingdom of love, of justice and of peace, will give peace and justice to this humanity. (December 10, 1976) [The earth] will be made arid and

---

[274] Carlo Acutis. *The Appeals of Our Lady: Apparitions and Marian Shrines in the World*. Apparitions of the Virgin Mary at Heede.

[275] Ibid.

[276] *The Writings of St. Maximilian Maria Kolbe*. Volume 1. Nerbini International. 2016. Chapter 14. Part b.

> desolate then "purified" by fire to be fertilized by the honest labor of the just escaped for the divine goodness to the tremendous hour of the divine anger. [Then] **there will be the reign of God in the souls, that reign the just ask from God invoking "Thy Kingdom come."** (January 2, 1979)

Sr. Natalia of Hungary. A 20th-Century nun whose messages bear a *nihil obstat* and an *imprimatur*, Sr. Natalia was given revelations from Jesus and Mary which read:

> The end of sin is close, but not the end of the world. Soon no more souls will be lost. My words will be fulfilled, and there will only be one flock and one Shepherd. (Jn. 10:16) Pray, so that before the holy peace, and the great mercy for the world arrives, sinners may be converted and accept my mercy, amending their lives ... [The Virgin Mary revealed:] The age of world peace is not delayed. The Heavenly Father only wants to give time to those who are able to be converted and find refuge with God ... [Sr. Natalia writes:] The Savior showed me that unceasing love, happiness and divine joy will signify [the] future clean world. I saw the blessing of God abundantly poured out upon the earth. Jesus then explained to me: "... **the arrival of the era of paradise, when mankind will live as without sin. There will be a new world and a new era. It will be the era when humanity will recover what it lost in paradise. When my Immaculate Mother steps on the neck of the serpent...**"[277]

Elizabeth Kindelmann (Flame of Love). The "Flame of Love" revelations to Elizabeth Kindelmann, a 20th-century Hungarian wife and mother, were approved by no fewer than four Archbishops (including two Cardinals). In them, we read:

> [After being shown a vision, Elizabeth wrote:] my heart overflowed with a huge cheerfulness ... I saw how **Satan becomes blinded, and also the beneficial effects that men will reap from it, in the whole world**. Under the effect of that gladness, I could hardly close my eyes during the whole night, and when a light sleep came on me, my guardian angel woke me saying: "How can you sleep like that, with **such a great gladness which will shake the world?"**[Immediately after her guardian angel said these words, Jesus revealed to Elizabeth more about what this blinding of Satan entails. Jesus said:] That Satan becomes blind means the world triumph of my Sacred-Heart, the liberation of

---

[277] Sor Maria Natalia Magdolna. *The Victorious Queen of the World*. Two Hearts Books and Publishers. 1987.

souls, and that the road of Salvation will open in all its plenitude. (November 13th-14th, 1964) [In an undated entry from August 1962, Jesus said to Elizabeth:] **Let the coming of my Kingdom be the aim of your life on earth.**

Alicja Lenczewska. A Polish mystic and saintly woman who received revelations from Jesus, Alicja died in 2001, and her messages were approved in 2017.[278] The following is a small selection of her messages from Jesus which prophesy a glorious Era of Peace:

> Satan and his servants will rejoice—as they rejoiced then in Jerusalem. But the time of their apparent victory will be short, for the morning will come of **the Resurrection of the Holy Church,** immortal, giving birth to new life on earth—the holiness of My children. (November 11, 2000) The Immaculate Heart of My Mother will triumph ... the dawn and spring of the Holy Church is coming ... A purification will be given that will bring the sons of darkness to the light of God's Truth, and every person will according to their own will in the light of that Truth will have to choose the Kingdom of My Father or give themselves over eternally to the father of lies ... **Mary is the one through whom will come the rebirth of My Church, so that it would shine with the full splendor of God's Holiness.** (June 8, 2002)

Servant of God Maria Esperanza (Betania). Maria was a wife, mother, mystic, and recipient of the approved apparitions at Betania, Venezuela. She died in 2004, and her beatification process has begun. Regarding her prophecies, Dr. Thomas Petrisko explains:

> In many interviews, Maria has spoken of the coming times. She indicates somewhat that she knows what the Era of Peace may be like and what it may bring... "The environment will be fresh and new, and we will be happy in our world, without the feeling of tension ... This century is purifying; after will come peace and love ... It will be in a way never before imagined by man, because the Light of His New Rising will be evident to everyone. And of course, man is still not ready for this, to accept these profound things, which actually are so simple and so clear... [The Lord told Esparanza:] "I will come among you in a resplendent sun. My rays will reach all nations to illuminate you, to enlighten you, that you may rise and grow as plants grow, with fruits. You all have the right to receive the grace of God the Father." (*Call of the Ages.* P. 469-470)

---

278 Anna Gębalska-Berekets. *A mystic from Poland and her conversations with Jesus.* Aleteia. May 31, 2017

Fr. Stefano Gobbi. The founder of the Marian Movement of Priests, Fr. Gobbi, was an Italian priest, mystic, and theologian who died in 2011 and was the recipient of revelations (locutions) recorded in "the Blue Book," the actual title of which is *To the Priests, Our Lady's Beloved Sons*. This book bears full ecclesiastical approbation; having *imprimaturs* from Bishops and Cardinals who not only approved these revelations, but also strongly encouraged their promotion. In the messages, we read multitudes of prophecies regarding the Era; a small selection of which are as follows:

> **Jesus, Who taught you the prayer for asking for the coming of God's kingdom upon earth, will at last see this prayer of His fulfilled, for He will establish His Kingdom. And creation will return to being a new garden in which Christ will be glorified** by all and His divine Kingship will be welcomed and exalted; it will be a universal Kingdom of Grace, beauty, harmony, communion, justice and peace. (July 3, 1987) In the hour of the great trial, *paradise will be joined to earth, until* the moment when the luminous door will be opened, to cause to descend upon the world the glorious presence of Christ, who will restore his reign in which the divine Will shall be accomplished in a perfect manner, as in heaven, so also on earth. (November 1, 1990) ***The new era,* which I announce to you, coincides with the complete fulfillment of the divine will, so that at last there is coming about that which Jesus taught you to ask for, from the Heavenly Father: 'Your will be done on earth as it is in heaven.'** This is the time when the divine will of the Father, of the Son and of the Holy Spirit is being accomplished by the creatures. From the perfect fulfillment of the divine will, the whole world is becoming renewed. (August 15, 1991)

Gladys Quiroga (San Nicolas). Ms. Quiroga was the recipient of approved apparitions of Mary under the title of Our Lady of the Rosary. World-renowned theologian Fr. Rene Laurentin both promoted and wrote extensively on these apparitions, and hundreds of thousands of pilgrims have visited the apparition site. Our Lady revealed to Gladys:

> If [man] desired to discover God, this would be an earth of peace for all, because only God can make peace reign, that peace so longed for by many! (June 7, 1985) The Holy Church will soon come to shine like the brightest of stars. Glory be to God. Make it known. (November 9, 1986) **The most intense Light of Christ will rise again. As at the Calvary, after the Crucifixion**

> **and death came the Resurrection, the Church will also be reborn by the strength of Love** ... You must make this known! (July 10, 1988)

Pedro Regis. A seer from Anguera, Brazil, Pedro has been receiving messages for decades and enjoys the support of his Bishop, who stated: "I have already reached the conclusion that, from the pastoral point of view, the meeting in Angüera [Pedro's revelations] is valid." Jesus and Mary said to Pedro:

> I want to make you saints for the glory of the reign of God. Open your hearts! **Very soon the world will be transformed into a new world, without hate or violence. The world will be a new garden** and all will live happily. (October 8, 1988) I want you to be a part of the Lord's victorious army. The Lord has reserved a great Grace for His own. He will transform humanity into a new garden. **When all this happens the world will be abound with goods and man will lack nothing**. It will be a time when the fruits of trees will be multiplied and there will be two crops per year. Hunger will no longer exist for humanity. (June 3, 2000) You still have long years of trials ahead of you, but the great day is coming. My Jesus will give you the grace to live in complete peace. The Earth will be completely transformed **and all will live joyfully**. (December 24, 2013)

Léandre Lachance is a Canadian mystic who recorded conversations with Jesus which now bear an *imprimatur* from both Cardinal Janis Riga and Archbishop Paolo Pezzi. Within them, the Lord told Léandre:

> **For two thousand years, I have taught My Apostles what believers repeat to the Father: 'Your will be done**... on earth as it is in Heaven.' **The hour has come! Blessed are you, children of the earth, for entering this new earth at this time.** Understand that nothing impure can dwell there. The purification has begun and it will be completed: it will be brought about either by the Love flowing through the hearts that give their 'yes' or through sufferings of all kinds. (January 14th, 1997) **Very soon, My Kingdom will burst forth on this earth: this hour belongs to My Father**. This great event is prepared by the purification of hearts. I want My chosen ones to be totally pure, something that is impossible on your own. With your consent, I purify. This is My work and not yours. (November 24th, 1996)[279]

[279] *For the Happiness of My Own, My Chosen Ones*. La Fondation des choisis de Jésus.

Virginie is a French mystic who founded an Ecclesial movement, *Alliance des Coeurs Unis* (The Covenant of the United Hearts), that works for spiritual renewal throughout the Church. She began receiving messages from Heaven in the year 1994, and her revelations are strongly supported by her Bishop, Marc Aillet. Jesus revealed to Virginie:

> **The Triumph of the Immaculate Heart of Mary will make the Kingdom of God come down to earth**… and all the powers will bow and acknowledge the Unity and Royalty of Our two United Holy Hearts. (August 22, 2013) My Church has no path other than to follow Me to Golgotha … The martyrdom of My Church will lead her to her Resurrection, to her Triumph! But I need each one of you." (February 10, 2015) "Divine Royalty … will triumph at the time chosen by God**, re-establishing the Kingdom of the Divine Will in the world**." (March 23, 2012)[280]

Queen of Peace (Medjugorje). The apparitions at Medjugorje, while neither approved nor condemned, have recently seen many positive developments in the Church and have become among the most famous and abundantly fruitful Marian Apparitions ever. In 2019, they became what appear to be the first *ongoing* apparitions in the history of the Church to enjoy expressly Vatican-authorized official pilgrimages.[281] One of the seers, Mirjana, recently published a book, the very title of which speaks of the Era of Peace. Entitled *My Heart Will Triumph*, we see in it the following:

> **Our Lady is planning to change the world**. **She did not come to announce our destruction;** she came to save us, and with her Son, **she will triumph over evil**. If our Mother has promised to defeat evil, then what do we have to fear? (Chapter 14) [Our Lady] asked for our prayers**, "so that as soon as possible a time of peace, for which my heart waits impatiently, may reign.**" (Chapter 26) After the events take place as predicted, it will be difficult for even the staunchest skeptics to doubt the existence of God. (Chapter 13) Some seem to think that all the secrets are negative. Maybe they have a guilty conscience; maybe they are afraid of how they've lived their life and so they fear God's punishment. Perhaps when we do not have enough good inside, we expect bad things ... The people who are concerned about the secrets have not seen Our Lady and do not know about God's complete

[280] *Les Secrets du Roi: Que ton règne arrive*! Resiac. 2012.
[281] Pope authorizes pilgrimages to Medjugorje. Vatican News. May 12, 2019.

project—why Our Lady comes here at all, or what she's preparing us for. (Chapter 14)

***

As elsewhere, limitations of space here demand that we leave untouched the vast majority of revelations which prophesy the Era. But even from this small sample, an overwhelming consensus emerges guaranteeing the coming of this Glorious Age, to be lived on earth before the end of time; an age which is initiated by a veritable Coming of Christ in grace to establish His Kingdom upon earth. While individual private revelations, of course, remain fallible (unlike Public Revelation), it is not possible that an entire century of prophets—trustworthy, saintly souls, across the entire world—could be systematically and radically deceived on one of their fundamental and unanimous tenets.[282]

Therefore, as no one can now harbor any doubt as to the imminent coming of the Kingdom of God on earth—guaranteed, as it is, by the Old Testament, the New Testament, the Fathers of the Church, Papal Magisterium, and private revelation—we turn our attention to discussing more about this Kingdom and the preparations made for it in light of the entirety of Salvation History.

[282] Any dismissal of the Era, therefore, is none other than a blanket dismissal of private revelation, thus implying that the *sensus fidelium* (sense of the faithful) can err (a notion which, in turn, is condemned by the Catechism (§492) and *Lumen Gentium* (§12)).

23. The Original Glory and the Penultimate Plan

"God made man right." –Ecclesiastes 7:30

We began the final part of this book by acknowledging the most fundamental realities which must describe the bookends of history in accordance with the perfection of its author: Almighty God. Now, we must delve more deeply into the details of the plan of the Greatest Author.

All Christians know how everything began: the Universe, the World, and most importantly *man himself* came out of God's Creative Hands perfect in every way. Whatever was essential to the nature of man was not lacking in man as God created him, for if it were lacking then God would have created an evil,[283] which could never be; therefore, all creation issued forth from its origin with absolute beauty. But beauty, the Angelic Doctor rightly teaches, "consists in due proportion."[284] Therefore, we call something "beautiful" if it contains within itself the symmetry necessary for the recognition of its proportionality. This symmetry, as an essential characteristic of beauty, applies not only to spatial considerations but, of utmost importance, to chronological ones. Accordingly, when we view all of creation's history from the perspective of eternity, we will see this symmetry between the splendor of the world's beginning and its conclusion stunningly displayed.

To learn about the penultimate destiny of the world, therefore, we should examine in more detail the nature of its opening. For as we have seen, the same Doctor taught that *all things find their perfection in returning to their origin.*

The Beginning, the Fall, and the Redemption

> "As the end of a thing corresponds to its beginning, it is not possible to be ignorant of the end of things if we know their beginning."
>
> –St. Thomas Aquinas[285]

The Universe predates man chronologically, but ontologically it takes a low second place; Jesus tells Luisa it only exists for man's sake (11/20/1929) and that man was to be its king (7/29/1926). This,

[283] The traditional (and most theologically and philosophically accurate) definition of evil is simply "the absence of a due perfection."

[284] St. Thomas Aquinas. *Summa Theologica*, I, Q5. A4.

[285] Ibid. Q103. A2.

indeed, Adam was upon his creation: the ruler of all things. And although the Universe was made to house man, *man himself was made to house God*. This reality also defined Adam before the Fall: his sanctity far surpassed any other possible sanctity (aside from Jesus and Mary, who far surpassed Adam), including both those of the Old Testament and the New (10/2/1927). The Liturgy of the Church testifies to the truth of this surpassing glory of prelapsarian Adam and Eve, for within it we pray: "**... you call human nature back to its original holiness** ..."[286] (Preface of Virgins. Roman Missal.) As a *call*, this prayer reminds us of an invitation to which we must respond; not an acknowledgment of some achievement already secured (in which case the prayer would instead say: "you *have*, through Redemption, *placed* our human nature back in the position of its original holiness"). Similarly, Cardinal Christoph Schönborn teaches, "deification is located in the **reestablishing** of fallen man in his innate dignity."[287] The Fathers of the Church, moreover, insisted upon the supreme standing of Adam's holiness, some even explicitly teaching that Adam possessed the Holy Spirit as his own "*vital principle*;" an assertion which, in light of Jesus' revelations to Luisa, is identical to saying that *Adam possessed the Gift of Living in the Divine Will*. As Fr. John Hardon teaches:

> The Fathers explicitly teach that the first man possessed [deification]... which Adam lost by the fall ... some of the Greek Fathers, like Basil and Cyril of Alexandria, believed that the supernatural sanctification of Adam is indicated in Genesis 2:7 ... **the grace of the Holy Spirit as [Adam's] supernatural vital principle...** the Fathers' common belief that Adam received both natural and supernatural life is a witness to Christian tradition.[288]

---

[286] Note: John Paul II did speak of original innocence as being "irremediably" lost *inasmuch as* Christianity *itself* does not entail a return to that state. Obviously, this is correct. Christianity *as such* removes the *guilt* of original sin, but not its *effects*: thus, all the evils among Christians we have seen during the last 2,000 years! It would be incorrect, however, to interpret the Pope's words to mean that (at least many aspects of) original justice *could not ever* be restored. Quite the contrary, John Paul himself insisted that they *would* be (as we saw earlier). Moreover, this Liturgical Prayer here footnoted makes it clear that part and parcel to the Christian calling is striving after original holiness; and it would be absurd to accuse this prayer of espousing a calling which is impossible to heed. Finally, if original innocence could *never* be restored, then it would be lacking in Heaven, also, which is clearly false. In sum, we mustn't regard the Pope as insisting that nothing about original holiness could ever be restored on earth.

[287] *From Death to Life: The Christian Journey*. 1995. Page 50.

[288] John A. Hardon, S.J., *God the Author of Nature and the Supernatural*. Thesis VIII. Part III.

We can see, therefore, that there is certainly something in Original Holiness which surpasses even Christian Holiness, and to which we thus must aspire.[289]

However, everyone must be tried; no creature with a free will is exempt from a test before confirmation in grace. Even though we know what transpired—and God knew what would transpire before it did—it would nevertheless be blasphemous to accuse God of so testing Adam and Eve without His ordained Will being that they pass the test. And He knew exactly what to do if they passed. Jesus tells Luisa that if Adam had obeyed, all future generations would have been confirmed in happiness, and at the proper time He would have come to earth as a triumphant King, not as a suffering Savior (4/1/1928, 3/31/1929).

Despite the horror of the Fall and the glory of the plan it ruined, we must not waste one moment in lamentation. God allowed the Fall *knowing* that an even greater good would come thanks to it. Accordingly, each Easter Vigil, the Church prays the Exultet, in which we joyfully proclaim: "*felix culpa!*", "O, happy fault! [of Adam], which gained for us so great a savior." Indeed, after the Fall, God was on the move to enact an even *greater* plan than He would have enacted if Adam had passed the test. But how, one might ask, is this plan *greater* if the plan itself can be said to be the *restoration* of what was lost at the Fall? The answer is that this new plan *entails* such a restoration, but *does not consist merely in* this restoration. The dénouement surely restores the glory of the original setting, but provides a still greater exposition.

God did not delay in enacting His new plan. Immediately, the *Protoevangelium* (Genesis 3:15) was announced, and Jesus tells Luisa that His Own foreseen merits preserved the world from dissolution

---

[289] The Catechism, however, refers to the "glory of the new creation in Christ" surpassing that of original holiness (§375). Accordingly, this is one of the many delicate theological matters that can only be addressed with the appropriate distinctions. True to form, St. Thomas Aquinas provides them: "Nevertheless he **[Adam] knew God with a more perfect knowledge than we do now.** Thus in a sense his knowledge was midway between our knowledge in the present state, and the knowledge we shall have in heaven ... **In the state of innocence [Original Holiness] man's works were more meritorious than after sin was committed**, if we consider the degree of merit on the part of grace, which would have been more copious as meeting with no obstacle in human nature: and in like manner, if we consider the absolute degree of the work done; because, as man would have had greater virtue, he would have performed greater works. But if we consider the proportionate degree, a greater reason for merit exists after sin, on account of man's weakness; because a small deed is more beyond the capacity of one who works with difficulty than a great deed is beyond one who performs it easily." (*Summa Theologica*. I. Q95. A4.)

(10/7/1929). Moreover, the Fall of Man ignited God's love for us *even more* than it was inflamed in the Garden itself (5/19/1931). Truly, therefore, we can say that as soon as the Fall had transpired, God was on the move not only to restore, but also to reorder in a greater way than would have been possible if the Fall had never occurred. We must take a moment to consider precisely why this is so.

God created Adam with the highest category of holiness (to claim God did not do so would be to contradict His Goodness by claiming He created a being without its due perfection). But God permitted Adam to fall because He foresaw a coming age in which Adam's holiness could be combined with sanctifying Christian grace through the merits of the Incarnation and Passion of His Son. In that coming age, treasures could now be built up in Heaven that could not possibly have existed without the Fall—treasures that will make the blood, sweat, and tears of their attainment seem like nothing. These treasures embellish our eternal home of Heaven. Were Adam to never have fallen, although we would never have lost the terrestrial paradise and the perfect state of our souls, the celestial paradise would not have received the same glorifications, and we would be eternally devoid of the crowns which we now have the ability to merit if we so choose—crowns that the angels themselves envy us for, since they love God but cannot suffer for Him.

These glorious crowns, therefore, proceed from our willing participation in the Passion of the Incarnate Christ. Without the Passion of Christ (and the Fall that called for it), God's infinite love for us also would never have had its most perfect and beautiful exposition; an exposition which will enrapture us *for all eternity*. Therefore, we can indeed say that, "thanks to" the fall of Adam, we will have the most glorious possible and imaginable exposition of Divine Love before our eyes forever in the marks that Our Lord continues to carry in His hands, feet, and side—even in Heaven.

When one prayerfully observes the details of this *Greatest Story Ever Told*, which is history itself, it becomes clear that there is no contradiction between, on the one hand, God's ultimate plan entailing the restoration of what was lost at the Fall and, on the other hand, Christian holiness being in a sense greater than original holiness. In fact, only now that Jesus has revealed this ultimate plan in detail to

Luisa do mysteries which have hitherto perplexed the greatest theologians throughout the history of the Church begin to become unveiled.[290]

Jesus tells Luisa that even though Adam was created holy, happy, and glorious, nevertheless when the wounds of Christ now cover a soul who accepts the Divine Mercy, that soul is rendered even *more beautiful still*. He goes on to tell her that if man's original holiness is like the creation of the heavens, then Christian holiness, won by Christ's Passion, is like studding that heaven with stars (2/26/1922). Accordingly, Christ promised in the Gospel: "**When I am lifted up from the earth, I will draw all men to myself**." (John 12:32)

By His being lifted up on the Cross, Christ won the salvation of the world. As He hung there, the Church was born from His Own Sacred Side, which gushed forth blood and water as a "fountain of mercy for us." This Church was destined to serve as the New Ark for the whole world, even *unto the end of time***.** With the Incarnation, Passion, death, and Resurrection of Jesus, and the institution of the Sacraments, the evils that had multiplied and grown for thousands of years began to diminish. The Gospel spread throughout the world, and with its proclamation came the transformation of entire nations, as well as individual lives, and everything in between.[291]

---

[290] In a nutshell: In the Original Glory, we see the exposition of the *type* of holiness God's ordained Will desires for us. In the Fall, we see God's permissive Will operative, knowing full well that a greater good would come. In the times of the Old Testament, we see 4,000 years of beseeching the coming of the Redeemer in preparation for the climax of history, in which Christ's Incarnation, Passion, death, and Resurrection would conquer sin and death, open the gates of Heaven, and introduce a totally new type of Sanctifying Grace that never would have been possible without the Fall. In the 2,000 years since, we see this Grace—and the Gospel that proclaims it, and the Church that administers it—spreading throughout the world and growing in sanctity during the preparation for the ultimate restoration of the Original Glory. When that Restoration comes—a time we stand on the cusp of—Christian holiness will be combined with the holiness of the Original Glory in such a way as to *both* embellish our celestial, Heavenly home (our only true ultimate destiny) as much as possible for all eternity, while at the same time sublimating the entire earth to the Reign of the very same Will which animates all of Heaven—the Divine Will.

[291] We should note that, even in the days of the Old Testament, God was preparing the foundations for His greatest desire: to give His very own Life to His children—that is, the Gift of His Will. He began this laborious process by putting in place the first step to Living in His Will; namely, revealing some key elements of its contents and demanding obedience thereto. Thus it was that the just life, though accessible to reason, was revealed to Moses and great promises accompanied its faithful observance. But God ultimately desired loving sons, not merely obedient servants. So, when the fullness of time had come, He sent His only begotten Son to earth in order that all who loved Him could be incorporated into His very Body and receive adopted sonship. Consequently, this work of preparing for the Gift exploded in intensity upon the Incarnation of the Word of God and the

Meanwhile, something amazing was happening; something unnoticed by history books, but which was truly unprecedented and far outshining all the grand events depicted within their pages. God began preparing the way for the Gift He would bestow upon the world. These preparations consisted in a sanctity that flourished and grew within the inner life of the Church—in her saints—in the very development of Sacred Tradition which we traced in Part Two.

Indeed, the fruits of Christianity are astounding—but they have not yet attained their full intent, which is to call down the Kingdom *conclusively and exhaustively* upon earth as the final preparation for its *definitive and perfect* enjoyment forever in Heaven. No one can deny that God's Will does not yet reign upon earth as fully as it should. But two thousand years' worth of effort will not go unrewarded. Jesus tells Luisa that the Our Father prayer contains the most sure and solemn promise He could possibly have made, and that we, today, must await the coming of the Kingdom of the Divine Will with *just as much* certainty as the Israelites had in awaiting the Redeemer (2/5/1928). He moreover assures us that every single Our Father that is prayed serves to water the seed of this Kingdom (8/25/1929), and that the difficult work is already done, whereas what is needed now is merely to make the Divine Will known.

Examining the nature of this absolute promise—and what must precede its fulfillment more proximately—will comprise the following sections.

The Third Fiat: Triumph of the Church

> "Although the end be last in the order of execution, yet it is first in the order of intention."
>
> –St. Thomas Aquinas (*S.Th.* I-II. QI. AI.)

Jesus repeatedly tells Luisa that this Kingdom upon earth which we await (and can already claim within our souls by virtue of the Gift) is none other than the *Third Fiat* of Almighty God (the first Fiat being Creation, the second being Redemption). It is what He now ardently desires to give to the world, but He is waiting for our response. He is waiting for us to strive sufficiently for it, pray for it, and yearn for it. He is waiting for us to live in His Will even now, and perform as many

---

founding of Christianity. We are, in this book, focusing on that "explosion" only due to limitations of space. But the efforts undertaken in the Old Testament must not be overlooked!

acts in His Will as we can, in order to prepare the ground for its universal reign. He is waiting for us to sufficiently spread knowledge of the Kingdom of His Will before He can institute its true triumph.

We are still in the Age of the Church—we will be until the end of time, and the Third Fiat in no way changes that fact. Jesus describes the Three Fiats of God as His three essential, fundamental works; that is, His three works *ad extra* (7/11/1923). No such work of God is ever subject to expiration or dispensation (the Old Covenant was *not* among these Three Fiats of God, hence its replacement with another dispensation—the New and Eternal Covenant, Redemption, which *is* one of the Three Fiats). Consider that the Second Fiat, Redemption, in no way replaced the First, Creation (Christianity did not give us another planet or cosmos!); rather, it took place entirely within the Fiat which preceded it. In the same way, the Fiat of Sanctification will take place entirely within the context of Redemption—entirely within the Catholic Church.

This continuity, however, does not imply that there will be no amazing changes. For we have now arrived at the moment when the Church is almost ready for her crown; the moment when the prayer she has been praying more fervently than all others—that is, the *Our Father*—is ready to be fulfilled. That Coronation of the Church will be a monumental event that will bring about her radical transformation.

The precise time of its arrival is unknown (for it depends upon our response), but its coming is an absolute guarantee. Jesus assures Luisa that the reign of His Will upon earth is not different from Redemption; rather, it is simply the second act of the same decree, and absolutely nothing can prevent its execution (1/3/1932). Since its coming cannot be stopped, it will plow through whatever stands in its way. Moreover, we know that it will be "soon," as Jesus promises Luisa that it will transpire *about* two-thousand years after Redemption (1/29/1919).

Therefore, we are left with two options. We can clear the way for its arrival: through repentance, prayer, evangelization, works of mercy, fasting, sacrifice, frequenting the Sacraments, praying the Rosary, and proclaiming and spreading knowledge of the Divine Will, and above all Living in the Divine Will. If we do this, then the Kingdom will be able to arrive more by way of love than by way of justice. Or, we can neglect these sacred callings, in which case Divine Justice will have to do all the work to bring the Kingdom upon earth. Jesus tells Luisa that these, and only these, are our two alternatives (11/19/1926), and it is entirely up to us regarding which one we choose.

It is already far too late for love to do *all* the work; man has spurned Heaven for so long that it is no longer possible to entirely avert the chastisements. They will come, and they will purge and purify both the Church and the world to prepare them for the reign of the Divine Will. But the details of the scope, duration, and severity of the chastisements is not set in stone, and therefore they can still be drastically mitigated by our response. In order to further encourage a wholehearted undertaking of this response, we should turn now to consider the chastisements themselves.

The Chastisements

> "Now when these things begin to take place, look up and raise your heads, because your redemption is drawing near." –Luke 21:28

In his book that we quoted earlier, entitled *Listen to My Prophets*, Fr. Edward O'Connor spends hundreds of pages analyzing dozens of the most important revelations, messages, apparitions, and locutions of the modern Era, and he relays the following about their *prophetic consensus*:

> The basic message is that of St. Faustina: **we are in an age of mercy, which will soon give way to an age of justice**. The reason for this is the immorality of today's world, which surpasses that of any past age ... **God has been sending prophets as never before to call us to repentance**. Most often, it is the Blessed Mother who speaks through them. She warns of an unprecedented tribulation that lies in the very near future. The Church will be torn apart. The Antichrist, already alive in the world, will manifest himself ... Not only the Church, but the whole world will experience tribulation. **There will be natural disasters,** such as earthquakes, floods, fierce storms and strange weather patterns. **Economic ruin** will plunge the whole world into poverty. **There will be warfare, perhaps even a Third World War. There will also be cosmic disasters** in the form of devastating meteors striking the earth or other heavenly bodies passing close enough to wreak havoc. Finally, a mysterious fire from heaven will wipe out the greater part of mankind, and plunge the world in utter darkness for three days. Before these terrible events take place, **we will be prepared, first by a "Warning" in which everyone on earth will see his or her soul as it appears before God,** and secondly by a miraculous sign. The disasters to come will purify the world and leave it as God intended it to be. The Holy Spirit will be poured out as never before and renew the hearts of all mankind. Most of the visionaries insist that the time left before

these things take place is very short. (P. 189-190)

I will not attempt to repeat here what Fr. O'Connor and others have already done by reviewing the details of what is coming before the Era, therefore suffice it to say that we are living in unprecedented times. Heaven is on the move like never before. The Kingdom of God is at hand. *Repent*. (Mark 1:15) There is no other way to be prepared for the veritable freight train now bearing down upon the world, as the events spoken of in the Book of Revelation are about to begin.

Jesus tells Luisa that He will turn everything upside down, generate astonishing new phenomena to destroy the pride of men, and allow turmoil of all sorts to transpire (6/18/1925). He explains that this is necessary because a more beautiful building can only be built if the collapsing one is first reduced to rubble (4/30/1928). No one who takes even a brief, though honest, look at the Church or the world today could dare dispute the necessity of the task Jesus here describes. There is scarcely one crevice of society left that is not utterly replete with mortal sin, inundated with blasphemy, defined by heresy, proud of its ugliness, and attached to its errors. If modern society is a building, then it is one infested with termites, filled with mold, and rotting in all of its beams. Let us not be so unwise as to lament the fact that God must, and soon will, tear it down.

We are, of course, not here talking about individual souls. These are eternal; society is temporary. Souls are an end; buildings, cities, nations, and all such things are mere means. Each will be little more than a memory even as a soul's enjoyment of Heaven feels like it has just started. When Luisa lamented about the beginnings of the chastisements observed in her own day—even Churches being destroyed—Jesus reminded her it is *souls* that He cares about, not buildings; the latter can all be rebuilt, He says, just as they were after the Flood. But if souls are lost, it is forever (11/20/1917), and this alone is what He agonizes over. Indeed, what use is anything temporal if it is not conducive to salvation and sanctification? The answer, of course, is: *no use at all*. God, entirely aware of this fact, will not tolerate society's continued degeneration at the expense of eternity.

Recall that, in the beginning of the 20th Century, Jesus lamented to Luisa that the efforts then beginning to liberalize divorce laws constituted the supreme sacrilege against Himself and His Church. Now, in the 21st Century, the process that began there has arrived at its culmination in the recognition of certain mortal sins, too perverse to even mention here, as "marriage." Increasingly, this perversity is being promoted within the Church herself (though in accordance with

Christ's promise, we can be certain it will never infect her Magisterium). Considering what Jesus would have said to Luisa about this if she were alive today does not require much imagination.

Marriage is the foundation and first vital cell of society itself (*Apostolicam Actuositatem,* §11), and since it has now been rendered scarcely recognizable in the understanding of society at large, we can for that reason alone conclude that there is nothing left to wait for in anticipating the arrival of the chastisements. As the Servant of God Sr. Lucia of Fatima said, "**The final battle between the Lord and the kingdom of Satan will be about Marriage and the Family.**"[292]

As this "final battle" is now witnessing the most extreme clashes, we can be sure the chastisements will arrive any moment. But we must understand that the chastisements do not detract one iota from the love that God has for all of us. Jesus tells Luisa that He would *eviscerate* Himself (6/6/1935) to not have to see *any* of His dear children suffer (which means each soul, no matter how sinful). He promises her that He has gone so far as to give His Own mother an unspeakable privilege: to entirely protect, from the chastisements, whoever she pleases (Ibid.). Whether that protection takes the form of an overwhelming outpouring of God's grace to easily shoulder any burden, or the form of actual physical protection from the harm that will come to the whole world, is not our business. All that matters in this regard is that we wholeheartedly consecrate ourselves to the Blessed Virgin, and never allow any diminishment in our devotion to her, our trust in her, and our love of her. Therefore, whenever seeing what is coming upon the world tempts us to fear, let us instead reconsecrate ourselves to her—fulfilling her requests at Fatima for the daily Rosary and First Saturday devotion and a life centered on prayer, the Eucharist, Confession, fasting, and Scripture.

Indeed, what really matters for us is that the chastisements can be mitigated and shortened, and the Era can be hastened, and above all, the salvation and sanctification of souls can be achieved more powerfully than ever in the midst of these imminent events—by the prayer and action of the Faithful who must devote themselves wholeheartedly to this task. Specifically, the chastisements will be proportional in duration, scope, and severity to the deficiency of the knowledge of the Divine Will among the people. Do you want, then, to mitigate the chastisements? Do you want to spare this world some of the historically unprecedented misery about to deluge it? Be a New

292 Catholic News Agency. "Fatima visionary predicted 'final battle' would be over marriage, family." CNA Staff. October 13, 2021.

Evangelist of the Third Fiat. Proclaim the Kingdom. Proclaim the Divine Mercy while we still have the benefit of the Time of Mercy, which is so quickly drawing to a close.

One who lives in the Divine Will—and truly, any soul in God's grace—has no fear of the chastisements (though he urgently desires to mitigate them for the sake of his brothers and sisters). For even at their most terrible, he approaches them like a person with dirt on his body approaches a shower. Jesus tells Luisa that just as a courageous soul uses the very waters of a storm to become washed and made more beautiful, we must be so courageous that the chastisements only compel us to be ever more resolute in our mission (4/16/1931). Commit now, therefore—the moment you hear on the news of the next war, or disaster, or persecution, or apostasy, or plague, or terrifying phenomenon that heralds the chastisements—to immediately *redouble* your zeal and resolve for saving and sanctifying souls; for Proclaiming the Kingdom.

This commitment, so very necessary, will become much easier if you remind yourself of the glory of Heaven (which, as Christians, we should be constantly meditating upon) and also if you consider what awaits us even on earth after the chastisements, during the Era of Peace. Let us consider just a small portion of that glory now.

On the Era Itself

> "When a woman is in travail she has sorrow, because her hour has come; but when she is delivered of the child, she no longer remembers the anguish, for joy that a child is born into the world."
> –John 16:21

As the life of the Church must follow the life of her Head—that is, Christ Himself—she, too, will have a time in her history that corresponds to His Passion, and also a time that corresponds to the period of His Resurrected Presence on earth (the Era of Peace; the Reign of the Divine Will) before His Ascension into Heaven (which, in turn, corresponds to the End of Time and the Church's definitive perfection in the Heavenly Wedding Feast).

Just as Jesus was recognizable after His Resurrection, and in some ways continued His life and teachings in a similar way as He did before His Passion, so too there will be a continuity between the Church and the world now and during the Era. Equally importantly, however, there will be great differences. (*Note: the most important thing about the Era is its orientation toward Heaven, which is to say, the salvation and sanctification of souls will be accomplished more powerfully than ever before, but we will discuss this more in the next section.*)

Regarding the Era, Jesus tells Luisa that:

- Creation is not yet finished, and will receive its *most* beautiful works during the Era (2/7/1938).
- Faith will become so clear during the Era that it will be like seeing the sun on a clear day; compared to this virtue now, which is so often like trying to convince others of the existence of the sun on a cloudy day (6/29/1928).[293]
- We will be given infused science in our intellects in order to have intuitive knowledge of natural things (5/22/1932).
- The variety of sanctities and beauties enjoyed by the citizens of the Era—though they will all be animated by the Divine Will—will be so diverse and numerous as to resemble the most astounding garden (5/15/1926).
- Bodily afflictions and infirmities will vanish, replaced by luminosity, strength, health, and grace (7/7/1928).
- *Everything* will be transformed to be enthrallingly beautiful (6/9/1929), including human beings, even physically, though of a beauty entirely pure like the Blessed Virgin's (7/30/1929).
- We will be able to *hear* the enchanting celestial music of the spheres; that is, the reverberations of the motions of the stars and planets which, upon our ability to sense, will far surpass in beauty even the greatest symphonies of Mozart (1/28/1927).[294]
- All animals will reacquire automatic obedience to man and their natural inclination to serve man (1/28/1927).
- All humanity will acquire the very dignity, nobility, happiness, and Heavenly peace forfeited by Adam (8/13/1923).
- Death will still happen, but not as the fearful and agonizing thing it is today; rather, as a mere peaceful transition from this life to the next, once we have completed our mission upon earth. More-

---

[293] I would add that conveyance of such Faith is, even now, quite feasible for reasonable and sincere people (we *can* prove God's existence even with reason alone, just as we could prove the sun on a cloudy day!), but unfortunately the task is far too often unsuccessful today; Jesus is here simply telling Luisa that Faith will still be needed during the Era (it is not Heaven; we will not have the Beatific Vision), but proving one's Faith to another then will be as straightforward as, for example, "proving" the rising of the sun on a clear day, or that 2 and 2 make 4.

[294] Note: even the ancient Greek philosophers posited the existence of this "Music of the Spheres." Unlike today's rationalistic, reductionistic scholars, the ancients were intelligent enough to recognize that it is only reasonable to suppose that the beauty and regularity of the motion of the heavenly bodies generates literal music.

over, He promises that the bodies of the dead will all remain incorrupt; fully composed in their tombs awaiting the day of the General Resurrection and Last Judgment (10/22/1926).

- The Sacraments, far from being discarded, will rather acquire their complete fruit in the Church and the world—serving no longer primarily as occasional medicine for the sick, but as perennial food for the heathy (11/2/1926).
- The union between Heaven and earth in the Communion of Saints will be so palpable that, during the Era, we will even be able to *see* and *hear* the blessed in Heaven. (7/10/1928) Consequently, when loved ones die during the Era, the farewell will not be the extremely painful thing it is for most people today.
- There will be an abundance of all goods; including natural ones—the immense riches of creation will be fully available to all (1/28/1927). Accordingly, Jesus tells Luisa that all the elements are in waiting—almost eager, as it were, to deliver to their king (man himself) the superabundance of beneficial effects they contain within themselves, but which they can only deliver a small fraction of now due to the present reign of sin (6/25/1928).

This is only a small taste of the glory of the Era destined to soon dawn upon the whole earth. Dive into Jesus' revelations to Luisa yourself, and you will come across a great deal more.

Some may be concerned about the last point above; supposing that such opulence of material goods would induce us to carnality, worldliness, and sin. This is a valid concern, and it is precisely why, as Jesus explains to Luisa, poverties and shortages of all sorts are often necessary now (1/28/1927). These circumstances of want help us remain detached from the earth and focused on Heaven. But during the Era, there will no longer be the same risk of sin in material goods that there is today, therefore there will be no need for Providence to allow them to be so often lacking. This is to say that during the Era, all will have finally learned the "secret" of St. Paul, who taught:

> **I know how to be abased, and I know how to abound; in any and all circumstances I have learned the secret of facing plenty and hunger, abundance and want.** (Philippians 4:12)

Another truth of the Era liable to misunderstanding must here be reiterated: there is nothing homogeneous, techno-dystopian, or Communistic about it. All, indeed, will have a baseline astonishing beauty and holiness, but the varieties that shall exist will far outshine the variety we now observe. Jesus assures Luisa that we will *always* be free, especially during the Era, and thus there will be great hierarchy in those days; some taking the highest of these beautiful paths by *best* using their free wills, others unfortunately choosing less noble ones—paths which, even if they do not include mortal sin, nevertheless are far less meritorious (4/25/1923). Struggle and conquest, therefore, will never depart from our calling as Christians until the end of time, whereafter everything will be enjoyment, without any struggle and without risk, for all eternity.

Descriptions of the Era could be continued for many pages, so for now it must suffice to say that the general paradigm for the Era is none other than Eden itself (though better, as we now have the Incarnation and Redemption); if it was a part of life in the Garden of Eden (or would have been had enough time passed before the Fall—such as the earth being filled with people—6/25/1928), then there is a good chance it will be a part of life during the Era. As already established, justice itself demands that humanity return to God in a similar state to that in which we came forth from Him. If we were to say this will not be so, then we fail to honor God by considering Him to be like ourselves; we who begin a task only to give up later with the end result being worse than that with which we started, like a worthless contractor who completes the demolition and brings in the new raw materials, only to leave them all in a few piles around the house he was supposed to completely renovate.

But we must not make too many assumptions about all the details of the Era based upon this paradigm. There will certainly be differences. We will still have the Church in her entirety—Sacraments, Hierarchies, Doctrines, etc. Baptism will still be needed to render one a Christian and remove the guilt of Original Sin. Jesus does *not* tell Luisa that the Gift removes the guilt of Original Sin, but only that it acts like cement against an infestation of pests; i.e., it stops Original Sin in its tracks from doing further harm through its effects (3/19/1926). On the contrary, He tells her that *everyone* (except the Blessed Virgin) inherits Original Sin (6/30/1931).

Many additional exceptions could doubtless be noted. Jesus tells Luisa very clearly that the Era will be *almost* a restoration of Eden (2/22/1921); it will not be a literal and complete accomplishment of the same. It is not important for us to know exactly what that means, so we should not get distracted by becoming overly curious. We need only know enough to inspire us to be zealous for hastening its arrival; while, even more importantly, always remaining entirely grounded in Catholic orthodoxy.

Nevertheless, I hope and pray that all are adequately—even *overwhelmingly*—inspired to be zealous by recognizing that just as

Creation came forth from God's hands in the beginning with nobility, beauty, and holiness, so too it will return to Him in a similar state. Thus, the words of Revelation will be fulfilled, and the Church, the Bride of Christ, will ascend to the altar of God for the Great Wedding Feast that commences upon the consummation of history. She will not be dirty, sick, and stained as she now is, but rather bejeweled and fully prepared "**as a bride adorned for her husband**" (Revelation 21:2)—thanks to the Era of Peace. In sum, as we have already seen in the teachings of Pope St. John Paul II, this Era will "re-establish the original harmony of creation."

The Original Harmony itself, however, was ordered toward Heaven! Even if Adam had not sinned, earth still would not have been our ultimate home; Heaven alone would have retained that distinction. We must therefore always remember that, far from eclipsing or duplicating Heaven, the Era holds—as its entire purpose—the aim of populating and glorifying our Heavenly Fatherland.

The Era: All About Heaven

> "May these mysteries, O Lord, in which we have participated, profit us, we pray, for even now, as we walk amid passing things, you teach us by them to love the things of heaven and hold fast to what endures."
>
> –Prayer After Communion. First Week of Advent. Roman Missal.

No one, on account of the Era, ought to allow one iota of focus to be taken away from living life with a Heavenly orientation as its predominant theme. The fundamental nature of the Era is the conforming of the earth to the law of Heaven, so as to glorify our eternal home and generate saints to populate this home. Therefore, no one should, as admonished against by the well-placed rebuke of Liberation Theology (which *does* detract from Heaven), "immanentize the eschaton." With this idea in mind, Cardinal Ratzinger astutely wrote:

> Faced with the urgency of certain problems, some are tempted to emphasize, unilaterally, the liberation from servitude of an earthly and temporal kind. **They do so in such a way that they seem to put liberation from sin in second place**, and so fail to give it the primary importance it is due... To some it even seems that the necessary struggle for human justice and freedom in the economic and political sense constitutes the whole essence of sal-

> vation. For them, the Gospel is reduced to a purely earthly gospel...[295]

To Luisa, Jesus confides similar lamentations, bemoaning the fact that even among priests there are so many modernists and hedonists who view a soul treading the path to perdition as if it were nothing to worry about, while temporal matters garner all their attention (1/15/1911). How at odds this approach is with everything about the Era! If the Era will provide an outpouring of justice that liberates those in bondage (as indeed it will), it does so merely secondarily to, and as an effect of, its casting out of Satan, its sublimation of the human will into the Divine Will, its triumph of the Church, its reign of the Sacraments, its motivating the repentance, conversion, and sanctification of all souls, etc. These latter realities of the Era are why we earnestly desire it and strive to hasten it, even though we remain aware of its other beneficial temporal effects (and there is nothing wrong with eagerly awaiting these as well).

Cardinal Ratzinger concludes the same document by quoting Pope St. Paul VI, who taught that the Kingdom of God…

> ... Cannot be confused with the progress of civilization, of science, and of human technology, but that it consists in knowing ever more deeply the unfathomable riches of Christ, to hope ever more strongly in things eternal, to respond ever more ardently to the love of God, **to spread ever more widely grace and holiness among men**.[296]

This *is* the Era, and this is why we long for it: *grace and holiness reigning among men*.

The greatest fact about the Era is that the earth will become a veritable *saint-making factory*. Jesus tells Luisa that the purpose of earth is to generate saints to populate Heaven (e.g., 6/6/1935, 11/5/1925). To be sure, Jesus—with His sacrifice on the cross 2,000 years ago—opened the doors to Heaven and showed us the "narrow way." During the Era, however, the way to Heaven will become a highway. Today especially, the only "eschatological highway" one generally finds is the proverbial "highway to hell." This path, as Jesus says even in the Gospel, is the one tread by "many," whereas only the "few" are treading the path to salvation. (cf. Matthew 7:14) But during the Era, holiness will be the norm, not the exception. During the Era, we will not be constantly tormented by fears that our loved ones will

---

[295] Cardinal Ratzinger. *Instruction on Certain Aspects of the "Theology of Liberation."* Congregation for the Doctrine of the Faith. August 6, 1984.

[296] Ibid.

not make it to Heaven. During the Era, these "small ways" that "few find" leading to salvation will become great and glorious roads trodden by the multitude. The Era, in a word, will be the time in which we see fulfilled the Fatima prayer, "... **lead all souls to Heaven**..."

Moreover, as we saw in the last section, there will be during the Era a superior and far more palpable bond between the three ranks of the Church. The Faithful on earth (the Church Militant), will join hearts with those in Purgatory (the Church Suffering) and Heaven (the Church Triumphant). Today, it is easy for even a sincere Christian to find himself going a long time scarcely thinking of eternity, much less living his life oriented towards it. During the Era, we will *always* be thinking of Heaven, and we will receive inescapable foretastes of it not only every Mass, but also every time we look at the stars, or the smile of a person, or the rising sun. No longer will the things of earth be enjoyed purely for their own sake; they will, as the Liturgical prayer above supplicates for, be approached rightly: as *veils* of the very Divinity which we will only experience in totality once we arrive in Heaven.

During the Era, therefore, *we will long for Heaven even more than we do now!* This longing will be different; far from being the painful thing that it sometimes is now, it will be pure joy and excitement, like the awaiting of Christmas morning with the eagerness of children. Indeed, the Church's beauty in the Era will make us *more* mindful of the fact that her full perfection is only in Heaven, which will in turn elicit greater cognizance of our ultimate destiny (the Beatific Vision of Heaven), and our longing for it will increase in stride and far exceed its present degree, just as the closer a magnet is placed to a piece of steel, the stronger is the pull.[297]

Allow me to illustrate by way of a personal testimony and "A Tale of Two Cemeteries." Focus on Heaven has always been my life's greatest joy. My greatest happiness has come from contemplating it, and my most overwhelming experiences in meditation have always

---

[297] Happiness will reign over the whole earth during the Era, and this happiness will be complete in a *terrestrial* sense; but such happiness was created by God as only the preparation for eternal happiness, and to enliven our desire for the happiness that is only possible in our Heavenly Beatitude. Therefore, during the Era our happiness will indeed be immense, but it will also involve a triumphant longing for Heaven—a longing that will, perhaps paradoxically, be another source of joy. Even now, any serious Christian can doubtless recall that his moments of greatest happiness were precisely in the moments when he most hoped for, longed for, and meditated upon Heaven. That will be doubly true during the Era: we will be much closer to Heaven, but this proximity will only make our ardent longing for it more inflamed.

come from either it or from the Passion. In keeping with this, one of my favorite routines is to prayerfully walk through cemeteries. There, surrounded by the remains of those who have passed, I am filled with excitement at their silent testimony: the utter fleetingness of this life, and the imminence of the day when, upon our own deaths, we get to leave all its troubles behind and enter eternity, and enjoy the Beatific Vision forever. I should note that I've never understood the use of the words "envying the dead" as a description of the consequence of some terrible event. I love my life, but I *already* envy the dead! For I know I will love life after death infinitely more.

My anticipation of the Era of Peace has only strengthened everything noted above in my own heart; an effect sure to result in anyone's heart who approaches the Era's themes correctly. That said, while strolling through any cemetery can provide edification—by virtue of its fundamental orientation to eternity—it is ideal to stroll through one that is quiet, peaceful, beautiful, adorned with edifying tombstone inscriptions and breathtaking statues which powerfully glorify Jesus, Mary, and the angels and saints.

Such a cemetery is more inspiring, indeed, than one frequented by gangs for sin and crime, unkempt and overgrown, inundated with noise and fumes from an adjacent highway, and filled with ugly modernist tombstones that, instead of bearing inscriptions and images directed towards eternity, are plastered with words and pictures of the deceased person's worldly hobbies.

Neither cemetery can escape the fact that, by nature, it is fundamentally "about" the afterlife—but only one properly comports itself in accordance with its nature. Unfortunately, the world, as it is now, far more resembles the latter cemetery than the former. During the Era, it will be the opposite. This earth, though glorified and far surpassing its present state even in temporal beauty and happiness, will still be entirely *about* Heaven; its surpassing glory will only render its Heavenly orientation *more* intense.

Finally, know that you will enjoy the Era more from Heaven than you will from the earth, so you should also not waste one second wondering whether you will "live to see" the Era. You *will* see it! Whether you see it from earth or from Heaven is not important. Despite their perfect happiness, the souls in Heaven are more eager to see the arrival of the Era than we ourselves are, since unlike us they are not subject to folly and shortsightedness. As we noted earlier, Jesus even tells Luisa that they are now engaged in a sort of holy competition with us to see who can do more—we from earth, or they from above—to hasten the arrival of the Kingdom on earth! (5/20/1928)

Yet, someone may still complain and say, *"If Heaven can be so powerfully glorified through the Era, why did God allow almost all of human history to be so painful? Why would He have allowed that if there was an easier way?"* As we already addressed that question in the preceding sections, its continued submission demonstrates only one thing: he who asks it has grown attached to his own cross.

I recall a priest sharing a story about an outdoor weekend retreat he once led for youth. At the beginning of the weekend, he instructed each youth to find a big ugly rock. After everyone had found such a stone, he told them they had to carry it with them everywhere. Though understandably annoyed at this directive, they nevertheless acquiesced and remained burdened with the task of hauling around a heavy hunk of rock everywhere they went. Close to the end of the retreat, the priest said, "Now throw this rock into the lake." Some happily and immediately did so, and greatly enjoyed their newfound freedom. Others complained and resisted. They had grown so accustomed to the burden presented to them by their rocks, and they had become so attached to this suffering, that they could not bring themselves to part with it.

Let us not be like that. God's plan is perfect. We do not need to micromanage it. In fact, we do not even need to completely understand it. We only need to trust it. Whatever He has done or allowed in the past was best, and whatever He *will* do or allow in the future will be best.

> For everything there is a season, and a time for every matter under heaven: a time to be born, and a time to die; a time to plant, and a time to pluck up what is planted; a time to kill, and a time to heal; a time to break down, and a time to build up; a time to weep, and a time to laugh; a time to mourn, and a time to dance; **a time to cast away stones**, and a time to gather stones together; time to embrace, and a time to refrain from embracing; a time to seek, and a time to lose; a time to keep, and a time to cast away; a time to rend, and a time to sew; a time to keep silence, and a time to speak; a time to love, and a time to hate; a time for war, **and a time for peace**. (Ecclesiastes 3)

My friends, there is a time for building up treasures in Heaven through great suffering, and a time for doing the same through a meritorious Faith which glorifies and thanks God for His blessings. There is a time for embellishing our eternal home through conquests on this earth against mortal sin and all manner of grave evils and errors, and there is a time for doing the same through striving after the very highest and best options presented to us out of many that are all good in themselves. There is a time for growing and meriting through conversion from *enemy of God* to *friend of God*, and there is a time for doing the same through the sanctification of proceeding from one glory to another glory. If we are so blessed as to live to see the time wherein the latter conquests are those which dominate on earth, then let us thank God for that, and not question His wisdom.

24. Certainty

"The Lord will win, because it is divine decree that His Kingdom will come upon earth."
–Servant of God Luisa Piccarreta

We will conclude this book with a meditation on the certainty we can and must have in the thesis presented within its pages. It is not my thesis, and it is not Luisa's thesis. It is not even the thesis of the Popes, saints, mystics, Church Fathers, and other authorities who likewise insisted upon it. It is, rather, the Almighty's greatest prerogative; the primary promise directly from Christ Himself, and it will be fulfilled so long as God is God.

Jesus tells Luisa that His entire message to her on Living in the Divine Will and its impending reign over the whole earth (despite the fact that it encompassed thousands of pages of revelations) is enclosed in the eleven words of the third petition of the Our Father (2/24/1933), "*Thy will be done on earth as it is in Heaven*" (Matthew 6:10). Jesus promised that He is so bound and committed to those words that nothing could possibly prevent their realization (2/5/1928). But on this point, the private revelations of Jesus to Luisa are just a confirmation of a fact we should have already regarded as certain.

> Since prayer is necessary to the Christian, the Son of God, yielding to the request of the disciples, 'Lord, teach us to pray,' gave them a prescribed form of prayer, **and encouraged them to hope that the objects of their petitions would be granted**. (Roman Catechism [The Catechism of the Council of Trent]. On the Lord's Prayer. Part IV.) **Christian hope sustains us ... and leads us to pray as Jesus taught us: "Thy Kingdom come. Thy will be done, on earth as it is in heaven."** (Pope St. John Paul II. *Redemptoris Missio*, §86)

Now, hope—being Divinely mandated—entails not wishful thinking, but rather a *certain* conviction. If we lack this conviction, we are not praying the Our Father in the way that Christ and the Church command us to pray it. For while "hopes" placed in men may amount to little more than wishes, *true hope*—hope in God—is never so tepid. Rather, it is always rock solid. The first indispensable necessity, therefore, *for any Christian to pray the Our Father as he must*, is that he do so with absolute conviction; with a *sure and certain hope* that what he prays for, in obedience to Divine Teaching, *will* come about. "**Truly,**

truly, I say to you, if you ask anything of the Father, he will give it to you in my name." (John 16:23)

Without this sure and certain hope, one is compelled to ponder what exactly he is doing by even praying the Our Father at all. It is only a deceitful, confused, or at best timid man who, upon proffering a certain request, actually hopes for it to be only *partially* fulfilled. A single-minded man will recognize that, just as only one who hopes for full health takes medicine, the axiom is true which holds that *willing the means is willing the end.* Why pray for—much less work for—the conversion of sinners and unbelievers, or for the end to various injustices (such as abortion, genocide, persecution, etc.), or for the sanctification of the Faithful, and so on, unless one truly *hopes* for (that is, *confidently expects*) the complete attainment of these things by God's grace—and not just in some instances, but everywhere on earth?

To fail to have true hope in the total fulfillment of the Our Father's third petition is to render all such prayers duplicitous. These prayers are each contained in that ultimate and all-encompassing aim of *God's Will being done on earth as in Heaven.* To doubt the fulfillment of the latter even while supplicating God for the former is to be double-minded. If we insist upon harboring such duplicity, then Scripture rebukes us:

> But let him ask in faith, with no doubting, for he who doubts is like a wave of the sea that is driven and tossed by the wind. For that person must not suppose that a double-minded man, unstable in all his ways, will receive anything from the Lord. (James 1:6-8)

We must not ask for God's Will to be only *partially* done on earth; or to be only done on earth in *some of the ways* it is done in Heaven. If that is what we are doing when we pray the Our Father, then, as Scripture admonishes, we should not expect to "receive *anything* from the Lord."

The jaded cynic protests that it is quite naïve to hope that the Lord's Prayer could actually be fulfilled. But Luisa was not naïve. She even dared to say to Jesus that it did not seem possible for the Kingdom to come on earth, considering how mankind was only becoming more and more sinful (a descent which, since her day, has sadly accelerated). Jesus gently rebuked her, and pointed out that such apparent impossibilities will melt like wax before Him (1/3/1932), that He has already done all the hard work (2/24/1933), and that His mother will work *miracles that will shake the entire earth* to bring the Kingdom about (7/14/1935). He reminds Luisa not to worry that man does not and will not merit the Kingdom; we did not merit our creation either, and Redemption itself was scarcely proportioned to the merits of mankind, but both happened nevertheless by virtue of God's gratuitous love. This, Jesus promises, is precisely why and how the Kingdom will come upon earth (3/26/1933). Therefore, banish all doubt.

In sum, as we have already seen the great Church Father St. John Chrysostom remind us: Jesus, in teaching the Lord's Prayer "... **did not at all say, 'Thy will be done' in me, or in us, but *everywhere on the earth*...**" No human preconditions are affixed to the fulfillment of these words; the attainment of their promise remains as certain as anything else that Jesus foretold would certainly happen, such as His Resurrection. Just as the accomplishment of that glorious event was put in doubt by those who heard it promised beforehand, so too is the fulfillment of the Our Father prayer put in doubt today—even by Christians.

But we must know better, and we must now become the boldest Witnesses to Hope that history has ever seen. For the world has never been so direly in need of hope as it now is. This hope in the fulfillment of the Greatest Promise of the Greatest Prayer—a hope which I pray now wells up from the very depths of your heart to the point of overflowing—is, I assure you, the remedy to the maladies of those around you. It is the balm that can heal those souls racked with pain and despair and who, upon observing the state of the world, only grow despondent and are ready to give up on life. *But you must apply the remedy for it to work.*

Not only is this hope the only remedy for individual souls, it is also the only remedy for the entire world. And although the Our Father's fulfillment will be gratuitous and unmerited, it will not come without sufficient cooperation from those called to be its heralds. Hence the incessant plea from Jesus to us all to proclaim this Kingdom. Jesus assures Luisa that the *only thing* needed, in order for the Kingdom to arrive on earth, is willing souls who will spare no expense, who will be bold and courageous, who are ready to sacrifice and even lay down their lives, in order to hurl these truths on the Divine Will—the coming of the Kingdom—the fulfillment of the Our Father—*across the whole world* (8/25/1929).

Perhaps, right now, the only thing needed is *one more* zealous soul; *one more* missionary of the Divine Will whose heart is on fire for the glory of God and the salvation and sanctification of His children. Perhaps that soul is you.

The time will come when Jesus will triumph over all, and His kingdom on earth will certainly come, because it is a decree of God, and He does not easily change His decrees because of the wickedness of men. However, **blessed are those who interest themselves in His Will, because the Lord will use them to open the ways which had been closed**, and will use their acts as many keys in order to open Heaven and to make It descend and reign upon earth. (Letter of the Servant of God Luisa Piccarreta to Federico Abresch)

... **If the Divine Fiat is known, the kingdom of the enemy is over. Here is all his rage.** But the Lord will win, because it is divine decree that His Kingdom will come upon earth. It is a matter of time, but He will make His way; He lacks neither power nor wisdom to dispose the circumstances. But I tell you: whatever you can do [to make the Divine Will known]—do it. (Letter of the Servant of God Luisa Piccarreta to "Irene." December 5, 1939)

Go, fortified by My grace, and fight for My kingdom in human souls; fight as a king's child would; and remember that the days of your exile will pass quickly, and with them the possibility of earning merit for heaven. I expect from you, My child, a great number of souls who will glorify My mercy for all eternity. My child, that you may answer My call worthily, receive Me daily in Holy Communion. It will give you strength... (Jesus to St. Faustina. *Divine Mercy in My Soul*, §1489)

FIAT

APPENDICES

25. Proclaiming the Divine Will for Priests

(Note: while this first appendix is addressed to priests in particular—those whom Jesus is *especially* calling to be heralds of the Divine Will message—it will also prove useful for anyone who is looking to promote the Divine Will using an approach that is particularly circumspect. All the faithful are called to proclaim this message, and we should always do so in a way that is prudent with respect to the nature of our audience.)

The USCCB's 2012 document "Preaching the Mystery of Faith," presents Jesus' Own preaching as the paradigm of a priest's homilies as follows:

> **The key motif of Jesus' preaching in the Synoptic Gospels is his announcement of the coming Reign of God ... Jesus makes the Kingdom of God the keynote of his mission and teaches his disciples to pray to the Father: "Thy Kingdom come" (Mt 6:10) ... All effective homilies have this sense of urgency and freshness, revealing the startling beauty and promise of the Kingdom...**

These sound directives on a priest's preaching will be well heeded by incorporating the Divine Will message into homilies. To be sure, all the faithful—wherever they happen to stand on any given private revelation—should feel at home at the Mass, including during the homily, and the *main thrust* of sermons should not *generally* consist in the *explicit* promotion of a *particular* private revelation. This does not mean, however, that private revelations (above all, one so glorious as those of Jesus to Luisa) must be pretended to not exist during the preaching of homilies! Whoever is of that opinion should consider just how often Popes have included private revelations in their own homilies. The greatest example of this is Pope St. John Paul II's zeal in proclaiming the Divine Mercy as revealed to St. Faustina, going so far as to insist that these revelations constituted the very mission of his whole Papacy. And, mark my words, the next great Papal passion for a private revelation will be for the Divine Will as revealed to Luisa. I know neither when this will be nor who will occupy the Chair of Peter, but whoever he is, he will approach his Pontificate as a mission to proclaim the Divine Will, just as John Paul the Great made it his to proclaim the Divine Mercy.

In the case of the private revelations of Jesus to the Servant of God Luisa Piccarreta, on the Gift of Living in the Divine Will and the coming reign of the Divine Will on earth as in Heaven, there are many ways to incorporate these themes into the public preaching of the Church even now (that is—as of this writing—even before Luisa's Beatification and the release of the full, approved, critical edition of her revelations) without any risk of imprudence or friction with the norms governing homiletics.

The first reason this can be done successfully is simple: the main theme of Jesus' revelations to Luisa is also the main theme of Scripture itself. These private revelations place Scripture's own nucleus under a microscope and therefore render more explicit its full power and beauty. Just as one's appreciation for the breathtakingly intelligent design of a leaf only increases when viewing its cellular structure under great magnification, so too one's appreciation for the Word of God will only be inflamed by delving more deeply still into this Word's ultimate word: "Thy Will be done on earth as it is in Heaven." (Matthew 6:10) Accordingly, priests can first develop a habit of bringing the supremacy of union with the Will of God into the main points of homilies: exhorting their congregations to trust in that Will, to submit to that Will, to love that Will, and the glorify that Will in all things. Jesus Himself did the same—in His Own public ministry—when He sought to drive home particularly central points. We see this not only in the climax of the Our Father prayer (itself the centerpiece of the greatest homily, the Sermon on the Mount), but also in many other places. (See Part One of this book.)

The Apostolic Exhortation *Evangelii Gaudium* dedicates many paragraphs to homiletics, some points of which are worth repeating here:

> ... Our own aim is not to understand every little detail of a text; **our most important goal is to discover its principal message**, the message which gives structure and unity to the text ... We must not think that in catechesis the kerygma gives way to a supposedly more "solid" formation. **Nothing is more solid, profound, secure, meaningful and wisdom-filled than that initial proclamation. All Christian formation consists of entering more deeply into the kerygma** ... (§147, 165)

While a multitude of "principal messages" exist throughout Scripture's various passages, all of them are summed up in the *supreme* principal message which is none other than God's Will, and the accomplishment of that Will is also the essence of the kerygma. If, therefore, you are wondering what exactly is needed to renew your preaching and render it more coherent, powerful, and *kerygmatic* than ever before, look no further than the Divine Will.

As you consider the details of how to work this into your preaching, this book may serve well as a resource. As I have not included within these pages so much as a single direct quote from Luisa's private revelations, you can freely quote anything in this book without worrying about any ecclesial notifications, or overstepping the bounds of private revelation's incorporation into your sermon, and certainly without worrying about contradicting Catholic orthodoxy. (Though I submit, without reservation, everything I have written in this book to the judgment of Holy Mother Church, and I ask that all Church teachings—past, present, and future—be preferred to anything I have ever written or will ever write.)

There are indeed other strategies, however, which you can begin with to express the main thrust of Luisa's revelations, while not referring to them directly. You could incorporate into your preaching and teaching the various works given throughout the history of the Church which build up to the Gift of Living in the Divine Will (see Parts One and Two). Whoever is well grounded in the following will have absolutely no problem understanding the Gift of Living in the Divine Will as soon as it is presented to them:

- The supremely important nature of the Our Father
- The theme of divinization in the Fathers of the Church
- The Teaching of St. Maximus the Confessor
- St. Bernard of Clairvaux, *On Loving God*
- St. Francis de Sales, *Treatise on the Love of God*
- St. Alphonsus Liguori, *Uniformity With God's Will*
- Fr. De Caussade, *Abandonment to Divine Providence*
- Marian Consecration (as taught by St. Louis de Montfort and St. Maximilian Kolbe)
- The Little Way of St. Thérèse of Lisieux

Once your flock is well grounded in these teachings, you can easily introduce them to the lofty spirituality (which truly does relay the Gift of Living in the Divine Will) in the mystics discussed in Part Three; especially St. Faustina and Blessed Conchita. I recommend securing for yourself a copy of St. Faustina's Diary, *Divine Mercy in My Soul,* and whatever materials you can find on Blessed Conchita. None of this, however, need be treated like a rigorous academic program; even brief introductions will suffice. Afterwards, your congregation will have no difficulty in comprehending the Gift of Living in the Divine Will, and you can feel more than ready to introduce them to Jesus' revelations to Luisa.

If all you can now manage to do is incorporate these themes into your homilies, that is fine. Jesus does not expect anyone to neglect the duties of his state in life for the sake of His revelations to Luisa, and He certainly does not expect this of priests who must, above all, ensure they are as available as possible for Mass, Confession, Anointing, Catechesis, etc.

But if more is reasonable for you, then you could next start a Divine Will cenacle in your parish—if there are enough parishioners available who are ready and willing to take on the various secretarial duties for the group. Unlike many other devotions, spiritualities, consecrations, programs, etc., now popular within the Church, the Divine Will has no flashy marketing campaigns—replete with DVDs, workbooks, professional brochures full of corporate stock images, custom smartphone apps, and the like. It is better that such things do not exist for the Divine Will, as their absence will elicit a more authentic zeal, joy, and love in approaching these revelations.

As you gather together around a table after an evening Mass, when the bustle of the day's parish busyness has subsided, with the buzzing tube-fluorescent lights turned off and nothing before you but a lit candle, a Bible, a Catechism, Rosary beads, and Jesus' revelations to Luisa, and overjoyed parishioners beside you whose hearts have similarly been set ablaze by Jesus' words to Luisa, you will with good cause feel just like the early Christian disciples did. And from these hearts on fire, you will see extraordinary graces spreading to others. Soon, you will see your parish transformed like you never thought possible.

Jesus is asking everyone who knows this message to proclaim it, but as a priest, you can be sure that you will be given special graces for doing so. The moment you feel ready, do not hesitate to proclaim these messages beyond the boundaries of your own parish. Get it out to the world. Put teachings up on a YouTube channel, blog, social media platform, or other media outlet. Submit articles on the Divine Will to your Diocesan newspaper. Record homilies in which you preach on the Divine Will. Make yourself available to give talks on the Divine Will at various Catholic events. Be creative and be zealous with other methods of getting the message out there. Your efforts will be superabundantly rewarded. I promise you that.

Forming a Divine Will Cenacle

Although I will present some suggestions below, there is no single structure that must be followed in order to host a Divine Will cenacle; whoever feels called to host such a prayer group should proceed in accordance with his or her discernment of the Holy Spirit's promptings—always, of course, in obedience to any norms which may exist from the local Ordinary. One criterion, however, is essential for any Divine Will group: zeal for and adherence to Catholic orthodoxy. Ideally, each Divine Will group would be led by a Catholic priest. If no priest is available, then someone with a solidly orthodox Catholic theological training should lead. If neither is available, then each meeting should at least be undertaken with the *Catechism of the Catholic Church* handy, and it—or other authoritative Catholic texts—must always be consulted, and the teachings therein submitted to, whenever questions arise regarding the proper understanding of a given passage in Luisa's writings. Needless to say, as soon as the official edition and translation of Luisa's volumes is available, it is this (and only this) version which should be used, and its own footnotes should always be consulted and respected.

A possible general format for the meetings is as follows:

1) Begin with prayer, perhaps a Chaplet of Divine Mercy or Holy Rosary.
2) Pray the Chaplet of the Divine Will. (This prayer, given to us by St. Hannibal, is like the Divine Mercy Chaplet, but on each "Hail Mary" bead, the leader says: "Thy Will be Done," and all respond: "On earth as it is in Heaven." On each "Our Father" bead, we pray a "Glory Be." Then we conclude with the prayer: "Lord Jesus, we praise You, we love You, we bless You, and we thank You Who are God with the Father and the Holy Spirit in Your Holy and Eternal Divine Will. Amen."
3) Read the Gospel from the day's Mass.
4) Select one or more passages from Luisa's volumes to discuss. A convenient way of selecting passages is by considering whatever entry in Luisa's diary was given on the same Month/Day as the meeting is being held (Luisa's volumes can easily be found organized in this manner by searching for a "Divine Will Calendar.")
5) Bring Scripture, Magisterium, the lives and teachings of the saints, etc., regularly into your discussion. Doing so is not "off topic;" it is necessary.
6) Bear fruit! Approaching Luisa's revelations properly will result in

more and better prayer, works of mercy, frequenting of the sacraments, etc. It will result in sins being repented of, virtues flowering, unruly passions diminishing, and peace, joy, happiness, and trust permeating one's days. It will result in evangelization, conversions, vocations, and even miracles (remember, too, that Luisa is a powerful intercessor!).[298] It will result in the Divine Will revelations themselves being proclaimed from the rooftops. Discuss how fruit like this will be borne by your group's dedication to Luisa's revelations, and work to implement your resolutions.

7) End with a concluding prayer or prayers of your group's choosing.

Some Pragmatic Notes Regarding the Volumes

All of Luisa's volumes are very easy to find, so I will not include here specific instructions on acquiring them. But do be aware that unless you are fluent in Luisa's dialect of Italian, you will be reading an unofficial translation of Jesus' revelations to her.

Each available translation of Luisa's volumes contains some translation errors which might make it difficult to properly understand and interpret a few details in them. Accordingly, it is important to focus on the main themes and avoid drawing too many inferences from small details. The release of the official, critical, footnoted edition of Luisa's revelations will resolve these issues. It is, however, imperative that we not sit around and wait for this to occur. Far too much is at stake, and while we can hope and pray the release will occur very soon, no guarantee exists here. Nor does the Vatican have a reputation for speed.

Some critics of Luisa attempt to argue that the existing "Moratorium" on the commercial *publication* of her complete volumes means that they cannot be read, shared, or promoted *at all* by Catholics. This is false and has been repeatedly contradicted by the sole competent Ecclesial authorities on the matter (who, within the very official documents the "Moratorium" is spoken of, openly advocate for reading and sharing this spirituality!); therefore, those who insist on repeating it should simply be ignored, and we should feel free to

---

[298] Do not forget to diligently document miracles received through Luisa's intercession, and submit them to your Bishop.

read and share the volumes no matter how much they continue to protest. (See the Appendices of *The Crown of Sanctity* for details).[299]

As we do this, the most important thing is what I have constantly repeated elsewhere: that we always read all of Jesus' revelations to Luisa in light of Catholic teaching, and whenever there appears to be the need to defer to one over the other, we choose Catholic teaching every time. *There are no actual cases of contradictions here.* But the imperfections in translation, and the open-endedness of how to interpret certain teachings in the volumes, does at least mean that those who fail to take this advice are at risk.

Some more minor matters should also be acknowledged. Though I am not qualified to scrutinize this issue, I nevertheless suspect that an overly literal approach to translation may have been taken in some points within some of the presently available English translations. To give just one example, the translation of Luisa's volumes that I most often read renders the Italian word "mamma" (for the Blessed Mother) in English as precisely that: "mamma." (Or as "mama.") While using this affectionate term in English is certainly not inappropriate for our tender Heavenly Mother (and anyone who does appreciate its use should feel no qualms continuing with it despite what I say here!), it also carries with it a *degree* of informality that it seems to not have in Italian. Now, I do not speak Italian, but I have consulted many Italian-English translation dictionaries, and almost all of them present either "mom" or "mother" as the first and most appropriate way to translate the Italian "mamma;" therefore, I say "mother" where the Italian of Luisa's writings say "mamma," and I have modified the document from which I print out the volumes for my own reading accordingly. There are other cases of similar potential translation issues that may be overly literal or otherwise imperfect. The release of the official translation will also resolve these issues; in the meantime, we must plow forward with what we have, and not become bothered by issues that are a mere nothing compared to the magnitude of the mission at hand. Perhaps I am right, and perhaps I am wrong, about this little point; either way, these are tiny matters and they mustn't become a distraction. Simply do what you must to get yourself "into" these revelations!

Similarly, I encourage you to proceed as you like and feel comfortable with regarding how exactly you read the volumes and, in

---

[299] Available for free at www.DSDOConnor.com (Nevertheless, I have written this present book with no direct quotes from the volumes in order to ensure that there is absolutely no impediment whatsoever to it being handed to any Catholic; even the most cautious.)

general, how you proceed with Divine Will spirituality. There is no need to burn yourself out, and as long as you've already taken the basic steps for receiving the Gift (steps outlined in Part Four), you can gradually approach the deeper aspects of the Rounds, Acts, etc. Jesus tells Luisa that holiness is found in the duties of your state in life; and not even a spirituality as lofty as the Divine Will shall succeed in sanctifying you if you undertake it in such a way as to detract from these duties. Furthermore, Jesus does not want already pious souls ever to simply supplant their spiritual lives and replace them with something new. He wants their spiritual lives to *grow*, and He wants them to remain committed to their usual spiritual practices (9/17/1905), including those which are not specifically "Divine Will prayers." (Moreover, everything can be, and does become, a Divine Will prayer by simply being undertaken with the intention of doing it in the Divine Will!) Do not forget that Luisa herself admonished to *never* neglect praying the Rosary.

26. Questions Answered and Concerns Addressed

Aren't these claims simply too great for a private revelation?

Although Luisa's writings do indeed contain the most glorious private revelations that Heaven has ever graced the Church with, nowhere within their thousands of pages is there any hint of dispensationalism, a claim to a new Public Revelation, or a claim to an improvement, completion,[300] surpassing, or correcting of Public Revelation. In each page, Luisa's writings present themselves as only a *private* revelation entirely subservient to—fitting within the framework of and resting upon the foundation of—Public Revelation in Christ (the Deposit of Faith), and unquestionably under the dominion of the Magisterium and hierarchical authority of the Catholic Church.

Recall, from our considerations in Part Three, that nowhere has the Church placed limits on how grand or glorious of a claim private revelation may make—the Church only teaches that a private revelation cannot claim to *itself* improve, complete, surpass, or correct Public Revelation (cf. Catechism §67). Nowhere do Luisa's private revelations assert anything resembling the latter. You will easily see this if you open their pages and read; but for now, a few comparisons will suffice, which are compiled in the table on the next page.

As you review the table's contents, a clear picture will emerge from even that brief consideration of some essentials of both the Definitive Public Revelation we have been given *in* Christ, and the private revelations on the Divine Will we have been given *through* Luisa: they are entirely and un-confusedly distinct in nature. The revelations given to Luisa fit squarely within the boundaries, given by the Church, which restrict the scope of authentic private revelation.

---

[300] It is true that the Gift is the "crown and *completion*" of sanctity, but this "completion" is none other than what the Our Father prayer *already* reveals. Luisa's revelations do not propose to themselves "complete" Public Revelation in this sense. They only *render explicit* (as the Catechism says private revelation is indispensable for!) the completion *already* embryonic in Public Revelation and developed by two thousand years of Sacred Tradition. This dynamic was carefully demonstrated throughout Parts One and Two.

Public Revelation in Jesus Christ	Private revelation through Luisa
God is revealed as Three Persons, not One.	No new revelation of God's essence. These Three Persons simply now wish to share Their life even more fully with us.
Jesus reveals Himself as Divine.	Luisa insists she is a sinner and the lowliest of all creatures.
A new, permanent Church is established on earth that is necessary for salvation.	A new *spirituality* is introduced, yet obedient to and fitting perfectly within this same Church.
Seven Sacraments are instituted.	*No Sacraments are instituted;*[301] the same Seven Sacraments remain the necessary path to holiness.
A new Priesthood is established.	No new priesthood is formed: these very same (Catholic) priests are called to be the primary heralds of these revelations.
Laws are altered.[302]	Laws are entirely unchanged.
Entirely new Liturgy is instituted.	The Liturgy is identical.
There is a total change in leadership away from the Levitical Priesthood and to the Petrine Ministry.	All authority remains with the Successor of Peter, all his Magisterium, and the entire Catholic hierarchy.

Isn't this too great? What about the errors of Meister Eckhart?

Some may be concerned that the soul simply *cannot* exceed "mystical marriage" on earth; that one cannot ever hope to, before death, enjoy the Divine Will as the very animating principle of one's own will. But in considering the ontological possibility of the Gift, all are forced to acknowledge that God is at least *capable* of working in anyone the same type of holiness that He has already worked in the Blessed Virgin Mary. Indeed, the Blessed Mother is the greatest creature that will ever exist (*far* greater than *anyone else* who has the Gift), but we must nevertheless acknowledge that Our Lady is a creature,

---

301 Any comparisons of the Divine Will to a sacrament in Luisa's volumes are not literal, but are similar to, for example, referring to the "Sacrament of the Present Moment;" a well-established theme in orthodox Catholic spiritual theology. Jesus' words to Luisa even refer to the Cross as *sacrament* (and *more than Sacrament*) in the same (non-literal) manner (4/21/1900).

302 E.g., Divorce made impermissible, juridical Mosaic precepts dispensed from, all foods declared clean, circumcision abolished.

thus whatever *type of holiness* she enjoys has been entirely given to her by God, and whatever type of holiness God gave to her, He is also capable of giving to others. There are simply no Magisterial, theological, Scriptural, philosophical, or any other grounds for denying this ontological possibility.

What, however, does her holiness consist in? Well, Scripture tells us, saying she is "*full* of grace" (Luke 1:28). The Catechism tells us; she adhered "completely" to the Father's Will (§967). The Magisterium tells us; she possessed such sanctity that "**one cannot even imagine anything greater.**" (*Ineffabilis Deus*, §1) The sanctity here described clearly far exceeds mystical marriage—and all other sanctities described before the 20th Century—and no Catholic can deny that Our Lady enjoyed it. Similarly, one cannot deny that it is possible for God to give this type of sanctity to His other children (in a way *categorically* similar, though *singularly* far inferior).

Some others, however, though acknowledging the truth of what is written above, may still insist that this holiness is so great that it contrasts with Papal teaching related to the errors of a certain monk who died almost 700 years ago. This may be a more abstract concern, but as it is related to the present matter, we should address it here.

***

The Papal Bull, *In Agro Dominico*, promulgated by Pope John XXII in the year 1329, condemns 28 propositions taught by Meister Eckart, a Dominican theologian who died only the year before. Not one of these propositions, however, is found anywhere in Luisa's writings (and most of them are not even related to anything in Luisa's writings). Nevertheless, some critics have accused the Gift of Living in the Divine Will of standing condemned by the 10th condemnation therein. In this critique, they display a misunderstanding of how Magisterial condemnations operate. One cannot simply extract a single *clause* from a condemned *proposition*, consider the clause in isolation, and then claim that whatever else contains this clause is also condemned. Rather, the substance of the entire condemned proposition must be present in an assertion for that assertion itself to likewise stand condemned.[303] Luisa's revelations do not teach what this Papal

---

[303] Consider, for example, this same Papal Bull's 14th condemned proposition, which reads: "**A good man ought so to conform his will to the divine will that he himself wishes whatever God wishes**; because God wishes me to have sinned in some way, I would not wish that I had not committed sins, and this is true repentance." Imagine how absurd it would be to extract only the first clause of that proposition and claim that whatever asserts it is heretical by virtue of this condemnation. Such a claim would anathematize virtually every saint in the history of the Church—not to mention Our Lord Himself.

Bull's 10th condemned proposition asserts;[304] in fact, they also affirmatively and repeatedly contradict it. Indeed, content is found in Luisa's revelations which resemble the 10th proposition's *first* clauses, but this says nothing: a long list could be drawn up—of saints, Fathers of the Church, Doctors of the Church, and even Magisterial documents—that have also taught those clauses.

It is the *last* clause of the condemned proposition (that there is "**no distinction**" between the Blessed Sacrament—or the Divinity, or the Word of God, etc.—and the sanctified human soul) which contains the heretical notion, and which imparts its own unorthodoxy to the preceding three clauses when annexed to them. Nowhere in Luisa's writings, however, do we find such an assertion. On the contrary, Luisa's writings (and those of countless other mystics, including St. Faustina)—though referring to the Gift as having the ability to make the soul a "living host"—make it clear that there are *many* distinctions (some of which we covered in Part Three) between the soul and the Eucharist itself. The same is true with the 11th and 13th condemnations found within *In Agro Dominico*, which condemn similar teachings. Jesus does not tell Luisa (or any of the 20th-Century mystics) that there is "**nothing excepted**" in the similarities described between His Humanity and the soul with the Gift, or the Divine Nature and the soul with the Gift; quite the contrary, *many* exceptions are noted!

In His revelations to Luisa, Jesus constantly qualifies that the marvels associated with the sanctity of one who lives in the Divine Will *only* exist *as much as is possible for a creature* (e.g., 9/4/1905, 4/28/1923, 5/23/1923, 9/7/1926, 8/3/1931). These revelations exist to bring us into His Will and accomplish their eschatological mission, not to provide a theology textbook; therefore, with the frequent repetition of this phrase (and many similar remarks), Jesus is reminding us to simply consult orthodox Catholic teaching in ascertaining the

---

All of them have admonished us to be thus conformed to God's Will. Clearly, it is the latter clause in this condemned proposition which is problematic; the notion that God affirmatively wills our sins, and that lacking contrition is therefore "true repentance." Indeed, that notion is not only heretical, but also blasphemous.

304 The condemned proposition reads: "We are transformed entirely in God, and we are changed into Him; in a similar manner as in the sacrament the bread is changed into the body of Christ; so I am changed into Him because He Himself makes me to be one with Him, not like (to Him); through the living God it is true **that there is no distinction there**."

finer theological details, and not wrongly suppose that the revelations alter any Church teachings.[305]

Tangentially, we should acknowledge that a source of Eckhart's errors may well have been the extreme emphasis he placed on *intellect*. He went so far as to claim that the human intellect is *uncreated* and thus equal to God Himself. Jesus' revelations to Luisa, far from affirming these errors, powerfully and explicitly refute them. We should also note that Eckhart, like Joachim of Fiore (who went too far in describing the Era, succumbing to an unorthodox dispensationalism), was a good Catholic, a good priest, and a good theologian. Both were obedient to the Church and likely would have abandoned any of their problematic opinions had they been formally condemned during their lifetimes. Both had legitimate insights. We should, therefore, not be surprised that some themes in their writings at least touched on valid points, despite the errors mixed in. Just as we do not discard all the teachings of Thomas Aquinas merely because he erred on the Immaculate Conception, so too we should not pretend that the errors of Eckhart or Joachim mean that everything they said was dangerous or wrong. In fact, their true teachings far outnumbered their errors. Twenty-eight propositions of Eckhart were condemned; a very small number compared to the thousands he proposed. While the temptation to "throw out the baby with the bathwater" is perennial, Christian wisdom rejects this sloppiness.

Finally, the criticisms claiming that the Gift is "too great" because it is higher even than spiritual marriage, or "too easy" because it is based primarily on sincere desire, are illicit on the sole grounds that they could be equally levied against the approved writings and revelations of St. Thérèse of Lisieux, St. Faustina, Blessed Conchita, St. Elizabeth of the Trinity, and a multitude of mystics of the 20th Century; many of whom are now Beatified or Canonized (see Part Three).

(Note: Some of the condemned propositions in Eckhart's teachings relate to Quietism, but that heresy is addressed in another section.)

---

[305] As we can see, no change to Catholic theology is conveyed in Luisa's revelations regarding what differentiates the creature and the Creator; what is intended, rather, is merely an end to the limits that some men have invented; insisting, without good reason, that all manner of absolute restrictions apply to our holiness which do not, in fact, exist. What is certain, however, is that Luisa's writings are worlds apart from the teachings of Eckhart, who not only failed to offer these qualifications, but, quite the opposite, repeatedly endeavored to oppose them by explicitly eradicating distinction between creature and Creator.

Isn't Our Lady exalted too highly in these revelations?

Having settled that one may not licitly criticize Luisa's revelations on account of their offering to others the same *type* of sanctity enjoyed by Our Lady, the next critic may proceed to instead insist that even Our Lady *herself* does not enjoy this great sanctity of Living in the Divine Will.

There is a debate raging among the theologians of the Church today regarding the degree of veneration and honors that are due to the Blessed Virgin. On one side are the theologians in line with the unanimous consensus of private revelation, in keeping with the clear direction of the entirety of Sacred Tradition's development in Mariology, and in accord with the many Magisterial proclamations which have touched on related issues. On the other side, there are those who, motivated by a false and lowest-common-denominator ecumenism, relentlessly oppose any efforts to render what is due to the Queen of the Universe. As Jesus' revelations to Luisa fall squarely in the former category, they have received much opposition from those who downplay or even reject the glories enjoyed by the Queen of Heaven. Whoever truly thinks with the mind of the Church, however, will not see this as an obstacle, but rather as a testimony to Luisa's authenticity.

Indeed, these revelations refer to Our Lady as the Co-redemptrix (5/1/1925). They insist that what God is by nature, Mary has been given by grace (9/26/1899). They insist that she is always *with* Jesus in everything He does in the world, thus clearly implying—even if that exact phrase is not found in the volumes—that she is the Mediatrix of *All* Grace that now flows from God (5/28/1937). They insist that she became the Queen of the Universe not at some later time in life or even after her Assumption, but rather immediately upon her Immaculate Conception, whereupon all the angels immediately saw in her their Celestial Sovereign. They insist that the Kingdom of the Divine Will can also be truly named the Kingdom of the Celestial Empress (7/14/1935). Much more can be said and, indeed, has been said.[306]

Despite these exaltations, Luisa's revelations do not once stray from realms of orthodoxy in describing the glories of Mary. Jesus tells Luisa that His Humanity's possession of the Divine Will was so much greater than Mary's as to utterly eclipse it (5/21/1926). He points out that often the Blessed Virgin was left in a state of pure faith—just like

[306] As of this writing, at least one book has been published which is entirely dedicated to summarizing just how tremendously these revelations exalt Our Lady.

us—not seeing directly, or with clarity, certain Divine Truths (5/23/1923), though she never succumbed to any doubts in this faith. He points out that until the moment of the Incarnation of the Word, Mary never previously assumed she would be the one chosen for this supreme privilege, so great was her humility. Luisa's revelations teach that even Mary, despite her Immaculate Conception, had to be tested—although she immediately and perfectly passed this test at that same moment her life began.[307]

For in truth, all of this exaltation is called for, and the time has come for Catholics to stop temporizing, and simply acknowledge it. The Blessed Virgin *is not God's "plan B."* Just as the Incarnation itself was an eternal decree, not *only* a remedy for sin,[308] so too Our Lady, who was of course essential to the Incarnation, is an eternal decree of the Almighty. She was willed by God before the foundation of the world, as the most perfect possible creature—the creature who, though finite, would be the *created* Immaculate Conception, in perfect union with her Divine spouse, the "*uncreated* Immaculate Conception," Who is none other than the Holy Spirit. From this it follows that if any glory is *even ontologically possible* to exist in a creature, it must exist in Our Lady. She—as the Magisterium teaches—is the greatest creature who can possibly exist, for "she approaches as near to God himself **as is possible for a created being**." (Pope Pius IX. Apostolic Constitution, *Ineffabilis Deus*). Therefore, for God to fail to bring about a given marvel in her would be for Him to fail to bring it about, *period.* For God to fail to bring about some perfection in Creation, however,

---

[307] It is worth noting here, in accordance with what we discussed in Part Four on a "theology too deep for human origin," that not even the world's most learned theologian of Luisa's time would have been capable of crafting a Mariology which succeeded in so accurately exalting Our Lady, while at the same time avoiding any unorthodox claims about her.

[308] Some theologians, most notably St. Thomas Aquinas, held that the Incarnation was merely "contingent," i.e., it would not have happened if man had not sinned. The Church, however, has never taught this, and it is moreover contradicted by many saints and private revelations since Aquinas' day. Indeed, if man had not sinned, then the Incarnation would have looked very different: Christ would have come as a victorious King instead of as a suffering Savior, but He would have come, nevertheless. For the Dominican tradition, the contingency of the Incarnation is just one opinion of many, and setting it aside entails no disrespect for what the Holy Spirit was and is doing through St. Dominic and the order he founded. But the absolute primacy of Jesus and Mary, in the Incarnation, is a teaching so fundamental to the Franciscan Tradition that it is known as "*The* Franciscan Thesis," and setting this aside *would* entail no small degree of disrespect for what God Willed to bring about through the Franciscans. For more information, I recommend A *Primer on the Absolute Primacy of Christ; Blessed John Duns Scotus and the Franciscan Thesis*, by Fr. Maximilian Mary Dean.

would be for Him to fail in the very purpose of Creation itself, and we must not dare attribute such a failure to the Almighty.[309]

The next thing we must know is that Our Lady is—as the yet-to-be declared Fifth Marian Dogma holds[310]—the Co-Redemptrix, Advocate, and Mediatrix of All Grace. As Co-redemptrix, Mary is the one who, *with* Christ (*not* above, or equal, to Christ), and more than any other creature, enables salvation itself. As Advocate, Mary stands with the Holy Spirit and therefore is, *with* Him (*not* above, or equal, to Him), our "helper." As Mediatrix, whatever grace anyone, anywhere, and at any time, receives, he receives it from Christ, but *through* Mary's hands. All these titles have been repeatedly used in the ordinary Magisterium to describe Our Lady, therefore no Catholic should have any hesitation in using them, and no one should regard their corollaries being displayed in a private revelation as a stumbling block to its authenticity.

Furthermore, none of this detracts from the primacy of Christ; it is He Who chose to so exalt Mary. None of this detracts from orthodox Catholic theology; even though she is the greatest possible creature, Mary nevertheless remains a mere nothing compared to her Son, and she enjoys all her privileges by *grace* (as a gift from God), not by nature (that is, not generated by herself). None of this detracts from ecumenism properly understood; whoever is unwilling to acknowledge Our Lady's glories should not be considered ready for union with the Successor of Peter, as "the Marian dimension of the Church precedes the Petrine." (*Catechism of the Catholic Church* §773)

Isn't Luisa exalted too highly in these revelations?

Just as St. Faustina is the secretary and earthly head of the very mission of Divine Mercy that will—as Jesus told her—"prepare the world for My Final Coming," (*Diary* §429) so, too, Luisa is certainly the same for the great mission of the Divine Will. Moreover, as a victim soul, Luisa—with Jesus—accomplished the hard work of preparing the way for its reign (though in an entirely secondary and subservient manner to what Jesus and His Mother did 2,000 years ago), therefore we are right to join ourselves with Luisa in this mission. Carmelites do the same for St. Teresa of Ávila, going so far as to invoke not only the traditional "JMJ," (Jesus, Mary, Joseph), but

---

[309] This assertion is not tantamount to a Leibnizian "most perfect of all possible worlds" hypothesis; for it does not entail an insistence that *all* things in Creation must be so perfected, but only that *at least one* creature must be.

[310] For more information on this proposed Dogma, I recommend *Mary: Coredemptrix, Mediatrix, Advocate,* by Dr. Mark Miravalle.

"JMJT," adding St. Teresa in to the invocation of the very Holy Family. One should not expect a different approach in how the children of the Divine Will regard Luisa.

But nowhere do Jesus' words to Luisa describe her as on par with, much less exceeding, the Blessed Virgin. Quite the opposite, Jesus Himself laments to Luisa that this slander had been levied against her writings even in her own day. He explicitly notes that He did *not* say Luisa was another Blessed Virgin, or even that Luisa was *like* her! Rather, He points out that He simply wants Luisa to *become similar to* the Blessed Virgin, just like He told many people to become similar to Himself, though this would never eradicate the distinction between Creator and creature (5/19/1931). Jesus indeed calls Luisa the Little Daughter of the Divine Will, but He reserves the title of *Big* Daughter of the Divine Will for His mother!

Luisa's inferiority to Our Lady is, in fact, a primary reason for her being chosen for this mission. Jesus explains to Luisa that if He had done all this work in preparing for the reign of the Divine Will only through His Mother, or even through someone else immaculately conceived (though no one else ever will be), then we would all be tempted to regard our own participation in its triumph as too lofty a task for us considering the utterly supreme holiness of the Blessed Virgin, which all should know is unreachable. Luisa, on the other hand, was not immaculately conceived; she was and is an entirely ordinary creature like us, and for Jesus to open the doors to the Divine Will through Luisa—as He did—is for Him to show us all that *we too* can enter through them by joining hands with Luisa (6/6/1926); by heeding the revelations Jesus gave to her.

What about St. Joseph? Why not earlier?

Another skeptic may acknowledge the possibility of the Gift, yet protest it with the following words, *"It is absurd to say that we can now receive a new Gift of sanctity that, before the 20th Century, only Jesus, Mary, Adam, and Eve had. What about St. Joseph? St. Francis? St. Augustine? St. Paul? Why now for so great a gift, given such great saints in Church history?"*

First, we must note that either one *does*, or one does *not* believe in the existence of the Gift. If he does not believe that this Gift exists, how, then, can he pretend to be offended at the notion of the saints of previous times in the Church not having it? If, on the other hand, he *does* believe that the Gift exists, how can he be so foolish as to allow pietistical concerns prevent him from desiring and asking for such a great good? We must beware duplicity. No one does any honor to these saints by neglecting to heed Heaven's calls on account of doing so allegedly detracting from their glory. These saints are *alive,* and they are watching us now from Heaven, begging us to accept this Gift!

As discussed in Part Three, having a greater gift does not make its recipient "greater" than one who has not received it merely because the latter did not live in the time of that gift. For example, St. Joseph always has been and always will be the greatest saint after the Blessed Virgin (cf. Leo XIII, *Quamquam Pluries* §3); Luisa's revelations make no attempt to alter that. Jesus even tells Luisa that His Kingdom was in full force in the home of Nazareth and that Joseph fully lived in the reflections of the Divine Will in this home, and that Joseph was *the* prime minister of this Kingdom (7/7/1928)—a sovereign dignity not given even to Luisa. Whether Joseph was fully given the Gift itself is not relevant to ascertaining *his* greatness. What *is* certain is that St. Joseph did not live in such a time as to allow him to receive the Eucharist, and yet the absence of this great gift from his life in no way detracts from his own greatness. Only a fool would castigate another who glorifies the Eucharist on account of this glorification allegedly detracting from the glory due to St. Joseph. Indeed, to such a person as that, Jesus would say the same thing He said in the Gospel, "**Are you envious because I am generous?**" (Matthew 20:15)

Should we begin walking on that slippery slope of questioning the Divine Wisdom in the timing He has chosen to employ for the dissemination of His gifts and graces, infinitely more questions immediately arise. Why didn't God reveal the Sacred Heart or Divine Mercy devotions earlier, perhaps to St. Mary Magdalene? Why weren't the Desert Fathers blessed with the Holy Rosary and its corresponding promises? Why was daily Communion not broadly encouraged before the reign of Pope St. Pius X in the 20th Century? Why weren't seven-year-olds permitted to receive before that same reign?

The answer is that *God has predetermined His timeline, and it is not ours to question.* It is only ours to ask (when an alleged revelation or development comes along), *"is this from God?"* (See the Church-sanctioned norms for discerning private revelations, included in Part Three.) If it is from God, then we must bend the knee and unclench the fist. Like the pivotal developments noted above, the Gift *is* from God, so let us not suppose His timetable requires our sanction.

What about the Purgative, Illuminative, and Unitive Ways?

The sanctity of the Divine Will does not dismiss the Purgative, Illuminative, and Unitive ways in the spiritual life. Quite the contrary, Luisa's own volumes carefully ascend these steps (insisting upon them just as John of the Cross and Teresa of Ávila did) before expounding upon the Gift itself, nor is any attempt made to supplant this tradition and the importance of its teachings for our spiritual lives. Luisa's writings *build* on this foundation of Sacred Tradition; they do not repudiate it. To criticize them as artificial would make as much sense as opening the Bible at random and, upon reading of the Incarnation, repudiating God for not first preparing the way with prophets and a moral law. Whoever has read Part Two of this book should have no problem seeing how perfectly harmonious Luisa's revelations are with Sacred Tradition as we know it.

Moreover, there is no hint of "leaving behind" the holiness of these three phases of the spiritual life by receiving the Gift of Living in the Divine Will. Throughout Luisa's later volumes—that is, well after Jesus had revealed much about the Gift to her—He repeatedly returns to the various virtues annexed to these three stages and exhorts us to acquire them.

A nearly exact analogy exists for the present matter. The graces of the Blessed Sacrament exceed the value contained in the exercise of the moral virtues, but they never dispense of or distract from these virtues. Additionally, one need not be perfected in virtue to receive these Eucharistic graces; he need only be a Catholic in a state of grace who believes in the Real Presence. So too, the Gift of Living in the Divine Will, though surpassing the traditional three stages of the spiritual life, never removes their importance from our lives. *Nor, however, does the Gift's superiority to them entail the prerequisite of mastering them before receiving it.* We simply need to be in a state of grace, desire the Gift, and ask for it. Even with the Gift, the soul may very well have much work to do within these three stages of the spiritual life; just as one who licitly receives the Eucharist may well very need much growth in moral virtue. In both respects, therefore, the Gift is analogous to Eucharistic graces, and in neither case should their superiority be treated as an affront to what is, in a sense, beneath them. Indeed, St. Paul's oft-quoted admonition, employing the analogy of parts of the body all being necessary, applies not only to those who wrongly compare individual members of Christ's Mystical Body, but also to those who needlessly set various themes in the Faith and Spirituality in opposition to each other:

> And if the ear should say, "Because I am not an eye, I do not belong to the body," that would not make it any less a part of the body. If the whole body were an eye, where would be the hearing? If the whole body were an ear, where would be the sense of smell? But as it is, **God arranged the organs in the body, each one of them, as he chose**. (1 Corinthians 12:16-18)

Let us permit God to do the arranging. Spiritual realities all have their place in His Providential ordering of all things, and the exaltation of one never entails the denigration of another.

Isn't this Millenarianism or Modified Millenarianism?

Regardless of what name one wishes to use to identify the time soon coming to earth—*The Imminent Glorious Era of Universal Peace, the Reign of the Divine Will on earth as in Heaven, the Triumph of the Immaculate Heart of Mary, the Coming of Christ in Grace and His Eucharistic Reign, the Coming of the Kingdom of God*—one thing is certain: so long as it is understood in the proper sense (which is indeed the sense given by Jesus to the Servant of God Luisa Piccarreta as well as the other mystics and seers discussed in this book), it is entirely in accord with Catholic Teaching. This fact has been affirmed directly not only by many Magisterial documents, but also by countless *imprimaturs*, Beatifications, Canonizations, and other ecclesiastical endorsements given to those works of the souls who have proclaimed the Era. (See Part Five.)

Turning our attention to Luisa's writings in the following table, we will find that they do not teach Millenarianism, modified Millenarianism, or anything of the sort, and even more, that they *specifically repudiate these errors.*

Errors associated with Millenarianism	Teachings of Jesus to Luisa
Jesus will visibly reign on earth.	The Era will be a *Sacramental* reign of Christ in *grace* (11/2/1926).
There will be a "rapture" of all believers before the chastisements.	Even if many of the faithful are protected, they will have to live through the chastisements on earth.
Dispensationalism, and the "*Spiritual Legacy of Joachim of Fiore*": The Church, along with her hierarchies and doctrines, will pass away for the sake of an "Age of the Spirit" that will replace it.	The Era is the Church acquiring her *full vigor;* not passing away (9/2/1901), *Catholic priests* will be its primary heralds (1/13/1929), and the Sacraments *flourishing*; finally bearing their *complete fruit* in the Church (11/2/1926).
The Eternal Resurrection will precede the Era, and there will be no more death.	There *will* be death during the Era, and the bodies of the dead will *await* the Day of Resurrection, at the conclusion of the Era (10/22/1926).
Jesus' literal presence on earth will give all the Beatific Vision, thus eradicating the need for faith.	There will still be the need for faith, although it will be clearer than it is today (6/29/1928).
All on earth will be ontologically confirmed in grace and categorically incapable of any sin or suffering	Only in Heaven does such ontological confirmation exist (9/29/1931), and even in the Era, there may be suffering (although of a triumphant and glorious nature) (8/22/1926).

Unfortunately, however, there are a few authors today who have published their own Era-free eschatological speculations which insist upon the imminent end of the world, and who systematically distort Scripture, Magisterium, and private revelation to try and popularize a false appearance in which the Era seems to be the heresy of modified millenarianism. But *the Church's own authority* has already defined even *modified* Millenarianism as consisting in the anticipation of Christ *visibly* reigning on earth (full blown *un*-modified Millenarianism, on the other hand, includes additional errors beyond this; e.g., the "rapture," the assurance of a literal 1,000-year duration, a pre-Era Eternal Resurrection, the Beatific Vision and definitive perfection of man on earth, an abundance of carnal fulfillments, etc.). For example, the July 21st, 1944 Declaration of the Holy Office specifically defines even *modified* Millenarianism as the system of teachings wherein:

> "[The teaching that Christ] will come **visibly** to rule over this world... cannot be taught safely." (Decree of the Holy Office on Mitigated Millenarianism. *Acta Apostolica Sedis*. Annus XXXVI—

Series II—Vol. XI. Page 212)

This condemnation itself was a follow-up to the Holy Office's earlier decree, issued only three years before, regarding the book of a certain Jesuit Priest, Fr. Manuel De Lacunza. The priest wrote *The Coming of Messiah in Glory and Majesty,* in which he painstakingly (and vainly) argued for a system of *modified* Millenarianism, which purged Millenarianism of a few errors, but staunchly maintained the visible reign of Christ on earth. On July 11th, 1941, the Holy Office condemned this book of Fr. Lacunza's, "**with specific reference to the book's *moderate* Millenarianism.**"[311]

That the Era's critics are attempting to supersede the authority of the Church by defining "modified" or "mitigated" in this context on their own terms—and in contradiction to how the Church has already repeatedly defined them—should immediately convey to any orthodox Catholic that these arguments ought not be credited. Due, however, to the popularity (in a few circles) of such arguments, a lengthy chapter is dedicated to their refutation in *The Crown of Sanctity,* and I encourage anyone who has been exposed to these positions to read it (pages 356-396),[312] as we do not here have space to address everything.

These critics offer the conjecture that the Catechism, by condemning even modified forms of Millenarianism (cf. § 676-677), is actually employing an "umbrella term" which denounces any sort of future glorious Era of Peace or Golden Age of the Church. This insistence, though repeatedly proffered, is never backed up with a single Magisterial teaching. Indeed, no such Magisterium exists. The critics only present various Church documents that, for example, speak of death, or the possibility of sin, or suffering, or struggle, or the need for faith, or any number of other similar things, enduring in some form until the end of time. The presentations of these in order to oppose the Era are red herrings and the conjectures made based upon them are non-sequiturs, since the prophecies of the Era *do not claim otherwise.*

The Catechism, in these sections and elsewhere, makes it clear that it is only condemning the following: 1) the notion of a visible reign of Christ on earth, 2) any placement of messianic hope for the *eternal* fulfillment of the Kingdom into the temporal sphere, 3) "Progressive ascendancy" teachings, and 4) secular messianism. The Era of Peace as relayed to Luisa (and all the mystics we have covered in

---

311 Lacunza Y Diaz, Manuel De. *New Catholic Encyclopedia.*

312 It can be downloaded freely from www.DSDOConnor.com

this book) bears no resemblance to what is forbidden by any one of these four condemnations. On the contrary, it succeeds in safeguarding the faithful *against* each of these errors. (A fact we saw repeatedly in Part Five.)

The subtle twist with which the Era's critics distort the Catechism's paragraph in question consists in ignoring some of its words, particularly "*that* messianic hope *which,*" in the following:

> The Antichrist's deception already begins to take shape in the world every time the claim is made to realize within history **that** messianic hope **which** can only be realized beyond history... (§676)

As we can see with an honest and straightforward reading of the text, the Catechism is only condemning a *specific type* of anticipation being directed within time; namely, *that* type *which* is only to be "realized beyond history." As no authentic prophecies of the Era place eternal hopes within history, it is fallacious to claim they stand condemned by this teaching.[313] Moreover, the Catechism's following paragraph only restricts the definitive perfection of the Kingdom to Heaven. This, again, is a fact that no one who anticipates the Era denies. As we saw, the Era is *all about Heaven*, and it does not detract one iota from the focus due to our eternal home, but only increases our heart's direction to it ever more.[314]

As the USCCB's "FAQ about the Catechism" states, "**By its very nature, a catechism presents the fundamental truths of the faith which have already been communicated and defined**." (Q17.)

---

[313] Moreover, this entire paragraph of the Catechism is concerned with "the Antichrist's deception," whereas the content of the Era of Peace is as contrary to Antichristic teachings as one could imagine. For that reason alone, it is absurd to suppose this paragraph can be directed at the Era.

[314] In a word, all that the Era's critics have here succeeded in, therefore, is employing circular reasoning: merely asserting that the Era duplicates Heaven in their very attempt to argue that this is the error of which the Era is guilty. In a similarly misleading move, some critics of the Era seek to leverage the dogmatic truth which we affirm in the Nicene Creed, that Christ's "**Kingdom will have no end**;" twisting it into a declaration that Christ's Kingdom cannot exist on earth, since earth ends. But this move itself is implicitly heretical, since it is tantamount to accusing the many other manifestations of Christ's Kingdom on earth (e.g., the Sacraments) of running afoul of the Nicene Creed. We know as Catholics that Christ's Kingdom is extended within the Sacraments, yet they will not exist in Heaven! Indeed, it is obvious that our Faith's affirmation of Christ's Kingdom having no end is a reference to *eternity having no end*. No honest Christian who recites the Nicene Creed fails to comprehend that this is what that line within it means. *Everything* on earth ends; both the Kingdom of God that is the Era of Peace, and all the other temporal realities held by the Catholic Faith as being signified by the words, "Kingdom of God" (the Sacraments, the proclamation and acceptance of the Gospel, the Church's hierarchy, etc.).

Therefore, one is sure to be in error if he supposes that, though incapable of finding any Magisterium affirming it, he has nevertheless deduced some doctrinal implication by reading between the lines of the Catechism, and, accordingly, insists that it really should *be seen as* condemning far more than what is described in its own wording.

In the case of the Era of Peace (the coming of the Kingdom), there is no Magisterium (before or after the Catechism's publication) confirming the hypothesis of the critics of the Era who denounce the Reign of the Divine Will as "modified Millenarianism." There is, rather, plentiful Magisterium expressly contradicting their stance. A number of such Magisterial statements were covered in Part Five of this book—wherein we reviewed *118 years* of formal Papal teaching that expressly affirms the reality of the Era of Peace in precisely the terms which the critics reject.

What about St. Augustine's Amillennialism and the Antichrist?

St. Augustine's famous "Amillennial" interpretation of Revelation 20 (as opposed to the "Millennial" one discussed in Part Five) regards the "thousand-year" reign of saints on earth spoken of therein as symbolic of the entire Age of the Church in general (from the birth of Christianity to the end of time) and therefore does not regard it as prophesying a future event. This interpretation is still popular, and certainly had been the most popular account during the Medieval and Modern periods of Church History.

But this interpretation has never been promulgated by the Church as doctrine or as the sole correct understanding of Revelation 20. This is itself telling, as it is almost strange for a teaching that was so common in the Church, for so many centuries, to fail to ever become Magisterial. The mystery vanishes, however, when one considers that this is not some enigma, but rather consists in the Holy Spirit preventing a doctrinal exposition of Amillennialism *for a reason.* Prayerful consideration suggests a quite reasonable understanding of why matters transpired as they did. The Holy Spirit, knowing the time would come in which a Millennial understanding of Revelation was essential, inspired it to become firmly established in Christianity in its early centuries. Once set down so solidly as to become a permanent element of Sacred Tradition,[315] the Holy Spirit moved the Church to focus on the understanding that was more relevant for their own

[315] Which, as we saw in Part Five, it indeed is, no matter how much today's mainstream theologians are embarrassed by it!

times (the Amillennial one), since He obviously knew exactly when the Kingdom would come. However, now that we stand on the cusp of its arrival, this same Spirit has caused the rebirth of Millennial interpretations.

None should regard the scenario above as tantamount to a suggestion that the Holy Spirit inspired error in the Medieval and early Modern periods! Far from it. Much powerful edification can certainly be found within Augustine's exposition of Amillennialism; therefore, we should here acknowledge some of its additional enriching content. Regarding—as St. Augustine does—Baptism as a type of "First Resurrection," and the Age of the Church as a type of "Reign of the Saints" during which Satan is "chained" is a perfectly valid way of meditating upon Revelation 20. Satan *is* more restricted, since Christ's sacrifice on the Cross, than he was before that moment. Baptism *is* a type of spiritual "resurrection." The saints *do* reign on earth at least *more* powerfully since the birth of Christianity than they did before it. Now that we are nearing the time of fulfillment of the *clear* sense of Revelation 20, however, it is important to no longer remain restricted to Augustine's view here. Therefore, while Amillennialism's commentary remains edifying,[316] we mustn't regard it as the sole legitimate way of understanding this Scriptural chapter, lest we become worthy of rebuke by the same encyclical of Venerable Pope Pius XII we have considered elsewhere.[317]

Indeed, recent faithful Biblical scholarship has refuted the view which regards Amillennialism as the sole or definitive understanding of Revelation 20. See, for example, Fr. Joseph Iannuzzi, SThD, PhD, *Antichrist and the End Times* (2005) and *The Splendor of Creation* (2011), Dr. Françoise Breynaert, *The Glorious Coming of Christ & the Millennium* (2019),[318] and Professor Jacques Cabaud, *On the End Times* (2019). As these and other scholars have demonstrated, sola-Amillennialism is both overly flexible with the clear sense of Scripture and at odds with the teachings of almost all the other Fathers of the Church. It is contradicted by many recent inescapable and unimpeachable developments, and it is even considered unacceptable by Augustine himself, who bluntly contradicted *sola*-Amillennialism by stating that his Amillennial view was just *one possible* interpretation of Revelation 20

---

[316] Accordingly, I discourage anyone from condemning this interpretation or rejecting it—it remains a fine interpretation, therefore we should only counter the insistence that this interpretation be the *only* allowed one.

[317] That is, *Divino Afflante Spiritu*, §47

[318] Bishop Dominique Rey extolled this book, writing that "it is a reminder for every Christian of the need to stand ready... to ardently desire the *Maranatha: "Come, Lord Jesus!"* (Preface)

that mustn't be regarded as ruling out the interpretation which regards the passage as meaning what it says:

> [The teaching that] the saints should thus enjoy a kind of Sabbath-rest during that period [the 'thousand year' reign], a holy leisure after the labors of six thousand years since man was created... **would not be objectionable, if it were believed that the joys of the saints, in that Sabbath, shall be spiritual, and consequent on the presence of God**. (St. Augustine, *City of God*, Book 20, Ch. 7)

As we can see, Augustine's only concern with the Millenarians of his day were the carnal and literalistic views of that time to come. It is, of course, impossible to use Augustine's words to argue against a reign of Peace if he himself has explicitly admitted there is nothing objectionable with such a view! (The view he presents as "not objectionable" is precisely how the Era is portrayed in all authentic private revelation—wherein the Era's joys are not carnal, but are associated with a new outpouring of God's grace.) Furthermore, what follows is the final paragraph in Augustine's famous treatment of eschatology, found in Book 20 of *The City of God*, in which he says:

> Elias the Tishbite shall come; the Jews shall believe; Antichrist shall persecute; Christ shall judge; the dead shall rise; the good and the wicked shall be separated; the world shall be burned and renewed. **All these things, we believe, shall come to pass; but how, or in what order, human understanding cannot perfectly teach us,** but only the experience of the events themselves. **My opinion, however, is that they will happen in the order in which I have related them** [i.e., his Amillennialism]. (Chapter 30)

St. Augustine was not one to bashfully pretend that the orthodox truths he defended were merely "his opinions," as he says here of his Amillennial take on Revelation 20. Moreover, he insists his opinion is open to correction by "*the experience of the events themselves;*" an experience which, since his own day, has rendered sola-Amillennialism indefensible.

It is not surprising that someone like Augustine—who died in the year 430 and lived during a golden age of Catholicism's explosive and uninterrupted growth (what Pope St. John Paul II referred to as the "millennium of Christian unity"), *after* its legalization by Constantine (313) and *before* its tearing asunder in the second millennium (especially beginning with the Great Schism of 1054)—would see his own Era as the one wherein Satan is chained and the saints reign, as written in Revelation 20.

But we have long since passed the time in which it was conceivable that this chaining might refer *merely* to the age of the Church in general. For the last 1,000 years, the Body of Christ has been torn apart by Schism. For the last 500 years since the Reformation, it has been ravaged so severely by sectarianism, heresy, and apostasy, that it makes the Arian Crisis of the early Church look minor. For the last 300 years since the so-called "Enlightenment," diabolical Modernism has begun dominating the world and much of the Church. Despite two thousand years passing since her founding by Christ, *His One True Church*, the Catholic Church, still only counts less than one-fifth of the world's inhabitants among its ranks. No stretch of the imagination and no faithful Scriptural exegesis could plausibly assert that the facts of the world's last 1,000 years of history paint a picture that remotely resembles what Revelation 20's "chaining of Satan" and "reign of saints" would look like.

The sola-Amillennial view has even been implicitly Magisterially rebuked by the Popes of the 20th Century who—as early as 1903 A.D., upon seeing the deluge of evil inundating the world—declared that the times had become more sinful than *ever* before.[319] It is not intellectually honest to assent to this Magisterial teaching and simultaneously hold that we are or were in the time of the binding of Satan spoken of in the Book of Revelation. One of those views must go. And it mustn't be the one which is Magisterially taught.

***

Insistence upon sola-Amillennialism is often bound up with the opinion about the Antichrist which regards his diabolical reign as *only* occurring immediately before the end of the world. Those who hold this view insist—by misinterpreting several Scriptural passages, while dogmatizing the opinions of some theologians—that the Antichrist's defeat will either itself be accomplished directly through the Second Coming of Christ in the flesh at the end of time, or will at least only occur almost immediately before that event.

The French 19th-Century seminary professor and missionary preacher, Fr. Charles Arminjon—in a book of which St. Thérèse of Lisieux said, "**This reading was one of the greatest graces of my life**..."[320]—carefully demonstrated the error of this view:

> Some have concluded from this passage [2 Thessalonians 2] that Christ is to come down in person to strike His great adversary,

[319] See, for example, Pope St. Pius X. *E Supremi* October 4th, 1903. Paragraph 3, wherein he teaches that society had become worse than in "*any* past age."

[320] Thérèse of Lisieux, *Story of a Soul: The Autobiography of Saint Thérèse of Lisieux* (Washington, DC: ICS Publications, 1996), 102.

> and that this will be the day when He will appear in His glory and majesty. **This interpretation is incorrect. St. Thomas and St. John Chrysostom explain ... that Christ will strike the Antichrist by dazzling him with a brightness that will be like an omen and sign of His Second Coming** ... What is certain is that Satan will be hurled back into the darkness of the abyss, the reign of the man of evil will be utterly destroyed ... **Will the resurrection of the body and the Last Judgment follow close upon that great event? Holy Scripture is silent on this point, and the Church has not wished to define anything.** Among the interpreters of Holy Writ, some affirm it and others deny it. Suarez expresses the view that after the death of the Antichrist, the world will not subsist more than forty-five days ... This opinion, however, does not seem to be the most certain. **The most authoritative view, and the one that appears to be most in harmony with Holy Scripture, is that, after the fall of the Antichrist, the Catholic Church will once again enter upon a period of prosperity and triumph** ... [referencing Romans 11] These **words are formal, and appear to leave no room for doubt.** They are in harmony with those of St. John [referencing the Book of Revelation]: '*I then saw ... those who had won the victory over the beast and its image and also the number that signified its name ... They sang the song of Moses, the servant of God, and the song of the Lamb.*' In other words, the Christians and the remnant of the Jews henceforth have only one spirit and one faith, they address the same praises and blessings to the Son of God and, together, proclaim His glory ... **Is it really credible that the day when all people will be united in this long-sought harmony will be the one when the heavens shall pass away with great violence...? Would Christ cause the Church to be born again, in all her glory and all the splendor of her beauty, only to dry up forthwith the springs of her youth and her inexhaustible fecundity?**[321]

Here Fr. Arminjon argues forcefully and correctly—not merely as his own eschatological speculation, but as the most *authoritative* view most in harmony with Scripture—that the Era of Peace will occur *after* the time of the Antichrist. Thus he skillfully corrects the common but mistaken opinion of theologians in centuries before him who did not have access to what Fr. Arminjon knew.

Even saints as great as Robert Bellarmine (born 1542) were mistaken on this point. In a remark contained within a large treatise dedicated strictly to proving that the Pope was not the Antichrist, he

---

[321] Charles Arminjon, *The End of the Present World and the Mysteries of the Future Life*. Pages 56-58.

wrote that the "last judgment will immediately follow" the Antichrist (*On the Roman Pontiff.* Book III. Chapter 7. §4), though he mitigated this claim in a later chapter of the same work.[322] Here, Bellarmine merely cites Matthew 24 as allegedly teaching this, but in fact that passage only depicts Jesus describing the *sun being darkened*, etc., as what "immediately" (v. 29) follows the Antichrist. This is surely a reference to some great Divine Intervention or catastrophic event, but it is not a portrayal of the end of time. The same chapter's *following* verses may be a reference to the Last Judgment itself (or they may not be—they could equally well refer to the "the Warning" or "Illumination of Conscience"[323]), but there is no indication of timing—only *ordering*—in those verses, therefore we are only justified in concluding that the events described therein will happen *at some point after* the defeat of the Antichrist.

Temporal eschatology is perhaps the single subject in all theology that is most prone to error when studied under the light of human understanding (as we just saw, Augustine himself openly testified to this difficulty) and outside of the boundaries of what the Church has dogmatically defined. We should, therefore, not be surprised to see that even many of the most learned saints in Church history gave opinions in this realm that should no longer be regarded as accurate—especially when the deficiency of these speculations has been made clear in light of what has happened *since* their own day in the Magisterium, in private revelation, and in the many eschatologically-oriented developments evident in the Church and the world.

But we are not left only the authority of Fr. Charles Arminjon's correction on this point. We also have the teaching of the highest authority in the Church. Shortly after Fr. Arminjon presented this teaching, Pope St. Pius X taught, in the same encyclical noted above (*E Supremi*), that the literal Antichrist himself *may* already be in the world, writing, **"... there may be already in the world the "Son of**

---

[322] In Chapter IX, Bellarmine changes his tone, and simply says that "the arrival of the Antichrist will be **a little before the end** of the world." (§1) He does not quantify "little," therefore it is clear that no one should use his arguments in an attempt to dispute the Era. We do not know how long the Era will endure before history concludes, but it is safe to say that it will indeed be "very little" time compared to the duration of history that precedes it, so one can even agree with Bellarmine here and still believe in a post-Antichrist Era of Peace.

[323] This is an extraordinary event, predicted by a multitude of private revelations, with which God will intervene by giving every soul alive an experience of a "mini-Judgment." It will not be the Last Judgment itself, but in many ways it will resemble that great event.

Perdition" of whom the Apostle speaks (II. Thess. ii., 3) ..."[324] No document appealed to by those who insist that the Antichrist can only come immediately before the end of time rivals, much less surpasses, the authority of this text. Nor is it possible to understand this text in any other way than the one which refutes them. For, as we saw in Part Five, the same encyclical clearly prophesies a yet-to-come Era of Peace, thus indicating that the Era—the "Restoration of All Things in Christ"—will *follow* the defeat of the Son of Perdition.[325]

Although presenting them would be outside of the scope of this book, a multitude of contemporary private revelations—many bearing forms of ecclesiastical approval and other verifications of authenticity—have asserted that the Antichrist is truly imminent, and that the Era of Peace will follow his defeat by a "coming of Christ" in grace. In the extensive reading and research I have undertaken regarding private revelations of late (ones which enjoy strong arguments in support of their authentic nature), I have not come across a single one which prophesies the Antichrist as arising after the Era of Peace. While it is easy to see how one who implicitly supposes that Heaven stopped speaking to souls around the dawn of the 20th Century could insist that the Antichrist only comes immediately before the end of the world,[326] it is difficult to comprehend how anyone who remains open to the Holy Spirit's continued intervention could arrive at similar conclusions. The theologian Fr. Edward O'Connor, summarizing his own extremely extensive study of contemporary private revelation, wrote the following in 2011 about their unanimously agreed-upon main thrust—their prophetic consensus[327]:

> The Church will be torn apart. **The Antichrist, already alive in**

---

[324] Pope St. Pius X. *E Supremi*. Paragraph 5. Note that the "Son of Perdition" spoken of in 2 Thessalonians is always understood as a reference to the literal, singular, personal Antichrist himself.

[325] If the Antichrist were only to reign immediately before the world's end, then it would be contradictory for the Pope to speculate that the Antichrist was so imminent that he may already be alive even while teaching that the Era (which he called "*The Restoration of All Things in Christ*") is yet to come. As we can be sure that no Papal Encyclical would contain so flagrant a contradiction, we can be equally sure that the Antichrist will arise *before* the Era. Finally, these straightforward conclusions are not weakened even if the Pope's comment regarding the Antichrist already being born in 1903 was incorrect; the implications that follow from these considerations do not depend upon the accuracy of what the Pope himself admitted—by saying, "*may be*"—as being speculative.

[326] Not because the earlier "prophetic consensus" in any way claims this, but only because the earlier prophecies do not in general paint a single clear picture of the order of these events. Therefore the various prophetic timetables developed from them are mostly the result of human efforts to force clarity upon what Heaven deliberately left unclear.

[327] Ten years' worth of authentic prophecy since Fr. O'Connor wrote this summary has only repeatedly confirmed its contents.

> **the world, will manifest himself ...** The disasters to come will purify the world and leave it as God intended it to be. The Holy Spirit will be poured out as never before and renew the hearts of all mankind.[328]

Not only, then, is the view here described most in accordance with Public Revelation; it is also the one forcefully taught by *all* of Heaven's messages today. As such, I would present a simple question to anyone who supposes that the Antichrist can only arise at the very end of time, and cannot possibly be imminent: *If not now, when?* If today's Dictatorship of Relativism and Culture of Death do not present the precisely ideal conditions for the rise of the Antichrist, then what conditions do?

***

Despite the confidence we can have in the Era on account of what is described in the preceding paragraphs on the Millennium, we must be equally careful to not regard it as a necessary thesis. The glorious Era of Peace, wherein the Our Father prayer will be fulfilled, *is* coming. This is an absolute fact, and its arrival in no way depends upon how exactly one interprets Revelation 20, or the various Biblical verses that refer to the Antichrist and the events surrounding his diabolical rule. Supposing that the Era would be called into question even by "sola-Amillennialism" being declared a Dogma of the Faith (whereas we can be safely assured that it will never even be doctrinally taught, much less dogmatically defined) would be like supposing that Christianity would be called into question if the Shroud of Turin were shown to be a fake. Like the Millennium, the Shroud is almost certainly authentic and is a helpful reminder of the authenticity of its subject, but in no way is it needed for us to have certainty in that very authenticity.

Neither Jesus' revelations to Luisa, nor most of the other private revelations considered in this book, say anything about the proper interpretation of the Book of Revelation, the "thousand years" described therein, or the timing of the Antichrist. Therefore, whoever wishes to—despite everything that has been written in the pages above—remain lock-step with a sola-Amillennial take on Revelation 20, and the notion that the Antichrist can only come immediately before the end of time, will still have no trouble acknowledging the reality of the coming reign of the Divine Will on earth as in Heaven.

Nor would the Kingdom's arrival be in any way called into question if the Antichrist (or *an* Antichrist) were to arise afterwards.

---

[328] *Listen to My Prophets.* Pages 189-190.

Heaven alone, not the Era, causes ontological confirmation in grace, therefore it is possible (whether *likely* is another question) even for the citizens of the Era to succumb to an Antichrist figure well in the future, after a final falling away, which God would perhaps allow simply to have one last chance to show the greatness of His Mercy.

Pragmatically speaking, it would be sensible for many of the faithful to simply leave these matters to the side, and instead focus on the Kingdom itself—the reign of the Divine Will itself—and the hastening thereof, without too much focus on the allusions to it in the Book of Revelation (the most difficult book of the entire Bible to accurately interpret!). The debates that too often ensue—instigated by those who treat certain common opinions of theologians in the Middle Ages as dogmas—become tremendous distractions from our mission.

Moreover, an enormous amount of grave error has recently been promoted by various Christian and quasi-Christian denominations in the name of Revelation 20's Millennium (e.g., Evangelical rapture-Millenarians, Jehovah's Witnesses, Mormons, Seventh Day Adventists). These groups promote deeply problematic Millenarian ideals, along with their own brands of Dispensationalism and other heresies, therefore great care must be taken—by any Catholic who promotes a Millennial understanding of Revelation 20—to ensure that these errors and related ones are solidly rejected in all expositions of the Millennium.

At the same time, however, I will add that it is precisely when Catholics fail to heed the guiding influence of the Holy Spirit that Catholicism bleeds members to other denominations or even other religions which, though lacking the fullness of the truth that exists only in Catholicism, often count among their ranks members who do a much better job heeding God's Will in those respects. When Catholics fail to be spiritual, the Church loses members to Pentecostalism. When Catholics fail to be reverent in Liturgy, the Church loses members to Eastern Orthodoxy. When Catholics fail to be appropriately rigorous with moral teachings, the Church loses members to Islam. The same is true when Catholic fail to regard the undeniably clear Signs of the Times and the utterly unavoidable elements of the prophetic consensus. Here, as most Catholics continue to neglect the imminence of the Coming of Christ in grace, the Church will continue to lose members to the denominations like those listed above, which, though they tragically espouse Millenarian and Dispensationalist heresy in so doing, nevertheless succeed in attracting members by their absolutely right and just focus on the fundamental Christian plea, *Maranatha!,* and their corresponding conviction and excitement in the imminent fulfillment of that petition.

Finally, it must be reiterated that the "*Millennial*" interpretation of the Bible simply holds that Revelation 20 prophesies a future Era of Peace to be enjoyed during the world's final millennium. A *Millenarian* interpretation, on the other hand, holds that this Era consists in the visible reign of Christ on earth. Only the latter—*Millenarian*—interpretation is condemned by the Church.

Isn't this the heresy of Monothelitism or Quietism?

Monothelitism, the heresy which holds that Jesus had only one will (the Divine Will) is expressly contradicted by Luisa's revelations: Jesus tells Luisa that He *did* have a human will (7/19/1928). Neither do these revelations treat Monothelitist presuppositions as paradigmatic for our own sanctity; He tells Luisa that He wants our wills *little* (just as St. Thérèse of Lisieux taught), but not annihilated; *active* (with His very own activity), not passive. In other words, there is also no *Quietism* in these writings—no hint of that heresy which holds that the pinnacle of sanctification is found in the will being rendered entirely passive through a type of psychological self-annihilation.

Not only do Luisa's writings neither teach nor imply any of the 43 propositions that the Church has condemned as constituting the heresy of Quietism (cf. *Coelestis Pastor*, Pope Innocent XI, 1687 A.D.), but also throughout them we see the *opposite* of Quietism being relentlessly taught. In fact, these writings present moral effort as being paramount, implore working in order to attain salvation and avoid Purgatory as extremely important, demand interceding for others and for diverse intentions, lament the loss of souls (and other evils), insist firmly on all the virtues traditionally upheld, exhort us to sacrifice for the mitigation of chastisements, and on the list goes. One of the encouragements Luisa was most fond of issuing in her letters were precisely those words one would never find on the lips of any Quietist, namely, ***"make yourself a saint!"***

In Luisa's volumes, we even read of a moment of misguided piety, in which Luisa herself, at the prospect of dying and being admitted to Heaven, protested to Jesus for a moment (quite contrary to her usual approach) that she did not care about the world and what transpires in it. Jesus corrected her, insisting that *He cares* about what happens on earth, and that *she therefore must also care* (5/15/1938). Indeed, there is scarcely a page among the thousands comprising Luisa's volumes that fails to refute Quietism, therefore it is quite astounding that some prominent critics have levied this charge against Luisa. Their doing so testifies to just how little they know about these revelations and thus reminds us not to be troubled by their critiques. Any allegations of Quietism could—more easily than against Luisa and her volumes—be levied against innumerable works of unassailable orthodoxy given to us by the many saints, Doctors of the Church, and other mystics quoted in Parts Two and Three of this book.

Much content in Jesus' revelations to Luisa do indeed speak of how repugnant the human *self*-will is, but all such exhortations are given with the foundational understanding, specifically conveyed in the volumes, that the human will is the *most beautiful thing God made,* and that only *on its own* (that is, lacking union with the Divine Will) does it appear degraded (1/31/1928). Jesus also tells Luisa that the Divine Will does not destroy the human will's operations, but rather does the opposite: it *embellishes* and *animates* them! (9/16/1931) This is entirely opposite to Quietism, whose main tenet is the annihilation of the human will's operation.

Finally, the "evil" of *not* Living in the Divine Will only applies to one who affirmatively rejects this grace of graces—not to one who, through no fault of his own, is unaware of it—and even less to one who only lacked it due to not living in its time! (1/10/1930) On the contrary, Luisa's revelations exalt the "ordinary" holiness (that is, the holiness of the "pre-Gift days") in the highest terms. Jesus even told Luisa that St. Aloysius Gonzaga (who died in 1591, long before the Gift was available) had such an astounding degree of holiness that *everything* in him was love; and Luisa herself, commenting on what Jesus showed her in Aloysius' soul, said that his love was so great as to be capable of reducing the world to ashes (6/20/1899). Though this message was given a full decade after Luisa was given the Gift, it nevertheless exhorts us to pre-Gift holiness as our model. Clearly, no one reading Luisa's revelations is justified in looking down upon "ordinary" holiness, as Quietists do.

Nor are the points above mere scattered assertions mined out of Jesus' many words to Luisa; they are, rather, the very sentiments left impressed upon Luisa's memory. For in her own words contained in the volumes, wherein she sought to summarize Jesus' teachings, Luisa affirmed that He only desires our wills *small*—not destroyed—*alive and operative*—not dead (3/26/1933).

Expanding our consideration of this concern, we can also see that Pantheism, Hinduism, and Buddhism teach a spirituality radically distinct from Luisa's revelations; these religions and philosophies teach that one need only *recognize* the "identity or sameness of the Atman—the deepest self—with the Braham—the Godhead" (Hinduism), or the "Godhead of everything" (Pantheism), or the "extinguishment or nirvana of the self" (Buddhism). Luisa's revelations teach not the extinguishing of the self, but the sacrificing of the *self-will* to God. They teach not the "recognition" of the divinity of the self, but the *attainment* of the divinization of the self through the ordinary Catholic spiritual life, *combined with* desiring the Gift of Living in the Divine Will. They teach not the Divinity *of* all things, but the Divine *impression left on* all created things by their Divine Craftsman, and how these things serve as *veils of*—not literal incarnations of—the Divine Will.

What about the bad followers of the Divine Will?

As with all the greatest movements which have existed in the history of the Church, the Divine Will[329] is not without a few followers who completely contort its teachings even while presenting themselves as authentic devotees, thus scandalizing the faithful.

They are, however, a miniscule fraction of the movement. I say this as one who, for over a decade, has attended and spoken at Divine Will conferences all across the United States (as well as Canada and Mexico), meeting thousands upon thousands of Divine Will devotees in the process. Without exaggeration, I can attest that well over 99% of the attendees of these events are the very best, holiest, most charitable, orthodox-minded, authentic Catholics and Christians I have found anywhere. I should add that I found this to be true well before I ever wrote or said anything publicly about the Divine Will.

Unfortunately, that leaves us with the fraction-of-a-percent remaining. No doubt it was the behavior of such people which inspired many of the attacks against Luisa's revelations still found circulating on the internet. These bad followers have generated and promoted bogus interpretations of Luisa's writings that are at odds with Catholic Teaching and are in no way faithful to the content of what Jesus actually revealed to Luisa. They go about with an entirely invented yet openly professed confidence regarding their own soul's status in relation to the Gift, even while their lives lack so many of the most rudimentary graces and virtues which any authentic Christian must have, and which an aspiring child of the Divine Will must especially

---

329 The Divine Will is, of course, much more than a "movement" or a "devotion," but considering it under that *aspect* will suffice for the present appendix.

have. They treat Luisa's revelations as a new Public Revelation—despite both Jesus' words to Luisa and Luisa's own example repeatedly contradicting that approach—and they refuse to understand their themes in light of Scripture, Tradition, and Magisterium. Some of them even do so by claiming that they enjoy direct supernatural enlightenment on how exactly Luisa's revelations should be understood, or at least "know someone who does" and defer to his or her "Heavenly" understanding. In a word, the one person on earth they perhaps *least* resemble is a certain woman from Italy named Luisa.

Therefore, to such people, I say: if you really believe that you have received direct supernatural enlightenment on Luisa's revelations, then *please be more like Luisa.* Open the very first page of Luisa's volumes, read the very first line therein, and remind yourself that she only allowed a single word of Jesus' revelations to her to become known because she was commanded to do so, under holy obedience, by the Church. Then, remind yourself how supremely Jesus exalted St. Hannibal within Luisa's volumes, choosing him alone as the primary apostle of the Divine Will—and recall that he always insisted upon (and Luisa agreed!) Jesus' words to Luisa being read in light of, and through the filter of, Catholic teaching. This approach did not inhibit St. Hannibal's zeal for living in and promoting the Divine Will one iota; it merely guided him on how exactly to do so. Jesus chose him, and no one else, as the Divine Will's primary apostle; therefore, woe to any supposed follower of the Divine Will who dares to approach it (or its promotion) in a way that contradicts the example of this great saint. As he declared, "With [the Gift of Living in the Divine Will,] in order to form Saints who surpass the ones of the past, it is important that the new Saints **possess all the virtues to a heroic degree, just as did the Saints of old**." As Jesus tells Luisa, if you clash with others and cannot be in union with your neighbor, you certainly are not in union with Him (10/10/1905). This is doubly true if you cannot be in peaceful union with other pious Catholics.

Returning now to address everyone: I must encourage those who have come across bad followers of the Divine Will to not be disheartened. If you are wise enough to refuse to allow bad Christians to turn you off to Christianity, bad Catholics to turn you off to Catholicism, bad devotees of Fatima to turn you off to Marian Apparitions, bad pro-lifers to turn you off to being pro-life, then please employ that same wisdom here with the Divine Will. If you have come across a bad follower, then simply ignore him, look elsewhere, and I am sure that you will find a true child of the Divine Will in the next place you look!

6,000 years since Adam? What about evolution?

A recurring theme in Luisa's revelations is the teaching that this "Third Fiat," (that is, the fulfillment of the Our Father prayer), has been 6,000 years in the making since the fall of Man.

However, nowhere in Luisa's revelations is either evolution or young earth creationism spoken of—on these questions, consistency with her writings only requires holding that Adam and Eve are indeed our first parents and that they did indeed fall from grace "about" 6,000 years ago. If even this appears too tall an order, bear in mind that—despite how unfashionable it is to acknowledge this today—the Catholic Faith essentially requires as much. In *Humani Generis §37*, Pope Pius XII condemned the notion that humanity proceeds from more than one set of parents (Adam and Eve). Furthermore, even if some of the Book of Genesis is intended symbolically (although the same Encyclical teaches that Genesis *does* indeed pertain to *history* in the *true* sense, cf. §38), the genealogy in the Gospel of Luke makes it impossible to claim that there are tens-of-thousands (much less hundreds-of-thousands) of years standing between the present day and Adam and Eve's begetting of their first son, Cain. There are absolutely no plausible grounds—historical, archeological, textual, social, semiotical, Patristic, allegorical, Magisterial, theological, or philosophical—to suppose that when the Evangelist, in this genealogy, writes "…the son of..." he actually means "the great, great, great, [x100] grandson of..." We are confronted with a simple choice of either treating that genealogy as true *as it is stated* (which yields about 6,000 years since Adam and Eve), or rejecting the inerrancy of Scripture. The latter is heretical. It has been repeatedly condemned as such in the strongest and most authoritative terms by the Church (e.g., *Divino Afflante Spiritu* §1, *Providentissimus Deus* §20-21).

What if I don't have time for another private revelation?

This is an understandable hesitation, but I hope that even those who feel it do at least have time to read the next few paragraphs. Whoever has read Part Four of this book has no need to hear what follows yet again, though I include it here knowing that some will turn directly to the present section to first assess the objection under consideration before learning about "yet another" private revelation.

Throughout the 2,000 years of her history, the Church has been blessed by Heaven with innumerable private revelations. Although each authentic revelation is certainly important, it is also true that a range of significance exists within this domain. Closer to one end, we find momentous and universally-relevant messages, like those of Our Lady of Fatima. On the other end exist lesser-known messages which, while significant and important to be heeded *in what they apply to,* nevertheless come with a relevance that is more or less provisional, localized, or temporary. Most other apparitions and mystical revelations enjoy a spiritual weightiness somewhere between these two ends of the spectrum, and one may therefore often be justified in making a "strategic" decision—matters of authenticity aside—on the question of whether to dedicate time to them.

An exception exists in the present case. These revelations on the Divine Will are either utterly and completely false, or they are, for lack of a better word, *everything*. No other private revelation in the history of the Church has, like this one, been given the express mission by Jesus of ushering in the fulfillment of the Our Father prayer itself.

Though quite an assertion, I present it as no mere newcomer to the realm of private revelation. If any reader is already acquainted with my efforts in various apostolates, he is likely aware that private revelation in general is a passion of mine, and that I have, for many years, promoted the messages of many apparitions, as well as the writings of many mystical private revelations—messages which themselves are only a fraction of what I have studied. (Here I take a very careful approach, and for various reasons, I've chosen to leave aside most of the private revelations that I have reviewed.) While I remain passionate for many apparitions and mystics, I have no hesitation in placing Jesus' words to Luisa head and shoulders above all others. If, therefore, you feel that your life does not have room for "yet another" private revelation, then I exhort you to reconsider that stance in this particular case. This is not "just another" of Heaven's messages any more than John the Baptist was "just another" prophet, and the invitation now presented to you is not "just another" unsolicited suggestion any more than a marriage proposal is "just another" word a man speaks to the woman he hopes to marry.

God, indeed, is ever capable of surprising us, and what wonders He *will* do is never limited by precedent. On the other hand, neither men nor demons manage to be surprising in their antics; for even when—*especially* when, rather—they regard themselves as novel, they are usually only repeating what has been done many times. "There is nothing new under the sun," (Ecclesiastes 1:9) as Solomon wisely observed regarding the things of this world. Whoever opens a history book—on Popes, Councils, Mystics, Saints, or what have you—will find confirmed the observation of this great man. Throughout Church history, we have just about seen it all.

But *not once* in this 2,000-year history has a mystic like Luisa—who had a canonized saint dedicate the most heroic years of his life to promoting her message; who had decades pass since her death only repeatedly confirming and authenticating her legacy of holiness; and who had a Cause for Beatification successfully accepted by the Vatican—nevertheless later had her entire life's primary mission and passion turn out to be a fraud, delusion, or deception. That has not ever happened, *and it will not ever happen*.

So, just as no one can deny that we are confronted with the simple dichotomy that these revelations are either utterly and completely false, *or that they are everything*—so too no one acquainted with the facts can deny that the first half of that dichotomy is impossible. This leaves us with the latter half, and God leaves it to our free wills to choose whether or not to live authentically in accordance with it.

Concluding notes on the concerns of Catholics

As a teacher myself, I am as tempted as anyone is to take the erroneous approach to mysticism—thus, I feel I ought to repeat here the very thing I must remind myself: mysticism should never be approached as a theology professor approaches the grading of a student's term paper. Mysticism is not primarily an intellectual exercise. It must be judged above all by its fruits, and its various literary forms (and the *mode of the receiver*) must be understood and considered, so that what the text *actually means* can be received in accordance with God's intended purpose. Otherwise, it will elicit an endless array of tempests in teapots thanks to neurotic scholars who obsess over quandaries which they themselves created by reading their own confused thoughts into a text that neither contains nor implies them. What would become of the entire 2,000-year history of Catholic Spiritual Tradition if a quibbling, literalistic, rationalistic, hair-splitting, obsessive-compulsive approach was taken to mysticism in general? It would be in shambles, and our glorious Faith—which *needs* mysticism—would have devolved into a mere systematic philosophy.

The only happenings in the life of the Church which do not receive any opposition are those initiatives carefully strategized by business and marketing experts who optimize their efforts strictly for worldly success and correspondingly know exactly how to make sure they offend no one. Offending no one and having no critics or enemies, in fact, is proof that a "revelation" or a movement or initiative of any sort is not from God, for the Almighty always has better goals in mind than merely confirming the status-quo.

***

Critics and quibbles aside, however, as you delve into Luisa's revelations, you will no doubt have honest and very good questions. They will not each have easy three second answers. But it is no different with the Faith itself, and I challenge anyone who thinks otherwise to open Aquinas' *Summa Theologica* or any other great work of Catholic Theology. There, he will quickly find that as soon as one confronts the dilemmas which arise even in Christianity and Catholicism themselves (not excluding *apparent* contradictions), resolving them is not always a cut and dry affair. An enormous number of distinctions must be issued, and these are sometimes very subtle. Just as the Pharisaical critic uses these distinctions as occasions to pounce, so too the easily frustrated dabbler, who is just looking for an excuse to throw his hands in the air and give up, will find plenty of opportunities to do so. Just as inexcusable as such an attitude is with the Faith itself, so too should it be avoided with Jesus' words to Luisa. I can assure you that every time I have taken sufficient care to explore any difficulties which occasionally arise in reading Jesus' words to Luisa, I have not been disappointed. But sometimes this requires time, care, and effort. It is okay if you cannot always afford to dedicate such attention to these matters. Simply know that the entire Catholic Faith and all its teachings remain, and that there *are* answers to all your questions. The Church—whose job alone it is to render such judgments—has already examined Luisa's revelations and found them orthodox (see Part Four).

Therefore, please do not delay living in and proclaiming the Divine Will until you feel you have definitively mastered each possible question! That is only a temptation which may just cause you to neglect this Divine task your whole life. No saint in the history of the Church would have ever proclaimed the Gospel if he waited to do so until he had all the answers to every difficulty any of his hearers could have suggested.

Who, for example, could proclaim Christianity without proclaiming the Father, the Son, and the Holy Spirit? No one. Yet we cannot even express this, the absolute highest Dogma of our Faith—the Trinity—without immediately committing ourselves to an enormous amount of subtle distinctions. God is absolutely One, we say. (And rightly so). But immediately we must qualify; well, He is one *nature*, but He is three *Persons*. But these Persons are identical in substance. "So they are really just one Person!?", a hearer shouts. No! Distinction between Them is found on the basis of relation. And so on, and so on. Soon, we find ourselves speaking of spirations, generations, notions, etc. Then, St. Patrick comes along and says, "**Behold the clover; it is one and three. So is God**."

The same is true with the Divine Will. Until the end of time, theologians will provide ever deeper, more subtle, and more distinction-laden expositions of its glory. This is a good thing. But the Divine Will, while infinitely deep and broad, is also simple, therefore proclaiming it can, and should, be simple. And just as St. Patrick presented the clover, so too we today can rest content that, with the Gift, it is absolutely true, but it also changes nothing about our Catholic Faith, and we can be confident that we have proclaimed it well even if in our proclamation we focus on giving something akin to "the message in a nutshell" as relayed in Part Four.

> "**If all things were within our grasp, the Higher Power would not be beyond us**." - St. Gregory of Nyssa

27. Epilogue: Pascal's Wager

"Never was a tale told that men would rather find true."
–J.R.R. Tolkien (on Christianity)

Pascal's Wager—that disarmingly simple consideration wherein God's existence is not itself proven, but Faith in the same is nevertheless rendered utterly compelling to any reasonable person—may not be the best way to arrive at belief in God. But if Faith still results from one considering this wager, then that undertaking is more than worthwhile. Let us apply it to the matter at hand, therefore, and consider two simple words: ***Why not?***

Why not approach *the greatest petition* of *the Greatest Prayer* with full faith and confidence? Why not believe that it really can be fulfilled in the *greatest possible* way? *Why not* trust that the Son of God will make good on His greatest promise?

"Because, well, what if we're wrong?" one may ask. I doubt anyone who has read Part Four of this book could truly suspect that is a likelihood, but I will still address the hypothetical here. *Even if* the Greatest Prayer ever prayed by the Son of God Himself was just a pipe dream that can never be realized, or a mere platitude that does not mean what it says, you still gain much by rejecting the lukewarm, Deist interpretation of the Our Father. For by doing so—by simply exercising the will (even if the intellect remains stubborn) and *choosing* to side with the truth of the matter—*choosing* trust that God desires, and is certain to bring about, the reign of His Will on earth as in Heaven (first in your own soul if only you let Him; and then, at the proper time, throughout the world)—your Faith will be strengthened, your Hope will be invigorated, and your Charity will grow in perfection. You will become a better Christian and a better Catholic than you were before you thought carefully about and heeded the full implications of the Lord's Prayer.

Firstly, because *charity will grow.* The height of charity is love of God, and love is strengthened by apprehending the goodness of what is loved, and acknowledging the magnanimity of God in the gloriousness of His plan (both for your own holiness and for the world's renewal) is an unparalleled way of appreciating His goodness. Secondly, because *hope will be invigorated,* as its proper ultimate object (confident expectation in Heaven) will not be deprived of its temporal support; that is, confident expectation in God's triumph on earth *as well as* His eternal one. Thirdly, because *faith will be strengthened,* as its own essential nature (belief in Divine Truths) will find its home in the human heart and mind cured of confusion, incoherence, and incompletion. You will find yourself expressing the very sentiments most do when they first truly receive the Divine Will message; namely, "*this caused everything else to suddenly make sense, and was like a key to unlocking the full power, beauty, and glory of the Faith that I previously did not sufficiently appreciate.*" Those exposed to the revelations on the Divine Will always come away from this experience with their Catholic Faith greatly strengthened.

But, if we are right—if indeed Jesus meant what He said in the only prayer He taught—then not only will the aforementioned benefits (and countless others) be yours, but also the task which now presents itself to you carries with it an urgency and an importance that could not—even theoretically—be matched, much less exceeded. For this task is none other than the Greatest Mission in History: "**... a mission so sublime that no other can be compared to it—that is, the triumph of the Divine Will upon the whole earth, in conformity with what is said in the 'Our Father.'**" -St. Hannibal di Francia

I humbly exhort you, therefore, to heed the content of these pages with awareness of its life-changing and world-changing potential; a potential which requires, for its own actualization, that those who know the message do not themselves fail to zealously proclaim it from the rooftops. I thus exhort you, certainly not on account of anything special about myself (I am the least worthy man to be proclaiming this message), but only because I am, in fact, very selfish: I want the Kingdom to come. I want God's Will to reign. I want the Divine Mercy to "triumph over the whole world," as promised in St. Faustina's revelations (§1789). I want the path to salvation to be opened in all its plenitude, so that "all souls may be led to Heaven, especially those most in need of His Mercy." (cf. Our Lady of Fatima). I want the Restoration of All Things in Christ (cf. Pope St. Pius X, *E Supremi*) to reach its fruition, so that Jesus may banish the evils which inundate the world today more than ever before in history. Through the Gift of Living in the Divine Will, I want souls to not merely arrive at Heaven, but to build up as many treasures as *possible* in Heaven (Matthew 6:20)—which is our only true home and ultimate destiny (*Catechism* §1024)—by becoming the greatest saints they can possibly become. I want all these things with every fiber of my being, but I know that they will only be attained when enough people know of Jesus' teachings on His Divine Will so that they may desire His Will, and earnestly beseech Him for His Will to reign in their lives and over the whole world. Until His Will reigns, souls will continue treading the path to perdition in terrifying numbers, evil will continue inundating this world while even turning people's temporal lives into foretastes of damnation, and the greatest adornments to our eternal home in Heaven will continue to be neglected.

Jesus *will* give the world this great Gift of the Reign of His Will—that much we can be solemnly assured of—but precisely when He bestows it upon us is determined by when we, in sufficient numbers and with sufficient zeal, ask Him for it.

In the prologue, I acknowledged that some readers of this book will doubtless be tempted to regard its primary claim as simply too grandiose. "Too good to be true," they may say. But that axiom only applies to the promises of man; for in such cases, what appears "too good to be true" is indeed always a fraud. But *all* the promises of God appear "too good to be true," however, *they are true*. Therefore, we must simply bend the knee in faithful gratitude when He issues them. In fact, if a promise did not seem "too good to be true," then it would not be from God, as His goodness and power are such that He "**pardons what conscience dreads and gives what prayer does not dare to ask**" (Roman Missal, Collect for the 27th Week of Ordinary Time), and the glory of His plans always far surpasses our own comparatively tepid aspirations. Jaded as modern man is from the relentless barrage of failed promises issued from the ivory towers of the Ivy League, the West Wing, Silicon Valley, Hollywood, and Wall Street, the perverse inclination to reflexively reject good news is—understandably—more prevalent today than ever before. But the failures of men must never seduce us into supposing that God is likewise inept, for "**The weakness of God is stronger than men.**" (1 Corinthians 1:25)

To project timidity upon the Almighty is to betray the Godlessness of one's own slant. Indeed, suspicion is warranted in response to the timid human promises which suppose that God's Will for the world merely consists in waiting for its consummation in flames at the end of time, while occasionally fixing a few scattered injustices—a reasonable agenda for a political party. God has much greater things in mind: *the Restoration of All Things in Christ*. Timid human hopes for the world presented as God's Will are mere political or corporate agendas masquerading as piety—wolves in prophet's clothing.

Suspicion is likewise warranted in response to the timid human promises which suppose that God is satisfied with our individual lives, so long as they become somewhat "successful" and a few of the more perverse disorders are removed from them—a reasonable accomplishment for a life coach to inspire in his client, or a psychiatrist to bring about in his patient. God has much greater things in mind here as well: that we become saints. "Be perfect, as your heavenly Father is perfect." (Matthew 5:48) Timid human hopes for our lives presented as God's Will are mere sales pitches masquerading as spirituality—wolves in sage's clothing.

In sum, the world needs Christians who are willing to reject Deism—that heresy distinguished by its haughtiness which holds that God's role in History was little more than to create the world, whereupon He leaves it to its own devices; a convenient notion for a modernist who above all does not want the Will of the Almighty interfering with his own plans. The world needs Christians who are moreover willing to reject all of Deism's *corollaries*—and are willing to believe that God is capable of *fully* bringing about His Will in the world and in our own lives.

God's Will is that His Own Divine Life be in our souls as fully as possible (1 Thessalonians 4:3), and that His Kingdom reign upon earth. (Matthew 6:10) And no purpose of His can be thwarted. (Job 42:2) We 21st-Century Christians are so blessed to be alive now, in the most exciting time in the history of the world: the time in which the very thing our ancestors in the Faith had waited for, had prayed for, and knew would one day arrive … is finally here.

So, I conclude with a word to the skeptic who, upon being handed this book and hearing of its thesis, might ask: "*Why should I believe this utterly extraordinary message which I frankly find too incredible?*" To learn the proper answer, turn this book over and begin reading it from the other side. But to attain an adequate provisional understanding, consider only this: confidence in God is never unrewarded, it is not even possible for us to overestimate His power, and Christ, the Son of God, is the King of All.

Because of this,
God highly exalted him
And bestowed on him the name
Above every other name,
So that at Jesus' name
Every knee must bend
In the heavens, on the earth,
And under the earth,
And every tongue proclaim
To the glory of God the Father:
JESUS CHRIST IS LORD!
-Philippians 2:9-11

Published on the Feast of Christ the King. November 21st, 2021

28. A Checklist for Living in the Divine Will

- **Repent, for the Kingdom of God is at hand.** Abandon your sins and remain always in a state of grace, ever trusting in His Mercy.
- **Be a good Catholic**. Believe and obey 100% of the Church's teachings. Undertake nobly the duties of your state in life; therein lies holiness.
- **Continuously converse with Jesus.** Constantly say, "Jesus, I Trust in You," "Thy Will be Done," and "Thy Kingdom Come!"
- **Do everything as an Act in the Divine Will** by asking that Jesus Himself act in you, and make your every act be one of pure love of God.
- **Ask God for the Gift of Living in the Divine Will every day.**
- **Grow in virtue every day. Live the beatitudes. *Be a saint!***
- **Zealously spread knowledge of the Divine Will to the whole world!**
- **Read, re-read, and meditate upon Jesus' revelations to Luisa** as much as you can. Live out their teachings! Do the *Hours of the Passion* often.
- **Consecrate yourself to Mary** and remain always close to her.
- **Pray the Rosary every day.** Pray it as a family. Pray from the heart; let prayer become your life's *continuous joy*.
- **Wear a Crucifix, Miraculous Medal, and Brown Scapular**.
- Gently, gracefully, and naturally **evangelize in every conversation**.
- **Attend Mass and receive Communion daily** if you can; taking time afterwards to pray while the Real Presence remains within you.
- **Pray the Divine Mercy Chaplet every day** and live the Divine Mercy revelations given to St. Faustina. Display the Divine Mercy Image everywhere.
- **Make a good confession at least once a month**; examine your conscience carefully and do not let it become mere habit.
- **Love each cross God sends you**, and bear it with resignation, patience, peace, and joy; offering it to Christ in union with His sufferings. Keep His Passion ever before your mind and foster a strong devotion to it.
- **Perform regular works of mercy**; both Spiritual and Corporal.
- **Do a daily or weekly Holy Hour before the Blessed Sacrament.**
- **Engage daily in mental prayer,** dedicated solely to spontaneously conversing with Jesus, meditation, contemplation, and the Rounds.
- **Do spiritual reading every day: Scripture, Magisterium**, saint biographies and writings, the Liturgy of the Hours (Divine Office), etc.
- Make sacrifices. **Fast Wednesdays and Fridays as you deem yourself called** in accordance with your particular duties, needs, and abilities.
- **Ensure that your home is a holy place**. The Kingdom will come *one Nazareth at a time.* Imitate the example of the Holy Family, consecrate your family to them, and pray daily for their protection. Never neglect to seek the protection of the Prime Minister of the Kingdom of the Divine Will—St. Joseph.

Jesus, I Trust in You

THY WILL BE DONE

Have you found this book helpful?

Kindly consider leaving a review for it on Amazon (simply search for this book's title and author on Amazon.com, or find it by going directly to amazon.com/Daniel-OConnor/e/B00UA0DJ4O or www.ProclaimTheKingdom.com.) Each review posted helps this book to be introduced to more people, which in turn will help spread the message of the Divine Will across the whole world, that God's Kingdom may come, and His Will may be done on earth as it is in Heaven. *Come, Lord Jesus!*

Are you interested in distributing copies of this book? See www.DSDOConnor.com for information on discounted bulk orders of the paperback.

About the Author

Daniel O'Connor is an adjunct professor of Philosophy and Religion at a State University of New York Community College. Originally a mechanical engineer, he switched careers and obtained a master's degree in theology from a Catholic Seminary in Connecticut. Now a Doctoral student working on a PhD in Philosophy, he is the author of *The Crown of Sanctity* and *The Crown of History*, the founder of the Divine Will Missionaries of Mercy (www.DWMoM.org), and writes for his personal website (www.DSDOConnor.com) where his books, talks, videos, and other works may be found. Daniel lives in New York with his wife, Regina, and their four children, Joseph, David, Mary, and Luisa.

Made in United States
Orlando, FL
05 December 2021